The Narrow Way

The Narrow Way

Biblical and Historical proof that GOD IS GREAT

by Diana Lesperance

VMI Publishers
Sisters, Oregon

The Narrow Way
Biblical and Historical proof that GOD IS GREAT
© 2009 by Diana Lesperance

Published by
VMI Publishers
Sisters, Oregon
www.vmipublishers.com

ISBN: 1933204923
ISBN 13: 9781933204925
Library of Congress Control Number: 2009929797

Unless otherwise noted, scriptures have been taken from the
HOLY BIBLE, NEW INTERNATIONAL VERSION. Copyright © 1973,
1978, 1984 International Bible Society. Used by permission of
Zondervan Bible Publishers.

Printed in the USA.

Contents and/or cover may not be reproduced in part or in whole without the
expressed written consent of the Publisher.

Cover design by Rebecca Barbier

Contents

PART I: The Narrow Way in the Bible

Chapter 1	The Narrow Way	1
Chapter 2	The Narrow Way in the Old Testament	21
Chapter 3	The Narrow Way in the New Testament	45

PART II: The Narrow Way in History

Chapter 4	The Narrow Way in the Roman Empire	71
Chapter 5	The Narrow Way through the Inquisition	93
Chapter 6	The Narrow Way in the Reformation	113
Chapter 7	The Narrow Way in a Time of Revolutions	137
Chapter 8	The Narrow Way Abolishes Slavery	163
Chapter 9	The Narrow Way on a Mission	187
Chapter 10	The Narrow Way Confronts Hitler	213
Chapter 11	The Narrow Way Confronts Communism	237
Chapter 12	The Narrow Way Confronts Terrorism	267
Chapter 13	The Narrow Way Cannot Go Astray	293
Endnotes		309
Bibliography		331
Index		343

Enter through the narrow gate.
For wide is the gate and broad is the road
that leads to destruction,
and many enter through it.

But small is the gate
and narrow the road that leads to life,
and only a few find it.

Matthew 7:13-14

Acknowledgments

To Kelly, whose willingness to listen eagerly during a drive on a warm spring night inspired me to write this book.

My thanks to my husband Greg, who has sacrificed, served, encouraged, and believed in me even in the darkest moments. I love you. To my friend Linda who is my Barnabus, Sam-wise, and my joy. I love you. To my children and all their friends, who I hope will someday read these pages and courageously choose to walk on the Narrow Way. I love you all so much. To my dad, who always debated with me while I was growing up. You planted a seed of righteousness in me. I love you. To my sweet friend Rabson, who helped heal my heart. I love you and miss you. And to Jesus, who arrested my mind. I love you.

I'd also like to acknowledge the Lakeland College Library staff for all their help and patience, Google Books for giving me access to obscure, outdated material I could never have found anywhere else, and to the Amazon chat rooms whose conversations on atheism and religion challenged and strengthened me. In particular I'd like to thank Walk, Thomas, Jayne, Emerson, Terri, Ariex, Mark, and G. Altier.

"As for God, his **way** is perfect;
the word of the Lord is flawless."
2 Samuel 22:31a

"My feet have closely followed his steps;
I have kept to his **way** without turning aside."
Job 23:11

"There are those who rebel against the light,
who do not know its **ways** or stay in its paths."
Job 24:13

"He guides the humble in what is right and
teaches them his **way**."
Psalms 25:9

"Whether you turn to the right or to the left,
your ears will hear a voice behind you, saying,
'This is the **way**; walk in it.'"
Isaiah 30:21

"And a highway will be there;
it will be called the **Way** of Holiness."
Isaiah 35:8a

"A voice of one calling:
'In the desert prepare the **way** for the Lord;
make straight in the wilderness a highway for our God.'"
Isaiah 40:3

"We all, like sheep, have gone astray,
each of us has turned to his own **way**;
and the Lord has laid on him the iniquity of us all."
Isaiah 53:6

"This is what the Lord says:
'Stand at the crossroads and look;
ask for the ancient paths, ask where the good **way** is,
and walk in it, and you will find rest for your souls.
But you said, "We will not walk in it."
I appointed watchmen over you and said,
"Listen to the sound of the trumpet!"
But you said, "We will not listen."'
Jeremiah 6:16-17

"This is he who was spoken of through the prophet Isaiah:
'A voice of one calling in the desert,
"Prepare the **way** for the Lord,
make straight paths for him."'
Matthew 3:3

"Jesus answered, 'I am the **way** and the truth and the life.
No one comes to the Father except through me.'"
John 14:6

"I persecuted the followers of this **Way** to their death,
arresting both men and women and
throwing them into prison."
Acts 22:4

PART I:

The Narrow Way in the Bible

CHAPTER ONE
The Narrow Way

"The Cosmos is all that is or ever was or ever will be. Our feeblest contemplations of the Cosmos stir us. There is a tingling in the spine, a catch in the voice, a faint sensation, as if a distant memory, of falling from a height. We know we are approaching the greatest of mysteries." —Carl Sagan, *Cosmos*

"Ah! How they still strove through that infinite blueness to seek out the thing that might destroy them!" —Herman Melville on the pursuit of Moby Dick

"The last temptation is hope." —Dietrich Bonhoeffer, *Letters and Papers from Prison*

"I've sweated through philosophy, jurisprudence, medicine, yes, and alas, theology through and through and out and in! Poor fool! Poor disillusioned man, no whit more wise than you began." —Johann Wolfgang von Goethe, opening statement of *Faust*

Religion is mankind's attempt to restore what was lost in the Garden of Eden without doing it God's way. It is independence with a capital "I." It's the universe's equivalent of a strong-willed child, and human history is merely the embarrassing record of all of its temper tantrums, messes, rebellions, and darts into the street… the ultimate struggle for power and control.

Although Voltaire saw history as merely a "series of crimes and misfortunes," I say history is the record of the world's attempt to regain paradise. It's like a little boy who was sent to his room on Christmas morning because he was disobedient, and now he can't bear his punishment and yearns to get back to the brightly wrapped gifts and the stocking he knows is stuffed with little treats. He's told that he must humble himself and admit that he did wrong and apologize so that the relationship can be healed, but this he can't bear to do, so he tries to get to the gifts his own way. He begs. He throws a fit. He manipulates. He sneaks. He tries to make a deal. He demands. He'll try anything except the way of humility. But nothing works. Futility is a word created just for the purpose of describing this process. And yet, in spite of the fruitlessness of this endeavor, he can't give up. He has to believe he can get back there on his own.

Like that little boy, we try everything to return to that joyful moment in time, the Christmas morning of history in the Garden of Eden. And nothing works. We keep hoping for a brighter future, but like a bad dream where we just can't seem to get where we want to be, we try harder, certain that satisfaction is just around the corner, only to have it vanish like an elusive ghost. The solution is there, but we refuse to give in. We defiantly jut out our chin and convince ourselves we'll figure something else out.

For those who hold a progressive viewpoint, who hope for and believe in a bright future for mankind, a restoration of Eden, history stands as an ugly reflection of reality. In the movie, *What Ever Happened to Baby Jane?*, Bette Davis plays a child star who's grown up, yet always hopes for a return to the limelight. She's so old that her face is wrinkled and her eyebrows are drawn onto her face, but she still wears little girl dresses and curls her hair in ringlets, unable to face the fact that she'll never make a comeback.

Instead of gray hair and wrinkles, historians must look in the mirror of the past and face gulags, inquisitions, greed, lust for power, wars, holocausts, and genocides. There's no hopeful and fresh face of youth gleaming out at us, just a weary, contorted, and aging face, and like Baby Jane, we want to scream in horror and frustration.

We've tried to make sense of the ugly image. Not wanting to accept the hopelessness for a comeback, and a return to the heyday, when everything glittered and shone with possibilities, we surge ahead with new plans. We develop think tanks so our best minds can be put to the task. We organize, thinking that our collective effort can bring it about. We dialogue, strategize, scrape, claw, and manipulate. "There must be a way!" we scream.

Maybe some kind of synthesis of human thought is the answer. Perhaps we can try to blend the thinking of the best and the brightest in the world. So Hegel blended Kant and Herder, but that just produced a holocaust. Marx thought it was Feuerbach and Hegel, but that just produced a gulag. Thomas Paine thought it was classical liberalism and anti-clericalism, but that just produced the guillotine. Failure. How can this be?! There *has* to be a way back!

Eden is in our hearts. Even though we think we're pressing forward in time toward our utopia, the goal isn't based on a future vision as much as it is on a memory, an inward recollection of how things *should* be. It's a primeval instinct, something out of the ancient past that hounds us and refuses to leave us alone, causing us to be obsessed with the attainment of the perfect day. We live under this tyranny of "what should be" and are unable, no matter how hard we try, to gain fulfillment. Mick Jagger wasn't singing only of himself when he bemoaned the fact that he couldn't "get no satisfaction."

This experience is common to all mankind, collectively and individually. How many of us wish that we could just get things in *order*? We want to arrange our garages, arrange our homes, arrange our society, our churches, our schools, businesses, and relationships. If we could just get organized, we would be successful. Somehow, we unconsciously know that there's been a breakdown. Something went terribly wrong, and now instead of order there's chaos. Entropy is a tiring reality.

Totalitarian governments are an expression of this desire for order. In fact, tyranny of all forms has its roots in this need for structure, the drive to create our idea of what *should* be, a self-willed attempt to overcome the consequences of the Fall. But human beings are flawed and cannot create perfection, so our attempts at designing an orderly world turn out more like the monster from Mary Shelley's *Frankenstein*: violent, cruel, and hideous.

And yet we must continue to try. We must hope. We devise bigger and bigger structures and grander organizations, which offer us temporary jubilation and success. But then the plan is mismanaged, runs out of money, peters out. It's almost impossible to overcome the second law of thermodynamics—the Curse. Consequently, the world goes through cycles of hope and despair. We have a bipolar disorder in this sense. When we're down, we're really down, and when we're up, we're often manic.

Nations also go through these fluctuating cycles. In the early twentieth century, the United States went through a period of progressive hopefulness. We had abolished slavery, and social reform was ablaze in our hearts. But then World War I came, and it produced a slew of despairing writers such as Willa Cather and Ernest Hemingway who sadly lamented the horrors of war. A bit of hope came in the development of the League of Nations, and the Roaring Twenties became known as an era of gaiety and prosperity, when Hoover promised a "chicken in every pot," but then fear gripped us on Black Tuesday and despair settled in again as businessmen jumped from the windows of tall buildings and we stood in soup lines and battled dust storms. FDR would deliver us, though, giving us hope again with his New Deal—and then tragedy struck as Pearl Harbor was bombed and Hitler rolled across Europe. Another World War.

But then victory! The boys were coming home, and we were moving to Levittown. Nothing could stop us now... except the Cold War and the threat of nuclear annihilation by communists who were intent on conquering the world. (Can we never get a break?) But we were too war-weary to really think about that. The 1950s were a time of optimism and idealism. A new prosperity *was* possible. All we wanted was to "Rock Around the Clock" and "Leave it to Beaver"... until the Korean War made us face the reality that there was indeed an enemy.

The early Sixties, in a sense, was an "up" time. Elvis Presley and Doris Day sang light-hearted songs on brightly colored sets. JFK had successfully stood down Kruschev in the Cuban Missile Crisis. Jobs were plentiful, and there was the prospect of creating a "Great Society," but then desolation and grief engulfed us as Camelot disappeared in a flash and a small war in a little place in Southeast Asia began to chew up our sons like a meat grinder.

A cloud of despair began to settle down on us again. Music and drugs offered an escape, but we had no solutions, no hope... until Martin Luther King, Jr., shared his dream and the Beatles invited us to "Imagine" a new world. Our hopes began to rise again. We began to sing about the dawning of "The Age of Aquarius" and teaching the world to "sing in perfect harmony."

And then, again, depression and failure. The U.S. loss in Vietnam, Watergate, the prospect of mutually assured destruction, and the backlash of free sex and drugs, led us to another moment of hopelessness. We began to accept the fact that we were just "Dust in the Wind."

THE NARROW WAY

Night after night, we were reminded by the newscaster of what day it was in the Iranian hostage crisis. Gasoline prices and interest rates skyrocketed. And in case we didn't realize how the deck was stacked against us, we watched great white sharks, towering infernos, hijacked planes, upside-down ships and earthquakes on the big screen. How could anyone be hopeful in this kind of world?

But then Ronald Reagan was elected, the hostages were freed, and old-fashioned American idealism—Mom, baseball, and apple pie—was recalled. It was "morning in America!" We forgot about the Cold War and began to create our free enterprise paradise. Capitalism thrived as we built bigger homes and bought bigger cars. Even the church got caught up in the euphoria of success and prosperity. And when the Berlin Wall came down, Francis Fukuyama declared with exhilaration that the world had finally experienced Hegel's "end of history," the final triumph of liberal democracy and freedom over totalitarianism. Now utopia was even possible on an international level. The solution was finally here: allow everyone to create their own *individual* Gardens!

We basked in the glory of our victory. Eden *was* possible! Tiananmen Square—oh well, what can we do about it? Rwanda—who wants to hear about that? Somalia—let's just get the heck out of there! The president lied and obstructed justice—who cares? It's the economy stupid! Y2K? No way! (See, we told you so!) Just show me the granite countertops and big screen TVs.

And then… 9/11.

On a perfect day—an Eden-like day—everything changed. We lost paradise, and we knew it. We couldn't deny reality anymore. We grieved not only at the loss of life, but also at the loss of Eden. Instead of "Capitalists of the world, unite!" we faced the prospect of a "clash of civilizations" just as Samuel P. Huntington, that Harvard prophet of doom, had warned us less than a decade earlier.

But why?

So now we scramble to make sense of it all. The solution is democracy, we say. After all, it seems that democratic nations aren't as likely to go to war. Bruce Russett's Democratic Peace Theory may work. Perhaps this will get us back. So we embark on another grand experiment, the success of which hinges on Muslims being capable of living at peace with one another and embracing the concepts of freedom and democracy.

In the meantime, the Israeli problem hangs like a noose around the neck of the world. How can we stop her enemies from wanting to "push her into the sea?" If we could just solve *that* problem, maybe hope could be restored. So we try a new angle—if the civilizations of the world are indeed "clashing," then let's try to stop this by forming an "alliance of civilizations," a United Nations-led attempt to merge and blend all religions and cultures into one huge dialogue of tolerance and understanding—a new Tower of Babel.

As King Solomon would say, "Vanity."

Atheism: The Hope of the World?

But wait! Now we have a new source of hope, a new voice crying in the wilderness. It's *religion*, they say, that's the cause of all our troubles. After all, what is the source of most wars? It's the religious divisions between Jews, Muslims, Christians, Hindus, and other sects. That's the albatross around our necks, holding us back from our progress toward utopia. Hitchens, Harris, Dawkins, and Dennett are crusaders who bring the prospect of a new hope for the world. Here is Hitchens describing this blissful future, which is dashed by the practitioners of "religion."

> In our hands and within our view is a whole universe of discovery and clarification, which is a pleasure to study in itself, gives the average person access to insights that not even Darwin or Einstein possessed, and offers the promise of near miraculous advances in healings, in energy, and in peaceful exchange between different cultures. Yet millions of people in all societies still prefer the myths of the cave and the tribe and the blood sacrifice.[1]

He then goes on to promote a new Enlightenment, in which he describes *his* Eden as a society which can experience "unfettered scientific inquiry," sexual freedom, and dependence on good literature, rather than sacred texts, for ethical insights. But this utopia, he tells us, is based "on the sole condition that we banish all religions from the discourse."[2] His thesis is that "religion poisons everything," and he writes a very convincing argument to this effect, but, he assures us:

> [O]nly the most naive utopianist can believe that this new humane civilization will develop, like some dream of "progress," in a

straight line. We have first to transcend our prehistory, and escape the gnarled hands which reach out to drag us back to the catacombs and the reeking altars and the guilty pleasures of subjection and abjection. "Know yourself," said the Greeks, gently suggesting the consolations of philosophy. To clear the mind for this project, it has become necessary to know the enemy, and to prepare to fight it.[3]

In other words, since religion is a great evil, he hopes to be part of a vanguard that will "fight the enemy," through reason, not violence (I presume), and convince mankind that atheism is the only hope. I must assume that he doesn't expect to transcend prehistory in his lifetime, so in his only hope for immortality, his legacy, he leaves behind a prophetic utterance.

Perhaps Hitchens believes that when religious clashes have led to massive destruction, people will hearken back to his astute analysis and give atheism, his final solution, a chance—a hope not put into a Tower of Babel, a unified attempt to climb up to God, but on an absolute rebellion, just as in the Garden. Only this time, there's no God creeping around, calling out our name while we hide in the bushes. *He's* banished this time, and we run the show. We *will* have paradise, and we don't need God here telling us what we can and cannot do. We'll eat of the Tree of the Knowledge of Good and Evil if we want! We'll decide what's right and wrong! We'll be as gods! Nietzsche's vision will be fulfilled. God *is* dead! We *are* supermen!

And yet, must we be reminded that Nietzsche went mad? Do we recall that the Berlin Wall was smashed down by the citizens of an anti-religious utopia? And does it really ring true to us that people of faith have only made evil contributions to world history?

Isn't Hitchens' proposal just another Baby Jane type of deception? Instead of facing the truth, isn't he just encouraging us to be like her as she deceitfully looks in the mirror at her aging, hopeless self and believes for another comeback?

In fact, I would argue that Hitchens is just contributing to the development of another religion, although he would deny it vehemently. But since I define religion as "mankind's attempt to restore what was lost in the Garden of Eden, without following God's way," isn't the pursuit of an atheist utopia just another religious effort? According to Hitchens, the Soviet Union and North Korea both degenerated into regimes that were religious in nature.[4]

Are we to believe that atheists will eventually get it right, that their other attempts at organizing society, which have deteriorated into quasi-religious nightmares, won't happen again, or that Hitchens' New Enlightenment won't produce another French Revolution?

On the other hand, whether religious people can face it or not, Hitchens is absolutely right. He speaks the truth—lucid, clear, hard truth. His depiction of religion in history is absolutely correct. It *is* evil. It does poison everything. Who can deny this? Even the most ardent believer would have to admit it. And they do. For example, William Wilberforce, the British parliamentarian whose tireless efforts led to the abolition of slavery in the British Empire, was a passionate evangelical Christian (not exactly an atheist or deist), and he asked: "To what else have been owing the extensive ravages of national persecutions, and religious wars and crusades; whereby rapacity, and pride, and cruelty, sheltering themselves under the mask of this specious principle, have so often afflicted this world?"[5]

Wilberforce, like Hitchens, wouldn't be afraid of following the advice of the German historian Leopold von Ranke, who said, "wie es eigentlich gewesen"—history should "show how things actually were."[6] In this Hitchens and Wilberforce aren't like Baby Jane. They're willing to face the truth, no matter how ugly.

But this truth puts us in a quandary. If religion can't get us back to Eden, if it truly is a source of so much evil, and atheism could never produce paradise, how can there ever be any hope for the world?

Hitchens describes a worldview that juxtaposes skeptics and believers: "Just as secularists and atheists have withstood clerical and theocratic tyrannies, so religious believers have resisted pagan and materialistic ones. But this would only be to split the difference."[7] So does this mean that the only options are atheism or religion, two sides that have both resorted to tyranny and hungered for power and control over their subjects? Are these the only possibilities? Or is there another option?

The Third Way

I would argue that there *is* another option, another way. And this way is the way back to Eden, but it's God's way back. It's not religion, and it's not atheism. It was what John the Baptist was ranting about when he shouted, "Prepare the

THE NARROW WAY

way for the Lord," (Matt. 3:3, emphasis mine). It was why Jesus declared that he was "the *way* and the truth and the life" (John 14:6, emphasis mine).

And this Way has also revealed itself in history. The followers of this Way have been at the forefront of political and religious freedom, civil rights, women's rights, scientific advancements, the abolition of blood sport, animal cruelty, human sacrifice, infanticide, slavery, child labor, and tyranny of every form. This is just a short list. They've also established orphanages, hospitals, refugee camps, soup kitchens, and so many other forms of charity and kindness that they're too numerous to mention.

Yet, for some reason, the world hates the followers of this Way. Emperors hate them. Popes hate them. Nazis hate them. Communists hate them. Muslims hate them. Hindus hate them. Jews hate them. Protestants hate them. Catholics hate them. And yes, atheists hate them. They've been boiled in oil, thrown to the beasts, hanged, shot, sent to concentration camps, banished to the Gulag, beheaded, and burnt at the stake. Jesus said of those who killed his predecessors who were on the Way:

> Therefore I am sending you prophets and wise men and teachers. Some of them you will kill and crucify; others you will flog in your synagogues and pursue from town to town. And so upon you will come all the righteous blood that has been shed on earth, from the blood of righteous Abel to the blood of Zechariah son of Berekiah, whom you murdered between the temple and the altar.
> —Matthew 23:34-35

Jesus, himself, was murdered by the political *and* religious leaders of his day. His death was a symbol of the Way that runs between the secular and the sacred. He called it a Narrow Way, and it's the Way of the ancient prophets, John the Baptist, William Tyndale, Dietrich Bonhoeffer, Martin Luther King, Jr., and countless others who have been woven like a blood-stained scarlet thread throughout the tapestry of history, shining in beauty for all to see.

The purpose of this book is to reveal this Way and to show that it is the way back to Eden that the world so desperately yearns for. I hope to show how both the Old and New Testaments point us to this Way. I'd also like to show how history bears the record of this Way.

THE NARROW WAY

The Narrow Way confounds. It baffles those who must ignore it in order for their worldview to make sense. On one side, those who are skeptics and haters of religion find it hard to admit that Martin Luther King, Jr., was a man of faith. They must rationalize that he wasn't a true believer, as Hitchens does, saying that because King never sought revenge when injured, he was "in no real as opposed to nominal sense... a Christian."[8] On the other side are those believers who must look at religion's brutal past and say that what happened was a fluke and not a true representation of religion. To appease their conscience, they point to the failures of the atheistic regimes and say, "You're much worse than us! We killed some people, but you killed a lot of people!" To which Hitchens arrogantly (and rightly) sniffs, "One would think religion had more sense of dignity than that."[9] I would agree.

I believe we must ask: why did Jesus say that religious leaders were responsible for the deaths of all the ancient prophets? Why did the apostle John speak of a "whore," a false religion that rivaled the "bride" and which was responsible for all the blood of the saints and martyrs? Why were believers such as Jonathan Huss killed during the Inquisition? And why did Jesus say religious authorities were responsible for the death of Abel? None of these things make sense if we don't develop a dividing line, something that reveals the characteristics of those who have traveled along the Way and separates them from those who follow religion. I hope this book will give a glimpse of what those dividing lines may be.

Is Religion the Way?

I'd like to make the case that religion was birthed in the Garden of Eden, and since it wasn't God's will for it to exist, *it truly is poisonous*. It turns God into a dictator who makes unbearable, impossible demands on us. It perverts justice and righteousness, turning faith into ritualistic acts: long prayers, fasts, lighting candles, swinging incense, eating certain foods, not eating certain foods, ritual hand washing, ritual bathing, wearing religious clothing, cutting hair, not cutting hair, circumcision, sacrifice, dancing, not dancing, ritual giving, not marrying, worshiping in a certain place, and on and on. Like Jesus said, we tithe down to our mint and cumin (thinking the ritual is all that God requires) and yet neglect the needs of our parents!

Religious activity is a show. It serves no real purpose except to demonstrate to others around us that we're "spiritual." It causes us to believe that if we do these certain petty little actions, we'll be right with God. We'll somehow please him—or appease him. But this isn't what God wants! Over and over the prophets assure us of this fact.

Jesus went up against the religious leaders of his day and showed them the inadequacy of their faith. He knew it was a show. That's why he said to the Pharisees that they were like those who cleaned the outside of the cup, but inside they were full of greed and self-indulgence. Jesus hated religion. It didn't create anything beautiful in the human heart. All it did was feed the pride of those who could keep up the show, or create despair and hopelessness in those who couldn't. The outside may look beautiful, but the inside is filled with greed, lust, cruelty, pride, and selfishness. This is the religion that Hitchens sees. He's right in saying it's poison.

But how does this explain the incredible contributions that have been made to the world by people of faith? Atheists would have us believe that religious people, particularly "fundamentalists," have made the world a backward, mean place. They point to the insistence of Christians in believing in creation rather than evolution as a position that has hindered scientific advancement. They blame fundamentalists for the witch trials and the Inquisition. They point to slavery as a Christian phenomenon, and they also try to equate Christianity with Nazism. I hope that this book will be able to present convincing arguments to the contrary. I'd like to explain why the truth is the exact opposite!

Christians were actually at the forefront in opposing this wickedness and were often attacked vehemently by systems and leaders who *claimed* to have God on their side. Yet these believers didn't compromise or give in, even to the point of death.

What inspired these people of faith to pursue righteous causes with so much passion? I would argue that it was their understanding of the Scriptures as a source of justice, love, and grace, rather than a source of ritual and religious ceremonies.

Although Old Testament Law is jam-packed with specific details about sacrifices, tabernacles, and priests, the apostle Paul told us that the Old Testament sanctuary was just a "copy and shadow" (Heb. 8:5) of the sanctuary in heaven. So, while the Jewish faith is rife with rituals, they weren't there as an appeasement to a petty God. Instead they stand as a glorious symbol of the hope that was to come... evidence that God was real. Every detail, down to the way they baked their bread to the simplicity of the tabernacle structure, was a reflection of God's truth and his desire for mankind.

These Old Testament symbols also revealed a contrast between the religious way and God's way. For example, while most of the world's faiths have temples that reach toward the sky, the Jewish tabernacle stays close to the ground. This reflects the fact that God doesn't want us to climb to him, with all the religious pride that rewards those who reach the top, but he wants to come down to us, where we can reach out to him in humility and simply receive. The tabernacle is also different from the temples of other faiths. M.R. De Haan II explains in his little booklet, *God's House of Symbols: A Walk Through the Old Testament Tabernacle* that "God purposely left the exterior of the tent drab and uninviting. But when the priests moved into the holy place, their eyes would gradually become accustomed to a new kind of light, to a rich variety of color, and to furniture overlaid with gold."[10] This is a reflection of the idea, spoken about by Jesus, that our religious life shouldn't produce outward pretense, but inward beauty. There's no tolerance of "whitewashed sepulchers" in the kingdom of God. We can't clean the outside of the cup and neglect the filth inside.

This idea of justice and mercy taking precedence over ritual was a major theme of the prophets. They saw that religious activity, as a way to please God, was replacing love and kindness, and they cried out against it. Isaiah voiced this exact concern:

> "The multitude of your sacrifices—what are they to me?" says the Lord. "I have more than enough of burnt offerings, of rams and the fat of fattened animals; I have no pleasure in the blood of bulls and lambs and goats. When you come to appear before me, who has asked this of you, this trampling of my courts? Stop bringing meaningless offerings! Your incense is detestable to me. New Moons, Sabbaths and convocations—I cannot bear your evil assemblies. Your New Moon festivals and your appointed feasts my soul hates. They have become a burden to me; I am weary of bearing them. When you spread out your hands in prayer, I will hide my eyes from you; even if you offer many prayers, I will not listen. Your hands are full of blood; wash and make yourselves clean. Take your evil deeds out of

my sight! Stop doing wrong, learn to do right! Seek justice, encourage the oppressed. Defend the cause of the fatherless, plead the case of the widow."

—Isaiah 1:11-17

In other words, faith in God should produce true righteousness, which is care for the oppressed and needy, and not just church attendance. The Old Testament rituals weren't empty; they were symbols that reflected the need for holiness. When they were used as a way to merely cover sin and make it easy to be unjust or unloving, they were a perversion of God's will.

Jesus said he came to fulfill the Law and the Prophets. He fulfilled the ritual law by becoming the sacrifice, the Lamb of God. He fulfilled the moral law by being sinless. He fulfilled the prophets in two ways: not only by fulfilling the Old Testament prophecies concerning the Messiah, but also by living a life of compassion and love toward the needy.

The ritual law, while seeming to point to senseless requirements and silly rules, were in truth a way that could reveal the Messiah, the way to God and the hope of the world. It contained what C.S. Lewis may have referred to in *The Lion, the Witch, and the Wardrobe* as the "deeper magic."[11] Within the outward expression, there was a hidden message that revealed the will and purposes of God. The Law would point to a new temple: the church, which was washed in the blood of the Lamb and lived a life of true righteousness, not religious show. Any religion that inverts this message is wrong, deceiving itself, and becoming an expression of the serpent, which produces deadly poison, rather than nourishment and life.

Life is what Adam and Eve gave up in the Garden. They could have eaten from the Tree of Life, but they ate of the Tree of the Knowledge of Good and Evil instead. When they did this, they traded that which would animate and give strength, movement, and enthusiasm for that which would produce a stench and cause them to be sick and anemic, remaining dull and empty. Religion has this effect. Although it can engender some enthusiasm, what is produced is fanaticism—a deathly, zombielike zealousness that takes the form of witch hunts and terrorism rather than love and kindness.

In the next chapters I hope that I can show how those who were traveling on the Way of Life, who understood the biblical message, produced amazing life and fruit. Jesus said "a tree is recognized by its fruit" (Matt. 12:33b), and history gives us glimpses of the fruit produced by those who eat of the Tree of Life. They were trailblazers, filled with compassion and yearning for freedom, because "if the Son sets you free, you will be free indeed" (John 8:36).

Does your faith produce a life of "love, joy, peace, patience, kindness, goodness, faithfulness, gentleness and self-control" (Gal. 5:22-23), or does it produce a life of selfishness, unconquerable sin, and futile attempts to please God through dead, empty ritual and sacrifices? For some Christians this could be the tyranny of the unkept "quiet time," the burden of tithing rather than paying the rent or spending hours tarrying at the altar until your mind is deadened and you have nothing to give except a show of your "spiritual passion" by being there so long. Religious ritual or show takes many forms.

My Experience with Religion

At this point, I think I should share a little of my experience with religion. When I was eighteen, I had an encounter with Jesus. It didn't happen in church. It happened in cockroach-infested military housing, a place dubbed the Slocum Slums by those who had the joy and privilege of living there. I was unhappily married and felt suicidal at the time. I had a little boy and fantasized that I would crash my car while we were both in it, but instead, right in the midst of my despair, I came across a comic book, entitled *The Real Jesus*. The words and pictures on the pages came alive, in a sense, and I began to weep with passion and regret all at once. I can't say I understood every detail of the commitment I was making, but I just knew that something offered me hope. It awakened something inside of me. Whereas before I was facing the prospect of death, now I had love and gratitude toward someone who did an extraordinary thing for me. If he had truly done this for me, as part of his gift to the world, could I deny it, reject it? No. I couldn't harden my heart. Every part of me felt only tenderness, pain, and sympathy for the one who took my place on the cross. My heart was grieved and filled with joy at the same time. I would embrace Jesus. I wouldn't look away.

At this point, (I can't say it happened all at once), I became a different person. I became strong. I committed myself to my marriage. I became stable. I had a little girl. I enjoyed life. I started going to church and learning the Bible. This kept on for a number of years... but then something else, almost imperceptibly, began to happen to me. I became religious. I was at the church in my best, fancy dress every time the doors were open. I took leadership positions and climbed up the associational, and then the state, ladder of success. I refused simple pleasures like music, movies, dancing, or an occasional drink. I prayed long, expressive, public prayers. I taught the Bible (without truly understanding its message). I became a proud, spiritual "prig" (in the words of Oswald Chambers, author of the Christian classic, *My Utmost for His Highest*).[12]

The church I was involved in fueled this religious zeal. They believed for a move of God, a great revival with signs and wonders that would usher people into the kingdom of God. Many churches believe something similar to this, but our church went over the edge.

We were visited by a man who claimed he was a prophet. He supposedly had special gifts from God that would allow him to know God's specific will for individual people or churches. He told our church that revival was surely coming and that it would begin in the youth group. He predicted that a "notable miracle" would occur on a specific Sunday, and gave many other "prophecies from God."

But none of these prophecies came to pass. He was a *false* prophet. In his desperation, he began to say that his failures were the result of the powers of darkness, that Satan was attacking the church and trying to hinder the move of God. And then, in an astounding, brazen attempt to preserve himself at all costs, he began to attack innocent women and accuse them of being witches who "quenched the Spirit" (1 Thess. 5:19, NAS).

I may have gotten caught up in this frenzy if not for two things: First, a knowledge of the Scriptures, which declare, "You may say to yourselves, 'How can we know when a message has not been spoken by the Lord?' If what a prophet proclaims in the name of the Lord does not take place or come true, that is a message the Lord has not spoken. That prophet has spoken presumptuously. Do not be afraid of him" (Deut. 18:21-22). Second, I had a love and concern for the accused women. I knew them as human beings, and I knew they were innocent. Most were women who had no men to defend them— women on the fringes who were easy targets.

I felt outraged. I couldn't believe that the church would accept this, but they did. My husband and I tried to influence others to take a stand against it, but instead the pastor and other "prayer warriors" led a campaign against us.

We were warned not to "touch God's anointed" or come against "the seat of Moses." And in the meantime, four women were branded as witches. For questioning the veracity of "God's prophet," my husband and I were called before the church board, stripped of our position as adult Sunday school teachers in the sanctuary, and ultimately kicked out of the church. My husband was characterized as being one who must have had a "demon leap on him," and I was referred to as being "poison" and having a "Jezebel spirit."

This was like an earthquake, which shook me down to the bottom of my soul. I had to make sense of it. I wasn't willing to abandon the sweet savior that I had met in that dumpy little apartment nearly two decades before, but if my church was following God's will and way, *God's way was wrong!* What a quandary!

It was then that I felt my eyes being opened. My best friend, who was also a Christian, but a member of a different church, helped me to patiently dissect what had happened. We began to search the Word and discovered truths we never understood before. The Scriptures, just like the book *The Real Jesus* had done so many years before, began to come alive in a new way, and all of a sudden I found myself being drawn away in excitement to study them. Before, the Bible was merely a guidebook, now it was a source of passion, even of romance. I felt myself being gently beckoned away to discover new little insights that would fill my heart with desire for more of the God who was becoming so beautiful to me.

Initially, I was especially intrigued by Matthew 7:21-23, which said to those who were claiming to be Christians that even though they said they did miracles, cast out demons, and prophesied in his name, Jesus would still say to them on judgment day, "I never knew you. Away from me, you evildoers!" How could he say this to "Christians"? What could this mean?

These words of Jesus sparked a revolution in my perspective and understanding. I discovered that outward religious activities, no matter how spiritual they might seem, were not the gauge of our faith. It doesn't matter what form your religious endeavors take (even prophesying or casting out demons!), if your faith only produces the gifts of the Spirit, rather than the fruits of the Spirit, it's not pleasing to God. This is why the Apostle Paul said, "If I speak in the tongues of men and of angels, but have not love … I gain nothing" (1 Cor. 13:1-3).

I realized that my church was vulnerable on this account. We had put so much stock into our gifts, particularly that of prophesying, that we ended up being easily deceived. When we decided to castigate innocent women, to scapegoat them for the sake of our great cause, we lost the heart of God. We put our collective goal of revival ahead of justice, mercy, and compassion toward individuals. James said, "Religion that God our Father accepts as pure and faultless is this: to look after orphans and widows in their distress" (James 1:27). When we abandoned widows, as some of these women were, we abandoned God.

But to our church, revival was the great white hope. It was our Eden. We had sign-up sheets where we publicly declared our willingness to fast for revival on certain days (clearly violating Jesus' admonition to fast secretly), we met at the church for early morning prayers for revival, we had passionate Friday night prayers for revival and fervent prayers for revival in all the services. We were committed to this cause. We walked around town and walked around the church pulling down the strongholds of "spiritual wickedness in high places" that would stop the revival. We had revival preachers as guests. We studied revivals of the past—all of us knew of Jonathan Edwards. We lingered at the altar. We worshiped and worshiped and worshiped. But no matter how much we tried, nothing happened. We were like the prophets of Baal. No matter how frenzied they became, they couldn't call down fire from heaven, and neither could we. The goal was so elusive. Like a carrot on a stick, it was always out of reach.

So when somebody who seemed so spiritual (by our standards), came to us and told us what we wanted to hear, we leaped on it. We believed it with all our hearts. But just as Jude described those who are false, our prophet was a cloud "without rain" (Jude 12)—promising much, but delivering nothing. Instead of getting more people, more money, affirmation from God for our efforts, recognition from others, and glory—our Eden—all we got was heartbreak, deception, division, and destruction. We had experienced our own Fall. Just as in the Garden, we had chosen religious effort over love, compassion, and justice… and it poisoned us.

This experience was the beginning of a journey that would lead to this book and to the understanding of the Bible and history found within these pages. It is an understanding birthed from tragedy, an attempt to make sense out of injustice, to bring goodness out of grief. My husband and I went to other churches and found similar problems, churches that followed goals based on elusive plans, promises of evangelical Edens found in books such as John C. Maxwell's *The 21 Irrefutable Laws of Leadership* or Tommy Tenney's *The God Chasers* that offer paradise, but produce the same results: heartache, deception, division, and destruction. Both of these books are attempts to bring about our idea of paradise (a strong, thriving church with lots of people and lots of money). One accomplishes the goal through developing strong leaders and the other, interestingly enough, through calling down fire from heaven by praying for a manifestation of God's power.

If my experience is any indication of what's going on in America's churches, there must be a great deal of confusion and pain brought about by what I believe is a religious pursuit of Eden, a grasping for paradise in our own way, rather than in God's way.

There's an obscure little law in the Old Testament that forbids us to wear any piece of clothing made of a cloth woven from a blend of woolen and linen (Lev. 19:19 KJV). It's used by some as an example of the absurdity of the Old Testament Law and how it should be tossed out, but within this little law is a precious truth. It can best be summed up by the example of Cain and Abel. Abel's offering was a blood sacrifice. Cain's was a grain sacrifice. God rejected the offering that came from Cain, because it represented the work of our hands (religion), and accepted the offering of Abel, which represented the sacrifice of Jesus. Linen, a cloth woven from a plant, represents using religious works to get to God, and woolen, the fur of a lamb, represents getting to God through Jesus.

It isn't pleasing to God when our churches blend the woolen and the linen together. Paul confirmed this when he exclaimed, "You foolish Galatians! Who has bewitched you?" (Gal. 3:1a). They had started out with complete trust in the work of the cross, but then reverted back to the practice of circumcision. He says they were now trying to reach their goal through "human effort" (Gal. 3:3). When the church resorts to any kind of activity that proceeds from the Old Testament Law, such as tithing, fasting, the priesthood, abstaining from certain foods or any other law that was merely a shadow of Christ, they make the death of Jesus null and void and even come under the curse they're trying so hard to avoid!

It is for freedom that Christ has set us free. Stand firm, then, and do not let yourselves be burdened again by a yoke of slavery. Mark

my words! I, Paul, tell you that if you let yourselves be circumcised, Christ will be of no value to you at all. Again I declare to every man who lets himself be circumcised that he is obligated to obey the whole law. You who are trying to be justified by law have been alienated from Christ; you have fallen away from grace. But by faith we eagerly await through the Spirit the righteousness for which we hope. For in Christ Jesus neither circumcision nor uncircumcision has any value. The only thing that counts is faith expressing itself through love.
—Galatians 5:1-6

So any time we do anything other than express our love for God or man (which Jesus said fulfills the moral law), we are in danger of blending the woolen and the linen.

How much joy would it bring to God if we simply began to love him, love each other, and love our neighbors? Instead, we're sold a bill of goods, being told by the latest charlatan that they have the silver bullet, the quick way to bring back Eden—when Eden is only love.

Time and again, the great thinkers devise grand plans and schemes to take us back to the Garden—and all they do, like a strong-willed child running into the street, is contribute to their own destruction (and ours). Yet throughout history those who have discovered the Narrow Way, God's way, have created their own humble little Edens wherever they have gone. They have created places of love, freedom, refuge, and care—bright lights shining forth *true* hope in a world that can be very dark and full of despair.

CHAPTER TWO
The Narrow Way in the Old Testament

> *"The Bible fights for God against religion. This fight is rather strong in the Old Testament, where it is most powerful in the attack of the prophets against the cult and the polytheistic implications of the popular religion. It's also evident in the New Testament... which is full of stories in which Jesus violates ritual laws in order to exercise love, and in Paul the whole ritual law is dispossessed by the appearance of the Christ."* —Paul Tillich, twentieth-century theologian

> *"'But let him who boasts boast about this: that he understands and knows me, that I am the Lord, who exercises kindness, justice and righteousness on earth, for in these I delight,' declares the Lord."* —Jeremiah 9:24

When I define religion as mankind's attempt to restore Eden without doing it God's way, I'm not only referring to a return to a place, a garden, but also a return to a relationship. In Eden, Adam and Eve had an intimate connection with God. He walked with them and talked with them. There was no separation or divorce. But when they disobeyed, the relationship was severed. There was a cut. Not only were they cut off from paradise, they were also cut off from intimacy with and acceptance from God. So the Fall encompassed being separated from both God *and* the Garden, and the return to Eden includes attempts to get both back. This is why I say that utopian pursuits are a form of religion. They take the form of an attempt to recover the physical aspects of Eden. But religion can also take the form of an attempt to restore the relationship with God and get back to a time when we were accepted, rather than rejected and forsaken.

In trying to heal this wound, we've invented all types of man-made activities that we hope will serve as a balm to assist in healing. But instead of embracing the Balm of Gilead, we end up getting out a knife and making the cut deeper. Religion is like a knife; it not only separates us further from God, but also from each other. It wounds and injures. It divides, cuts, and separates.

Yet it doesn't need to be this way. God has revealed a way we can be restored, but we refuse to submit to it. We hate being told this. I'm sure that there are those who will read this book and find it to be very offensive. There will be a vitriolic reaction that causes hatred to rise up inside some readers as I tell them that the Way to God involves only the acceptance of the blood of the Lamb, and that Christianity is not just another religion but is absolutely different because it doesn't involve any self-effort whereby pride can be birthed. It's Good News! It's available to all, no matter how hopeless your condition. Just reach out and receive the work of Christ on the Cross, the shed blood of the Lamb, and you will be accepted by God, allowing new life to flow into you and make you new.

This is anti-religion. It's the opposite of poison and death. It's life. It puts everyone on a level playing field before God. There's no more need for priests. The blood has been shed, and the Way is now opened. No mediator is needed between man and God anymore. The veil in the Temple was torn. There's no need for ritual law. It was merely a vessel, like a shell, which would be cracked open, revealing that the purpose of its existence was to produce something lovely: the pearl of great price. There's no need to climb to get up to God, like Martin Luther who crawled on bloody knees up the steps of the Lateran in Rome, but instead God came down to us and did it all. His own blood was shed. It is finished.

Religion has always taken the form of the older brother, Cain, who, in his jealousy and hatred toward Abel, took out that cutting knife and shed his little brother's blood. This is the continual record of history. It's seen in the clash between all of the older and younger brothers in the biblical story. Ishmael and Isaac. Jacob and Esau. Joseph and his brothers. The prodigal and the older brother. All were at odds with one another. Even Jesus, in being referred to as the Second Adam, symbolized the younger brother Abel, rather than the older brother Cain, and he was killed by those bearers of man-made ritual, the religious leaders of his day.[13]

THE NARROW WAY IN THE OLD TESTAMENT

Religious self-effort is hated by God because it's rooted in pride. It's dependent upon our ability to gear up and perform. As I said in the first chapter, it's *independence*. It isn't submission, but rebellion. It refuses to obey. After all, God's Way does nothing to build up our ego. It doesn't provide any titles or positions. It doesn't let us form any special classes or divisions. Special clothing is out—it only divides. It doesn't provide any rituals for religious leaders to perform except to lovingly care for the flock and serve them. In the Kingdom of God, recognition isn't given to those holding positions but to whom honor is really due—the honorable.

This leveling of religious divisions or classes would lead John the Baptist to cry out (as Isaiah did): "Prepare the way for the Lord, make straight paths for him. Every valley shall be filled in, every mountain and hill made low" (Luke 3:4-5). And Mary would marvel at the work of God, mentioning this same concept of exaltation and humiliation: "He has performed mighty deeds with his arm; he has scattered those who are proud in their inmost thoughts. He has brought down rulers from their thrones but has lifted up the humble" (Luke 1:51-52).

The way of God is democratic. It's an equalizer. It's not the way of the Nicolaitans (Rev. 2:15). ("Nico" means "to rule" and "laitans" is the root word for "laity," so Nicolaitans means "to rule over the laity.") God doesn't want anyone to rule over his sheep. He wants them to have a shepherd who will lead them to restful green pastures and beside still water, not a cruel shepherd who will use them and drive them to steep, rocky places.

The characterization of God as a cruel dictator rather than a good shepherd, by those who reject God, would be correct if the only reason the ritual law existed was to make mankind jump through hoops at the whim of a controlling tyrant, like some great dog trainer in the sky. But that's not why the Law existed. It would be pointless and petty standing alone. But within it was proof of God's existence, evidence that he was at work in history for anyone who wanted to see it. Jesus said "seek and you will find" (Matt. 7:7), and within these carefully conveyed and detailed laws was a revelation that even ~~Michael~~ Dan Brown, author of *The Da Vinci Code*, couldn't have conceived of—evidence for the reality of God in history.

The Jewish people were to carry out this special task in history. They were so detailed in their work that the Talmudist had to follow a number of minute regulations that detailed the way to copy the Scriptures. Everything from the ink to the skins that made up the scrolls to the number and length of columns down to the fact that "the copyist must sit in full Jewish dress, wash his whole body, not begin to write the name of God with a pen newly dipped in ink, and should a king address him while writing that name he must take no notice of him."[14]

The Hebrew Scriptures have been preserved so perfectly that the Dead Sea scrolls, hidden over a thousand years ago but discovered only in the 1940s, contained only minute, inconsequential variations from the modern texts.[15] What a precious responsibility! And the Jewish people didn't fail. They were faithful. They were preserving a precious treasure that would point to the Messiah, the hope of the world. They may not have understood everything they were doing, but as Abraham was promised, through them "all peoples on earth will be blessed" (Gen. 12:3b).

How else could we know with any level of certainty who the Messiah was? Any David Koresh or Sun Myung Moon could claim to be the Christ. We would have no standard to lead us. But there was a way! The Old Testament is merely a proof. It validates the proposition put forth by the New Testament that Jesus was the Christ. This is why Jesus would take his disciples to the Old Testament in order to explain who he was. On the road to Emmaus after he was resurrected, he would begin with Moses and all the prophets and explain to Cleopas and his fellow traveler all that was said in the Scriptures concerning himself. And as the two, who began by walking with him and ended by dining with him, reflected on their encounter, they asked each other, "Were not our hearts burning within us while he talked with us on the road and opened the Scriptures to us?" (Luke 24:32).

When we understand what the Old Testament revealed, we become passionate about it. Something deep within our hearts is filled with wonder, making it difficult to grasp the reality of what we're learning. To have evidence that something more than us exists in the cosmos is mind-boggling.

The Old Testament was created to reveal this "something more" to us. It would show that the way to God was indeed through Jesus and assure us that we could put our trust in him. Without this proof, we would be like a ship without a lighthouse or a traveler without a map. Any person who has taken the time to understand the connection between the Old and New Testament can't help but be amazed. The Law that was so tenderly preserved by those precious Jewish scribes would culminate in the life of Jesus, the "Lamb of God, who takes away the sins of the world" (John 1:29). He was the Way, hidden within the Law, and foretold by the prophets.[16]

This chapter will attempt to reveal this Narrow Way in the Old Testament and to show how God hates the other way, the religious way. It will begin in the Garden and culminate in the writings of the Minor Prophets. It is the message that burns within all of God's servants throughout history, and it's what led to them being murdered.

The Two Trees

There were two trees in the Garden. One tree was the Tree of Life. By eating of this tree mankind could have eternal life and live a holy life. The other tree was the Tree of the Knowledge of Good and Evil. By eating of this tree we were also able to have eternal life by living a holy life, but the difference between the trees is this: the Tree of Life gives us *power* to live a life of holiness, while the Tree of the Knowledge of Good and Evil gives *knowledge* of what the expectations are for holiness, but doesn't empower us to live it.

If Adam and Eve had eaten of the Tree of Life, they would have been infused with God's life—a power that would have produced a spiritual energy filling them with the spiritual fruits of "love, joy, peace, patience, kindness, goodness, faithfulness, gentleness and self-control" (Gal. 5:22-23). They would have produced fruit in keeping with the tree they had eaten from. Holiness—pure living—would have flowed from them as a result of this life, rather than as a result of merely knowing the law.

When Adam and Eve ate of the Tree of Knowledge, they put themselves in a position where their eyes were opened to the law. Their conscience was awakened, and they knew right from wrong. But they didn't have any power to live a law-abiding life. They only had knowledge. Their obedience to the law was dependent on their own strength. Paul spoke of them as having a form of godliness but denying its power. Therefore, since they had rejected the power of God and embraced self-power, they were doomed to failure.

God knew this, and that was why he told them they would die if they ate of the Tree of Knowledge. It wasn't that they had displeased God and were now worthy of death. He told them this, because their choice would lead to death.

It would lead to sin, which would separate them from him—the source of Life. He is a holy God, and sin, which is selfishness, can't infect his realm. He doesn't want to give any space to evil in his Kingdom. It would only spread. Jesus said it was like yeast that would expand and touch everything. (This is why the Jews were told to eat unleavened bread for Passover. It represents sinlessness.)

Lucifer

In order to understand the Fall, we need to realize that Adam and Eve weren't the first in the universe to rebel. The Bible tells us of another of God's creations, the angels, as having rebelled. They were led by Lucifer (which means "light-bearing one"). He was God's most beautiful creation. He lived in the presence of God. But Lucifer, impressed by his own beauty and abilities, became arrogant. He wanted to be like God. He convinced one third of the angels to follow him in rebellion. At this point, sin, rooted in pride, was given place in the universe.

But this left God in a difficult position. If there were no consequences for the actions of these angels, sin would spread. Like a virus out of control, it would move across the cosmos and infect everything. If this happened, there would no longer be any heaven, just a *Mad Max* kind of universe where the strong and evil would run rampant over the weak. The pride and rebellion in Lucifer's heart would spread and permeate creation, causing war, division, hatred, and injustice.

On the other hand, if God were to destroy the rebellious angels, there would be fear in the universe. God would have a dictatorial relationship with his creation, rather than the love relationship he desired. What could he do? Ignore them and let the universe become infected, or destroy them and make creation live in fear of him? It seemed there was no way out.

Love requires liberty. It can't be forced. And yet it appeared that the angels were forced to love God… or else. Lucifer had forced God's hand. The corrupt seed of thought had been planted, and Lucifer had prevailed. Through the life—or death —of the fallen angel, God would lose. Checkmate.

Or so Lucifer thought. But God *wasn't* trapped. He devised another way. It was a beautiful plan that included a display to the universe of his great love. It would show his creation that he was a loving God and not a dictator, revealing his selflessness and humility. It would show them that they could trust his heart and that he was worthy of their allegiance and love. It would even inspire passion for him, not just lip service and lifeless obedience.

The Scriptures say that God wants a bride, but he isn't interested in an arranged marriage. He wants love rooted in passion and romance, the kind that produces life and joy. (This is why Christianity doesn't encourage arranged marriages, but instead recognizes the power and mystery of attraction as the foundation for a strong marriage.) Through this plan God would reveal himself to be a friend, rather than a dictator, and instead of a tyrant, he would be a bridegroom so full of passion that he would even die for his bride.

As with the angels, God had to give his creation a free will, or there would be no true love. He created a new race called humans and put them in a perfect environment so that there would only be satisfaction and sufficiency. There would be no excuse for rebellion. He would provide a way for them to have eternal life with him. All they had to do was eat of the Tree of Life.

But he also had to give them another option. It had to have within it the same temptation as that experienced by the angels—to "be like God" (Gen. 3:5)—and the same consequence—death. This would allow God to show the justice of his decisions. If the angels could watch this drama unfold and see the consequence of sin, perhaps it would make them long for justice and righteousness and would set their hearts in agreement with God.

Lucifer watched as God set up this new world. He regarded the two trees and probably pondered what God was doing. He knew disobedience and rebellion had left God on the horns of a dilemma in the past, and perhaps thought God was banking on the fact that this different type of creation—a creation made in his own image—wouldn't be as easily tempted. It's difficult to say what led Lucifer to creep into the Garden and begin his seduction. (Seduction is an interesting word to use because it implies that there was an intimacy between God and humanity that would be corrupted by a betrayal, an adultery.) Nevertheless, Lucifer went in for the kill, hoping to have victory over the defeated God again!

But this time, God would put *Lucifer* on the horns of a dilemma. No matter what choice humanity made, God would have the victory, not Lucifer. If they chose the Tree of Life, they would live in union with God forever, but if they chose the Tree of the Knowledge of Good and Evil, there would be provision for them to have life also. Lucifer wouldn't understand this, though. It was a "deeper magic."

It's the principle of the seed. Inside the outer shell a form of life lies dormant. Likewise, within the outer shell of the seed of the Jewish religion would lie dormant a glorious form of life. It was a magnificent plan that would finally conquer Lucifer and his fallen angels and restore a just and righteous peace to the universe.

Adam and Eve

At the Fall, religion was birthed. (Having its source in a serpent, it's no surprise that it's poisonous.) By eating of the Tree of Knowledge, Adam and Eve were cut off from the source of life. They were now aware of their sin and felt convicted before God. So they covered themselves with fig leaves and hid. This was the first religious act. They were trying to figure out a way to be with him, but they knew they would be too humiliated to stand there naked, so they picked leaves and sewed them together to make clothing.

The word "religion" means "to reconnect." (It comes from the same root word as "ligament," a connecting tissue.) When Adam and Eve covered themselves, instead of running away completely, they showed that they were trying to reconnect to God. They didn't want to be separated from him. But the problem was that they did it their own way. They didn't know any other way, so God showed them the way he wanted—the way that was necessary for justice. He sacrificed animals and used their fur as clothing to cover Adam and Eve's shame. This was the first time we see a glimpse of the Way that God had planned to restore order, justice, and righteousness in the universe. But surprisingly, the restoration wouldn't be accomplished only by pure justice or righteousness, but by a tender, sweet, little word, perhaps new to the universe: "grace."

Instead of a Pharisaical self-righteous God who blusters against every infraction of the law, God revealed that he wants mankind to live. So he offered Adam and Eve grace. They would be exiled so that they couldn't eat of the Tree of Life and live forever in their sinful condition, and they would have to pay a temporal consequence for their sin (pain and work), but they wouldn't pay a spiritual consequence. The Blood took care of that. This would be the Way to God now. There could be nothing added to it. It had to be blood because it would point to the loving sacrifice that he, himself, would one day become on our behalf in order to prove that he wasn't a dictator, but a beautiful, compassionate, loving, servant.

Cain and Abel

The sons of Adam and Eve, Cain and Abel, would know of this requirement also, because they brought offerings to the Lord, but the Scripture says that Cain's offering wasn't acceptable. Why not? After all, he probably worked hard to prepare it. But God wants a blood offering. He wanted this blood offering to be a type and shadow that would point to the final offering—Jesus. This is why Hebrews 11:4 says that Abel's sacrifice was a better source of righteousness.

Cain was angry that God didn't accept his offering, so the Lord asked him, "Why are you angry? Why is your face downcast? If you do what is right, will you not be accepted? But if you do not do what is right, sin is crouching at your door; it desires to have you, but you must master it" (Gen. 4:6-7).

God was saying that even though Cain's offering was unacceptable to him, all he had to do, since he didn't want to do it God's way, was "do what was right." The only problem was, if he messed up once, sin was "crouching at the door," ready to leap on him. All Cain had to do was master the sin desire—and never slip up—and he would be accepted by God. This is the condition of mankind. Either we do things God's way, which is receiving the Blood as a covering for our sin, or we always do what's right. It's our choice.

Since none of us are perfect (Cain went out and killed his brother immediately after this admonition from God to do the right thing), that means we can try to reconnect to God, to get back to Eden, our own way (fig leaves, grain offerings—which symbolize religious works or human effort) or by doing it God's way. Most of humanity has chosen their own way. The prophet Isaiah said, "We all, like sheep, have gone astray, each of us has turned to his own way" (Isa. 53:6a). Religion is mankind going its own way. It's a refusal to embrace God's way. It's the way of Cain. And it produces murder. Instead of life, its fruit is death. God is against it. It is rebellion, and it doesn't bring him pleasure. The basket of vegetables put together by Cain did nothing to produce goodness in his heart. It was a form of godliness, a form of the offering God required, but it wasn't the right offering, and it didn't give him any power to live a righteous life. It was just another form of disobedience.

Noah

If we would just submit to God in this one thing—getting to God through the Blood alone—life would flow through us. We would be able to access the

Spirit of God and have the power to live a life pleasing to God—not a perfect life, only Jesus did that—but an overcomer's life that isn't in bondage to hatred and sin.

As we look at the rest of the biblical narrative, we see the Blood as a consistent presence. In the story of Noah, God considered him to be a righteous man in the midst of a very violent world. He had "found favor in the eyes of the Lord" (Gen. 6:8). He wasn't pleasing to God because he was perfect. (He was lying drunk and naked in a tent at one point in his life.) But Noah offered blood sacrifices. He did things God's way. And God was pleased with him. He was used to preserve mankind from judgment and total destruction. There's no record that Noah lit any candles or wore any special clothes. He didn't perform any religious ritual except the shedding of an animal's blood.

The Tower of Babel

The Tower of Babel is the story of mankind's first collective effort to bring back Eden. They all spoke one language, so they organized themselves, building a city, and in its midst they built a tower that would reach up to heaven. They attempted to get back to paradise by bringing order (a city) out of a chaotic world, and they tried to reconnect to God by climbing to heaven. By joining together they would make a name for themselves (Gen. 11:4), but this proud effort wasn't pleasing to God. They were trying to get back to paradise their own way, so God would scatter them. Religious efforts, which are characterized by so many cities, temples, and towers throughout the world, would not make men acceptable to God.

As those rebels from Babel spread out across the globe, they took their religious inclinations with them. Galatians says that the whole world is under this curse of the law—knowledge of good and evil without power—*religion*. All of us, like sheep, have gone astray and have gone our own way. The human race developed countless religious systems, but none of them were devised by God, *except one*. The Jews would be called God's chosen people, not because they were so holy (we know they weren't!), but because although they too would set up intricate laws and rituals which had no power, their laws would be given to them by God as shadows and symbols that would point to the Messiah. Humanity could now know that faith had substance and evidence based on the revelation given through the seed of Abraham.

The Christian faith isn't just a leap into thin air with the hope that God may someday uphold us in the by and by. Rather, Christianity can put out the challenge to others to explain the content and formation of the Word. How could it all point to Jesus—the Lamb of God? We're told that the Old Testament was merely a type of the reality found in Christ. All of the religious rituals were there for a purpose. They would become a source of faith, not one that's made up of just puffs and whiffs, but one that is living and real in history.

The apostle Paul, a Pharisee who knew the Law, would be chosen to unfold and explain these symbols to us. He would explain how the blood sacrifice was there to point to Jesus, the Lamb of God. He would explain how the priesthood was only a shadow of Jesus, our mediator and high priest before God. He would explain that the Temple was merely a type of the Church. He would show us how the Old Testament stories were even symbols that pointed to Christ, explaining that Jesus was the Second Adam and as a symbol of this, all of the second-born sons of the patriarchs would receive the blessing rather than the first. Abel rather than Cain. Isaac rather than Ishmael. Jacob rather than Esau.

Paul would explain how none of us, even Abraham or his descendents, could be saved by obedience to the law, since none of us could keep it. We could only be saved through faith. And does God demand that we have faith with no evidence? No! We may not see God, but we can see his handiwork. We can see his plan… a plan that could only be orchestrated by something higher than us. Humans could not have woven together such intricate magnificence over the course of history.

Abraham

God would sovereignly choose Abraham to be the father of this faith. He was told to leave Ur and go to the land God would show him. He would end up in the land of the Canaanites, a place where blood was shed to appease the gods. But it wasn't animal blood the Canaanites wanted. It was the blood of children. This was how far humanity had gone astray! It was in this environment that God spoke to Abraham and told him to sacrifice Isaac. It wasn't unusual for a god to demand this, but God didn't ask that Isaac be sacrificed because he was a cruel god, rather it was to set himself apart from other gods by showing that he *didn't* want child sacrifice. He had already explained to Noah that he didn't want human blood to be shed: "Whoever sheds the blood of man, by man shall his blood be shed; for in the image of God has God made man" (Gen. 9:6). God wanted Abraham to know that his way was through the blood of an animal. It was this place called Mount Moriah that Abraham would call Jehovah Jireh, meaning "the Lord will provide," a symbol pointing to the Lamb that would be provided for all people who would trust in his shed blood. Later this would become the spot where the Temple would be built. This Temple would be the place where the blood of lambs would be shed for the atonement of the sins of Israel.

The Exodus

We see the Blood again in the story of the Exodus. God told Moses that the death angel would pass over any homes that had the blood of a lamb applied to the doorposts. The blood was to be put on the top and both sides, symbolizing the Cross. The whole Passover story is symbolic of Christ. Even the preparation of a spotless Lamb would point to the sinless Jesus. Life would come through the blood of a lamb. This was God's Way. The whole nation of Israel was saved through obedience to this command.

When God gave the ritual law to Moses, the first step necessary to come into the tent of God's presence was to offer an unblemished male from his herd at the door so that he'd be accepted by the Lord. This again pointed to the sinless Lamb, Jesus.

It's necessary to note that the blood of animals couldn't actually make atonement for sin. The same way that the Temple was just a symbol that pointed to the future Church, the blood of animals was just a symbol that pointed to the *future* blood of Jesus: "For the life of a creature is in the blood, and I have given it to you to make atonement for yourselves on the altar; it is the blood that makes atonement for one's life" (Lev. 17:11).

Hebrews 10:19 says that we can have "confidence to enter the Most Holy Place by the blood of Jesus." The Blood would make atonement (reparation). Atonement is a way to repair, or heal, the cut between God and man. It's a symbol of justice being restored. If "the wages of sin is death" (Rom. 6:23), then death was necessary for justice.

Rahab

The Blood appears again in the story of Jericho. Rahab, a prostitute, hid the two spies on her roof. She had heard how the Israelites were saved miraculously from the bondage of Egypt, and she was concerned that she would be on the wrong side of a battle with them. So when the king of Jericho asked her if she knew where the Israeli spies were, she said they had been there, but that they had left already, even though she was still hiding them. When the spies thanked her for hiding them, she requested that they would have mercy on her and her family when they attacked the city. They told her to place a scarlet cord out her window, and she would be saved. Rahab's choice would lead to her salvation and even to her being included in the lineage of Jesus Christ. For this to happen to a prostitute points again to that precious word: grace—acceptance by God through the Blood, which was symbolized in this case by the scarlet cord. The book of Hebrews would even place Rahab in the Hall of the Faithful, which included Noah, Abraham, Joseph, and Moses, just to name a few.

Isaiah

There's a Narrow Way, a lineage of Jesus Christ, which winds through the Old Testament. Matthew tells us that Seth, the third son of Adam and Eve, was the ancestor of Jesus and that a special family tree existed which traced its way through Noah, Abraham, Isaac, Jacob, Judah, Jesse, David, Solomon, Josiah, and other figures of the Old Testament. This was a bloodline, a scarlet thread that could be traced through history. God's Way is always symbolized by the blood. Even in this, the bloodline never ran through the oldest son, but the younger. The first Adam represented the bondage of religion, while the second Adam, Jesus, represented freedom and Life. The Old Testament, though characterized by the lifeless religious symbols of temples, rituals, and sacrifices, would give way to Life. The Tree of Life didn't die. Its seed just went into the ground for a time, only to awaken and blossom forth into new glory. Isaiah would proclaim, "Forget the former things; do not dwell on the past. See, I am doing a new thing! Now it springs up; do you not perceive it? I am making a way in the desert and streams in the wasteland" (Isa. 43:18-19).

Though Israel had been eating, along with the rest of the world, from a type of the Tree of the Knowledge of Good and Evil, in the form of ritualistic religion, John the Baptist said, "The ax is already at the root of the trees, and every tree that does not produce good fruit will be cut down and thrown into the fire!" (Matt. 3:10) God was about to do a new thing. The seed that had lain dormant was now a tree, and the old tree, which had produced bad fruit, death, could be cut down to give place to a new one that produced life. This is a paradox. The tree that was cut down to be used as a cross would hold the Lamb, whose shed blood would lead to Life, a restoration of Eden.

Even within the Old Testament Law is another indication of God's plan: "Anyone who is hung on a tree is under God's curse" (Deut. 21:23). The Cross would be part of God's plan for atonement. Jesus would become a curse for us, and those who accept his atonement will be set free from the curse given in the garden (Gal. 3:13).

Jesus would also be a type of scapegoat. In the Old Testament, the sin of the people of Israel was to be placed on a goat and sent out of the city. Jesus would die outside the city of Jerusalem in the "place of the skull" on Mount Calvary. Isaiah would prophesy this moment when he said:

> Surely he took up our infirmities and carried our sorrows, yet we considered him stricken by God, smitten by him, and afflicted. But he was pierced for our transgressions, he was crushed for our iniquities; the punishment that brought us peace was upon him, and by his wounds we are healed. We all, like sheep, have gone astray, each of us has turned to his own way; and the Lord has laid on him the iniquity of us all. He was oppressed and afflicted, yet he did not open his mouth; he was led like a lamb to the slaughter, and as a sheep before her shearers is silent, so he did not open his mouth.
> —Isaiah 53:2-7

Jesus was the Lamb! He was foretold by the prophets. He would make many righteous with a true righteousness, rather than ritual. This is the heart of God. What good are empty rituals if they don't produce goodness? The prophet Isaiah was burdened with this exact concern. The Israelites had neglected to love their neighbor, and yet they still maintained a form of godliness. It was superficial, though, and relied on false standards of righteousness. It sickened God. Even he can be sickened by the poisonous fruit of religion.

> "Why have we fasted," they say, "and you have not seen it? Why have we humbled ourselves, and you have not noticed?" Yet on the day of your fasting, you do as you please and exploit all your workers. Your fasting ends in quarreling and strife, and in striking each other with wicked fists. You cannot fast as you do today and expect your

voice to be heard on high. Is this the kind of fast I have chosen, only a day for a man to humble himself? Is it only for bowing one's head like a reed and for lying on sackcloth and ashes? Is that what you call a fast, a day acceptable to the Lord? Is not this the kind of fasting I have chosen: to loose the chains of injustice and untie the cords of the yoke, to set the oppressed free and break every yoke? Is it not to share your food with the hungry and to provide the poor wanderer with shelter—when you see the naked, to clothe him, and not to turn away from your own flesh and blood?

—Isaiah 58:3-7

Their religious effort didn't produce anything pleasing to God. Isaiah echoes God's frustrations concerning this matter. The sins of the people had separated them from God. He couldn't hear their prayers. They were murderers, bearing false witness in lawsuits against one another. They were violent and actually ran to do evil and shed blood. Isaiah said:

Their feet rush into sin; they are swift to shed innocent blood. Their thoughts are evil thoughts; ruin and destruction mark their ways. The way of peace they do not know; there is no justice in their paths. They have turned them into crooked roads; no one who walks in them will know peace.

—Isaiah 59:7-8

Jeremiah

The message of Jeremiah was similar, only more heart wrenching. At this point in history Israel had not only forsaken righteousness and pursued her own way, she had also pursued other gods. Instead of Jehovah Jireh, their provider, they were worshiping the gods of the Amalekites, Canaanites, and Philistines. These were brutal gods, Baals (there was one for each city) who demanded human sacrifice, especially children. They also demanded temple prostitution (indeed the root word of "priest" is the same as that for "prostitute") to reenact fertility rites. So the people of God were giving in to the surrounding nations and adopting their ways. They had left God's Way, the way that pointed to Jesus, and it broke his heart.

God was so passionate about Israel that he considered their betrayal to be adultery. "I remember the devotion of your youth, how as a bride you loved me and followed me through the desert" (Jer. 2:2). They had forgotten their deliverance from Egypt and instead turned to false gods that didn't satisfy. He actually compared them to a nymphomaniac prostitute (Jer. 3:3)!

Israel wasn't just a subject that God demanded worship from. She was a bride. She was part of his heart. He knew that her betrayal to other gods was going to hurt her. She was like a woman married to a stable, faithful, beautiful man, who leaves him to become a drugged out groupie for a rock band. God asked Israel why she left him: "What fault did your fathers find in me, that they strayed so far from me?" (Jer. 2:5a). How vulnerable was this tender God! Any person who has had a mate cheat on them has asked the same question.

But why was God so concerned about Israel's betrayal? Why couldn't they just worship these other gods? What was the big deal? Perhaps, living in the twenty-first century as we do, it's difficult to imagine religion in its most base form. The Canaanite religions were poisonous. They were brutal, and they produced cruel, warring societies. Filled with violent and sexually immoral rituals, Baal worship was the opposite of the worship desired by God. They set up high places. They gave grain offerings. And when they did offer blood sacrifices, it was of living children. They sacrificed their babies, roasting them alive in brass idols. Loud drums were pounded in order to cover their cries and to work the people into a religious frenzy.

The question that needs to be asked is: what would have happened to the world if this type of religious practice were to prevail? Instead of worshiping a God who took interest in the oppressed and needy, a God who was interested in justice and mercy, and loved his creation with passion, who wasn't interested in false religious ritual that didn't produce righteousness, the Baals basked in perverted religious ritual that didn't care about the needs of people. Worshiping these gods led to a hardening of people's hearts—even against their own children. If people were defeated in battle by those who followed these gods, they were often treated sadistically; having their eyes gouged out, their skin peeled off, or hooks put in their backs so they could be dragged away. We can judge God's admonition to war against them and destroy them, but it seems to me that it's merely a luxury that we can enjoy only in retrospect.

And is it perhaps hypocritical of Hitchens to criticize the Jews as they came out of Egypt and battled against these tribes, to put a different standard on modern civilization? He criticizes Moses and the Israelites because they carried out the pillage and murder of other tribes, and yet sets a totally different standard for himself. In a debate with Alistair McGrath he said:

> The worst kind of immorality yet is the wicked idea of non-resistance of evil, and the deranged idea that we should love our enemies. Nothing, nothing, could be more suicidal and immoral than that. We have to defend ourselves and our children and our civilization from our enemies. We have to learn to educate ourselves in a cold, steady dislike of them and a determination to encompass their destruction.[17]

In other words, to battle against religious tyrants is alright for us, but it was wrong for God to allow (or even encourage) the Israelites to go into battle. Hitchens supports the war on terror, because the combatants are evil Islamofascists who dishonor women, suppress free speech, and produce tyranny. These sins are bad, but how would Hitchens respond to poisonous religious societies that worshiped Baal and were determined to annihilate the Israelites, challenging them in the most blatant ways? Does Hitchens believe the Israelites should have left them alone and then waited for their own destruction? Was God unjust for helping the Israelites? Or perhaps God (just like Hitchens) also hated these perverted religions and knew that they were deadly in so many ways to a people who were being taught to love justice, compassion, and mercy.

Can Hitchens see that if Israel had been destroyed, the world would have most certainly become a religious dictatorship? There would be no freedom, no kindness, no grace, no love. These are the values enshrined in the Jewish faith and carried into the Christian faith, pictured most fully in the life of Jesus. Wasn't Israel's battle similar to the one we're fighting now in the war on terror? What is life like under the Taliban? Is it a life of freedom, kindness, grace, and love? Would Hitchens have wanted to live in a Canaanite society? Why is it alright to battle the Taliban and not the Canaanites?

Hosea

When the Israelites began to mingle with the surrounding nations, God had to yank them back from the precipice. If they had blended the Jewish faith with the Canaanite religion, God's plan would have been destroyed. The religious way would have prevailed over God's Way, so God had that generation carried off into captivity in Babylon. He disciplined them because he loved them, but it wasn't easy for him. He said that his "eyes overflow with tears night and day without ceasing; for my virgin daughter—my people—has suffered a grievous wound, a crushing blow" (Jer. 14:17). They were separated from him again, and he wept.

Over and over, the prophets, speaking for God, had this indictment against the people: Your festivals and rituals don't mean anything to God. Instead, be true to him and live righteous lives. Stop chasing after religion. God wants your heart.

In one of the most beautiful verses of the Bible, God voices this concern: "What can I do with you, Ephraim? What can I do with you, Judah? Your love is like the morning mist, like the early dew that disappears" (Hos. 6:4). His people were chasing after other gods, and it broke his heart. He wants love, rather than religion. "For I desire mercy, not sacrifice, and acknowledgement of God, rather than burnt offerings" (Hos. 6:6).

Whenever a religious ritual becomes more important than righteous living, God is upset. In this case, Israel was even offering a blood sacrifice, but instead of the sacrifice being offered with a grateful heart for the grace the people were to receive, it was used as a justification to continue in their sin. This is a religious attitude, whereby the gods must simply be appeased, rather than a humble attitude that acknowledges our actions separated us from God and hurt others. It's flowers and candy, rather than a heartfelt apology.

Joel

Joel spoke of this heart attitude when he declared, "'Even now,' declares the Lord, 'return to me with all your heart, with fasting and weeping and mourning.' Rend your hearts and not your garments" (Joel 2:12-13). God wants our hearts. He's such a precious God. He mourns when he must discipline. He's wounded when we betray him. He's generous beyond measure. He weeps. This is a lovely God—not a dictator, but a tender lover and a doting father.

Amos

This attitude of a God who rejects religion for righteousness is summed up perfectly by the prophet Amos: "I hate, I despise your religious feasts; I cannot stand your assemblies. Even though you bring me burnt offerings and grain offerings, I will not accept them. Though you bring choice fellowship offerings, I will have no regard for them. Away with the noise of your songs! I will not listen to the music of your harps. But let justice roll on like a river, righteousness like a never-failing stream!" (Amos 5:21-24).

Never let ritual take the place of righteousness. Even our music and worship is disgusting to God if it's only a ritual. True faith in God should result in tenderness, compassion, sympathy, and kindness. If it doesn't, your religion is poison; it's proceeding from the serpent, rather than the Lamb.

Micah

This admonition falls heavily on the ears of religious leaders. Where are you leading your people? Are you urging them to love God and do justice, or are you using them to further your own agenda, getting as much as you can from them? The leaders of Israel were rebuked for this attitude. Instead of feeding the flock, they were eating the flock:

> Listen, you leaders of Jacob, you rulers of the house of Israel. Should you not know justice, you who hate good and love evil; who tear the skin from my people and the flesh from their bones; who eat my people's flesh, strip off their skin and break their bones in pieces; who chop them up like meat for the pan, like flesh for the pot? Then they will cry out to the Lord, but he will not answer them. At that time he will hide his face from them because of the evil they have done. This is what the Lord says; "As for the prophets who lead my people astray, if one feeds them, they proclaim 'peace'; if he does not, they prepare to wage war against him."
>
> —Micah 3:1-5

Ezekiel

Ezekiel would also rebuke the "fat shepherds" for leading the people astray. Instead of leading them to a life of holiness and goodness, the priests actually ignored sin, because more sin offerings meant more meat for them to eat! So they actually benefited from the sins of the people:

> Woe to the shepherds of Israel who only take care of themselves! Should not shepherds take care of the flock? You eat the curds, clothe yourselves with the wool and slaughter the choice animals, but you

do not take care of the flock. You have not strengthened the weak or healed the sick or bound up the injured. You have not brought back the strays or searched for the lost. You have ruled them harshly and brutally.

—Ezekiel 34:2-4

Instead God wanted the shepherds to use their staff to guide the flock in the right pathways. When the sheep began to wander away, it was the concern of the shepherds to bring them back, but in this case the shepherds were actually driving the flock and ruling over them with cruelty. Rather than leading the sheep, searching for those who had wandered away, tending to them, and helping them to bind their wounds, they were driving the sheep to another way, putting them on a dangerous and even deadly pathway. Isn't this why religion is so horrible? Religious leaders haven't cared for the flock. They've driven the sheep to hopeless religious effort. Jesus said "Woe to you, teachers of the law and Pharisees, you hypocrites! You shut the kingdom of heaven in men's faces" (Matt. 23:13).

Jonah

Even the story of Jonah, the prophet from the fish's belly, confirms the antireligious attitude of God. Jonah was sent to Nineveh, a brutal and wicked city, known for its cruelty toward those it conquered. They impaled their victims, insuring a slow and painful death. They stacked up their victims like firewood at the gates of the city. They tied people down and slowly flayed them alive. They were also known to put their fists down their victim's throat and pull out their tongues by the roots. They were the enemies of Israel. This wasn't a place Jonah wanted to be. But God wanted to give them an opportunity to turn toward him. God forgave them, not because of any ritual they performed, but because of their humble attitude when rebuffed, revealing again that God was gracious. It wasn't adherence to particular details of the Law that God wanted, but a contrite heart.

Isn't this something that we find to be true in our own personal lives? None of us are perfect. When we hurt other people, the only hope for the restoration of the relationship is humility. We need to humble ourselves, admit we did wrong, and then ask for forgiveness, not as a ritual, but with a heartfelt attitude, acknowledging the pain we caused the other person, saying we're sorry for it, and then trying not to do it again. If we remain hard and arrogant, there's no hope for restoring the relationship. If we're not willing to honestly face our own shortcomings, and try to make it better, we'll only end up detached and separated from others. Pride separates. Humility heals.

King David

This is why King David was called "a man after his own heart" (1 Sam. 13:14a). When he committed adultery with Bathsheba and murdered her husband (by sending him to the front lines of battle), he humbled himself before God and cried out for forgiveness. Notice the attitude of David's heart: "Have mercy on me, O God, according to your unfailing love; according to your great compassion.... For I know my transgressions, and my sin is always before me... wash me, and I will be whiter than snow.... Create in me a pure heart, O God, and renew a steadfast spirit within me" (Psalm 51:1-10).

But King David also knew the non-religious heart of God. He knew that God was most interested in the heart and wasn't hard like other gods who just wanted sacrifice and ritual. He wanted tenderness and purity in the inner being, not just offerings to appease: "You do not delight in sacrifice, or I would bring it; you do not take pleasure in burnt offerings. The sacrifices of God are a broken spirit; a broken and contrite heart, O God, you will not despise" (Psalm 51:16-17).

And yet the ritual of shedding blood still stood as a requirement of the Law. David knew this and mentioned it, but he also knew that it couldn't become a ritual without any heart. He began his life as a shepherd who defended his flock against the attacks of lions and bears, and this still symbolizes the Good Shepherd who leads the sheep in the right way and defends them from predators. David was such a good king that the Star of David is still enshrined as the national symbol on Israel's flag.

God's Way is the humble acceptance of the blood of the Lamb. Why? Because the justice of God requires life for life. This is the way of blood. But this blood can't be demanded or confiscated; it must be received humbly in order for true healing to occur. We'll never make the universe a better place if we're not willing to face our faults. We only frustrate others and delude ourselves. Anyone who has ever been in a relationship with someone who won't face his or her faults knows what kind of special hell this is.

Humility isn't the demand of an unreasonable God who wants to see us grovel, but an acknowledgment that heaven is only possible when its citizens are willing to be humble. Arrogance was what led to Lucifer's rebellion. Selfishness and pride only produce misery, and people who are incapable of humility are incapable of maintaining paradise. Consequently, "God opposes the proud but gives grace to the humble" (1 Pet. 5:5), and Jesus said the meek "will inherit the earth" (Matt. 5:5).

This tender God desires a tender bride, someone he can be happily married to. He doesn't want a hard-hearted wife. King David actually danced in his underwear in the streets and worshiped the Lord with passion and songs of love. He and his men celebrated with all their might before the Lord. They also sacrificed an animal as they carried the Ark back into the city. When David got home his wife Michal conveyed the disgust she felt for him because of his passionate display. He was a king, but he had thrown off the royal robes and made himself equal with his men. This wasn't distinguished to Michal, but King David replied, "I will become even more undignified than this, and I will be humiliated in my own eyes" (2 Sam. 6:22). And then the Scriptures relate this simple verse: "And Michal daughter of Saul had no children to the day of her death" (2 Sam. 6:23). She was a symbol of religion. She loved her position, despised humility, lacked passion, and produced no life, but King David forsook his position and was willing to come passionately and humbly to the Lord through the Blood.

The Lamb

Jesus was crucified between two thieves. One of them was hard, telling Jesus to save himself (representing all religious effort) and the other one was humble, admitting that they were being punished justly, and "getting what our deeds deserve" (Luke 23:41a), merely asking that Jesus remember him in his kingdom. And Jesus answered the dying man by saying, "… today you will be with me in paradise" (Luke 23:43). Eden, for this sinning thief, was restored through humbly receiving the Lamb.

Will you harden your heart toward this tender God—especially if you realize that the one who died was Immanuel, "God with us" (Matt. 1:23)? God died for us! How can the universe possibly consider that he is a cruel dictator when they find out that he himself was willing to pay the price for our sins?

Think of the angels as they looked on and saw him dying. What tenderness and respect must have welled up inside of them as they saw him love his creation so much that he would be willing to pay the price for them, so that rather than judgment, the creation could experience his life-giving presence and not have to be separated from him. Instead of a harsh judge, he could now be known as the passionate lover, the tender father, the good friend-- all that is sacrificial and loving in the universe. What joy and grief mixed together they must have experienced as they saw him bleeding and dying. There was no mistaking it now: God really was love.

Now think of the fallen angels, and the frustration they must have felt at being deceived by Lucifer. They made the wrong choice, and yet they didn't have regret for their decision as much as they had rage toward the victorious God. Hatred, anger, fear, jealousy, frustration… these are just a few of the ways these messengers of darkness express themselves in the world today, especially toward those who have embraced this sacrificial God and are on the Narrow Way.

CHAPTER THREE

The Narrow Way in the New Testament

"The bride eyes not her garment, but her dear bridegroom's face;
I will not gaze at glory, but on the King of grace.
Not at the crown he giveth, but on His pierced hand;
The Lamb is all the glory of Immanuel's land." —Anonymous

"For it is by grace you have been saved, through faith—and this not from yourselves, it is the gift of God—not by works, so that no one can boast." —Ephesians 2:8-9

"Unstaid and fickle in all other things, save in the constant image of the object that is beloved." —William Shakespeare, *Twelfth Night*

"The Pharisee is that extremely admirable man who subordinates his entire life to his knowledge of good and evil and is as severe a judge of himself as of his neighbor, to the honor of God, whom he humbly thanks for this knowledge." —Dietrich Bonhoeffer

The New Testament is the ultimate non-religious message. It begins with a man in the desert (not a temple) screaming at religious leaders and calling them names. He describes these leaders as being poisonous snakes, calling them a "brood of vipers" (Luke 3:7). (This man, known as John the Baptist, and Christopher Hitchens may have more in common than many think!) It then goes on to say that Jesus, the Messiah, the hope of the world, had this same message. He also got upset with religious leaders. In Matthew 23 he pronounced seven "woes" against the Pharisees with these complaints against them:

1. They shut the kingdom of heaven in men's faces, not letting in those who are trying to get in.

2. They travel far and wide to make a convert, but then he only becomes twice the *son of hell* as themselves!
3. They are blind guides who are more interested in temporal gain than in spiritual devotion.
4. They give their money to the temple, but neglect their poor parents.
5. They emphasize following religious rules, but neglect mercy, justice, and compassion.
6. They look spiritual on the outside, with their religious clothing and rituals, but on the inside they're full of greed, self-indulgence, hypocrisy, and wickedness.
7. They reject and kill God's messengers.

Then Jesus also shouts at the Pharisees and calls them "snakes" and a "brood of vipers!" (Matt. 23:33).

Jesus taught that religion, with all of its shows and rituals, was poisonous. He warned his followers to obey what religious leaders teach about the Word, but not to do what they do. They put heavy burdens on peoples' shoulders. They do everything for men to see. They wear special clothing. They love to be honored and receive the best seats at banquets. They love being called by spiritual titles such as "Rabbi" or "Father." To Jesus, this kind of religious show was sickening. He was *not* religious.

Finally, the New Testament takes us to the converted Pharisee, Paul, whose entire message was one of opposition to religious works. He explained that men are saved by grace through faith in Jesus, rather than in works, lest any man should become proud and boast. He called religious rituals "dead works" and even said that the first foundation of true faith is to *repent from religion!* "Therefore let us leave the elementary teachings about Christ and go on to maturity, not laying again the foundation of repentance from acts that lead to death" (Heb. 6:1).

Paul's letters were sent to churches that were getting the message of Jesus wrong. The Galatians wanted to blend religious effort (circumcision) in with the "Good News" that no religious effort was needed. The Colossians also wanted to blend in fasting and ascetic practices with the Good News, but Paul warned against it, encouraging them to pursue good, kind, loving lives rather than religious works. Paul was mostly concerned that the church would be lured away from the simple message of faith in Jesus as the Lamb who died for them to set them free from religious bondage and effort—which had no power to help them conquer sin, he said:

> Since you died with Christ to the basic principles of this world, why, as though you still belonged to it, do you submit to its rules: "Do not handle! Do not taste! Do not touch!"? These are all destined to perish with use, because they are based on human commands and teachings. Such regulations indeed have an appearance of wisdom, with their self-imposed worship, their false humility and their harsh treatment of the body, but they lack any value in restraining sensual indulgence.
>
> —Colossians 2:20-23

This message of "Good News," that we don't have to act religious or do religious things to gain access to God, has been perverted by the church over and over again. There's always some new teacher or some old church that gets it wrong. It's the simplest of messages, but has the church really embraced it? No! We may say we believe in grace and the sacrifice of Jesus, but then we still blend in the woolen with linen, the blood with works, and put people on religious hamster wheels where they can get no rest.

We say repetitive prayers, even though we were told by Jesus not to (Matt. 6:7-8). We practice public fasting, even though we were warned by Jesus not to (Matt. 6:16-18). We set up religious hierarchies and priesthoods, forgetting that Jesus was our high priest and that now "there is one God and one mediator between God and men, the man Christ Jesus" (1 Tim. 2:5). We abstain from eating certain foods and getting married, even though we were told that was wrong (1 Tim. 4:3). We make people tithe, convincing them that if they don't they'll be under a curse, even though we were told to allow men to be "cheerful givers" and not put them under "compulsion" (2 Cor. 9:7). We call religious leaders "Father" even though Jesus said explicitly that we should call no man "father" except our Father in heaven (Matt. 23:9). We run around seeking signs and wonders, even though Jesus said, "A wicked and adulterous generation asks for a miraculous sign" (Matt. 12:39). We use our faith to get prosperity, even though we were warned not to use the Gospel for personal gain (Jude 1:11). We also suppose that grace means we have the right to sin even though we were warned that grace doesn't abound for the purpose of allowing sin to abound (Rom. 6:15).

When you look at the Christian church, you would think that Jesus never came!

It's as though the whole Gospel message has been obscured. Mainstream churches on the Left have a "new revelation" from God that sexual sin is now alright, taking advantage of the grace of God (Rom. 6:1-2).[18] The Right has gone off half-cocked chasing after anointings, miracles, power, signs, and prosperity, using the Word as a way to get what they want. And the Catholic Church continues to stand on its traditions, rather than on the pure teaching of the Gospels.

It's no wonder that skeptics are rising up and calling Christianity a crock. We have nothing to offer anymore. We've become caricatures… worthy of nothing but disdain. We've used the New Testament and the teachings of Jesus to create another religion, even though the Good News was that we've now been set free from religion! The whole heart of Christianity has been perverted. (Marcus Borg, whose book, *The Heart of Christianity: Rediscovering a Life of Faith*,[19] even has the gall to say that Christianity is merely another religion, a way to get to God through "dying to self,"[20] and promotes "Christian community"[21] and "practicing"[22] worship, daily devotionals, daily prayer, retreats, pilgrimages, journaling, church attendance, liturgy, hymns, meditation, contemplative prayer which involves the "repetition of a mantra,"[23] and brief rituals such as "washing one's face in the name of the Father, and of the Son, and of the Holy Spirit" as the Christian path. He is a false teacher who has forgotten the Good News of the Lamb's sacrifice and is merely leading us astray into self-effort under the guise of the new "emerging paradigm."[24] Calling this the "heart of Christianity" is pure bunk!)

The tree of Christianity is bent and hanging low. It needs to be tied back up to a straight pole. It has gone astray, veered off on an exit and gotten tangled up in thorny bushes. It needs the plumb line of Amos (Amos 7:7-9) to show it where it's supposed to be. It needs to be yanked back up into position where it can grow straight and tall, getting light and water and producing fruit. It's necessary for the church to look clearly at itself and pull no punches. We're only deluding ourselves if we don't acknowledge our sin.

If we expect to convince skeptics that Jesus has any beauty, we must admit that we've perverted his message. We must share the true Gospel. We need to find out why the teachings of Jesus caused men's hearts to burn within them as he taught them the Scriptures.

Why has Jesus inspired so much courage, passion, goodness, and love in humanity? Was it because he gave us freedom to sin? Was it because we could have "our best life now"[25] and join in on some kind of giant Amway meeting? Is this what Jesus was crucified for? Is this why Paul was beheaded? Is this why Huss was burnt at the stake or why Luther was willing to risk death in order to declare, "I cannot and will not recant" before the Inquisition?

No!

There is a message that burns in the hearts of men and women that causes them to be willing to face death, poverty, persecution, and rejection. And the message of all the prophets, apostles, and even Jesus is the same as Christopher Hitchens: Religion poisons everything. It exists as a result of the Fall, and its father is Satan, the serpent. All it produces is more of its offspring—poisonous snakes whose bites result in death.

Instead, the challenge to Christianity is to stop her selfish, poisonous religious pursuits and lift up Jesus and his finished work on the Cross. We claim to want revival, but the revival we want isn't like the revivals of Luther, Wesley, Whitefield, or Finney—who preached the gospel of grace. No! Instead we're pleading for a *new* move of God, which reveals itself in power displays. We've forgotten our first love—the passion found in the gospel of grace—and we're running off searching for a new lover who will give us signs, anointings, and miracles. Spiritual goose bumps. We're adulterers.

Isn't the Lamb of God enough? Can we just cast him aside so easily?

If we don't go back to him, how many will be lost because of our lust and perversion? How many more will join the atheist crusaders and skeptics?

When we present an image of a petty God, demanding religious ritual, or being some kind of force that we can manipulate to get what we want, we paint a shallow image and understanding of who he is. We don't reveal him in all his beauty as the savior, lover, father, brother, or friend. We don't show how magnificent his plan for mankind is. We don't cause men's hearts to long for him. Where are those who, like the wise men, search for him and worship him? He's no longer the mysterious promised King who was foretold by ancient prophecies. Instead, we've made him a laughing stock, someone to disdain. But this promised One is a precious treasure, a pearl of great price, a rose of Sharon, a beautiful gem. If we "call out for insight and cry aloud for understanding, and if [we] look for it as for silver and search for it as for hidden treasure, then [we] will understand the fear of the Lord and find the knowledge of God" (Prov. 2:2-5).

The Miraculous Word

As a church, we need to show the beauty of the Word. Instead, parts of the church on the Right are using it like some kind of tool to *conjure up* what they lust for and other parts on the Left are discounting it in order to *justify* their lusts. But God says that studying the Bible is like digging for buried treasure and those who search it with a willing heart will find him.

The purpose of the Word is to lead men to God and keep them there so they don't go astray. It isn't there to fulfill our lusts. It's there to reveal the Way to God. It's a message from an intelligent being in the universe that we call "God," for lack of a better term. It reveals his heart and his purposes. Its depth and symbolism is rich beyond measure, showing that there was indeed a plan, something that was woven through the fabric of human history to show us that he's real.

When atheists say that there is no proof of God's existence, all I can do is wonder how they explain the Bible and its message. Perhaps they don't realize what it says or haven't studied it before. Perhaps they've only been shown the petty God who we've been told is happy to hear a bunch of celibate women repeating the same words over and over again. Perhaps they've only been shown the God who seems to want them to dress up and go to a building where they sit in a pew and give him their money. But this is not the God of the Scriptures! The God of the Word is a God of justice and love who is trying to reveal himself in a lock-tight way to humanity. The life of Jesus is profusely interwoven with the Old Testament. He said he came to "fulfill the Law and the Prophets" and this he did this with precision. He is the sacrifice. He is the Sabbath. He is the tithe. He is the bread. He is the wine. He is the light. He is the manna from heaven. He is the rock. He is the living water. He is the Tree of Life. He is the Lion of the Tribe of Judah. He is the Root of Jesse. He is the Truth. He is the Life. He is the Way. He fulfilled it all!

Christopher Hitchens thinks that "the study of literature and poetry, both for its own sake and for the eternal ethical questions with which it deals, can now easily depose the scrutiny of sacred texts that have been found to be corrupt and infected."[26] (I guess this is regardless of the fact that much of great literature deals with and is inspired by biblical themes.) But no matter how rich and deep the literary symbolism of a great work such as *The Brothers Karamazov* is, nothing can compare to the unbelievably rich symbolism found in the Scriptures. The biblical narrative contains layer after layer of meaning and symbols. The first symbol discussed in this book was that of the Lamb. It runs as a consistent theme of both the Old and the New Testament. Other consistent themes include the blood, the fruits, the tree, the seed, the bride, the oil, and of course the Way.

These themes exist, not as a result of the literary genius of a brilliant writer such as Dostoyevsky, but in spite of the fact that the Bible was written over a 1,500-year time period by people as diverse as kings, farmers, tax collectors, doctors, shepherds, generals, and fishermen. They were written on three different continents in places as diverse as dungeons and palaces, and included different types of writings such as history, law, poetry, parables, allegory, biography, letters, prophecy, and persuasive argument. And yet every one of these authors revealed God's plan of redemption through Jesus Christ.

The author of Genesis gave us the first glimpse of God's plan when he revealed God's judgment against the serpent: "And I will put enmity between you and the woman, and between your offspring and hers; he will crush your head, and you will strike his heel" (Gen. 3:15). This spoke of the relationship between Lucifer and Jesus and the fact that humanity would be part of the plan to defeat that great traitor and heavenly rebel. Mankind is no little maggot or worm to God. We are part of a divine plan which will restore peace, justice, and righteousness in the universe.

Jesus Is the Passover Lamb

Moving on to Exodus, the author reveals the characteristics of this One who saves from death. "Go at once and select the animals for your families and slaughter the Passover lamb. Take a bunch of hyssop, dip it into the blood in the basin and put some of the blood on the top and on both sides of the doorframe. Not one of you shall go out the door of his house until morning. When the Lord goes through the land to strike down the Egyptians, he will see the blood on the top and sides of the doorframe and will pass over that doorway, and he will not permit the destroyer to enter your houses and strike you down" (Exod. 12:21-23). But this blood would only be a shadow (or symbol) of the reality, the blood of Christ, who would become the mediator of a New Covenant when he said, "This is my blood of the covenant, which is poured out for many for the forgiveness of sins" (Matt. 26:28).

Jesus Fulfills the Feasts of Israel

Leviticus 23 would speak of special feasts that would be appointed by God:

1. The Sabbath, which would symbolize Jesus, our Sabbath (Heb. 4:9-11), giving us rest from religious (or dead) works.
2. The Passover and Unleavened Bread, which would represent a memorial to the deliverance of the Israelites from Egypt, and the meal of the unblemished lamb and bread made without yeast (it being a symbol of sin or false teaching [1 Cor. 5:6-8, Matt. 16:12]). When the blood of the lamb was applied to the doorpost of the home, the death angel would "pass over" that home. This bread would symbolize the sinlessness of Jesus and his being the broken bread, the bread of life, and the manna from heaven. The lamb and its blood on the doorpost would symbolize the death of Jesus for us on the Cross in order to deliver us from death (Hebrews 9).
3. The First Fruits, which were characterized by the tithe (Lev. 23:10), but would symbolize Christ's resurrection and his becoming the first fruit of the dead (1 Cor. 15:20).
4. The Feast of Weeks, which would be characterized by a time period of fifty days and a command to leave behind the gleanings of the harvest for the poor and aliens (Lev. 23:22). It would symbolize the coming of the Holy Spirit at Pentecost (Acts 2) and the preaching of reconciliation and salvation to the Gentiles, who will be able to glean the fields of the Jews (the "crumbs" as Jesus called them!) a time period when there would be an opportunity for all nations to hear the Good News and receive salvation (Acts 10:34-35).
5. The Feast of Trumpets, which would be characterized by the blowing of a trumpet, a blood offering, and no work, and would symbolize that those who would be caught up with Jesus would trust in the blood of Jesus rather than dead works (Heb. 6:1).
6. The Day of Atonement, which would be characterized by self-denial, no work, and rest (Lev. 23:26-32). This would symbolize the salvation of the Jews, when they (who were "blinded" for a while for the sake of the Gentiles [Rom. 11:25-32, KJV]) will look on him "whom they have pierced" (Zech. 12:10) and repent. They would no longer come to God on the basis of their self-effort, but would come on the basis of the completed work of Christ on the Cross, meaning they could now rest.

7. And finally the Feast of Tabernacles, which would be characterized by a holy convocation at harvest time where no work is allowed and rejoicing and praising continues for seven days while the participants live in tents (booths) or miniature tabernacles. This feast symbolizes the completion of God's temple, or tabernacle, the body of Christ, his Bride. It would symbolize a time of ingathering, an assembly filled with joy, when the Jewish believers will be joined with the gentile believers as they're all set free from the bondage of sin and disobedience and led into the Sabbath rest of the new millennium, relying together on the Blood of the Lamb rather than their works (Joel 2:28).

On the Jewish calendar, the first four feasts were to be celebrated during the early rains. Then there would be a long, dry summer with no rain. This is a description of Jewish history. The feasts of the Sabbath, Passover, Unleavened Bread, First Fruits, and Weeks all symbolize the "early rains" (Joel 2:28) and what happened in the life of Jesus and the early church. Jesus fulfilled them all 2,000 years ago. But then there would be a long dry season for the Jews until "the full number of the Gentiles has come in" (Rom. 11:25). The latter rains would then fall on the house of Zion (Israel). At the return of Christ, when the trumpet sounds, the Jews will be saved. In the book of the Revelation it says 144,000 will be marked immediately after the sun is darkened and the moon no longer gives it light (Rev. 6:12-7:17). Zechariah said that the Jews will look upon him whom they pierced and weep (Zech. 12:10). Joel also described this moment when he spoke of the sun being darkened in the second half of the prophecy about God's Spirit being poured out upon all people (Joel 2:28-32).

What a magnificent story of history! Beyond magnificent. How could this story, told with such intricate details and rich symbolism, confirmed by so many historical facts, be so hated and scorned; especially when the main message is that of a gift? You don't have to do anything to be part of this glorious plan other than accept the gift. You don't have to fast for it, give money for it, sacrifice your child for it, commit suicide for it, bow in prayer five times a day for it... *nothing*!

And everything you do offer to God in exchange for this gift he characterizes as giving him a filthy "menstrual cloth" (Isa. 30:22). In other words, presenting your works to God is like laying a dirty Kotex in front of him; it represents blood that is dead and lifeless. It's worthless. What can you really do with it?

Jesus Is the Lamb That Saves

As the Old Testament goes on, we learn the story of Joshua, whose name translates to Yeshua or Jesus, and means "Jehovah saves." He would be the one to lead the people of God into the Promised Land (Josh. 1:3). Zechariah would also reveal a high priest named Joshua who would be accused by Satan as he was dressed in filthy clothes. He would be a "burning stick snatched from the fire" (Zech. 3:2b), meaning that he was in the process of receiving judgment but then was rescued and called before the heavenly council. There his guilt would be taken away from him and he'd be clothed as a priest and given rule as a king over the house of God. Zechariah said this was a symbol of the future servant of God, the "Branch." God would set a stone before Joshua engraved with the inscription: "I will remove the sin of this land in a single day" (Zech. 3:9). Only grace could achieve this!

Isaiah would describe this Christ, saying, "For to us a child is born, to us a son is given, and the government will be on his shoulders. And he will be called Wonderful Counselor, Mighty God, Everlasting Father, Prince of Peace. Of the increase of his government and peace there will be no end. He will reign on David's throne and over his kingdom, establishing and upholding it with justice and righteousness from that time on and forever" (Isa. 9:6-7).

What a plan! Who wouldn't want this? Is it so far-fetched to believe that in a universe that is so expansive and immeasurable, there might be something more than us? Carl Sagan said we were arrogant if we thought so, but how else can we explain the unity of the Word? There are those who get so involved in the small details of the Scriptures that they overlook the main theme: the Lamb of God. From Genesis to Revelation, the Lamb is the centerpiece. He is the Way, the Anointed One, who heals the wound between God and man. Through him, the concept of grace was made known to the universe. How else could grace be revealed? Could a just judge ever insist that one person pay for the crimes of another? *Only if the one willing to pay for the crime was the judge himself.*

Justice

But why, you may ask, is justice so important? Why can't crime be ignored? Ask a parent whose child was murdered by being buried alive if they think justice should be ignored. Ask a little boy who's had his iPod stolen if justice should be ignored. If it is ignored by those in authority, a posse will be organized, revenge will be sought, and society will break down into warring factions. The strong will rule over the weak. This is the logical consequence of a universe with no justice. It's the opposite of a universe that cares for the oppressed and needy. To coin a phrase, if there's no justice, there's no peace. An orderly society must contain an efficient court system, which provides "liberty and justice for all." There must be a sense that reparation was achieved, mending the damage that was done. This is also why repentance involves making things right (as much as we can) with those we've injured. For example, Zacchaeus, a tax collector who began following Jesus, returned the money he had taken unjustly from others (Luke 19:8-10).

Because of this need for justice, we needed a savior. We needed someone to take our place, to receive our judgment, or we would all be destroyed in a just universe. We would be hopeless. Unable to bring back Eden. Ever. And God could never have a Bride, someone to love him with absolute passion and commitment. He'd just have fearful angels. God's plan solved all of these problems. It was airtight. And it all hinged on the precious concept of grace.

Grace

Until Christ, though, there was no grace. There was mercy—the lessening of a punishment according to the whim of God—but no grace, nothing that would make us *pleasing* to him. This is why the "reeking altars"[27] (as Hitchens calls them) and blood sacrifice were necessary—for the sake of justice. They pointed to the One who would pay the price for the crimes committed by mankind. This was the gift of God. All we have to do is reach out and receive him with a humble heart. When we do, we invert the Fall. In the Garden we started out innocent and became guilty, but now we are guilty and become innocent. We are clean, holy, and pure through the blood of the Lamb. We've made it back to Eden. We're restored.

The Deity of Jesus

This is also why it's necessary to understand the deity of Christ. If Christ wasn't God, then God committed the sin of child sacrifice—offering up a child to appease a god, which in this case happened to be his son. This was the sin of the Amalekites that so grieved the heart of God! But Christ was called Immanuel (Matt.1:23) by the angels, which means "God with us." As John said,

"In the beginning was the Word [Jesus], and the Word was with God, and the Word was God" (John 1:1). In the Old Testament, God, who is one God, still spoke in the plural when deciding to scatter those building the Tower of Babel. "Come, let us go down and confuse their language so they will not understand each other" (Gen. 11:7). Jesus was a member of the Godhead. He said that "before Abraham was born, I am!" (John 8:58) The words "I am" were a reference to the most holy name of God in the Old Testament. When Moses asked God what his name was, God answered, "I am who I am" (Exod. 3:14). This claim to divinity was the blasphemy that caused Jesus to be killed by the religious leaders (Matt. 26:64-65; Luke 5:21, 6:5-11, 22:67-70; John 5:16-18, 8:57-59, 10:31-33). If his deity weren't so, then how could the angels possibly see any beauty in the sacrifice? How could we?

The Works of Satan

There are certain things Satan tries to pervert in order to turn people away from God:

1. He tries to pervert the sacrifice, causing children to be offered up, or suggesting that a continual sacrifice is needed, such as in the Catholic doctrine of transubstantiation.
2. He attacks the deity of Christ, causing so many religious groups to argue that Jesus was only the physical son and not God.
3. He attempts to substitute the humble acceptance of the blood of Jesus with religious works as a way to be accepted by God.
4. Finally, Satan tries to get us to doubt the Word. He casts aspersions on it, just as in the Garden. Why? Because the Word, cover to cover, reveals the sinless and holy Lamb, the Way to God. This is also why he hates the Jews, those who preserved that Word and carried the seed of the Lamb, and Christians who proclaim the Good News that Christ did it all. Evangelicals are particularly repugnant to him, what with their talk of grace and blood and their commitment to the inerrancy of the Bible.

Is it any wonder that Satan does his greatest work within the church? If the church is supposed to bear the truth of God, then all he has to do is pervert *their* message and he'll send people off the straight way into a crooked and thorny path, where they get caught up in futility and hopelessness. The church has always had to battle to preserve sound doctrine. The serpent is still trying to seduce, to lead the Bride astray so that she betrays God. Paul talked about this when he had to leave the church in the hands of the Ephesian elders:

> Keep watch over yourselves and all the flock of which the Holy Spirit has made you overseers. Be shepherds of the church of God, which he bought with his own blood. I know that after I leave, savage wolves will come in among you and will not spare the flock. Even from your own number men will arise and distort the truth in order to draw away disciples after them (Acts 20:28-30).

Paul realized that the church would be targeted. Not by those looking like demons and devils, but by those appearing like lambs and angels. Posers. We fall for beauty. The outward appearance. The show.

Paul had to warn the Corinthian Church about this very thing. They were being seduced by "super-apostles," who put on a great show in order to profit for themselves:

> I am jealous for you with a godly jealousy. I promised you to one husband, to Christ, so that I might present you as a pure virgin to him. But I am afraid that just as Eve was deceived by the serpent's cunning, your minds may somehow be led astray from your sincere and pure devotion to Christ. For if someone comes to you and preaches a Jesus other than the Jesus we preached, or if you receive a different spirit from the one you received, or a different gospel from the one you accepted, you put up with it easily enough. But I do not think I am in the least inferior to those "super-apostles." I may not be a trained speaker, but I do have knowledge.
> —2 Corinthians 11:2-6a

The pastor's (shepherd's) job is to keep watch over the flock so that he can present her as a virgin bride to Christ. A virgin hasn't been seduced. She is faithful and true to her first love. There's only one Narrow Way, and it's like the aisle of a church as a bride walks to her bridegroom on her wedding day. She isn't scanning the audience as she walks by, trying to steal a coy glance. Her eyes are fixed on the bridegroom. Her heart and body and soul are presented to him. She's consumed with him.

Jesus Fulfilled the Law

Are you a faithful shepherd? Are you preparing your church to meet her Bridegroom? What does this mean? It means preaching the Gospel, the Good News that Jesus was the Lamb and he did it all. This will sound offensive to some, but it has to be said. It means laying aside all of the Old Testament ritual law. The law has no power to give life, only death. Everything must be consummated in Christ. If we set aside ritual circumcision, because it was only a symbol of the circumcision of our hearts (Rom. 2:25-29, Deut. 10:16), we must set aside the tithe. It was only a symbol of Christ's resurrection (Lev. 23:10-12, 1 Cor. 15:20). If we set aside the sacrifice of animals because it was only a symbol of Jesus, the Lamb of God, we must set aside the priesthood. It was only a symbol of Jesus, our heavenly mediator. If we no longer need to celebrate the feasts because they were only symbols of Israel's history, then we no longer need a temple, a building where God resides, because we are now the temple. If we're no longer forbidden to eat meat that was previously considered unclean, because the prohibition was only there as a symbol to reveal that the Gentiles would now be acceptable through Christ, then we no longer must perform ritual fasting. It was only there as a symbol of humble contrition (Isa. 58:1-7, Col. 2:16). All of these Old Testament laws merely pointed to Jesus. (Remember: "He sets aside the first to establish the second" [Heb. 10:9b]). If we try to mix any of these things in with the Gospel, we're guilty of putting new wine into old wineskins, blending the woolen and the linen, something forbidden by God (Lev. 19:19). The law merely existed, as explained in Galatians 3:24, to "lead us to Christ."

Although the ritual law must be set aside, the *moral* law has been given new life. Because Christ repaired the Way to God, we're no longer in a condition of having knowledge of the law without power. The relationship between God and man is a two way street. Not only are we able to go before God; now he can also come to us. The Holy Spirit, which could only come once Christ did his work (he says he *had* to leave so the Spirit could come [John 16:7]), can now live in us. The Tree of Life, bountiful with the fruits of the Spirit (love, joy, peace, patience, kindness, goodness, faithfulness, gentleness, and self-control) can finally be eaten from! Hebrews 10:16 describes this new life: "This is the covenant I will make with them after that time, says the Lord. I will put my laws in their hearts, and I will write them on their minds." And we are reminded by Paul that "if anyone is in Christ, he is a new creation; the old has gone, the new has come" (2 Cor. 5:17).

Paul lamented over the condition of sinful man. As a religious leader, he knew the law, but knowing the law gave him no power to conquer sin. He said he even delighted in God's law, but still he cried out in helplessness, "What a wretched man that I am! Who will rescue me from this body of death?" (Rom. 7:24). The thing he wanted to do, he couldn't, and the thing he didn't want to do, he kept on doing. But the next declaration of Paul is this: "Thanks be to God—through Jesus Christ our Lord… the law of the Spirit of life set me free from the law of sin and death. For what the law was powerless to do in that it was weakened by the sinful nature, God did by sending his own Son in the likeness of sinful man to be a sin offering" (Rom. 7:25-8:3). Knowing the Law doesn't empower us to obey it. Only the Spirit of Life can accomplish this.

This is why self-help books are such an insidious part of the church landscape. No matter how much knowledge we have about how to perfect ourselves, we can't do it! We can't have our "best life now" merely through obtaining knowledge. We only set ourselves up for failure when we're told *how to* "enlarge our vision," *how to* "develop a healthy self-image," *how to* "discover the power of our thoughts," *how to* "choose to be happy," etc.[28] Knowing how to do something doesn't empower us to do it. The Christian pastor or teacher who focuses on giving their congregation "steps to… " information is leading their flock to a steep place, causing them to climb to get to God's blessings. They squelch the Life of the Spirit by leading them to laws. They are snake oil salesmen, encouraging us to eat of the wrong tree… again.

The New Way to Righteousness

Instead, we need to understand why John the Baptist said, "The ax is already at the root of the trees" (Luke 3:9a). It wasn't cut down yet because Christ hadn't shed his blood, but the ax was already poised and ready to cut down the old tree, the tree of self-effort for salvation, to be replaced with a new shoot, the Tree of Life, which is Jesus. John was the ultimate anti-religious prophet. He told the Jews that their religious heritage meant nothing to God and that "every tree that doesn't produce good fruit will be cut down and thrown into the fire" (Luke 3:9b). And yet, with all this anti-religious language, Jesus still said, "I tell you, among those born of women there is no one greater than John" (Luke 7:28).

Jesus said it was impossible for new wine to be poured into old wineskins, because the new wine will burst the old wineskins and the wine will pour out onto the ground, ruining both the wine and the wineskins (Matt. 9:17). But then he also mentioned how difficult it is to give up the old wine for the new. Those who have tasted the old wine don't want to switch to the new; the old tastes better to them.[29] This could be why Jesus went to those who never tasted any of the old wine (religious effort) and went instead to the non-religious: the lepers, tax collectors, prostitutes, and fishermen. They thought the new wine was great. They weren't fussy.[30]

In fact, Jesus said to the chief priests and elders, "I tell you the truth, the tax collectors and the prostitutes are entering the kingdom of God ahead of you. For John came to show you the way of righteousness, and you did not believe him, but the tax collectors and prostitutes did" (Matt. 21:31-32). The Way of righteousness declared by John was through the "Lamb of God, who takes away the sin of the world" (John 1:29), which restored the Tree of Life, empowering us to produce the fruits of the Spirit—love and compassion.

And yet Jesus told us he didn't come to abolish the law, but to fulfill it. This is the paradox. While the law in its lifeless form produced no good fruit, through Christ it would be fulfilled and become like a fruitful vine. Jesus said that "unless a kernel of wheat [representing the old religious system] falls to the ground and dies, it remains only a single seed. But if it dies, it produces many seeds" (John 12:24). That which was hidden in the law would now be unveiled. The Tree of the Knowledge of Good and Evil could be set aside for the Tree of Life. Jesus would even be the seed that would go into the ground and die, so that it could come forth and produce fruit. He would be the First Fruits from the dead! This is why he said to the chief priests and Pharisees that "the kingdom of God will be taken away from you and given to a people who will produce its fruit" (Matt. 21:43).

To illustrate this further, the parable of the Good Samaritan contrasts the religious leaders with the most despised people of their day, the Samaritans (who were half-breeds and rejected the placement of the Temple in Jerusalem). Jesus told the story of a man who was robbed and lying on the side of the road. The priest and Levite passed him by, but the Samaritan helped him. He was the one that pleased God. To love God and love our neighbor fulfills the law, not religious position or activity.

Tradition

The Pharisees and teachers of the law were upset with Jesus and his disciples, because they had broken a "tradition of the elders" and didn't perform ritual hand washing before they ate. (This was not a biblical admonition. It was one of many man-made regulations and rules, created after the Israelites returned from the exile of Babylon, for people to follow on a daily basis. Like little tyrants, the religious leaders watched everyone closely to see if they slipped up.)[31] Jesus wasn't impressed with their religious effort, though. Instead he asked them:

> And why do you break the command of God for the sake of your tradition? For God said, "Honor your father and mother" and "Anyone who curses his father or mother must be put to death." But you say that if a man says to his father or mother, "Whatever help you might otherwise have received from me is a gift devoted to God," he is not to "honor his father" with it. Thus you nullify the word of God for the sake of your tradition. You hypocrites!
>
> —Matthew 15:3-7a

The Temple

Religious leaders said that monetary gifts to God should be devoted to the Temple, whereas Jesus said it should be given to the needy. When God judges us, he no longer asks how much we've given to the Temple treasury or the church; instead we'll be asked when we clothed the naked, fed the hungry, visited those in prison, or cared for the sick (Matt. 25:31-46).

This is a hard word to any religious establishment. After all, if there's no tithe, how will the leaders be paid, and how will the buildings be kept up? But Jesus didn't have a building. John the Baptist didn't have a building. Amos didn't. Jeremiah didn't. Abraham didn't. David didn't. Paul didn't. There's not even a temple in heaven (Rev. 21:22)! Why must we burden people with heavy loads? How much money could have gone to the poor and needy around the world rather than our marble-floored, stained-glassed, gold, ivory, and silk-laden cathedrals?

I realize that there needs to be a place for the church to meet together. The Scriptures say, "Let us not give up meeting together, as some are in the habit of doing" (Heb. 10:25). This doesn't mean that we need to build expensive, extravagant buildings, which burden the people of God.

The building design that God gave to his people was that of a tent, a tabernacle that represented the Spirit of God. It was mobile. It moved. Jesus said that God's Spirit was like that. It moved where it wanted. When speaking to the religious leader Nicodemus about being born again of water and spirit, he explained: "The wind blows wherever it pleases. You hear its sound, but you cannot tell where it comes from or where it is going. So it is with everyone born of the Spirit" (John 3:8). He explained this further in his conversation with the Samaritan woman at the well. She wanted to embrace Jesus, a Jew, but she knew the Jews and the Samaritans disagreed over where the temple should be built. The Samaritans thought that since Abraham and Jacob had built altars nearby, that Mount Gerazim was the place to worship God. But the Jews insisted that Jerusalem was the temple site. Notice Jesus' answer to the woman:

> Believe me, woman, a time is coming when you will worship the Father neither on this mountain nor in Jerusalem. You Samaritans worship what you do not know; we worship what we do know, for salvation is from the Jews. Yet a time is coming and has now come when the true worshipers will worship the Father in spirit and truth, for they are the kind of worshipers the Father seeks. God is spirit, and his worshipers must worship in spirit and in truth.
> —John 4:21-24

The Old Testament Temple was merely a shadow of that which was fulfilled at the resurrection of Christ. Jesus said, "I am able to destroy the temple of God and rebuild it in three days" (Matt. 26:61b). Just as Jesus fulfilled the tithe, the Sabbath, the sacrifice, the circumcision, and the feasts, he fulfilled the temple. How many precious people have suffered because they didn't understand this? How many gave their money to build so many extravagant churches and cathedrals,[32] having the life sucked out of them, when they should have been using that money to help the poor and needy? Or even to care for their own families, as Jesus commanded (Matt. 15:3-9)? Instead, they thought that somehow they were accruing credit in heaven if they gave to enrich a religious establishment. This is religious effort—an attempt to please God in a way other than what he wants. It has caused so much suffering over the centuries and is akin to putting people in bondage—like the Jews in Egypt who were forced to build pyramids, a type of temple for the Gods.

Instead, we're now part of a new temple where Jesus is the cornerstone, the apostles are the foundation, and each of us is a stone. This isn't a man-made temple. It's a spiritual temple, fitted together by Christ himself. This is what Peter said about this new temple: "As you come to him, the living Stone—rejected by men but chosen by God and precious to him—you also, like living stones, are being built into a spiritual house" (1 Pet. 2:4-5). God's Spirit doesn't reside in buildings. It resides in people. There's no "cloud of glory" in any of our sanctuaries. This is part of the Old Covenant. The attempt to conjure up God's "manifest presence," as Tommy Tenney's "God Chasers" do, is akin to the religious effort of the prophets of Baal. It's unscriptural and religious. We can "approach the throne room of grace with confidence" (Heb. 4:16) through the blood of the Lamb. According to Hebrews 12:18-24, we no longer look for God in lightning, thunder, or clouds. Any kind of fleshly activity done to gain God's attention, even if it's "tarrying at the altar," is mixing the woolen and the linen. (Why is an altar needed?! Christ's blood was sprinkled on the altar in heaven once for all.)

Jesus Gives Us Rest

Paul says in his letter to the Colossians that we shouldn't let anyone judge us "by what [we] eat or drink, or with regard to a religious festival, a New Moon celebration, or a Sabbath day. These are a shadow of the things that were to come; the reality however is found in Christ" (Col. 2:16-17). If we do any of these things, we are *unspiritual*, and we've lost connection with the Head.

Religious activities that seem spiritual aren't bringing us closer to the Lord; they're actually cutting us off. Paul says they are the works of the flesh, equivalent to worshiping idols (Gal. 4:8-11). (Fasting and praying long prayers for revival will get you nowhere with God. Is it any wonder so many of our churches have failed—even after pleading and begging in prayer, worshiping, fasting, and marching?)

If we continue to dabble in the works of the flesh, we'll only continue to get death, but if we preach the grace received through the blood of the Lamb, life can flow to us from God. This is what Luther, Wesley, and Whitefield did in the past moves of God. Stop striving and start preaching the precious blood, rather than the drivel that has come out of Christendom over the last decades. Prosperity, success, laughter, power, leadership, dominion, chasing, contemplation. Aren't these the words that characterize the modern church? Where is the passionate preaching that reveals the grace and goodness of God? We need to repent of our pursuits, throw off the yoke, and rest. This is why Jesus came—to set us free from religious effort. "Come to me, all you who are weary and burdened, and I will give you rest. Take my yoke upon you and learn from me, for I am gentle and humble in heart, and you will find rest for your souls. For my yoke is easy and my burden is light" (Matt. 11:28-30).

Love

We've been set free to live holy lives that follow the two greatest commandments: to love God and love our neighbor as ourselves. Jesus said the whole Law could be summed up by obeying these two laws. Paul said that as "God's chosen people, holy and dearly loved" we should clothe ourselves "with compassion, kindness, humility, gentleness and patience" (Col. 3:12). These aren't religious activities; rather they are the fruits of the Spirit of Life.

Yet human nature continues to rise up and assert itself. In his letter to the Galatians, Paul warns us to stay away from religious rituals to please God. "It is for freedom that Christ has set us free. Stand firm, then, and do not let yourselves be burdened again by a yoke of slavery. Mark my words! I, Paul, tell you that if you let yourselves be circumcised, Christ will be of no value to you at all" (Gal. 5:1-2). If it's true for circumcision, it's also true for those other parts of the law, such as fasting, feasts, sacrifices, tithing, etc. Paul continues in the book of Galatians: "The only thing that counts is faith expressing itself through love" (Gal. 5:6).

He even says in 1 Corinthians 13 that even if we "speak in the tongues of men and of angels" and don't have love, it won't be of any spiritual profit to us. Love is the primary concern of God, not spiritual activity. The measurement of our intimacy with God is the love we have for others. Remember, even if we cast out demons and prophesy in Jesus' name, if we don't do good to others, he'll say, "I never knew you. Away from me, you evildoers!" (Matt. 7:23)

Spiritual Adultery

We must take this admonition seriously! If we attempt to access God in any way other than through the blood of Jesus, Christ will be of no value to us at all. Do we truly understand this? Our faith needs to be in Jesus and his finished work, not in our own efforts. In fact, this may be another hard word, but to push it home even further... if we don't rest and receive, the Scriptures say we are like whores. (Not my word—God's word!) If we attempt to get God's attention in any way other than Jesus, we are like women who dress up in promiscuous clothing and go out into the street to get a man's attention. But God is interested in a bride, not a whore!

The Scriptures are filled with sexual imagery concerning the relationship between God and his people. When Israel worshiped idols, God said it was like she committed adultery. He told Hosea to marry a whore, Gomer, to symbolize the relationship between himself and Israel. He talks about Israel being a virgin when he led her out of the bondage of Egypt. In Ezekiel, he talks about how he cared for her and clothed her in fine clothing and jewelry, admiring her beauty, but then he says Israel became a prostitute, even offering her children to the fire (Ezek.16). She was now defiled. She was religious. And it caused her to neglect righteousness and justice. As she turned toward other gods, practicing their ways, she turned away from concern for justice and caring for the poor, even becoming their oppressor (Ezek.16:49). (As the church neglects God's way, aren't we becoming less concerned for the poor and more concerned with our own beauty and success?)

There's also the contrast between the adulteress in the book of Proverbs and the bride in the Song of Solomon. In one book, we're warned to avoid the pitfalls of a whore, while in the other, the joy and passion of true love is conveyed. In the book of Proverbs, Solomon begs his son to be wise and follow his advice. He says if he does this, he'll "understand what is right and just and fair—every good path" (Prov. 2:9). This advice will also save him from "the adulteress, from the wayward wife with her seductive words, who has left the partner of her youth and ignored the covenant she made before God. For her house leads down to death and her paths to the spirits of the dead. None who go to her return or attain the paths of life" (Prov. 2:16-19).

In the same way that there's a marriage covenant between a husband and wife, there's a covenant between God and his people. Since the death of Jesus we live under the New Covenant. Jesus said, "This cup is the new covenant in my blood, which is poured out for you" (Luke 22:20). But when the church forgets the Blood and makes it a byline, she becomes a whore. She forgets the covenant she made and becomes a prostitute. This is how Solomon describes this loose woman:

> Then out came a woman to meet him, dressed like a prostitute and with crafty intent. (She is loud and defiant, her feet never stay at home; now in the street, now in the squares, at every corner she lurks.) She took hold of him and kissed him and with a brazen face she said: "I have fellowship offerings at home; today I fulfilled my vows. So I came out to meet you; I looked for you and have found you! I have covered my bed with colored linens from Egypt. I have perfumed my bed with myrrh, aloes and cinnamon. Come, let's drink deep of love till morning; let's enjoy ourselves with love! My husband is not at home; he has gone on a long journey. He took his purse filled with money and will not be home till full moon." With persuasive words she led him astray; she seduced him with her smooth talk.
>
> —Proverbs 7:10-21

This prostitute tries to turn people away from the right path. She's very religious and fulfills her ritual obligations, but they don't produce faithfulness and loyalty to her husband. She seduces and lures. She takes the initiative. This is what religion does. It attempts to lure the church away from her covenant. This is why the Book of Revelation describes the false church, religion, as a whore. She isn't a passionate, pure bride. She's manipulative and crafty. She's out to get something. She doesn't look to God for who he is, but for what she can get. Isn't this the church of today? (Even our quest for revival and outpourings are a type of whoredom!)

Do we think we can ever please God when we're unfaithful to his covenant? John tells us that the whore, the opposite of the bride, doesn't rely on the Blood, but instead is bloodthirsty. He even says, "In her was found the blood of prophets and of the saints, and of all who have been killed on the earth" (Rev. 18:24). This confirms the words of Jesus as he pointed to the religious leaders of Israel and declared that they were responsible for the blood of all the prophets. Religion is what's poisonous. It leads to murder, death, war, division. This is Christopher Hitchens' worldview. And it's correct. It's affirmed by the Bible.

The Bride

God's people are told to "come out of" the whore (Rev. 18:4). Come out of her adulteries, her betrayal of the Bridegroom, her neglect of the Covenant.

Instead be a Bride, dressed in pure white, eyes fixed on your beautiful Bridegroom, prepared to consummate your relationship with him, with a fire burning in your heart like the passion of a first love.

And he will greet his Bride, as a true knight rescuing the damsel in distress. He will be on a white horse. He will be called Faithful and True, a good husband. His eyes are blazing with passionate fire, and he's dressed in his covenantal robe. It's dipped in blood, and he's called the Word of God, King of Kings, and Lord of Lords. "The wedding of the Lamb has come, and his Bride has made herself ready. Fine linen, bright and clean, was given her to wear. (Fine linen stands for the righteous acts of the saints)" (Rev. 19:7-8).

Good Works

Now we know that the "righteous acts of the saints" doesn't refer to religious acts. It refers to the times when we live out the life of Jesus as he described himself in the synagogue and declared himself to be the Messiah. "The Spirit of the Lord is on me, because he has anointed me to preach good news to the poor. He has sent me to proclaim freedom for the prisoners and recovery of sight for the blind, to release the oppressed, to proclaim the year of the Lord's favor" (Luke 4:18-19).

The same Holy Spirit that anointed Jesus anoints us to do these works of righteousness. They are also *our* righteous works. And as Jesus gives spiritual blessings, they manifest in society as political and economic blessings, also.

As we walk through history in the rest of this book, we'll see how the church has lived out the anointing that Christ had from the Holy Spirit. We'll see how she has cared for the poor, set the captives free, opened the eyes of the blind, released the oppressed, and proclaimed the grace of God. This is her testimony. And it's beautiful.

When I see how intricately the Scriptures are woven together, I marvel at their consistent symbols and message. How could this book not be inspired? How could so many people, in so many places, over so much time, with so many different styles and types of messages, be so consistent in pointing to that One person?

When atheists and skeptics belittle this message, I'm sure they don't understand it. It reminds me of a redneck trashing Martin Luther King, Jr. Certainly, they don't understand him if they can besmirch him like that. King was glorious. To belittle him shows a complete lack of understanding, insight, and education. I would say it's the same for Jesus and the Bible. Tread softly when making flippant criticisms of the Word. It could be that you just don't understand.

The New Testament is against religion from beginning to end. It only points to Jesus as the Lamb, whose death would restore the relationship between man and God. All other attempts to reconnect with him are worthless. Jesus alone is the Narrow Way. Nothing else will do. But this is Good News, because it means all we have to do is receive him, like the thief on the cross, and we'll be made right with God. He did it all.

The prophet Haggai called Jesus the "desired of all nations" (Hag. 2:7). And he is! He alone sets men free from religious bondage and sin. Religion has no power to change the human heart—only the Life of Christ can do that. And nations who revel in that Life are blessed! Those on the Narrow Way are salt and light to the world. Any corner of the planet where they are allowed to thrive becomes more civilized and more liberated.

But none of these believers tries to bring about utopia through human effort. They live their lives in a way that brings about justice, righteousness, and freedom, but they know that their hope for perfection is only in Christ. Only through him can they be in paradise, reconciled to God.

Order. Newness. Light. Security. Life. Love. Joy. Peace. Humble, caring citizens. All the things we've tried to accomplish in history will finally be restored (Matt.19:28).[33] To get there, humanity only has to forsake religious effort and trust in the Lamb. Jesus stands at the door of all hearts and knocks. You have the power to open the door to him and receive his Life. But he's a gentleman and won't force his way in. It's your choice. He promises if you do let him in, though, he'll dine with you (Rev. 3:20). He'll be intimate with you. He'll be your friend. If you'll let him in, Eden will be restored.

PART II:

The Narrow Way in History

The unfolding of your words gives light…
Psalm 119:130

They overcame [Satan] by the blood of the Lamb and by the word of their testimony; they did not love their lives so much as to shrink from death.
Revelation 12:11

CHAPTER FOUR
The Narrow Way in the Roman Empire

"In those days the church was not merely a thermometer that recorded the ideas and principles of popular opinion; it was a thermostat that transformed the mores of society. Whenever the early Christians entered a town, the people in power became disturbed and immediately sought to convict the Christians for being 'disturbers of the peace' and 'outside agitators.' But the Christians pressed on, in the conviction that they were a 'colony of heaven,' called to obey God rather than man. Small in number, they were big in commitment. They were too God-intoxicated to be 'astronomically intimidated.' By their effort and example they brought an end to such ancient evils as infanticide and gladiatorial contests." —Martin Luther King, Jr., "Letter from a Birmingham Jail"

"You have won, Galilean." —Julian the Apostate's last words as he was dying on the battlefield in a war fought to prove the preeminence of the Roman gods.

The followers of the Narrow Way forever changed Western civilization. While the Greeks and Romans contributed much to philosophy, governmental structure, architecture, community planning, military strategy, art, and various other secular pursuits, they didn't contribute to the ethics or heart of the Western world. The ancients enjoyed blood sport. Over half of the population were slaves. They led aggressive wars. They were polytheists, and emperor worship was demanded—upon pain of death. There was no religious freedom. They practiced infanticide, exposing unwanted babies, especially girls, to the beasts and the elements. They were brutal and used force to control their subjects. Floggings, crucifixion, burning, impaling, and torture were commonplace. The ancient world may have had a form of order, but they were *not* civilized.

Piercing through the darkness of this time was the Light of the World, a simple carpenter from the Middle East, Jesus of Nazareth. He would become the most powerful civilizing influence humanity has ever known. He would inspire more books, more music, more artwork, more universities, and more places of refuge and help than any other person in history.

Did Jesus Even Exist?

Considering the profound impact Christ has had on the world, there are still those who make the absurd claim that he never existed. For example, the "historians" at www.religionislies.com assert: "Jesus Christ did not exist. If he did there is no acceptable evidence for it."[34] Even Christopher Hitchens refers to Christ as "the *supposed* Jesus of Nazareth."[35] But true historians don't take this line seriously for a moment. H.G. Wells, the skeptic historian and author of the classic *Outline of History*, acknowledged the existence of Christ. He described the personality of Jesus as being "like some terrible moral huntsman digging mankind out of the snug burrows in which they had lived hitherto. In the white blaze of his kingdom there was to be no property, no privilege, no pride and no precedence; no motive indeed and no reward but love. Is it any wonder that men were dazzled and blinded and cried out against him?"[36]

And even Wells, when asked which person he considered to have made the greatest impression on the world, according to historical standards, replied, "By this test Jesus stands first."[37]

Jesus would speak words never heard by the pagan world. Indeed, even the temple guards who were sent by the Pharisees to arrest Jesus said they hadn't done it, and when asked why they replied, "No one ever spoke the way this man does" (John 7:46). He would speak of kindness, love, peace, and justice, revealing that the heart of God was merciful and understanding rather than petty and demanding. The temple guards would hear this offer of Jesus: "If anyone is thirsty, let him come to me and drink. Whoever believes in me, as the Scripture has said, streams of living water will flow from within him" (John 7:37b-38). What man speaks like this?

Yet Ken Humphreys, the historian at www.jesusneverexisted.com tries to make the case that the Christian message was nothing unique or new. He claims that:

> ...nothing in the "Christian message" was original. Brotherly love and compassion had been taught by the Stoics for centuries. The Christian faith was a vulgarized paganism, set to the theme of the Jewish prophets and debased by religious intolerance... a "life" conjured up from mystical fantasy, a mass of borrowed quotations, copied story elements and a corpus of self-serving speculation, does not constitute an historical reality.[38]

He makes this assertion, based on no evidence, mind you, only on a declaration of his own interpretation of history, which ignores the accounts found in Matthew, Mark, Luke, and John, and even denies the testimony of those who weren't Jesus' followers, such as the first-century Jewish historian Josephus Flavius who wrote in his *Antiquities*:

> Now, there was about this time Jesus, a wise man, if it be lawful to call him a man, for he was a doer of wonderful works—a teacher of such men as receive the truth with pleasure. He drew over to him both many of the Jews, and many of the Gentiles. He was [the] Christ; and when Pilate, at the suggestion of the principal men amongst us, had condemned him to the cross, those that loved him at the first did not forsake him, for he appeared to them alive again the third day, as the divine prophets had foretold these and ten thousand other wonderful things concerning him; and the tribe of Christians, so named from him are not extinct at this day.[39]

And Pliny the Younger, governor of Bythinia, writing about 110 AD to Trajan, the Roman emperor, says that he didn't know how others dealt with the Christians, but describes how he decided to handle them:

> I have never been present at the examination of the Christians [by others], on which account I am unacquainted with what [used] to be inquired into, and what, and how far they used to be punished; nor are my doubts small, whether there be not a distinction to be made between the ages [of the accused]? and whether tender youth ought to have the same punishment with strong men? Whether there

be not room for pardon upon repentance?" or whether it may not be an advantage to one that had been a Christian, that he has forsaken Christianity? Whether the bare name, without any crimes besides, or the crimes adhering to that name… be… punished? In the meantime, I have taken this course about those who have been brought before me as Christians. I asked them whether they were Christians or not? If they confessed that they were Christians, I asked them again, and a third time, intermixing threatenings with the questions. If they persevered in their confession, I ordered them to be executed; for I did not doubt but, let their confession be of any sort whatsoever, this positiveness and inflexible obstinacy deserved to be punished.[40]

The Roman historian Tacitus writes in his *Annals* that the Christians were persecuted in 64 AD by Nero. After the fire that destroyed much of the city of Rome, he attempted to squelch rumors that he had started the fire by shifting the guilt away from himself and onto the Christians.

To get rid of the report, Nero fastened the guilt and inflicted the most exquisite tortures on a class hated for their abominations, called Christians by the populace. Christus, from whom the name had its origin, suffered the extreme penalty during the reign of Tiberius at the hands of one of our procurators, Pontius Pilatus, and a most mischievous superstition, thus checked for the moment, again broke out not only in Judea, the first source of the evil, but even in Rome, where all things hideous and shameful from every part of the world find their centre and become popular. Accordingly, an arrest was first made of all who pleaded guilty; then, upon their information, an immense multitude was convicted, not so much of the crime of firing the city, as of hatred against mankind. Mockery of every sort was added to their deaths. Covered with the skins of beasts, they were torn by dogs and perished, or were nailed to crosses, or were doomed to the flames and burnt, to serve as a nightly illumination, when daylight had expired.[41]

Seutonius, another Roman historian, writing in *The Twelve Caesars*, affirms the words of Pliny, saying about Nero that after the fire of Rome, "punishments were also inflicted on the Christians, a sect professing a new and mischievous religious belief."[42] There are also references to Jesus by the second-century playwright, Lucian. In the play, *The Passing of Peregrinus*, he mocks the simplistic and gullible church, whose leader was crucified in Palestine,[43] for embracing a scoundrel who takes advantage of their generosity.

To say that the Christians "created" a religion by pasting together myths, fictional narratives, and borrowed phrases is a ridiculous claim, because the sayings of Christ were so sublime and so revolutionary that the creator of this narrative would have had to be one of the most brilliant persons that ever existed. As Joseph Parker wrote in *Ecce Deus*, "only a Christ could have conceived of a Christ."[44]

Is it possible that the polytheistic ancient world, which heretofore had created no real morality, could have possibly given birth to the Christ myth and now produced the ideal man? One of the problems with Stoicism, for example, was its inability to produce their "wise man" in human shape. They looked in vain for this "man," and in a parody to Zeno, the founder of Stoicism, who had said, "It is reasonable to honour the gods: it is not reasonable to honour the non-existent: therefore the gods exist," they found it necessary to resort to the same circular reasoning when it came to finding the perfect role model, "It is reasonable to honour wise men: it is not reasonable to honour the non-existent: therefore wise men exist."[45] But they couldn't find the wise man. They couldn't even imagine him. Their gods fell far short of the ideal.

But now, are we to suppose that an obscure writer of unknown origins was somehow able to create the Stoics' "wise man," and yet no mention is ever made of this mastermind? If this person, who created the perfect God narrative, exists, why doesn't some person somewhere mention this writer? Instead, posterity has been given four different accounts of the actual life of this man, Jesus Christ. Should we toss these testimonies aside so easily, especially when they agree so precisely with the secular historical record, and believe instead in the existence of a hidden author, when there's no evidence whatsoever that this writer ever existed? In other words, in order to *not* believe in the historical Jesus, we'd rather believe in a brilliant unknown author when there's no record this person ever existed. Which takes more faith?

It's also worth asking how, since the gospels weren't written down until thirty years or so after the death of Jesus, the concept of the mythical Christ got communicated to all the Christians who were already dying in the arena, stoned by the Sanhedrin, and burning on Nero's stakes. Was it merely through the hearing of a mythical story, or was it because they *saw* and knew Jesus? If it was a myth, wouldn't this be common knowledge? Who would die for that?

Regardless of whether or not there was a secret writer, or whether or not the testimonies of the secular historians were embellished, as some skeptics claim, those who deny the existence of Jesus can't deny that a group of people known as "the Christians" exists.

As I hope to show in the rest of this chapter, this small group of "believers" would burst onto the world scene with a passion and moral fervor that would shake an empire and finally conquer it without lifting a weapon. These followers of "The Way" claimed that their zeal came as a result of the teachings and life of a man named Jesus. Those who deny the historical existence of Christ would have us believe that the church's fervor was the result of a type of fairytale or myth that was merely a mishmash of paganism and philosophy. But the content of the Christian message was contradictory to these "sources" that the gospels were supposedly formed from.

So the question is: Where did these Christians come from? Are we to believe that they were "spontaneously generated" like flies from rotten meat or that they sprung forth from the primordial soup?

The Greek myths had their source in Homer, and the Mormon scriptures had their source in Joseph Smith. Buddhism had a Buddha and communism had its Karl Marx. Again, I ask, was the source of Christianity found in Jesus, as so many testify, or in an unknown ghostwriter who made up the whole story? Who is "conjuring up a 'life'?"

And is it not worth mentioning that nearly all of the disciples referred to in these fictional narratives were put to death for their beliefs? Would they all have died for a fairytale or a lie? John Foxe, in his *Book of Martyrs*, describes the works and deaths of Jesus' disciples. In their allegiance to the "fairytale" character, Jesus:

> Thomas preached to the Parthians, Medes and Persians, also to the Carmanians, Hyrcanians, Bactrians and Magians. He suffered in Calamina, a city of India, being slain with a dart. Simon, who was brother to Jude, and to James the younger, who all were the sons of Mary Cleophas and of Alpheus, was Bishop of Jerusalem after

James, and was crucified in a city of Egypt in the time of Trajan the emperor. Simon the apostle, called Cananeus and Zelotes, preached in Mauritania, and in the country of Africa, and in Britain: he was likewise crucified."[46]

According to Clement, James, the brother of John, was beheaded. And Foxe goes on to say that tradition has it that Mark was burnt alive in Egypt. Bartholomew was "beaten down with staves, then crucified; and after… he was beheaded."[47] Andrew was crucified by Aegeas in the city of Patrae. Matthew preached Jesus "the fairytale" in Egypt and Ethiopia, after which King Hircanus "sent one to run him through with a spear."[48]

Philip was crucified and stoned in the city of Hieropolis. And James, the brother of Jesus, was thrown off the pinnacle of the Temple during Passover, but didn't die and started to pray for his persecutors when he was struck on the head by somebody in the mob with a blunt instrument and killed.

These were real people in real places, not gods on Mt. Olympus! And unlike Muslim terrorists, who die to gain heaven, while not actually seeing Allah or knowing Muhammed, who lived centuries ago, the disciples lived contemporaneously with Christ. If he wasn't real, if he was instead a character created by a ghostwriter, would they still have given of themselves so passionately? To them, Jesus was a man, their friend, their brother, and after the resurrection, their God. If he wasn't real, wouldn't someone have squealed? Yet there's *no* record anywhere of anyone—Roman, Jew, Greek, or otherwise—declaring that he didn't exist. Wouldn't there be an outcry or a response from the Roman world somewhere that all these men were delusional? Wouldn't somebody mock them? Wouldn't somebody mention that their story was contrived? After all, the Christians were being killed and crucified by kings, priests, and mobs all over the ancient world—they didn't remain obscure—and yet there's no attempt anywhere to discredit them by saying that Jesus was just a myth!

The story of Jesus is an actual account in real time with real people who had names and lived in actual cities and towns. It wasn't a fairytale with imaginary names and imaginary figures. There was no fantasy house in an unknown woods where Snow White would encounter seven dwarves and be protected from a witch. Instead, the gospel accounts mention Augustus, Herod, the Sea of Galilee, the Temple, real people who go on to be recorded in history, such as

Pontius Pilate, and events such as the census taken during the time Quirinius was the governor of Syria. Anyone in the ancient world could have disputed these facts and declared them to be lies. They could have interviewed anyone mentioned in the gospels and asked them if what was recorded was true, but nobody did. Instead, there are references to Jesus in secular sources, which treat his existence as a matter of fact.

Those who claim that Jesus didn't exist arrogantly suggest that those who "ignorantly" believe in Christ need to be enlightened. Listen to the attitude and tone of those who claim that Jesus never existed: "Do you really think it all began with a sanctimonious Jewish wonder-worker, strolling about 1st century Palestine? Prepare to be enlightened."[49]

But it seems to me that those who need to be enlightened are those who proudly insist that Jesus is made up—with no evidence to stand on except their own "conjured up 'life'"—the mystery writer. Who truly are the "self-serving" speculators who can't face historical reality?

Whereas the mythological Greek and Roman gods were caught up in selfish intrigues and manipulations, Jesus was a historical person who led a sinless life of blessing and selflessness toward others.[50] The followers of Jesus would permeate the ancient world with the Good News of a God who loved them and wanted to be with them. They would give hope to those who only knew the gods to be creatures that demanded subjection in exchange for blessings. Pagan religions existed merely as a way to receive from the gods. Humans would perform a ritual with the hope that the god would respond. This is the opposite of Christianity, which taught that "While we were still sinners, Christ died for us" (Rom. 5:8b), and he hopes that we will respond to him!

Charity

The Book of Acts tells us that these followers of Jesus were known as "The Way" (Acts 19:9, 23; 22:4; 24:14, 22). The simplicity of their message and the purity of their lives would alter the religious and cultural landscape forever. As a result of their passion and love for Jesus, the West would no longer be polytheistic. It would no longer practice blood sport. A new standard of humanity would develop, causing infanticide to end, the poor to be provided for, the sick cared for, and widows and orphans taken in. Their attitude toward slavery would eventually lead Europe to completely abolish it (until 1,500 years later).

When Jesus told them they were to be the salt of the earth, he meant that they were to be sprinkled throughout the world and serve as its preservative, keeping it from rotting and decaying.

For example, these simple and lovely words of Jesus would revolutionize the world without even striking a blow or firing a shot:

> "For I was hungry and you gave me something to eat, I was thirsty and you gave me something to drink, I was a stranger and you invited me in, I needed clothes and you clothed me, I was sick and you looked after me, I was in prison and you came to visit me." Then the righteous will answer him, "Lord, when did we see you hungry and feed you, or thirsty and give you something to drink? When did we see you a stranger and invite you in, or needing clothes and clothe you? When did we see you sick or in prison and go to visit you?" The King will reply, "'I tell you the truth, whatever you did for one of the least of these brothers of mine, you did for me."
>
> —Matthew 25:35-40

Instead of treating the poor as outcasts who were spiritually inferior and therefore worthy of being despised (as the Hindu religion teaches), Jesus taught that when his disciples looked upon the least of society, they were looking on *him*. So they saw beauty in the face of the needy instead of ugliness. This was radical! R.R. Palmer explains, "Where the Greeks had identified the beautiful and the good, had thought ugliness to be bad, had shrunk from disease and imperfection and from everything misshapen, horrible, and repulsive, the Christian sought out the diseased, the crippled, the mutilated, to give them help."[51] Instead of rejecting the unattractive, Christians loved and helped them, sacrificing themselves for the benefit of the least.

This was in contrast to the ethics of Plato, who said that his Republic should set up judges "which will care for those of your citizens who have good natures in body and soul; while as for those who haven't, they'll let die the ones whose bodies are such."[52] Contrary to the claims of those who declare Jesus never existed, the Christian ethic didn't evolve from either Greek philosophy or Roman religion. It came from a Jewish man named Jesus who also said:

> "When you give a luncheon or dinner, do not invite your friends, your brothers or relatives, or your rich neighbors; if you do, they may

invite you back and so you will be repaid. But when you give a banquet, invite the poor, the crippled, the lame, the blind, and you will be blessed. Although they cannot repay you, you will be repaid at the resurrection of the righteous."

—Luke 14:12-14

This attitude of Jesus would be faithfully acted out by his disciples from early on. Acts 6:1-6 says that one of the first things the early church did was appoint seven deacons (table servers) to handle the daily distribution of food to the needy. James, the brother of Jesus, would echo this concern for the least in society. He said, "Religion that God our Father accepts as pure and faultless is this: to look after orphans and widows in their distress" (James 1:27).

He also said that favoritism was forbidden in the church, saying, "Suppose a man comes into your meeting wearing a gold ring and fine clothes, and a poor man in shabby clothes also comes in. If you show special attention to the man wearing fine clothes and say, 'Here's a good seat for you,' but say to the poor man, 'You stand there' or 'Sit on the floor by my feet,' have you not discriminated among yourselves and become judges with evil thoughts?" (James 2:2-4).

James would also claim that faith without these works of charity would be dead. Just as the Old Testament prophets encouraged the people of God to be compassionate, loving justice and mercy, James would echo the words of John the Baptist, who told us that "The man with two tunics should share with him who has none, and the one who has food should do the same" (Luke 3:11). He asks: "Suppose a brother or sister is without clothes and daily food. If one of you says to him, 'Go, I wish you well; keep warm and well fed,' but does nothing about his physical needs, what good is it?" (James 2:15-16).

This attitude toward the least in society would continue in the early church. Justin Martyr, one of the earliest defenders of the faith, described the purpose and method of giving: "Those who prosper, and who so wish, contribute, each one as much as he chooses to. What is collected is deposited with the president, and he takes care of orphans and widows, and those who are in want on account of sickness or any other cause, and those who are in bonds, and the strangers who are sojourners among [us], and, briefly, he is the protector of all those in need."[53]

Tertullian also described the giving of the early church:

> There is no buying and selling of any sort in the things of God. Though we have our treasure-chest, it is not made up of purchase-money, as of a religion that has its price. On the monthly day, if he likes, each puts in a small donation; but only if it be his pleasure, and only if he be able: for there is no compulsion; all is voluntary. These gifts are, as it were, piety's deposit fund. For they are not taken thence and spent on feasts, and drinking-bouts, and eating-houses, but to support and bury poor people, to supply the wants of boys and girls destitute of means and parents, and of old persons confined now to the house; such, too, as have suffered shipwreck; and if there happen to be any in the mines, or banished to the islands, or shut up in the prisons....[54]

As mentioned before, Lucian mocked the generosity of the Christians, saying that their devotion to Christ even left them vulnerable to charlatans:

> The activity of these people, in dealing with any matter that affects their community, is something extraordinary; they spare no trouble, no expense.... You see, these misguided creatures start with the general conviction that they are immortal for all time, which explains the contempt of death and voluntary self-devotion which are so common among them; and then it was impressed on them by their original lawgiver that they are all brothers, from the moment that they are converted, and deny the gods of Greece, and worship the crucified sage, and live after his laws. All this they take quite on trust, with the result that they despise all worldly goods alike, regarding them merely as common property. Now an adroit, unscrupulous fellow, who has seen the world, has only to get among these simple souls, and his fortune is pretty soon made; he plays with them.[55]

Unfortunately, there will always be charlatans who will prey upon the flock, but at least the hearts of the sheep are tender, unlike the heartlessness of pagan ladies, says Clement, who are abandoned to luxury and "bring up parrots and curlews [a bird], but will not take in the orphan child."[56]

Ignatius described heretics as those who "care nothing about love: they have no concern for widows or orphans, for the oppressed, for those in prison or released, for the hungry or the thirsty."[57] And Tertullian rebuked pagans by declaring that "our compassion spends more in the streets than yours does in the temples."[58] This principle was also confirmed by Paul who said, "Let us do good to all people, especially to those who belong to the family of believers" (Gal. 6:10).

But doing good to *all*, and the good will that was engendered by the church's displays of charity, was becoming a problem for those who held pagan beliefs. Julian the Apostate was flustered with the church, writing in a letter to Arsacius that he observed "how the kindness of Christians to strangers, their care for the burial of their dead, and the sobriety of their lifestyle has done the most to advance their cause." And beyond that, he lamented, "the impious Galileans support our poor in addition to their own."[59] This inspired him to lead a campaign to get the pagan temples to care for the poor, but it failed miserably.

Lawrence, one of the seven deacons of Rome during the persecution by Emperor Valerian in the third century, was a distributor of church money to the poor. He was arrested and his persecutor demanded to know where the church's treasure was. In the meantime, a number of poor Christians had followed him to his trial. John Foxe described the ensuing scene:

> Then valiant Lawrence, stretching out his arms over the poor, said: "These are the precious treasure of the church; these are the treasure indeed, in whom the faith of Christ reigneth, in whom Jesus Christ hath His mansion place. What more precious jewels can Christ have than those in whom he hath promised to dwell? For so it is written, 'I was hungry and ye gave me to eat; I was thirsty, and ye gave me to drink; I was harbourless and ye lodged me.' And again, 'Look, what ye have done to the least of these, the same have ye done to me.' What greater riches can Christ our Master possess, than the poor people, in whom he loveth to be seen?"[60]

This angered the persecutor so much that he became enraged and tortured Lawrence with beatings, fiery tongs, burning plates, chains, fire-forks, and the grated bed of iron, on which the torturers were commanded to "roast him, broil him, toss him, turn him."[61]

The first admonition in the catalogue of virtues found in *The Shepherd of Hermas* is to care for widows and orphans. Again, this passionate attitude toward the lowly and poor did not proceed from Stoic philosophy or pagan religion. It came from the man Jesus. This compassion and courage would also reveal itself in times of calamity. During the plague in Alexandria, in the third century, the Bishop Dionysius wrote:

> Most of our brethren did not spare themselves, so great was their brotherly affection. They held fast to each other, visited the sick without fear, ministered to them assiduously, and served them for the sake of Christ. Right gladly did they perish with them.... Indeed many did die, after caring for the sick and giving health to others, transplanting the death of others, as it were, into themselves. In this way the noblest of our brethren died, including some presbyters and deacons and people of the highest reputation.... Quite the reverse was it with the heathen. They abandoned those who began to sicken, fled from their dearest friends, threw out the sick when half dead into the streets, and let the dead lie unburied.[62]

Cyprian also contrasted the attitudes of pagans with those of Christians. Speaking to Demetrianus about the plague at Carthage, he says that the pagans, "shun the deathbeds of the dying, but make for the spoils of the dead."[63]

In contrast, Eusebius spoke of the Christian attitude during an anthrax plague that occurred under the reign of Maximinius Daza:

> At the same time every race was given clear proof of the zeal and piety of Christians in all things. Amid the onset of these evils they alone revealed compassion and humanity in their deeds. Every day they carried on, nursing the dying and burying the dead, for there were countless numbers with no one to look after them. Into one place in every city they gathered the multitude of those who were wasted by hunger. They issued food to everyone. And all men began to speak of their work, and they gave glory to the God of the Christians.[64]

Slavery

Another change brought about by Jesus was the attitude toward slavery. In Athens, where nearly three-fourths of the population were slaves, Aristotle merely looked upon them as living tools. He said that men could be possessed by other men even though they are human beings because some men are merely "instruments of action" and that it was natural for some to be slaves "for that some should rule and others be ruled is a thing not only necessary, but expedient; from the hour of their birth, some are marked out for subjection, others for rule."[65] Plato also thought that the need for slavery was a natural condition of humanity (perhaps a necessary evil), but Jesus said that he came to set the captives free! He stands alone in ancient history as the friend of the slave.

In a world that had no energy supply, slaves were a form of power. Those who owned them had a source of production, a way to earn money or obtain goods. There were those who did manual labor and those who didn't. Work was scorned. It was looked down upon as the destiny of those in the lower class. But when Jesus came, he changed this attitude. How? By being a common laborer—a carpenter. If the King of Glory can work with his hands, how can we despise hard work? His disciples were also common laborers. Peter was a fisherman. Paul was a tentmaker. There were no upper-class disciples. They were all laborers (or in Matthew's case, a tax collector) who would have been despised in the ancient world.

The letters of Paul also reflect this changing attitude toward labor. In his second letter to the Thessalonians, he tells the church not to feed those who won't work even though they are able. (*The Didache* [a book claiming to be the teaching of the twelve apostles] even says that the church should consider a traveling prophet to be false if he wouldn't work.)[66] The example of Jesus made honest employment admirable, not despicable. The effect this had on the labor force was tremendous. It lessened the need for slaves, because more people were now willing to work in allegiance and service to their King.

Paul also pointed out that on a spiritual level all were equal before God. "There is neither Jew nor Greek, slave nor free, male nor female, for you are all one in Christ Jesus" (Gal. 3:28). This was different for the Roman religion, which wouldn't even allow slaves to venerate their gods because they would have defiled the worship. But Christianity had such a leveling effect on society that slaves had to be encouraged to not look down on their masters (1 Tim 6:2). Slaves would become full members of the church. They would be treated as equals. After Peter and Paul, the next bishop of Rome was Linus, a slave. Callistus, another early bishop of Rome, was also a slave. The church, unlike the Roman Empire, would recognize slave marriages, and while pagans were always sure to distinguish the tombs of the slave from the tombs of the free man, Christianity would make no such distinction.

While the church only consisted of a small band of poor, weak Jews in a huge, powerful, and somewhat monstrous empire, there was certainly no hope that they could overthrow the slave system through force or revolution. Certainly, rebellion had been tried before. The third time it was led by Spartacus, whose forces included trained gladiators, and yet they failed. Their bodies, crucified by the thousands, would line the Appian Way for miles. Paul had no hope of overthrowing a system or empire that was capable of striking such a crushing blow. So he taught Christians how to live as free men within the slave system—how to live above the tyranny with dignity, and for a higher purpose: the glory of God. But, beyond that, he did something else—he taught the church to live as equals. Perhaps in the outer world there was injustice to contend with, but within the walls of the church there was love and brotherhood. Thus we see Paul, writing in the letter to Philemon about Onesimus, his runaway slave:

> Although in Christ I could be bold and order you to do what you ought to do, yet I appeal to you on the basis of love. I then, as Paul—an old man and now also a prisoner of Christ Jesus—I appeal to you for my son Onesimus, who became my son while I was in chains. Formerly he was useless to you, but now he has become useful both to you and to me. I am sending him—who is my very heart—back to you. I would have liked to keep him with me so that he could take your place in helping me while I am in chains for the gospel. But I did not want to do anything without your consent, so that any favor you do will be spontaneous and not forced. Perhaps the reason he was separated from you for a little while was that you might have him back for good—no longer as a slave, but better than a slave, as a dear brother. He is very dear to me but even dearer to you, both as a man and as a brother in the Lord.
>
> —Philemon 1:8-16

These "brothers in the Lord" who were bound by love for God and one another would be equal in martyrdom also. H.G. Wells describes the effect of Christianity on the "lowly and unhappy" classes of "slaves, soldiers, and distressed peoples": "Christianity has been denounced by modern writers as a 'slave religion.' It was. It took the slaves and the downtrodden and it gave them hope and restored their self-respect so that they stood up for righteousness like men and faced persecution and torment."[67]

One example of a slave and free person facing martyrdom together is that of Felicity and Perpetua. Felicity was a slave girl who had just given birth in the arena jail, and Perpetua was a free woman who was still nursing her baby. They were arrested and told to renounce Christ, but refused and were sentenced to death in the Coliseum. Robert Ellsburg tells the story of their martyrdom:

> Perpetua and Felicity were set in the arena together. At first they were stripped, causing the crowd to shudder "seeing one a tender girl, the other her breasts yet dropping from her late childbearing." And so in a final ironic concession to their womanhood they were permitted to cover themselves. They were then exposed to a savage cow, which tossed them about on its horns. When they had survived this ordeal the executioner was ordered to put them to the sword....
> A final poignant image remains. The narrator notes that before meeting the sword the two young women, formerly mistress and servant, now sisters in Christ, turned to one another before the jeering crowd and exchanged a kiss.[68]

Christianity was a leveler. It made all people equal before God. Age, gender, nationality, and income weren't important in the kingdom of God. The only thing that mattered was the heart. A Christian was one who had humbly received the grace of God through Jesus and then lived a life of purity and love toward others. It didn't matter where a person was in life. Young, old, rich, poor, black, white, educated, uneducated, male, female, Jew, Greek, slave, free. Every life was special, created by God, and worthy of love and respect.

Perpetua and Felicity would face death together, holding hands, as equals before God. This attitude permeated the church, inspiring them to be compassionate to the slave and do noble and courageous deeds in order to deliver captives out of their bondage. This virtue didn't come from the Greek philosophers. It came from the Nazarene who said, "if the Son sets you free, you will be free indeed" (John 8:36).

The early church would go overboard to fulfill these words of Jesus. Clement described the willingness of the believers to extravagantly help others: "We know many of our own number who have had themselves imprisoned in order to ransom others; Many have sold themselves into slavery and given the price to feed others."[69] This great love would be written about in all the early writings of the church. Aristides, the Athenian orator, noted that "if they hear that anyone of their number is imprisoned or in distress for the sake of their Christ's name, they all render aid in his necessity, and if he can be redeemed, they set him free."[70] The *Shepherd of Hermas* expressed this passion simply: "Therefore, instead of fields buy ye souls that are in trouble."[71]

The early church may not have led a slave rebellion in the physical sense, but in the spiritual sense they were revolutionaries. They couldn't *overthrow* the Empire, but they could *undermine* it. And the heart of Jesus would eventually prevail. Goodness would defeat evil. Freedom would conquer tyranny. Because of Him. To whom else can we attribute the source of the attitude found in these words found in the Apostolic Constitutions: "All monies accruing from honest labour do ye appoint and apportion to the redeeming of the saints, ransoming thereby slaves and captives, prisoners, people who are sore abused or condemned by tyrants."[72]

The church would continue in this passionate thrust toward releasing captives and setting them free until slavery no longer existed as an institution. Melania would be one of many wealthy converts who would sell their possessions and give them to the poor. She would also be one of many who released their slaves. In her case, she is reported to have set 8,000 slaves at liberty. During the Barbarian invasions of the fifth to seventh centuries, captives from conquered cities were hauled away into slavery and the church intervened, redeeming them by the thousands.

Would the church have acted in this way if they condoned slavery? If, as many modern commentators declare, the church was indifferent to or even advocated slavery (since Paul told the slaves in the Ephesian Church to "obey their earthly masters"), would believers have acted so extravagantly in their eagerness to set slaves free? Redemption of slaves, as the Christian had been redeemed from the bondage of sin (symbolized in the Old Testament by the Israelite deliverance from the bondage of Egypt), was such an important aspect of the mission of the early church that slavery would finally be expunged completely from the Roman Empire.

Infanticide

In the same way that the church found value in the lives of the slaves, it also found value in the lives of children. This was in direct contrast to the pagan societies of the ancient world. To them, children, especially infants, were expendable. It wasn't unusual for babies to be exposed to the elements, ravaged by wild animals, drowned, sacrificed, eaten by cannibals, or even left on top of a tower to starve or be eaten by predatory birds.

According to Plutarch, writing on the subject of superstition, the ancient Carthaginians sacrificed children to Saturn. Poor parents would sell their babies "witting and knowing they killed their own children... as if they were lambs, young calves, or kids, for the said purpose. At which sacrifice the mother that bare them in her womb would stand by without any shew at all of being moved, without weeping or sighing for pity and compassion." The priests would threaten to not pay the parents if they showed any emotion. And to make sure that no sympathy could be mustered as the baby was roasted alive, "the place resounded and rung again with the noise of flutes and hautboys, with the sound also of drums and timbrels, to the end that the painful cry of the poor infants should not be heard." Human life was cheap in the ancient world. Those who were weak, deformed, or inadequate in any way were put out. Little girls were often thrown away, because boys were preferred.

Plato and Aristotle both accepted infanticide as part of Athenian law. The Spartans also practiced infanticide, but the decision on whether or not to expose the child was left up to public officials. Roman law, the Twelve Tables, condoned infanticide if a child was deformed and even gave fathers the right to expose their infant daughters. Cicero would defend infanticide merely because it was the law, and Seneca stated, "we drown children at birth who are weakly and abnormal."[74]

In a letter written by a Hilarion to his wife, the ancient attitude toward infanticide is captured: "I'm still in Alexandria... I entreat you and beg you to take good care of our baby son, As soon as I receive payment I'll send it to you. If you go into labour and childbirth before I get back home, if it's a boy keep it, if a girl discard it."[75]

Exposed infants were often picked up and raised by slave traders who cared nothing for them. They were so worthless that they were even named after waste. The *Cambridge Ancient History* describes how little value ancient societies placed on their children:

In Egypt we know that children were exposed in local garbage pits, cesspools and dumps where, in many cases, they were left to die. But these same venues could also serve as places where collusory acts of acquisition could be undertaken by parents and slave-dealers. In fact, there would seem to be a clear relationship between the "picked-up" children and a significant group of Egyptians who bore what are politely labeled "copronyms," that is, names derived from the word κο'προδ ("shit").[76]

The Christian attitude toward infanticide didn't proceed from the philosophers or pagan religions. It came from Jesus. While King Herod would flippantly slaughter little boys in order to rid himself of his competition (Matt. 2:16), Jesus would embrace the innocents, saying, "Let the little children come to me, and do not hinder them, for the kingdom of heaven belongs to such as these" (Matt. 19:14). This was a new ethic. It was revolutionary! Because of these words, the church would set itself to the task of saving exposed infants.

The New Testament doesn't mention infanticide, but that could be because Jesus and the disciples lived in Israel where Jewish law didn't allow babies to be exposed. In fact the Jewish rejection of infanticide angered the Roman historian Cornelius Tacitus, who noted in his *Histories* that "it was a crime among them to kill any newly-born infant" and that it was just another of the many "perverse and disgusting" customs of the Jews.[77] But even though infanticide isn't mentioned in the writings of the apostles, the church still garnered a particular ethic from the teachings of Jesus that inspired them to spread out amongst the ancient world and collect exposed babies and rear them as their own.

This ethic is expressed in the "Letter to Diognetus." Speaking of the Christians, the writer says: "Like other men, they marry and beget children, though they do not expose their infants."[78] The *Didache*, written around 100 AD, said "Practice no... abortion, or infanticide."[79] The Epistle of Barnabus says that followers of "the Way" should "never do away with an unborn child or destroy it after its birth."[80] This belief would become further strengthened in the fourth century under the newly converted Emperor Constantine, who changed Roman law. The Theodosian Code would make it easier for poor people to keep their children by giving them money from the imperial treasury to care for the baby and also entitle those who rescued a baby to have property rights over the child.

Christianity provided the world with a tenderness it hadn't known before. And as the Good News of God's grace through Christ spread around the world, as we'll see in subsequent chapters, it brought a new light into some of the harshest corners of the world. Those who hungered and thirsted for righteousness rather than brutality and perversion found a resting place in Christianity's branches. If we are to know a tree by its fruit, as Jesus said, rescuing abandoned children, redeeming slaves, caring for the needy, nursing the sick, and opposing an irrational religion were all fruits of this tree. Birthed out of love for its great founder and king, Jesus, who first loved them and gave all he had for them, the church would now go forth with this same passion toward others and attempt to let him live his life of great love through them.

Opposition to Religion

This chapter was about the original followers of the Narrow Way. And it isn't a coincidence that they were forced to confront "religion." In the same way that the prophets confronted religion in the Old Testament (the Baals, the Pharoah, and their own corrupt priesthood) and John the Baptist and Jesus confronted religion in the New Testament (the Pharisees and the religious class of Scribes and Sadducees), these new followers of the Narrow Way would confront religion of another form.

The early church lived in a polytheistic society that worshiped mythical gods and considered the emperor (Caesar) to be a god. There were many religions in the Roman Empire, since it covered such a vast area, but other than the Jews, who refused to worship Caesar, others could give their worship to the emperor because their religion didn't demand loyalty to a person. As T.R. Glover explains in *The Conflict of Religions in the Early Roman Empire*: "So far in dealing with the religious life of the ancient world, we have had to do with ideas and traditions—with a well-thought-out scheme of philosophy and with an ancient and impressive series of mysteries and cults. The new force that came into play is something quite different. The centre in the new religion is not an idea nor a ritual act, but a personality."[81]

In Christianity, there was an allegiance to a man. How could a Christian worship an emperor as God when Jesus, who gave all for them, was their God? How could they deny Jesus, their great love?

This was an absolute threat to the empire. Whereas the Jews wouldn't worship Caesar either, they were not only a religion, but a nation and a race, so they remained isolated and were easier to leave alone. The Christians were universal, though. They were spreading the Good News everywhere and appealing to all. This was dangerous to the order of the realm and had to be confronted.

One of the main purposes of the Roman Coliseum and the practice of blood sport was an attempt to make a public display of order in the empire. Thus wild animals, which were a threat to safety and security, were captured and used at the arena. Criminals were also rounded up to face their fate in the Coliseum. Execution of beasts and criminals, who were considered plagues on society, were symbols of good government. It was a way to express to the public that justice was being carried out. The crowds could easily justify their excitement, since they were merely involved in the administration of justice.

The emperor of Rome not only represented religion, but also the state. Christians, by not worshiping the emperor, were disrupting public order—something that had become very important in the minds of the Romans as a way to justify their blood sport. So when the believers and their children were tossed to the lions, there was no sympathy. They deserved it. After all, order was necessary.

And because Christians wouldn't bow to the Roman gods, the pagans believed the gods were angered, so any time anything bad happened, such as famine, pestilence, earthquakes, wars, or other disasters, the church was blamed. This was another reason to hunt the church down and get rid of believers. To the Romans, they were "atheists" who were invoking the wrath of the gods.

Christianity, as weak as it was (its membership consisting of the poor, laborers, slaves, orphans and widows) was the only force that confronted the Roman religion. Those on the Narrow Way were the only ones who had the Truth and were able to courageously stand up to the poisonous religion of their day. And it cost them greatly. In the same way that Cain killed Abel, the prophets were killed, and the Pharisees plotted to kill Jesus, the Roman Empire mercilessly tortured and murdered the church. John Foxe describes the hatred and vitriol of the Roman persecutions:

> The kinds of death were divers… Whatsoever the cruelness of man's invention could devise for the punishment of man's body, was practised against the Christians—stripes and scourgings, drawings, tearings, stonings, plates of iron laid unto them burning hot, deep dungeons, racks, strangling in prisons, the teeth of wild beasts, gridirons, gibbets and gallows, tossing upon the horns of bulls.[82]

But it was the church that confronted this tyrannical and poisonous religion that worshiped madmen and produced such brutality. The emperors, who were supposedly gods, were mentally ill, wicked men that Seutonius writes extensively about in *The Twelve Caesars*. Foxe also gives a short description of some of these Caesars:

> Claudius Nero, who reigned thirteen years with no little cruelty; but especially the third of these Neros, called Domitius Nero, who, succeeding after Claudius, reigned fourteen years with such fury and tyranny that he slew the most part of the senators and destroyed the whole order of the knighthood of Rome.... Such was his wretched cruelty, that he caused to be put to death his mother, his brother-in-law, his sister, his wife and his instructors, Seneca and Lucan.[83]

And yet the Christians were put to death for not worshiping these Caesars as God. Were they wrong? With the benefit of hindsight we don't think they were. But how did they have the insight and courage necessary to oppose this evil? I would say that it's because they had discovered the Way, the Truth, and the Life. As we walk through history, we will see a consistent trend: those who were able to oppose poisonous religion most effectively were always those on the Narrow Way of grace and love.

It was only when the church became religious that it lost its great power to be the salt of the earth and the light of the world. But when the life of God flowed through them, Christians loved their neighbors, seeing Jesus in the most detestable of faces and weakest of bodies. They remembered the words of their Savior: "I tell you the truth, whatever you did for one of the least of these brothers of mine, you did for me" (Matt. 25:40).

Perhaps Polycarp best summed up allegiance to this man, Jesus. When he was told to reproach Christ or face death he replied: "Eighty and six years have I served him, and he never once wronged me; how then shall I blaspheme my King, Who hath saved me?" Polycarp was then burnt alive at the stake. Many more would willingly face death because of their great love for this King.

But notice one thing: Polycarp didn't die in vain. Roman polytheism and emperor worship is now dead. And it took the followers of the Narrow Way to oppose and conquer it.

CHAPTER FIVE
The Narrow Way Through the Inquisition

In the last chapter I hope that I was able to reveal the beauty and power of the early church in a time when it was closest to the words and teachings of its Founder and describe what kind of fruit was produced in the ancient world as a consequence. Unfortunately, this chapter must trace how the church went astray from the teachings of Jesus and began the process of developing into another "religion."

Just as I describe my own Christian walk in the first chapter of this book, the church started out in the Spirit, filled with joy and life, but as in my own life, slowly, imperceptibly almost, the church became religious. Religion has always been the greatest temptation. It was for Adam and Eve in the Garden and it is for the church. Paul was warning the Galatians against this very thing when he asked: "You foolish Galatians! Who has bewitched you?... After beginning with the Spirit, are you now trying to attain your goal by human effort?" (Gal. 3:1-3) Even in the earliest stages of its life, the church was being seduced to obtain salvation by religious works rather than by trusting in Jesus and his Word.

In this chapter, I would like to trace the ways in which the teaching of the church was pulled away from the standard of Truth, and then document this effect of wrong doctrine on society. Because the church didn't understand that the mission of Christ was not only to set us free from our sins, but also to set us free from "religion," it became grotesque, and what was once alive and bursting with beauty, attracting all, was now perverse, monstrous, and evil, abandoning the Word for tradition and ceremony and neglecting the gospel of grace. The religious "Christianity" of the Middle Ages would culminate with the occurrence of witch hunts, inquisitions, and cries for reform. It was now a ravenous beast, preying upon the flock rather than tending it. H.G. Wells described this deterioration well:

> It is necessary that we should recall the reader's attention to the profound differences between this fully developed Christianity of Nicea and the teaching of Jesus of Nazareth. What is clearly apparent is that the teaching of Jesus of Nazareth was a *prophetic teaching* of the new type that began with the Hebrew prophets. It was not priestly, it had no consecrated temple, and no altar. It had no rites and ceremonies. Its sacrifice was "a broken and contrite heart." Its only organization was an organization of preachers, and its chief function was the sermon. But the fully fledged Christianity of the fourth century, though it preserved as its nucleus the teachings of Jesus in the Gospels, was mainly a priestly religion, of a type already familiar to the world for thousands of years. The centre of its elaborate ritual was an altar, and the essential act of worship the sacrifice, by a consecrated priest, of the Mass. And it had a rapidly developing organization of deacons, priests, and bishops.[85]

Having begun in the Spirit, the Church was now functioning in the flesh. It was no different than any other religion in the world. It was now poisonous and deathly. How could this have happened?

The paradox is that the attempt to preserve the purity of doctrine actually contributed the most to the contamination of doctrine. The final words of Paul to the elders of the church at Ephesus expressed the great concern of Paul to preserve the truth of the teachings of Jesus:

> Keep watch over yourselves and all the flock of which the Holy Spirit has made you overseers. Be shepherds of the church of God, which he bought with his own blood. I know that after I leave, savage wolves will come in among you and will not spare the flock. Even from your own number men will arise and distort the truth in order to draw away disciples after them. So be on your guard! Remember that for three years I never stopped warning each of you day and night with tears.
>
> —Acts 20:28-31

Protecting the flock from the wolves of deception was of the utmost concern to Paul. He knew that all Satan had to do was draw men away from the historical teachings and reality of Jesus and into illuminism (new revelation) and/or mysticism (divine union with God through ascetic effort). This would destroy the testimony of truth given by the apostles, opening the door to any teaching or new revelation given by anybody in any time claiming to have had a word from God or a new message from an angel or a vision of Jesus. This would have decimated sound doctrine and Truth. And the other danger, that men would seek union with God through something other than the blood of Jesus, for example, by obedience to Old Testament law or through other forms of self-effort, was also a profound threat to the church, because it undermined the doctrine of grace.

Unfortunately, both corruptions would be introduced to the church in its earliest stages. Because Paul was a Jew, he was very active in countering Judaism by explaining how Christ had fulfilled the law and provided a way of grace, but as the Gospel traveled throughout the ancient world, there were other religions to contend with. One of the most insidious was that of the Gnostics.

Gnosticism

The Gnostics believed that the material world was evil. Instead, they believed there was a "great abyss of unknowing," a place that was unfathomable and incomprehensible. This place was the supreme God, the *pleroma*, and it gave off "emanations," one of which was Wisdom. In the same way that curiosity killed the cat, Wisdom wrongly attempted to understand the unknowable and in a moment of "distress" for her offense, gave off matter, which Demiurge, a lesser god, used to form into the visible world. This was the opposite of the biblical creation account, whereby "the world was created good, and evil appeared later with the fall of man. In the Gnostic account, the fall of Wisdom came first and the creation followed in consequence. Hence, the material world was the result of the Fall and, therefore, bad."[86] At this point, Wisdom became a redeemer and liberated man by communicating the "gnosis" (knowledge or illumination), which would help him to detach his spiritual man from its evil fleshly bonds and cause it to ascend to be reunited with the *pleroma*.

According to the great church historian, Roland Bainton:

> Gnosticism absorbed Hebrew myths, but completely reversed

their values. Since the world is evil, Yahweh, who created the world, must be the evil demiurge. The serpent, who told Eve to eat of the tree of knowledge of good and evil is precisely the saving Gnosis. All those persons commended in the Old Testament were evil servants of the evil Yahweh, and those reproved, like Cain, belonged to the illumined.[87]

The Gnostics were willing to let their beliefs be syncretized (blended) with other religious systems and attempted to develop a Christian amalgam. But in this mixture, although Christ was the Redeemer, his role was to "deliver man from the thralldom of the flesh."[88] Therefore Christ had no real body or flesh. It only appeared that he did. He was really just a ghost. This was known as Docetism.[89] According to Bainton this teaching "subverted the whole Christian doctrine of the Incarnation and the Crucifixion." He says that "the greatest fight in the early church was to establish not the divinity, but the humanity of Christ. Again, the Incarnation was an event in time, but what the Gnostics sought was release from time; Gnosticism thus stripped history of all significance."[90]

So, instead of offering a revelation grounded in open, eyewitness accounts, the Gnostics claimed to have a *secret* revelation given through certain disciples that Jesus had taken aside and taught separately. This secret knowledge, the *gnosis*, would offer salvation by giving them magic passwords and keys which would allow them to get by "monstrous powers barring the ascent to open their doors and allow him to pass onward and upward to the realm of light."[91] This is an excerpt from the Gnostic *Gospel of Mary*:

18) When the soul had overcome the third power, it went upwards and saw the fourth power, which took seven forms.
19) The first form is darkness, the second desire, the third ignorance, the fourth is the excitement of death, the fifth is the kingdom of the flesh, the sixth is the foolish wisdom of flesh, the seventh is the wrathful wisdom. These are the seven powers of wrath.
20) They asked the soul, Whence do you come slayer of men, or where are you going, conqueror of space?
21) The soul answered and said, What binds me has been slain, and what turns me about has been overcome,

22) and my desire has been ended, and ignorance has died.
23) In a aeon I was released from a world, and in a Type from a type, and from the fetter of oblivion which is transient.
24) From this time on will I attain to the rest of the time, of the season, of the aeon, in silence.[92]

This wasn't a gospel rooted in history! It was a spiritual concoction based on transcendental experiences. If the church had embraced these documents and teachings there would no longer be a standard of truth based upon *reality*. The door would be open for all to develop their own religion with no need for a historical basis to their assertion. Anyone could claim to have authority based on a new vision, dream, or feeling. In fact, this is exactly what happened. The pursuit of new revelation would even make them competitive, each Gnostic teacher trying to outdo the other. This rivalry would express itself in other ways also. Some sects would demand "an ascetic life, with rules for the mortification of the flesh and a special prohibition on marriage"[93] so that the soul would "turn itself toward higher things." Some sects would do the opposite. Because the flesh wasn't important to the spirit realm, and only flesh was evil, it didn't matter if the body was involved in immorality.[94] After all, only the spirit was to attain union with God, therefore what men did with their bodies was unimportant. John countered this Gnostic Docetism by opening his letter with these words:

> That which was from the beginning, which we have heard, which we have seen with our eyes, which we have looked at and our hands have touched—this we proclaim concerning the Word of life. The life appeared; we have seen it and testify to it, and we proclaim to you the eternal life, which was with the Father and has appeared to us. We proclaim to you what we have seen and heard, so that you also may have fellowship with us.
>
> —1 John 1:1-3a

John was saying that Christianity existed in the real world and served in the real world. It wasn't an escapist religion that sought for God in supernatural or transcendent experiences. Rather, it found Jesus in the "least of these." The face of God was to be found in the poor, hungry, and sick, not in attempts to bring about a "divine union" through ascetic practices. Chadwick explains that the Gnostic ethic was "one of complete freedom from any constraint or any obligation toward society and government—regarding which he entertained the most pessimistic opinions."[95] If the Church had embraced the wrong doctrine of Gnosticism, it wouldn't have had the dynamic ministry of love that it manifested in the first few centuries of its existence.

Bainton explains that "gnosticism was one of the religions of contemplation, which despised the world of matter and sought salvation by way of emancipation from the flesh."[96] This wasn't the religion of the apostles. Their salvation was through faith in Jesus and his completed work on the cross—which manifested itself in their lives as the spirit of love.

Whereas the Narrow Way was democratic in its effect on society, Gnosticism developed elites that Paul called "super-apostles" (2 Cor. 11:5, Gal. 1:6-9). They had clandestine initiations for their membership, and within this secret society there were levels that could be attained through ascetic practices such as silence, fasting, denial of sexual fulfillment, etc. The leaders (those "super-apostles") were getting special visions and revelations from angels, which Paul said were leading the church to another gospel and another Jesus (2 Cor. 11, Gal. 1). They weren't leading the church to the gospel of grace and love; instead they were leading it to a self-centered and "perverted" (Gal. 1:7) way of works. To the apostles this was horrifying. We see that Paul cried over it (Acts 20:31). The apostles attacked it and tried to defend the Gospel against it, and Peter said these false teachers were "slaves to depravity" (2 Pet. 2:19), because their religion didn't produce true righteousness. It only produced a competitive religious show and "where you have envy and selfish ambition, there you find disorder and every evil practice" (James 3:16, also note 1 Cor. 14:33).

Gnosticism didn't lead the flock to green pastures and still waters where the sheep could find rest and refreshment; it led to mountainous, thorny, and rocky places where the flock would have to climb and sweat. It was a place of danger where a fall could occur at any moment and those who were stronger and more capable could make it to the top, whereas those who were weak or sickly would tire out and give up, leaving them in a place of failure and despair. This is the fruit of religion: it either leads to pride (for those who reach the top) or despair (for those who fail or won't even try). But the Good News of Jesus is that we can rest in what *he* did!

The Gnosticism that sprang up in the early church, like new weeds in a garden, had the appearance of truth. The Gnostics had their own apostles, their own scriptures, and they used the name of Jesus, but they weren't true. They were false. James said that the "wisdom" that comes from heaven is "first of all pure; then peace-loving, considerate, submissive, full of mercy and good fruit, impartial and sincere" (James 3:17). He then said, "Peacemakers who sow in peace raise a harvest of righteousness" (James 3:18). In other words, if the true and the false were left to grow, the fruit of the true gospel would be righteousness, while the fruit of the false would be immorality. This is why Jude cried out that false teachers were those who "are godless men, who change the grace of our God into a license for immorality and deny Jesus Christ our only Sovereign and Lord" (Jude 1:4b).

Through the false teaching of the Gnostics, Marcionism was also introduced to the church. Because Gnosticism taught that the Old Testament was the creation of the Demiurge, rather than of the true God, Marcion "proposed to cut the Gordian knot by throwing the Old Testament bodily out of the church, and substituting in its place a strictly Christian collection of writings." The Marcionites, consequently were "vigorously anti-Semitic."[97] They adopted Paul's writings, in particular, because he advocated the way of grace, rather than that of Jewish law. But Marcion's belief that Jesus was a completely new revelation from the Gnostic God meant that there was no proof of his divinity. Paul taught that the Old Testament was the veiled revelation of Christ, but Marcion's rejection of allegorical interpretation left the church with no evidence to support its case that Jesus was the Christ, the Messiah who was the Promised Deliverer.

Even though Marcionism was a danger to the early church, its propensity for isolation (it would set up separate communities) meant that it was easier to discount, while the permeating nature of the Alexandrian Gnostics, Basilides and Valentinus, seemed more dangerous because they didn't have any desire to detach themselves. As philosophers, rather than church men, to the apostles, they were like a virus that was infecting the church with the teaching that Valentinian mythology "had been secretly taught by Jesus to the disciples, and from them had been passed down by an esoteric oral tradition side by side with the public teaching of the church."[98] Supposedly this information had been given to the disciples during the forty days Jesus spent on the earth after his resurrection. In response, the apostles emphasized the fact that the Gospel was public rather than secret.

Maintaining Doctrinal Purity

Because of the fear that the truth of the Gospel would be corrupted by these various false teachings, the church took a defensive mode. This can be seen in the earliest writings of the apostles. They encouraged the flock to remain faithful to their overseers and avoid teachers who taught new doctrines. "Now we ask you, brothers, to respect those who work hard among you, who are over you in the Lord and who admonish you. Hold them in the highest regard in love because of their work. Live in peace with each other" (1 Thess. 5:12-13).

It was also important to the early church that the unity of the faith be maintained. Paul instructed Titus, "Warn a divisive person once, and then warn him a second time. After that, have nothing to do with him" (Tit. 3:10). And John warned the church that those who taught Docetism had run ahead of the teaching of Christ, saying that if anyone even welcomed one of these teachers into their home they would share "in his wicked work" (2 John 9:11).

The principle of the authority of the overseer was established by Paul in the letter to the Hebrews when he told them, "Remember your leaders, who spoke the word of God to you. Consider the outcome of their way of life and imitate their faith" (Heb. 13:7). Further on in the letter he flatly states: "Obey your leaders and submit to their authority. They keep watch over you as men who must give an account. Obey them so that their work will be a joy, not a burden, for that would be no advantage to you" (Heb. 13:17).

The Gnostic infiltration forced the church to establish a source of authority. Who spoke for God? As the first generation of believers died out, and the apostles were no longer present to explain the Gospel, the second generation of believers was in a quandary. How could they determine who or what the new authority on doctrine would be?

The church responded in two ways. One was to establish the authority of the bishops as the direct successors of the apostles, and the other was to develop the Canon of Scripture. Obviously the Gnostic teachers hadn't received the endorsements of the apostles. They were renegade teachers who had a certain appeal, but they hadn't received the "laying on of hands." Therefore one way to ensure doctrinal purity, the Patristic Fathers thought, was to establish ministerial authority.

For example, Ignatius of Antioch responded to false teachers by stating that only the approved local bishop could administer the sacraments, claiming that the bishop is God's representative on earth, an earthly counterpart corresponding to the heavenly Monarch, so that "we ought to regard the bishop as the Lord himself."[99]

Unfortunately, in their attempt to establish a form of authority and maintain sound doctrine, the early church fathers were developing the rudimentary beginnings of the Roman Catholic Church. Although they were simply trying to preserve the faith, they were also instituting an organization that would one day abandon the doctrines taught by the apostles and look upon the established traditions of the Roman Church as having more authority than the content of the Word. By making the Bishop of Rome the spokesperson for God, they were actually opening the door for human corruption of truth—the very thing they were trying to guard against.

Clement, another of the Patristic Fathers, responded to the Corinthian Church's overthrow of its leaders by saying what they did was a scandal and that it was wrong to depose those leaders who stood in direct succession to the apostles. According to Chadwick, this teaching on the authority of the bishops would be a strong weapon in future conflicts with Gnosticism.

Against any heretical claim to possess secret traditions of what Jesus had told the apostles in the forty days after the resurrection, there was the clear argument that the apostles Peter and Paul could not have failed to impart such doctrines to those whom they had set over the churches, and that by the line of accredited teachers in those churches of apostolic foundation no such heretical notions had been transmitted. The succession argument carried the implication that the teaching given by the contemporary bishop of, say, Rome or Antioch was in all respects identical with that of the apostles. This was important, for two reasons. In the first place, the faithful were thereby in some sense assured that revelation was not only knowable by a retrospective historical knowledge derived from either the apostles' occasional writings or anecdotal gossip, but had in the bishop a contemporary authority, able and authorized to speak God's word in the present.[100]

This ministerial authority was especially important also, since there was no established "Scripture" called the New Testament—only oral traditions or letters passed from church to church—making sound doctrine particularly difficult to maintain.

In response to this, the church developed its first statement of belief, called "The Rule of Faith." This was a short summary of Christian beliefs, derived from the apostolic writings and taught by the bishops. Irenaeus declared, for example, that "the whole Church believes 'in one God, the Father Almighty, Maker of heaven, and earth, and the sea, and all things that are in them; and in one Christ Jesus, the Son of God, who became incarnate for our salvation;'"[101] This "Rule" would be taught in all of the "official" churches. (Note the attempt to counter Gnostic teachings by the reference to Christ's flesh and that the Almighty God is the Creator, rather than Demiurge.)

The process of determining the Canon (which means "measuring stick") was also important to the early church fathers because of the infiltration by false teachers. Ireneaus developed his own canon based on the premise that any Scriptures had to have been written by the apostles who lived contemporaneously with Jesus and heard his teachings firsthand in order to have the mark of true authority. The one exception was Paul's writings, which were accepted as being as authoritative as the apostles. (In the debate with Peter over whether the church could demand circumcision of its adherents, Paul actually had *more* authority than Peter, and his position prevailed.)

Ascetic Mysticism and Contemplation

Slowly, but surely, though, the church began to rely more on rituals and traditions than on the teachings of Christ. They began to go astray. In Ireneaus we see the beginnings of the doctrine of transubstantiation. In Origen we see the worship of Mary and the teaching on her perpetual virginity. Tertullian promoted the clergy class and defended the central authority of the Roman Church. Cyprian would also argue that the church needed strong leaders and even went so far as to say that "no one can have God for a father who has not the church for a mother."[102] In Athanasius we see the doctrine of salvation through baptism. Augustine of Hippo would promote infant baptism and purgatory.

We also see the rise of asceticism at this time. Anthony of Egypt, one of the first "Desert Fathers," would end up living in tombs and "battling devils" that he said looked either grotesque or seductive. His unusual lifestyle would draw attention from the public, and he unwillingly gathered a following, causing him to go down in history as the father of Christian monasticism. Jerome, who translated the Greek Septuagint (Old Testament) into the Latin Vulgate, would live in a cave in Bethlehem for thirty-four years. The Cappadocian Fathers of the East would also lead an ascetic lifestyle.[103]

The monks were a movement separate from the established church. Some lived as hermits, some formed communities, and some traveled from place to place. They would try to outdo themselves in their asceticism. Some would beat themselves with chains, some would go on long fasts, and some would act like animals and feed on grass. Symeon the Stylite would live atop a column for thirty years. Not to be outdone, Daniel would imitate him and live on top of a column for thirty-four years. In response to some of these excesses, Benedict would develop his "Benedictine Rule." In particular, it would demand that monks ate. Many of the ascetics had destroyed their digestive systems by their harsh practices.

One of the results of the ascetic lifestyle was the entrance into mysticism. While some of the monastic orders developed charitable organizations, some of the hermit monks became mystics. Evagrius would become one of these early mystics. He traveled to Egypt and studied Origen. Robert Ellsburg describes him:

> Evagrius provided many practical hints on the best way to practice the ascetic life. But he never suggested that the main business of the monk was self-denial. All this was merely a means of focusing on his true business, prayer—the path to union with God. Through prayer the monk burnished the "mirror of his soul," the better to reflect the image of God. Evagrius's particular contribution here was in promoting the value of *contemplative prayer* [emphasis Ellsburg's], a state of pure openness to God without words or mental images.[104]

Evagrius' disciple was John Cassian, who would further entrench the ascetic monasticism of the Eastern Church into the Western Church. He would write his *Institutes* to describe the outward monastic order and his *Conferences* to describe the inward ascetic life. Even though he held several leadership positions in the Western Church, his orthodoxy would finally be questioned when he criticized "Augustine's doctrine of grace."[105]

The church had been seduced. It had become completely immersed in religious effort. The Word was no longer predominant. There were booklets on rules of conduct and prayer. Grace was no longer a precious teaching. Instead, works were necessary to please God. And now the pathway to "union with God" was ritualistic, mind-emptying prayer—rather than the blood of Jesus. (Even the goal of "divine union" is questionable, since the church isn't married yet! We don't have the right to attain divine union. It's a form of spiritual fornication. It's also a form of Gnosticism, since its goal is to be one with God through detaching the spirit from the body. Jesus taught us how to pray, and it was simply a prayer of relationship. The Lord's Prayer involved worship and requests for spiritual and physical help. It didn't involve soaking in silence to absorb the presence of the god-force.[106] Our prayers should be respectfully intimate, since we're only betrothed to God. We're the Bride, not the Wife.)

The organized institutional church would grow, and theologians would gradually change the apostolic message. Christ's work on the cross was no longer considered complete and finished as Paul taught in Hebrews: "Christ was sacrificed once to take away the sins of many" (Heb. 9:28). "He entered the Most Holy Place once for all by his own blood, having obtained eternal redemption" (Heb. 9:12). "For by one sacrifice he has made perfect forever those who are being made holy" (Heb. 10:14). Instead Tertullian would suggest a system of "satisfaction and merit," and Cyprian would then expand this idea and create accounts in heaven where religious works could be done by one person and drawn upon by another—laying a foundation for the idea of purgatory. Those who fasted, lived in celibacy, or followed ascetic practices could save up more credits than they needed for their own salvation and let others draw on them.

Note that the works of righteousness were no longer those of loving our God and our neighbors, but of religious efforts such as fasting and celibacy. Note also that the unpaid debt for sin was paid through human effort, rather than the blood of Jesus.

As a result of this abandonment of the Way, Western civilization, which was vibrant and ablaze with righteousness, would now enter into a time of darkness. The Light of the World would be covered up by layers of ecclesiastical pomp. While the church, which had been hounded, harassed, and persecuted for hundreds of years, was so grateful to now rest in the peace brought about by Constantine's conversion, an unfortunate result of this rest would be a syncretization with the Roman pagan religion, bringing further corruption to the body of Christ.

Constantine would change many laws, which would strengthen the church in the Empire, but Constantine was still a Roman politician whose main interest was in procuring the blessings of the Deity for his realm. Nevertheless, Foxe sums up this moment in time well, when the Cross prevailed over the Sword, and the Galilean prevailed over the Roman. He describes how so many emperors conspired against the Lord and his church, sparing nothing to "extirpate the name of Christ and all Christians," using policy, torment, cruelty, death, laws, proclamations, and edicts against the weak Christians, but concludes: "And yet, not withstanding, to see how no counsel can stand against the Lord, note how all these be gone, and yet Christ and his Church doth stand."[107]

But the condition of the standing church was questionable. It had strayed away from apostolic teaching, a rock and firm foundation of truth, and instead built on men's teaching. One step in the wrong direction doesn't seem that far off, but if there's no turning back, it can lead to a place that's a hundred miles away from the original destination. And yet, now, when someone, such as Helvidius or the former monk, Jovinian, rose up and used the apostolic writings to oppose the ascetic slide toward celibacy, they would be condemned as heretics by the Roman Church. Jerome would bluster against Jovinian and claim that Mary was a perpetual virgin and, without Scriptural evidence, would claim that her other sons were actually cousins or other close relatives. But Jerome's position was unpopular, because it encouraged convents—which many Roman families feared would be a threat to their very existence (since nuns didn't have children)—and his popularity was further destroyed by the death of Blesilla, a woman who died of "rigorous fastings" imposed upon her by Jerome. As a result of her death, he and other monks would be "set upon by the people and barely escaped alive."[108]

In Jovinian we see an attempt by someone on the Narrow Way to oppose the corrupt religion that had developed in the Roman Church, but he would be tossed aside and rejected by the followers of ritual and works. He joined the ranks of those other resisters of religion—from Abel onward.

The Dark Ages

With no Light to guide the Way, the West was now plunged into the Dark Ages. The church, as an institution, had strayed, and, paradoxically, any attempt to shine the Light would actually be squelched by the new ecclesiastical structure. Consequently, depravity and superstition would reign. Many authors have described the political and societal squalor or this age. It was a time of barbarian invasions, plague, political and religious intrigue, war, scientific decay, and intellectual stupor.

Because of the continual attacks by the Visigoths, Vandals, Franks, Ostrogoths, and Burgundians, the Roman Empire was weak. And because of internal corruption, its emperors were weak, its people were weak, and its senate was weak. It was a time when the church was able to step in and fill the leadership void. Since the Imperial Court had run away to safety behind the marsh at Ravenna as Attila the Hun was about to invade Rome in 452 AD, legend claims that Leo the Great, bishop of Rome, went out to meet Attila and somehow turned him and his hordes away. And again, in 455 AD, Leo was able to stop the Vandals from completely destroying Rome.

This time of fear and confusion allowed men like Leo to come to the rescue and gave them an opportunity to lead, something for which the people were very grateful. Because this made Leo into somewhat of a hero, it was difficult to oppose him on other issues. As the leader of the Roman Church, it was his job to insure the purity of doctrine, so when the Manicheans (a Gnostic sect that Augustine was once part of that relied on obedience to laws rather than grace) were scattered at the invasion of the Vandals in northern Africa, and started showing up in Rome, Leo was determined to stop what he considered to be their cancerous spread. He spoke out against them in the churches, burned their books, arrested their leaders, and banished them to perpetual exile. Thus, in the hero, Leo the Great, we see the beginnings of the Inquisition.

Again, a religious leader would abandon the teachings of Christ in order to preserve them. If Leo had correctly handled "the word of truth" (2 Tim. 2:15), he would have obeyed Jesus' admonition to let the wheat and the tares grow up together and be sorted out by the angels at his return (Matt. 13:24-30). He would have realized that Jesus never forced himself on anyone—he stands outside and knocks, but the door can only be opened by the tenant inside. So now, in a strange twist of affairs, the church had become the persecutor rather than the persecuted. Satan had prevailed. The visible church of Jesus was now a bully.

Also, the attempt to make Christianity more palatable to the ancient world would cause many of the church fathers, such as Clement and Augustine, to vigorously blend Hellenistic philosophy in with the Gospel. According to Will Durant, author of the classic *The Story of Philosophy*:

> Much of the politics of Catholicism was derived from Plato's "royal lies," or influenced by them: the ideas of heaven, purgatory, and hell, in their medieval form, are traceable to the last book of the *Republic*; the cosmology of scholasticism comes largely from the *Timaeus*; the doctrine of realism (the objective reality of general ideas) was an interpretation of the doctrine of Ideas; even the educational "quadrivium" (arithmetic, geometry, astronomy and music) was modeled on the curriculum outlined in Plato.[109]

This blending of Greek philosophy with the Word would continue and become known as medieval scholasticism. While Thomas Aquinas is probably one of the best known of the scholastics, Duns Scotus (whereby we get the word "dunce" from) would eventually epitomize the maddening arguments which would decline into so many senseless details that they served no real purpose. Their nominalist vs. realist debates were said to deteriorate into how many angels could dance on the head of a pin!

Because the church had blended so much of Greek philosophy into its theology, it also embraced Ptolemy's geocentric view of the universe. In the future this would cause the church to reject Galileo's heliocentric discoveries. Galileo was a Christian, not an atheist, and what he came up against was a church that had blended Aristotelian thought in with biblical doctrine. This meant that they had decided to rely on philosophical reasoning rather than empirical evidence. Believe it or not, Galileo's defense of the heliocentric Copernican viewpoint as laid out in the book, *Dialogue Concerning the Two Chief World Systems*, wasn't a debate about Scriptures, but rather a conflict over the truthfulness of the Aristotelian geocentric view of the solar system. The showdown wasn't one of science against religion, but one of scientific evidence against a philosophy that was only interested in discovering truth through the process of reason, rather than through empiricism. The sense that the book was disrespectful to the church would bring him before the Inquisition, and they would accuse him of going against the Bible, but Galileo never thought his position conflicted with the Word, only with the Aristotelian geocentric view.

It wasn't the Scriptures that brought about the darkness of the Middle Ages, but the merging of the Word with philosophy and man-made traditions into a false theology. It was false teaching that squelched science. It was false teaching that perverted education. It was false teaching that gave the popes so much money and power, allowing them to live in splendor while the common man lived in squalor. It was false teaching that led to the escapism and isolationism of the monasteries. It was false teaching that would lead to the pursuit of mystical experiences to find the face of God rather than trusting in the blood of Jesus and finding it in the faces of the "least of these." It was false teaching that led to religious wars and crusades. It was false teaching that led to the Inquisition. It was false teaching (particularly as found in the handbook *Malleus Maleficarum*) that led to the witch hunts and it would take those on the Narrow Way to restore sound teaching and break the stranglehold of poisonous religion. Foxe describes the condition of the church at this dark moment in history:

> In these days the whole state of religion was depraved and corrupted: the name only of Christ remained amongst Christians, but his true and lively doctrine was as far unknown to the most part as faith, consolation, the end and use of the law, the office of Christ, our impotency and weakness, the Holy Ghost, the greatness and strength of sin, true works, grace and free justification by faith, the liberty of a Christian man, there was almost no mention.[110]

Grace had been abandoned, and the Gospel was lost. Instead, Foxe says the church had become *religious* and, consequently, cruel and tyrannical:

> The world, forsaking the lively power of God's spiritual Word, was altogether led and blinded with outward ceremonies and human traditions; in these was all the hope of obtaining salvation fully fixed; insomuch that scarcely any other thing was seen in the temples or churches, taught or spoken of in sermons, or finally intended or gone about in their whole lives, but only heaping up of certain shadowy ceremonies upon ceremonies; neither was there any end of their heaping.
>
> The Church did fall into all kind of extreme tyranny; whereas the poverty and simplicity of Christ were changed into cruelty and abomination of life. With how many bonds and ceremonies were

the consciences of men, redeemed by Christ to liberty, ensnared and snarled! The Christian people were wholly carried away as it were by the nose, with mere decrees and constitutions of men, even whither it pleased the bishops to lead them, and not as Christ's will did direct them. The simple and unlearned people, being far from all knowledge of the holy Scripture, thought it quite enough for them to know only those things which were delivered them by their pastors; and they, on the other part, taught in a manner nothing else but such things as came forth of the court of Rome; whereof the most part tended to the profit of their order, more than to the glory of Christ.[111]

Walter Russell Bowie also describes the spiritual wasteland that existed at the time in his classic *The Story of the Church*:

But how could people get rid of their sins and hope for the blessing of God? The answer of the church was clear. Be baptized. Confess your sins to the priests. Come to the church and listen to the saying of the Mass.[112]

Following rituals for salvation could give a measure of security (for those who faithfully fulfilled them), but they didn't have the power to give Life. Unfortunately, since the common man had no access to the Scriptures, they were in bondage to the teachings of the clergy. Popes, bishops, priests, and monks held the "keys to the kingdom," and heaven's gate would only open, they claimed, if people followed their rules.

This lack of scriptural knowledge led to superstition and fear. Bowie says "they lived in what seemed not only a hard world, but a haunted world. They believed in demons and in witches and in evil spirits that hovered in the air."[113] Bowie says the fears of the people only empowered the Roman Catholic Church more because:

The less they knew, the more they imagined. They could not read the Gospels and learn about Jesus for themselves. Most of what they thought about him was that he would be the judge at the last day. Then he would reward the good, but sinners he would send to a hell that they were sure was full of devils waiting to torment them. Perhaps the church could persuade him to have mercy. Perhaps the

Virgin Mary, his mother, would plead with him. The Church said she would help everybody who turned to her if she was honored enough. And so there were prayers to the Virgin and prayers to the saints that they would ask Christ, the judge, not to be too hard. Only the church could tell poor sinners how to get the Virgin and the saints to be on their side and to help them. Therefore, nothing could be more fearful than not to be in good standing in the church.[114]

John Wycliffe

Into this darkness would shine the first glimmer of light. John Wycliffe, known as the Morning Star of the Reformation, would be one of the first to oppose the corrupt religion of the Middle Ages. There were other individuals and groups who were victimized by the Inquisition and witch hunts, such as the Jews, the Cathars, the Albigenses, and the Waldensians,[115] but Wycliffe was a scholar from Oxford University and a priest in the Catholic Church. He was a particularly serious threat, because he had the benefit of being able to read the Word for himself and he knew what Jesus taught. What he saw instead in the church disgusted him. He said, "They love worldly riches and labor for them night and day, in thought and deed; and labor little for God's worship and the saving of Christian souls."[116] Wycliffe's outcry began in the 1370s. He began by denouncing clerical abuses and as time went by became more radical and even attacked the Catholic Church as an institution saying that they had no authority apart from the grace of God. Some of the declarations of Wycliffe:

1. That the Eucharist is not the body of Christ.
2. That the Church at Rome is not the head of all other churches and that Peter was equal to the other disciples.
3. That the Pope didn't have the keys to the kingdom any more than other priests.
4. That the Gospel was sufficient and no other rules were needed to govern the Christian life.
5. That additional rules don't perfect the Gospel any more than white paint can add more color to a wall.
6. That neither the Pope nor any other leader in the church should have prisons.[117]

These views of Wycliffe, a follower of the Narrow Way of grace and love, were condemned by Pope Gregory XI in 1377. While he would eventually lose his position as a lecturer at the University because of his stand, Wycliffe would be preserved from the fires of the Inquisition because he had a measure of protection from John of Gaunt, the King's son, and Lord Henry Percy. His followers would be called the Lollards, and they would *not* be rescued from the fire. He died in 1384, but in 1428 Wycliffe would posthumously be condemned as a heretic and his bones would be dug up and burned.

John Huss

Wycliffe would influence John Huss, a priest at the University of Prague in the early 1400s. Huss read the works of Wycliffe and, agreeing with him, began to preach the same things at his church, the Bethlehem Chapel. Huss was a Bohemian polemicist who made a statement about the condition of the Roman Church by hanging pictures of the Pope in all his rich clothing next to the image of the "poverty-stricken Christ."[118] According to Caroline T. Marshall in *Eerdman's Handbook to the History of Christianity*, Huss "stressed the role of Scripture as an authority in the church" and "believed that neither popes nor cardinals could establish doctrine which was contrary to Scripture, nor should any Christian obey an order from them which was plainly wrong."[119] He also criticized the clergy and rebuked "his people for worshipping images, belief in false miracles, and undertaking 'superstitious pilgrimages.'"[120] He even condemned the sale of indulgences.

For opposing the Roman Catholic religion, Huss was called before the Council of Constance to defend his beliefs. The emperor had assured him that he would be given safe conduct, but instead he was condemned for heresy and burnt at the stake without even being given an opportunity to speak. The word "huss" means "goose," and this is where the term "his goose is cooked" comes from.

Foxe tells an interesting story about the trial of John Huss. He says that Huss tried to answer a question, when the following happened:

> As he was about to open his mouth to answer, all this mad herd began so to cry out upon him, that he had not leisure to speak one only word. The noise and trouble was so great and so vehement, that a man might have called it a bruit of wild beasts, and not of men, much less was it to be judged a congregation of men gathered together, to determine so grave and weighty matters.[121]

The crowd that was out of control wasn't an angry mob of commoners; it was the council of cardinals and bishops! Religion has a way of becoming irrational. It can easily be worked into a murderous frenzy. This, according to Jesus, is exactly what happened to Abel, the prophets, and even to him. It also happened to Stephen, the apostles, and the early church. Now it had happened to Huss.

Again, it took a person on the Narrow Way to courageously rise up and oppose poisonous religion, which is characterized by rituals and false teachings. Huss cared about the poor and opposed the lavish lifestyles of the prelates. He regarded the Scriptures as the truth and believed in grace, rather than ceremonies and rituals, as the way to God. For his beliefs he would be martyred. But notice one thing: Huss didn't die in vain. The religion of the Roman Church would soon lose its powerful stranglehold, and because of the followers of the Narrow Way the Cross would soon prevail wonderfully over the Flame, and the world would become closer to Eden than ever before.

CHAPTER SIX
The Narrow Way in the Reformation

While the previous chapter attempted to show what happened when the church strayed away from the Word and the knowledge of God's grace through Jesus, this chapter will attempt to reveal what happened to society as a result of this knowledge being restored. The impact on Western civilization was profound. A combination of events occurred over a short period of time which had immeasurable effects: the Renaissance plea for a return to the original sources ("ad fontes"), the rise of nationalism, Gutenburg's invention of the printing press, the advent of the age of exploration, and the attempt to reform the Catholic Church, led by the humanist Erasmus and continued by Luther.

As a result of these circumstances, the world would be catapulted from its age of darkness and despair into a period of hope and light. Because of the Renaissance admonition to return to the original documents, not only of the Greek philosophers, but also of the Scriptures (rather than church teachings and traditions), the Bible would receive a fresh perusal. And now, because of the printing press and attempts by Wycliffe, Luther, and others to translate the Scriptures into the common language, the Good News could go out, untainted, into the world.

This age of hope and light wouldn't come easily, though. There would be theological battles that would lead to denominationalism and division within the church, which would lead to horrifying wars, but this period would culminate in the Western concept of religious freedom and toleration. It would produce a new respect for family, the development of the work ethic, the expansion of education, the growth of secularism, the loss of papal power, the explosion of science, and the discovery and settlement of America.

Erasmus

As a result of the clear abuses and indulgent behavior of the popes, bishops, monks, friars, and priests, there were fervent calls to reform the Catholic Church. In the previous chapter, we saw that there were brave souls who would rise up to confront Roman teachings—taking great risks to preach the gospel of grace. Even from within the church, there were men, such as Erasmus, who recognized the need for reform. His essay, *In Praise of Folly*, would mock the church and describe her stupidity and foolishness. Speaking of the monks, Erasmus points out how petty their faith had become:

> Yet what is more pleasant than that they do all things by rule and, as it were, a kind of mathematics, the least swerving from which were a crime beyond forgiveness—as how many knots their shoes must be tied with, of what color everything is, what distinction of habits, of what stuff made, how many straws broad their girdles and of what fashion, how many bushels wide their cowl, how many fingers long their hair, and how many hours sleep; which exact equality, how disproportionate it is, among such variety of bodies and tempers... who is there that does not perceive it?[122]

Erasmus was so outspoken in his criticism of the Catholic Church that as time went on the saying would go around that "Erasmus laid the egg that Luther hatched." He also had a desire to see that the average person could read the Bible and made translation part of his life's work:

> I wish that the Scriptures might be translated into all languages, so that not only the Scots and the Irish, but also the Turk and the Saracen might read and understand them. I long that the farm-laborer might sing them as he follows his plough, the weaver hum them to the tune of his shuttle, the traveler beguile the weariness of his journey with their stories.[123]

Erasmus loved the Word and despised petty religion.

Luther

It was Luther that would be the cause of most of the church's trouble, though. He was a monk trained in scholasticism. He took his faith seriously, since he joined the clergy as a result of the near-death experience of being struck by lightening. Luther was concerned for his soul. It was this concern for his salvation that motivated him, rather than a desire to reform the church. Yet, as a result of Luther's passion, the church would never be the same. Indeed, the world would never be the same.

Luther followed in the ascetic footsteps of the Augustinian monks. He wore rough garments, fasted, went without sleep, worked during the day, and was celibate. But this wasn't enough. He would *really* prove himself to God and wear a hair shirt. He'd fast much longer than what was required. He would beat himself, like the albino member of Opus Dei in the book *The Da Vinci Code*. He would confess minute details of his life to the priests, looking for sin, in fear that he would forget something and not be forgiven. He would crawl on his knees until they were bloody up the steps of the Lateran in Rome.

Luther only knew poisonous religion, and it tormented him. He felt he could never be good enough for God, and like many superstitious people of the day he feared devils and the threat of hell.

But Luther, as a monk, had access to the Word of God. He was reading the Bible one day when the phrase "The just shall live by faith" leaped off the pages. It was then that Luther had a revelation from God: he wasn't saved by anything he did, but he was saved because of what God did through Christ! He didn't have to do anything more for God's approval. Jesus did it all. In his *Preface to Complete Works* he describes the moment when his spiritual eyes, so to speak, were opened:

> I began to understand that this verse [Romans 1:17] means that the righteousness of God is revealed through the Gospel, but it is a passive righteousness—that is, it is that by which the merciful God makes us righteous by faith, as it is written: "The righteous person lives by faith." All at once I felt that I had been born again and entered into paradise itself through open gates. Immediately I saw the whole of Scripture in a different light.[124]

THE NARROW WAY

Around this same time, Luther was a lecturer at the university in Wittenberg. He began to teach and preach this new doctrine, and students flocked to him to hear his message of hope. He had no idea that this would lead him into a conflict with the church!

But one day he heard that the Dominican monk, Tetzel, had come to a nearby town to sell indulgences for Pope Leo X, who needed money for, among other things, the building of St. Peter's Cathedral in Rome. The church, since Tertullian, you'll remember, had taught the idea of "satisfaction and merit." Therefore, if you bought an indulgence, you could draw from an account of excess good deeds that had been performed by the saints. The Pope could then declare that you or your family member would be relieved from spending time in purgatory to pay for your sins. Tetzel's motto was, "As soon as the coin in the coffer rings, the soul from purgatory springs!"

This enraged Luther, who wrote up his "Ninety-five Theses" and pounded them on the door of the Wittenberg Church. The door served as a type of bulletin board for the community, so everyone was able to read them. And because of the printing press, they were able to be circulated throughout Europe. According to Bowie, Luther didn't deny that the Pope was an earthly authority, initially, only that "he had no authority over purgatory."[125] He also said that "if any man was truly sorry for his sins and trusted in God's mercy through Christ, he would be forgiven, so there was no need of any indulgence from the pope. But if the pope thought he did have power to grant indulgences, why didn't he give them instead of having Tetzel get money out of the poor German people?"[126]

Luther was an overnight sensation. He didn't realize it, but he was speaking for many little sheep who were being sheared by the Catholic Church. At first the fat shepherd, Pope Leo X, didn't take Luther seriously and accused him of being a "drunken monk," but as Luther's "Theses" spread, the people stopped buying indulgences. Word of this got back to the Pope, and he began to harass Luther, ordering him to stop speaking. Then he sent his representatives to Germany to see what was happening. Luther didn't understand why the Pope was so concerned. He just wanted to bring Tetzel's false teaching to the Pope's attention, after all. But Luther didn't realize that Pope Leo X actually supported the selling of indulgences.

As a result of Luther's snowballing notoriety, John Eck, a well-known theologian, challenged him to a debate. He hoped to prove that Luther wasn't just attacking Tetzel, but was also attacking the Pope's authority. Since only the Pope could determine church doctrine, and Luther was turning to the Scriptures as a source of authority for doctrine, Eck would accuse Luther of the same heresy that John Huss was condemned for: denying the authority of the Pope.

This was preposterous to Luther! He was an Augustinian monk, a Christian, not a heretic! But in the debate with Eck he explained that the early church had no papal system and that this concept wasn't found in the Bible, either. In fact, he felt he needed to go even further. He said that the Bible had more authority than popes or councils and that forgiveness for sin came through Christ's sacrifice, *once for all*, on the cross, not through the so-called "miracle" in the Mass. He also said a person could be saved without the help of the church and that the Pope could be wrong, indeed he had been in the past, and "everybody knew it." Therefore, Christians needed to follow their own consciences no matter what the priests and the popes said.

Luther was so passionate about his position that he became a pamphleteer. In a work addressed to the Holy Roman Emperor, Charles V, called *To the Christian Nobility of the German Nation*, he attacked the entire Roman Catholic system, saying that the New Testament taught that all were priests in the church (the doctrine of the priesthood of the believer) and therefore all Christians could read the Scriptures for themselves without needing the church as a mediator.

By 1520, the Pope could take it no more, and he condemned Luther's views, ordering him to appear in Rome and recant before the Inquisition. In response, Luther called a public meeting and threw the papal bull onto a bonfire. The Pope then excommunicated him.

The following year, though, Luther would appear before a council (or diet) held in the city of Worms, known as the Diet of Worms. Even Charles V would be in attendance. The council would attempt to get him to recant his earlier claims about the authority of the Pope. They would ask him to denounce his writings. Eck (not the same Eck he debated) would ask him again if he defended what he said in his books. In one of the most humble and beautiful responses I've ever read in history, Luther replies: "This touches God and his Word. This affects the salvation of souls. Of this Christ said, 'he who denies me before men, him will I deny before my father.' To say too little or too much would be dangerous. I beg you, give me time to think it over."[127] The emperor gave him another day. Even though Luther would seem unsure of his position and even felt fearful, he would still appear before the Diet and make his famous declaration:

> Your imperial majesty and your lordships demand a simple answer. Here it is, plain and unvarnished. Unless I am convinced by Scripture or by clear reason—for I do not trust the Pope or church councils, since everyone knows that they can make mistakes and contradict themselves—I am bound by the Scriptures I have quoted. My conscience is held captive by the Word of God. I cannot and will not recant anything, because it is neither safe nor right to go against conscience. On this I take my stand. I can do no other. Here I stand. I cannot do otherwise. God help me. Amen.[128]

Roland Bainton, the author of the definitive biography of Martin Luther, records that the Diet required him to repeat his assertion in Latin and that Luther "was sweating."[129] The Spanish members of the council were reportedly so angry that they began to move toward him with rage, but the German knights who accompanied him there surrounded him and kept him safe.

Luther was allowed to go home while the Diet was determining his fate. But on the road back to Wittenberg, Luther was kidnapped! Fortunately, it was by a friend and supporter, Duke Frederick, who had his knights carry Luther back to his castle at Wartburg. Luther pretended he was a knight while he was there and also translated the Scriptures into German so the common man could read them. He called this period of time his "Patmos."[130]

This was a wise move on the part of the Duke, because the Diet had issued their Edict of Worms, which condemned Luther and would have led to his death. Here is a portion of what it said: "Luther is to be regarded as a convicted heretic. When the time is up, no one is to harbor him. His followers also are to be condemned. His books are to be eradicated from the memory of man."[131]

James Atkinson explains the importance of Luther's stand in *Eerdman's Handbook to the History of Christianity*:

> In his monastery Luther had been searching for God's pardon and peace. He faithfully observed punctiliously the spiritual techniques. Yet he found himself no nearer to God. He began to see that the way of the monk was merely a long discipline of religious duty and effort. Mysticism was an attempt to climb up to heaven.

Academic theology was little more than speculation about God, his nature and his character. Luther found one basic error in all these techniques of finding God. Ultimately they trusted in man's own ability to get him to God, or at least take him near enough to God to accept him. Luther realized it was not a matter of God being far from man, and man having to strive to reach him. The reverse was true. Man, created and sinful, was distant from God; God in Christ had come all the way to find him. This was no new truth, but simply the old gospel of grace, which had been overlaid.[132]

Through Luther, years of false teaching, spiritual sickness, obfuscation, and tyrannical authority were peeled off the church and tossed aside. Like blindness being dissolved and the light bursting into view, the Truth could now move forward and be a blessing to mankind.

Negative Consequences of the Reformation

Of course, this wouldn't happen without a struggle. As Luther wrote about in his famous hymn: "and still our ancient foe, doth seek to work us woe"[133] Luther's movement would be open to criticism, because religious radicals would rise up, such as Thomas Muntzer, who would reject the authority of the Word and embrace instead the revelation of the Spirit. In the end he claimed to have had a word from God that instructed him to "wipe out the ungodly"[134] with the sword. When the authorities tried to stop him, his followers were encouraged to fight back with the promise that bullets wouldn't hurt them. The bullets did hurt them, though, and 5,000 of them were killed. Muntzer tried to escape, but instead was captured, tortured, and beheaded.

The Catholic Church had always said that they needed to be the established authority because of the concern over false doctrine. They predicted that a church without unity would be out of control, with anyone and everyone claiming to be an expert and speaking for God. In Muntzer they were proven correct. (Erasmus wouldn't join Luther because of this danger.) Muntzer had gone beyond the Word, though, and claimed to have a revelation from the Spirit. In this, the Catholic Church was also guilty. They no longer relied solely on the written revelation of the apostles, but on the Bible *and* tradition. This is why the rallying cry of the Reformation was "Sola Scriptura," or "Only the Scriptures."

The Reformation was also one of the factors that led to the horrible and bloody Thirty Years War. This was a devastating conflict that would cause the land to be ravaged, producing pestilence, disease, and famine. Untold numbers of people died. It began as a religious war, but then became political and then religious again. But there's no denying that the conflict between the Catholics and the Protestants led to a vicious war.

Religious Tolerance

At the end of the hostilities, tired and demoralized, the Europeans would develop a peace agreement known as the Treaty of Westphalia. It would encourage religious tolerance between Catholics and Protestants, undermining the power of the Holy Roman Empire,[135] and it would become the foundation for a diplomatic system of states, ending medieval feudalism and establishing a balance of power amongst nations.

This new attitude of toleration toward religious diversity would find its fullest expression in John Locke's *Letter Concerning Toleration*. Locke was a believer who found no conflict between faith and reason. In his book called *The Reasonableness of Christianity* he posited that faith could only be birthed from reason. He argued in *Letter* that:

1. States have no authority or ability to discern truth amongst competing religions. Not that all are true or equally valid, just that it's not the role of the state to determine this.

2. Even if one religion did appear to be superior to others, that religion wouldn't want to force itself on others. It was better to use "inward persuasion"[136] than to be "compelled to the belief of anything by outward force."[137]

3. Trying to impose one religion on others would result in something worse than allowing religious diversity, because even within the "true" religion, disagreements would arise and, as seen in Europe, could lead to civil war.

Locke's *Letter* would have a profound impact on the founders of the United States. They learned from European mistakes and rejected the concept of church/state "Christendom." This would lead to the development of one of America's most precious Constitutional rights—religious freedom.

William Tyndale

The Reformation would also spread to other European nations. In England, many at Oxford and Cambridge read Luther's writings and agreed with him. One of these was William Tyndale. An expert in Greek and Hebrew, as other Reformers, he would also translate the Scriptures for the common man. He believed in the gospel of grace, saying "Evangelio (that we call 'gospel') is a Greek word, and it signifies good, merry, glad and joyful tidings, that make a man's heart glad, and make him sing, dance and leap for joy." Tyndale had discovered the Narrow Way of grace and love and, as others before him, would die for it. He would be arrested, imprisoned in a cold, damp, dungeon for eighteen months, and then strangled and burned because he maintained "that faith alone justifies… that to believe in the forgiveness of sins, and to embrace the mercy offered in the gospel, was enough for salvation."[138]

Thomas Cranmer

Under the reign of "Bloody" Queen Mary, a Catholic, the Protestants in England were persecuted. All the bishops and clergy were required to pledge allegiance to the Pope. If they didn't they could be condemned to death. Bishops Latimer and Ridley refused and were burnt at the stake. Thomas Cranmer, the archbishop, was also imprisoned for his beliefs, but he cracked under the pressure and recanted.

Although he had a moment of weakness, Cranmer's final stand would be much more dramatic. Forced to read a statement admitting his error in believing in the Protestant faith, he would instead make a confession of his embarrassment at wavering in his faith. And knowing that he would also face the flames as Ridley and Latimer had, he still declared: "And as for the pope, I refuse him as Christ's enemy and Antichrist with all his false doctrine." To which the crowd, gathered in the church at Oxford, would respond by screaming and demanding he be burnt. When Cranmer was put into the flames, he held out his right hand to be burnt first since he had used it in a moment of weakness to sign a document that renounced Christ. Cranmer was on the Narrow Way and, of course, would die for it at the hands of irrational religionists.

Those who condemn the entire church for the Inquisition need to understand that those who battled most successfully against the poisonous religion of the popes and bishops were those who knew the Gospel of grace and love.

After Queen Mary's death, the Protestant Queen Elizabeth would rule, and religious peace would be preserved through agreeing to a blend of Protestantism and Catholicism within the Anglican Church. During this period, Francis Bacon would write his *Essays*, Shakespeare would write his plays, Sir Walter Raleigh would be sent to settle America, and there would be peace and prosperity. Elizabeth's reign is still considered to be one of the greatest periods in English history and is known as "The Golden Age." Even so, the Catholic Church would excommunicate her and attempt to assassinate her.

Ulrich Zwingli

Another division in the church caused by the Reformation was of Zwingli in Zurich, Switzerland. He was a humanist, as Erasmus, and agreed that the Roman Church and its clergy had become abusive. He agreed with Luther that the Bible was the only source of spiritual authority. He would lead a reform movement to abolish all Catholic traditions in his church, including ritual fasting, pilgrimages, indulgences, confession, and worship of icons, celibacy for priests, and even the Mass, replacing it with the "Lord's Supper." (In this he would separate himself from Luther, who insisted that an actual incarnation occurred in the Eucharist.) In a stance against the Roman Catholic practice of fasting on Lent, Zwingli would publicly eat a bratwurst! He thought that the only standard was the Bible and joined in the Reformation rallying cry of "Sola Scriptura!" He said, "We will test everything by the touchstone of the Gospel and the fire of Paul. Where we find anything that is in conformity with the Gospel, we will preserve it; where we find something that does not conform to it; we will put it out.... because one must obey God rather than man."[139]

Like Elizabeth, Zwingli also promoted religious freedom for the Catholics. As one of the Magisterial Reformers, he even believed in a democratic form of government, going further than Luther, who was satisfied with supporting the prince. He would risk his own life to care for others during a plague in Zurich. He cared for widows and orphans and believed that Christians should be law-abiding and love justice. He would turn monasteries into hospitals and orphanages. The school system was reformed, and instead of an economy that relied on mercenaries, he would encourage agriculture and trade.

Zwingli would also be one of the first to preach from the Bible during church services rather than merely performing the Mass. He was humble and would confess that at one time he had an affair with a nun. He would translate the Scriptures so the common person could learn from them. And because priests couldn't marry, he secretly wed a young widowed woman with three children and had three more children with her. He would go out into the town square to preach the Gospel. Finally, he took the responsibility of caring for the flock seriously, saying he remained convinced that he "would give an account of the blood of the sheep which would perish as a consequence of my carelessness."[140]

In 1529 a Protestant missionary was burnt at the stake in one of the Catholic cantons (districts) of Switzerland. In response, Zwingli persuaded the leaders of Zurich to cut off trade with the area. As a result, the Catholic cantons declared war. Eight thousand of them attacked 1,500 of Zwingli's followers in the battle of Kappel. His successor Bullinger would relate this story of Zwingli's last moments:

> While the Catholic forces were looting the bodies of the dead and dying, they found Zwingli still alive, lying on his back, with his hands together as if he was praying, and his eyes looking upward to Heaven... he was stricken with a mortal wound, so they asked whether a priest should be fetched to hear his confession. At this, Zwingli shook his head.... they encouraged him to call upon Mary, the Mother of God and upon the Saints.[141]

According to Peter Hammond, author of *The Greatest Century of Reformation*:

> When Zwingli again shook his head, the Catholics cursed him, and said that he was one of the obstinate, cantankerous heretics and should get what he deserved. One of the Catholic captains then drew his sword and thrust Zwingli through. When his body was identified, there were tremendous shouts of joy throughout the Catholic camp. It was decided to quarter his body and burn the portions, throwing into the fire the entrails of some pigs and mixing the pig offal with Zwingli's ashes, scattering it to prevent a burial of the great Reformer.[142]

Again, zealous, irrational religionists would react to a person on the Narrow Way and kill him. It wasn't the Way of grace and love that became unreasonable. It was those who denied or added to the Word and trusted in their rituals and works who became venomous. As Hitchens says, "Religion poisons everything."

The Anabaptists

The Anabaptists were another group that grew as a result of the Reformation. Deridingly called the Re-baptizers because they wouldn't accept infant baptism and instead demanded a "believer's baptism" (since only adults could believe and not babies), the Anabaptists would suffer persecution because they didn't fit into the church/state molds that were developing. In Switzerland, Zurich was Protestant under Zwingli, and the other cantons were Catholic. In Germany, the princes in some areas were Catholic and others were Protestant. In England, there was a blend of Catholicism and Protestantism under Queen Elizabeth, and so on… but all of these churches were enforced by the authority of the state, just as Catholicism had been, and uniformity of belief in each territory was required. If you were living in Zurich, you believed as Zwingli believed. If you lived in Bohemia, you believed as Luther believed. There was no real religious freedom. And since all the other Protestants and Catholics practiced infant baptism, the Anabaptists didn't fit in anywhere and were a threat to political/religious unity. As it was, there was no centralized authority for the Anabaptists; they were a loose coalition of several groups.

Adding to their problems, at Munster, in 1535, a group of radical Anabaptists seized power, predicted the imminent arrival of Christ, and declared that the Old Testament Law was still valid, including polygamy.[143] The uprising was squelched by the Catholics, and as a result of it the sect had a horrible reputation. The Anabaptists would repent of this zealotry and under the leadership of Menno Simmons would become pacifists. They would develop into the Amish, the Mennonites, and the Moravians.

The Anabaptists were accused of denying the doctrine of "justification by grace," because they believed that faith should produce discipleship and a pure walk with God, but they vehemently denied this was their position. Rather, they believed purity was a consequence of having faith. The Anabaptists wanted to return to the brotherhood of the earliest church and expressed themselves in love and concern for their neighbors, some even going so far as to practice a Christian communism.

Again, because they didn't fit into the church/state societies, they were early defenders of the concept of the separation of church and state, saying that Christians were a "free, unforced, uncompelled people" and because faith is a free gift of God "the authorities exceed their competence when they 'champion the Word of God with a fist.'"[144] They didn't believe in the concept of "Christendom." As a result, Catholics would burn them at the stake and Protestants would drown them. An Anabaptist, thirty-year-old Felix Manz, would become the first person martyred by the Reformers because he rejected infant baptism.[145] Taken to a nearby river, he would be bound, weighted down, and tossed into the freezing water.

As you can see from the last paragraph, Protestantism wasn't immune from committing spiritual abuse. As I wrote in the first chapter of this book, religion is mankind's attempt to regain Eden in its own way. It's a striving for order and perfection at all costs. Catholicism had fallen into this chasm in its attempt to preserve sound doctrine through the use of force, and now Protestantism was about to follow. What began as a burst of light and freedom was now going astray and becoming systematized and ordered, demanding submission to somebody's ideal… or else. This is what happened when Geneva invited John Calvin to bring his brand of Protestantism to their city.

Calvinism

Calvinism would be another offshoot of the Reformation. While John Calvin was a Reformer who believed in Luther's Protestant message, his desire to bring about Eden on earth would go too far. His vision: that the church in Geneva was to be a disciplined army of the Lord, chosen to fight off the Midianites and Canaanites (the Catholics), because they were the new inheritors of the Abrahamic covenant, and therefore obedience to God's laws was imperative in order to secure the blessings of God. It was a return to the old religious system that had been cut off and replaced by Jesus. (Remember! "He set aside the first to establish the second" [Heb. 10:9b].) Christians live under a new covenant of grace, provided for through the blood of Jesus. We no longer live under an "if/then" covenant.

The city council of Geneva had decided to become Protestant, and the local population was glad to be free from indulgences and paying money to Rome, but, unfortunately, they would end up under another form of bondage. Calvin's preaching would be so stern that the people of Geneva would respond with rioting, threats, and curses. The city council would vote to banish Calvin (and his partner Farel) from Geneva, only to invite them back three years later, after which Calvin would begin to construct his Eden. According to Bowie:

> Religion was no empty form or easy word for Calvin, he wanted all Geneva to live seven days a week according to what he believed to be God's commandments.... he wanted the laws of the church to determine the laws of the city.... Therefore Calvin tried to order life in Geneva according to what he thought was the pattern of holiness. There were stern punishments not only for the wicked but also for the careless and easygoing. A man could be fined or imprisoned for playing dice for a bottle of wine or for laughing in church or going to sleep during a sermon, for doing anything he wasn't supposed to do on the Sabbath or for wearing more showy clothes than what were allowed. It was a grim and stern kind of obedience that Calvin required. It could not be kept up for long.[146]

In matters of conscience, the Protestants, it would seem, should have learned a lesson from their experience with the Inquisition, but concerning Michael Servetus, they didn't. The Catholic Church had already condemned him, but he escaped their prison and traveled to Geneva. The Calvinists considered him to be an anti-Trinitarian, therefore upon spotting Servetus attending a church in Geneva the town council had him arrested and put on trial. With the help of Calvin, they concluded he was guilty of heresy and should be burnt at the stake *in the name of the Father, Son, and Holy Spirit!*

Calvin would also overhear Jerome Bolsec oppose his doctrine of election (or predestination), saying it turned God into a tyrant. (Bolsec had no idea Calvin was in the room.) When Bolsec finished, Calvin spent an hour speaking on the subject, and Bolsec was sent to jail, only to be banished from Geneva. This was a kind of control that was reminiscent of the Roman Church's attempt to maintain sound doctrine.

The main opponent of Calvin was Sebastian Castellio. While previously exiled from Geneva, his outspoken opposition to the burning of Servetus caused him to be excoriated as a heretic and have his books censored, but his biblically based writings against the right of the church to convict and punish heretics would have a lasting impact on the Enlightenment concept of liberty of conscience.

Calvin went astray from the Scriptures in so many ways, even so, the part of Calvin's theology that aligned with the Word, as presented in the New Testament, would impact the world in a number of positive ways. His lasting contribution would be his *Institutes*, an orderly attempt to interpret the Scriptures, to overthrow the Catholic transcendent (mystical) view, and give tribute to the majesty of God—especially in the physical realm.

The Pilgrims

Geneva would become a place of refuge for many Protestants as persecution continued throughout Europe. For example, as Queen Mary persecuted English Protestants, they would escape to Geneva for safety. What they experienced and learned there would be brought back to their native countries. In Scotland, John Knox was influenced by Calvin, and in England the Puritans would form as a direct result of being exposed to Calvinism.

As stated before, the Reformed Tradition would also have a strong influence on the United States, because the Calvinists who returned to England under the safe reign of Queen Elizabeth would divide into two camps: those who wanted to purify the Church of England along Calvinist lines and those who wanted to separate themselves from the Church of England. The latter would decide to climb on board a little ship known as the Mayflower and travel to America to start a new colony as the first pilgrims. And as persecution of the Puritans increased because of their insistence on reforming the Anglican Church, they would also come to America and try to set up their "city on a hill."

Discrediting Mystical Monasticism

One of the most important aspects of Calvin's theology was that it moved Western civilization away from the monastic/mystical views that were prevalent in Catholicism. The monastic view insisted on isolation and separation from an evil world of temptations. The mystical view was that God could be found in ecstatic attempts to accomplish divine union through contemplative activity. But Calvin insisted that Christian living should occur in the real world. Abraham Kuyper offered this explanation for the change in attitude toward the new emphasis on the physical realm:

> For this reason the clergy, severing the earthly tie in celibacy, rank higher than the laity, and again, the monk, who turns away from earthly possessions also and sacrifices his own will, stands, ethically considered, on a higher level than the clergy. And finally the

highest perfection is reached by the stylite, who, mounting his pillar, severs himself from everything earthly, or by the yet more silent penitent who causes himself to be immured in his subterranean cave. Horizontally, if I may use this expression, the same thought finds embodiment in the separation between sacred and secular ground. Everything uncountenanced and uncared for by the church is looked upon as being of a lower character, and exorcism in baptism tells us that these lower things are really meant to be unholy. Now, it is evident that such a standpoint did not invite Christians to make a study of earthly things.[147]

The Scientific Revolution

This belief that a Christian was to live in the real, material world, rather than try to escape to otherworldly experiences would also contribute to the phenomenal growth of science. The Catholic Church had insisted on blending the Bible with the Aristotelian view of the universe when it came to scientific opinions, but the Reformation allowed for scientific discovery without the fetters of classical thought holding them down. Calvin reminded us that Christ is the Lord over *all* creation, not just the church, and that nature was "the theater of God's glory." The slide toward a Gnostic view of the universe through contemplative mysticism caused the church to forget that God looked at what he created and said it was good. Calvin would specifically encourage Christians to find proof of God in creation: "In attestation of his wondrous wisdom, both the heavens and the earth present us with innumerable proofs not only those more recondite proofs which astronomy, medicine, and all the natural sciences, are designed to illustrate, but proofs which force themselves on the most illiterate peasant, who cannot open his eyes without beholding them."[148]

This newfound respect for the material world, coupled with the thought that God had revealed himself through his creation,[149] opened up a whole universe filled with excitement and new revelations as men now attempted to find God in the world around them. In this, the Scriptures didn't act as a hindrance, but a help.

Francis Bacon, who developed the scientific method of using experiments, observation, and induction from the data, rather than through Aristotelian deduction, would declare: "There are two books laid before us to study, to prevent our falling into error; first, the volume of Scriptures, which reveal the will of God; then the volume of creatures [his creation], which express his power."[150]

Johannes Kepler, who was a Lutheran, was excommunicated by the Catholic Church in 1612. He discovered the laws of planetary motion because he wanted to understand the mind of God, and he was thrilled to find out that God was a designer! He said he saw "how God, like a human architect, approached the founding of the world according to order and rule and measured everything in such manner."[151]

Robert Boyle, whose *Skeptical Chymist* would become the foundation of modern chemistry, was a charter member of the Royal Society of Great Britain (and whose motto was "Nullius in Verbia" which means "nothing in word," emphasizing the importance of experimentation), and would overturn the Aristotelian viewpoint that all things were composed of the four elements of earth, air, fire, and water. He rejected the Greek (Hellenistic) basis for science and preferred using a truthful method of experimentation in order to know how God designed the universe, saying, "I ignore not that not only Leucippus, Epicurus, and other atomists of old, but of late some persons, for the most part admirers of Aristotle's writings, have pretended to be able to explicate the first beginning of things, and the world's phenomena, without taking in or acknowledging any divine Author of it."[152]

John Ray, one of the earliest biologists, opposed the Aristotelian concept of spontaneous generation, saying: "My observation and affirmation is that there is no such thing in nature."[153] He said it was "the atheist's fictitious and ridiculous account of the first production of mankind and other animals."[154]

Louis Pasteur, the founder of modern medicine and one of the founders of microbiology, who developed the process of pasteurization and a cure for rabies, is also known for discrediting spontaneous generation. His attempt to stop milk from spoiling came as a result of his desire to prove that life could only come from life. Consequently, he invented a way to heat liquids enough to kill the bacteria and then not let them be exposed to the air where bacteria would thrive. He was a Christian who was inspired to find God's handiwork in nature, and he said, "The more I study nature, the more I stand amazed at the work of the Creator."[155]

Joseph Lister, who developed a method of sterile surgery, would also disprove Aristotle's belief in spontaneous generation by stopping infection through a combination of the use of carbolic acid (which kills bacteria without being too harsh on the skin) and covering the wound with bandages. He also introduced the use of sterile catgut, allowing the thread to dissolve without having to upset the abrasion. Lister was a Quaker who gently affirmed: "I am a believer in the fundamental doctrines of Christianity."[156]

Attempts to associate the origins of the Scientific Revolution with the Renaissance or Enlightenment periods are disingenuous. The Renaissance was a rebirth of the Aristotelian worldview, which had been recovered in part as a result of contact with the Muslim scholar, Averroes, but science didn't advance as a result of this knowledge. In fact it was stunted as the medieval church attempted to blend this knowledge in with the Scriptures (just as they had also blended Greek philosophy in with the Word and formed medieval scholasticism). Instead, it was the direct attempt to overthrow Hellenism by men of the Reformation that led to the explosive growth in science. And the Enlightenment was a *consequence* of the Scientific Revolution, particularly as found in the work of Isaac Newton.

It was Isaac Newton's belief in the First Cause that led to deism and Enlightenment philosophy, but Isaac Newton was not an atheist. He was a believer who said that he was motivated by a desire to prove the existence of God when he wrote *Principia Mathematica*, saying, "When I wrote my treatise about our Systeme I had an eye upon such Principles as might work with considering men for the beleife of a Deity & nothing can rejoyce me more then to find it usefull for that purpose."[157] He was inspired by his desire to know the mind of God (much as Stephen Hawkings is) and believed that "this most beautiful system of the sun, planets, and comets, could only proceed from the counsel and dominion of an intelligent Being."[158]

Modern day skeptics point to the trial of Galileo as evidence that having faith in God is a hindrance to science,[159] but the truth is that the Scientific Revolution was precipitated by men of faith. It was their desire for truth based on physical evidence, rather than philosophy or reason, which led them to discover and understand the workings of the universe—from the smallest atom to the limitless galaxies. Because the Scriptures told them that God was a God of order rather than disorder (1 Cor. 14:33), they began to search for that order, and as a result of their studies, Isaac Newton, for one, could confidently assert: "He is a God of organization not of disarray."[160] The list of scientists who would declare that it was their faith in God that led them to their scientific knowledge could read like a virtual Who's Who of Scientific Advancement and Discovery.

Antiseptic Surgery—Joseph Lister (1827-1912)
Bacteriology—Louis Pasteur (1822-1895)
Calculus—Isaac Newton (1642-1727)
Celestial Mechanics—Johannes Kepler (1571-1730)
Chemistry—Robert Boyle (1627-1691)
Comparative Anatomy—Georges Cuvier (1769-1832)
Computer Science—Charles Babbage (1792-1871)
Dimensional Analysis—Lord Rayleigh (1842-1919)
Dynamics—Isaac Newton (1642-1727)
Electronics—John Ambrose Fleming (1849-1945)
Electrodynamics—James Clerk Maxwell (1831-1879)
Electromagnetics—Michael Faraday (1791-1867)
Energetics—Lord Kelvin (1824-1907)
Entomology of Living Insects—Henri Fabre (1823-1915)
Fluid Mechanics—George Stokes (1819-1903)
Galactic Astronomy—Sir William Herschel (1738-1822)
Gas Dynamics—Robert Boyle (1627-1691)
Genetics—Gregor Mendel (1822-1884)
Glacial Geology—Louis Agassiz (1807-1873)
Gynecology—James Simpson (1811-1870)
Hydraulics—Leonardo da Vinci (1452-1519)
Hydrography—Matthew Maury (1806-1873)
Hydrostatics—Blaise Pascal (1623-1662)
Ichthyology—Louis Agassiz (1807-1873)
Isotopic Chemistry—William Ramsey (1852-1916)
Model Analysis—Lord Rayleigh (1842-1919)
Natural History—John Ray (1627-1905)
Non-Euclidean Geometry—Bernard Riemann (1826-1866)
Oceanography—Matthew Maury (1806-1873)
Optical Mineralogy—David Brewster (1781-1868)
Paleontology—John Woodward (1665-1728)
Pathology—Rudolph Virchow (1821-1902)
Physical Astronomy—Johannes Kepler (1571-1630)

Reversible Thermodynamics—James Joule (1818-1889)
Statistical Thermodynamics—James Clerk Maxwell (1831-1879)
Stratigraphy—Nicholas Steno (1631-1686)
Systematic Biology—Carolus Linnaeus (1707-1778)
Thermodynamics—Lord Kelvin (1824-1907)
Thermokinetics—Humphrey Davy (1778-1829)
Vertebrate Paleontology—Georges Cuvier (1769-1832)[161]

This list could go on and on. Recently, a scientist who helped to decipher the genetic code through the Human Genome Project, Francis S. Collins, explained that he felt as though his work was like learning the language of God. He declares in the introduction of his book, *The Language of God: A Scientist Presents Evidence for Belief,* that "belief in God can be an entirely rational choice and that the principles of faith are, in fact, complimentary with the principles of science."[162] His faith didn't hinder his scientific work. It motivated him and filled him with awe. This was a common experience of believing scientists. Isaac Newton said that his work was like child's play. "I was like a boy playing on the sea-shore, and diverting myself now and then finding a smoother pebble or a prettier shell than ordinary, whilst the great ocean of truth lay all undiscovered before me."[163]

To these great scientists, unlocking the secrets of the universe was like an adventure. It inspired wonder and respect for the sheer genius and elegance of the Creator. Is there not magnificent order in the universe? And is it not governed by powerful and dependable laws such as the point at which water freezes or the gravitational pull necessary to keep things in place? The Scientific Revolution was an attempt to discover evidence for God in the material realm. And the efforts of these scientists have blessed humanity in ways too numerous to count. The Royal Society recentlty described the benefits that humanity has reaped from science:

> As a direct consequence, we live in the best of times: healthier, better fed, and with more energy subsidies than ever before. Basic understanding of the life sciences, especially with respect to infectious diseases, has resulted in average life expectancy at birth on the planet today being sixty-four years, up from forty-six years only fifty years ago; the gap in life expectancy between the developed and developing worlds has correspondingly shrunk from twenty-six years to

a still disgraceful twelve. Over the past thirty-five years, global food production has doubled, on only ten percent more land, while the human population has increased sixty percent; the problem of malnourishment is one of inequitable distribution, a problem which has been with us since the dawn of agriculture.[164]

Prosperity

Calvin's insistence on emphasizing a Christianity that exists in the real world within community rather than withdrawal and isolation also led to the wealth and prosperity of Western cultures. For example, while the monk may seem spiritually superior because of his fasting, celibacy, and "spiritual" service to God, Calvin would insist that *work* is honorable and a person can receive a "calling" to be a blacksmith as much as he might receive a calling to be a pastor. All vocations are equal and good if they bless others and are done "as unto the Lord." (This attitude also led to the growth of science, as Kepler put it: "I had the intention of becoming a theologian… but now I see how God is, by my endeavors, also glorified in astronomy, for the 'heavens declare the glory of God.'")[165]

The growth of a middle class would occur as a result of this new respect for work. Instead of society being divided into rich landowners, the clergy class, and the poor peasant, another option began to develop. The "Puritan work ethic," as it would come to be known, would contribute greatly to the wealth of Protestant Europe and America. Status wouldn't simply be determined by a person's class, but by the quality of their labors and the content of their character. This was an enormous change in attitude that greatly benefited the American settlers, for example.

Family

Another transformation that was encouraged by the Reformation was the changing attitude toward the family. In the past it was more spiritual to remain single and celibate, but after the Reformation, marriage was considered sacred also. The Protestant leaders contributed to this attitude by getting married and having children themselves. Luther married a former nun, Katherine von Bora, who was rescued from a convent through means of an empty fish barrel. Together, they would have six children and an active home life. Zwingli and Calvin also had families.

Education

The democratization of education also occurred as a result of the Protestants' insistence that individuals have the right to read the Bible for themselves. This led to a huge explosion in education. Coupled with the advent of the printing press, the common man would no longer be at the mercy of priests to know what the sacred texts revealed. Later, the emphasis on education would be spread to all nations, translating languages that were previously only known as an oral tradition and writing them down so the tribal peoples would also be able to read the Bible. As a result of these mission schools, the colonial resistance movements would be strengthened. (For example, Nelson Mandela attended Fort Hare, a Methodist mission.)

Civil Disobedience

Samuel Rutherford wrote *Lex Rex* as a result of his Calvinist understanding that unjust rulers can be overthrown. In the past, governments were "divinely ordered" and unable to be challenged by believers, but Calvin believed that Christians were subject to rulers, only in the Lord. The immoral king has no right to command the church to do something against God's will. This was Calvin's understanding of civil disobedience. Rutherford, a Presbyterian, would certainly be influenced by Calvin, and his discourse on the power of kings would contribute greatly to the American Revolution.

The followers of the Narrow Way, those who trusted in the Word and followed the way of grace and love, were given an opportunity to shine as a result of the Protestant Reformation. They wouldn't be perfect, but their emphasis on returning to the original Scriptures, rather than the traditions that had built up within the Catholic Church, would lead to a whole new understanding of family, work, religious freedom and tolerance, scientific discovery, expansion of education, freedom from tyranny, human rights, new diplomatic structures, exploration of foreign lands, and ultimately, a release from the bondage of the poisonous Roman Catholic religion into the way of grace. Because of the Scriptures, an age of darkness, bondage, and intellectual foolishness would be vanquished for an age of knowledge, freedom, and wisdom.

The work of translating the Bible into common languages by Wycliffe, Tyndale, Erasmus, Luther, Zwingli, and countless others wasn't in vain. As

THE NARROW WAY IN THE REFORMATION

John tells us: "In the beginning was the Word, and the Word was with God, and the Word was God. He was with God in the beginning. Through him all things were made; without him nothing was made that has been made. In him was life, and that life was the light of men" (John 1:1-4).

CHAPTER SEVEN
The Narrow Way in a Time of Revolution

> *"Those with the power to elect our presidents and congressmen—and many who themselves get elected—believe that dinosaurs lived two by two upon Noah's ark, that light from distant galaxies was created en route to the earth, and that the first members of our species were fashioned out of dirt and divine breath, in a garden with a talking snake, by the hand of an invisible God.*
>
> *"Among developed nations, America stands alone in these convictions. Our country now appears, as at no other time in her history, like a lumbering, bellicose, dim-witted giant. Anyone who cares about the fate of civilization would do well to recognize that the combination of great power and great stupidity is simply terrifying, even to one's friends."* —Sam Harris, *Letter to a Christian Nation*

Those on the Narrow Way played an integral part in the founding of America. In fact, I would argue that it's even questionable whether the United States would have been able to succeed without their active presence in the colonies because Enlightenment thought wasn't part of the knowledge possessed by most colonists and was a belief held only by the most educated in society. Consequently, there had to be something else that unified them, inspiring them to be willing to lay down their lives. I say that the "something else" was the way of grace and love—the Narrow Way.

If the Founders' political philosophies were that different from the beliefs of the colonists, there could never have been the passion that most Americans feel for their history and founding documents, but the American vision has always caused the hearts of her people to burst with enthusiasm. This wasn't because a vanguard of philosophers carefully and meticulously developed a slew of political documents, but because the highest and most rational thought that these learned, scientific men could produce merely aligned with the biblical concepts of those on the Narrow Way.

This may even seem shocking to those who think it's wise for our nation to abandon "fundamentalist" Christianity and align itself with secular Enlightenment thought, but I would even argue that the Founders would have failed, as the "philosophes" did in France, if they hadn't planted their seed in the fertile ground of American evangelicalism.

Authors of books such as *The Godless Constitution: The Case Against Religious Correctness* and *The Moral Minority: Our Skeptical Founding Fathers* emphasize the fact that the Founding Fathers weren't Christians. They detail all of the Founder's writings and show how "skeptical" they supposedly were. This, they say, should quiet the religious right, who diabolically want to create a state church through reciting the "Pledge of Allegiance" in the classroom, keeping "In God We Trust" on our money, or saying a prayer at a high school graduation.

These authors claim that they're staying true to the original intentions of the Founding Fathers and since the Founders were skeptics, they wouldn't want there to be any mention of God by the secular government. They say "the creche or the menorah on public property becomes the nose of the camel sneaking into the tent where Americans have carefully enshrined the constitutional separation of church and state."[166]

Were the Founders Atheists?

While I would agree that many of the Founders were products of Enlightenment rationalism, I think there needs to be an understanding that the term "skeptic" doesn't mean atheist. The Founders would not have declared that "God Is Not Great." They may not have even agreed completely with Hitchens' proposition that "religion poisons everything." Even though they were vehemently anti-clerical in most cases, they also recognized the important role that religion played in governing the people. This would become even more important after the failure of the French Revolution. Even so, Hitchens feels justified in claiming Enlightenment thinkers such as Voltaire, Jefferson, Paine, and Franklin as his own and explains the following:

> Arguments for atheism can be divided into two main categories: those that dispute the existence of God and those that demonstrate the ill effects of religion. It might be better if I broadened this somewhat, and said those that dispute the existence of an intervening God. Religion is, after all, more than the belief in a supreme being. It is the cult of that supreme being and the belief that his or her wishes have been made known or can be determined. Defining matters in this way, I can allow myself to mention great critics such as Thomas Jefferson or Thomas Paine, who perhaps paradoxically regarded religion as an insult to God.[167]

He also implies that the reason the Founders were deists rather than atheists was because Darwin hadn't come on the scene yet, giving them an alternative explanation of origins.

While Hitchens does acknowledge that he has "no right to claim past philosophers as purtative ancestors of atheism,"[168] he goes on to say that he may still be justified in making the claim that they were atheists:

> Because of religious intolerance we cannot know what they really thought privately, and were very nearly prevented from learning what they wrote publicly... in view of the terror imposed by religion on science and scholarship throughout the early Christian centuries... and the fact that most intelligent people found it prudent to make an outward show of conformity, one need not be surprised that the revival of philosophy was often originally expressed in quasi-devout terms.[169]

In other words, these anti-religious philosophers were able to express their disdain for the organized church, which could have really done harm to them, but not express their disdain for God, who if he wasn't real, could do nothing to them.

This attempt by the atheist Hitchens to claim those who clearly have accomplished great things as his own, even though they believed in a Supreme Being, could be seen to be an illegal seizure, a confiscation of something that isn't truly his. The word atheist is defined as "a person who believes there is no God."[170] So either Hitchens, who authors the book *The Portable Atheist*, is not an atheist, or he is trying to redefine the term. Anti-religious attitudes do not an atheist make. If that were the case, as I demonstrated earlier in this book, God would be an atheist!

Anti-Religion—Not Anti-God

Instead, I believe what all of these men had in common was a search for a *religionless* God. They saw all the abuses of religion, just as Hitchens does, but in spite of what Hitchens thinks they would have done, they didn't go as far as Hitchens. They didn't throw out the baby with the bathwater. Their contempt for religion didn't lead to contempt for God. Instead, I would argue that Franklin, Jefferson, Voltaire, and Paine, all men who earned Hitchens' respect, were searching for the non-religious Narrow Way.

Some of them rejected parts of the Scripture. There were two reasons for this. As deists they believed that the world was governed by natural law. They admired the work of the scientists, especially Isaac Newton, who revealed the laws of physics. To them, God was Newton's "first cause." He designed and set the universe in motion like a grand watchmaker and then stood back. So then, God revealed himself in nature, hence the term "Nature's God" referred to in the Declaration of Independence.

But they were also children of the Age of Exploration and realized that a multiplicity of religions existed in the world. The Judeo-Christian faiths weren't universal, the explorers had discovered, so to reconcile themselves to the idea of a just God, they held that there must be a Supreme Being—pure, simple, and rational—that in light of new discoveries, men would be able to embrace. They were also educated men who knew history and were familiar with the corruption of the church. From these perspectives—advances in science, exploration, and knowledge of history—deism was birthed.

Because God was revealed in the laws of nature and had merely set the universe in motion and stood back without intervening, miracles, prophecies, and other mysteries were cast off. God, they believed, wouldn't have interjected himself in history; he would have only let it progress naturally. This is why Jefferson's Bible had the verses about miracles removed. The deists also rejected parts of the Bible, because they believed much of the justification for the persecutions, witch hunts, and inquisitions had their source in verses such as "Do not allow a sorceress to live" (Exod. 22:18).

They also knew that after the Thirty Years War that devastated so much of Europe (it's reported that the fields were so ravaged by war they couldn't even produce crops), the Treaty of Westphalia, guaranteeing a measure of religious tolerance, was the culmination of the wisdom gleaned as a result of the carnage. The devastation caused by the war would pressure Catholics and Protestants to reconsider the use of force in resolving religious differences. With these religious ordeals still in their minds, deists all advocated the tolerance of different religions. John Locke's *Letter Concerning Toleration* would succinctly express their viewpoint.

Their faith was one of reason based on the highest that human knowledge had attained. History, science, exploration, philosophy, and a general increase in knowledge culminated into what was to become Enlightenment thought. But the Founders weren't atheists and it's wrong for Hitchens and others to claim them as their own.

Thomas Paine

Instead these men tried to plow out a different path, one in which Thomas Paine would join with the prophet Micah and declare, "I believe in the equality of man, and that religious duties consist in doing justice, in loving mercy, and endeavoring to make our fellow creatures happy."[171] He would also look at history and observe that "all national institutions of churches, whether Jewish, Christian, or Turkish, appear to me no other than human inventions set up to terrify and enslave mankind and monopolize power and profit."[172] His pamphlet *Common Sense* inspired Americans to rebel against British tyranny (by use of the Old Testament story of Samuel and Saul—whereby Israel wanted a king in spite of God's warning against it). But he also wrote *The Age of Reason* and supported the French Revolution, which ultimately led to him being despised by the same country that was once so inspired by his writings.

And yet ... Paine believed. In spite of the ugliness produced by religion, he saw beauty in the creation of God and hoped for immortality. But he refused to submit to religious leaders or be involved in their sins. I believe Paine was searching for a non-religious way to God. And while he may have abandoned some of the Word, therefore fashioning a god out of his own wisdom, he didn't abandon humanity or the principles of Christianity. Paine wasn't an unbeliever, and it's wrong for modern day atheists to parade him around as one of their trophies.

Thomas Jefferson

The same goes for Thomas Jefferson. He was also a believer. He may have rejected the miraculous portions of the Bible because of his commitment to natural law and knowledge of church corruption in history, but he didn't reject Jesus. In a letter to Benjamin Rush, he explains: "To the corruptions of Christianity, I am indeed opposed; but not to the genuine precepts of Jesus himself. I am a Christian, in the only sense in which he wished any one to be; sincerely attached to his doctrines, in preference to all others; ascribing to himself every human excellence, and believing he never claimed any other."[173]

While Jefferson may not have embraced the divinity of Jesus, he could still see his beauty. The fact that Jefferson refused to be a part of the religious system doesn't make him an atheist, and therefore I don't believe it's right for Hitchens and others to try to claim him as their own.

Voltaire

Voltaire is another deist that atheists try to hitch unto their wagon. But he was a believer. When atheists attempted to make claims on him, he revolted. He said that religion was the problem, not God, and that those who try to come against the corrupt church must be careful not to harm God in the process:

> Religion, you say, has produced countless misfortunes; say rather the superstition which reigns on our unhappy globe. This is the cruelest enemy of the pure worship due to the Supreme Being. Let us detest this monster which has always torn the bosom of its mother; those who combat it are the benefactors of the human race, it is a serpent which chokes religion in its embrace. We must crush its head without wounding the mother whom it devours.[174]

Voltaire realized that the enemy of God was religion (he called it "superstition"). He distinguishes between the true and the false just as Jefferson and Paine do. He wasn't an atheist, but an anti-religionist. This is how he describes his faith:

> [The theist] believes that religion consists neither in the opinions of an unintelligible metaphysic, nor in vain shows, but in worship and justice. To do good is his worship, to submit to God is his creed.

The Mohammedan cries out to him, "Beware if you fail to make the pilgrimage to Mecca!"—the priest says to him, "Curses on you if you do not make the trip to Notre Dame de Lorette!" He laughs at Lorette and at Mecca: but he succors the indigent and defends the oppressed.[175]

Voltaire would definitely not want to be held up as an atheist as though he was one of their own. He wasn't. He embraced another way between atheism and religion.

Benjamin Franklin

Benjamin Franklin is also portrayed as an atheist in much of atheist writing, which uses the deceptive term of "skeptic" to lump together atheists, deists, and agnostics, all as unbelievers. Franklin would insist on differentiating them from one another: "I oppose my theist to atheist, because I think they are diametrically opposite; and not near of kin, as Mr. Whitefield seems to suppose, where, (in his Journal) he tells us 'Mr. B was a deist, I had almost said an atheist;' that is, chalk, I had almost said charcoal."[176]

Franklin resented the fact that Whitefield, the evangelist, was lumping him together with atheists. Instead, he would agree with Voltaire that religion was the problem and not God. I think it may be helpful to read a letter that Franklin wrote to Joseph Huey on the matter of his faith. It's rather long, but I think Franklin expresses the heart of God in a beautiful way.

> The Faith you mention has doubtless its use in the World. I do not desire to see it diminished, nor would I endeavor to lessen it in any Man. But I wish it were more productive of Good Works than I have generally seen it: I mean real good Works, Works of Kindness, Charity, Mercy, and Publick Spirit; not Holiday-keeping, Sermon-Reading or Hearing, performing Church Ceremonies, or making long Prayers, fill'd with Flatteries and Compliments, despis'd even by wise Men, and much less capable of pleasing the Deity. The Worship of God is a Duty, the hearing and reading of Sermons may be useful; but if Men rest in Hearing and Praying, as many do, it is as if a Tree should value itself on being water'd and putting forth Leaves, tho it never produced any Fruit.

Your great Master tho't much less of these outward Appearances and Professions than many of his modern Disciples. He prefer'd the Doers of the Word to meer Hearers; the Son that seemingly refus'd to obey his Father and yet performed his Commands, to him that profess'd his Readiness but neglected the Works; the heretical but charitable Samaritan, to the uncharitable tho' orthodox Priest and sanctified Levite: and those who gave Food to the Hungry, Drink to the Thirsty, Raiment to the Naked, Entertainment to the Stranger, and Relief to the Sick, & co. tho' they never heard of his Name, he declares shall in the last Day be accepted, when those who cry Lord, Lord; who value themselves on their Faith tho' great enough to perform Miracles but have neglected good Works shall be rejected. He profess'd that he came not to call the Righteous but Sinners to Repentance, which imply'd his modest Opinion that there were some in his Time so good that they need not hear even him for improvement; but now a days we have scarce a little Parson, that does not think it the Duty of every Man within his Reach to sit under his petty Ministration, and that whoever omits them offends God, I wish to such more Humility, and to you Health and Happiness, being Your Friend and Servant.[177]

Franklin wanted Christians to do good works of charity and kindness, rather than religious rituals, and he says this was the way of Huey's "great Master," yet Hitchens dismisses Franklin's obvious admiration for the teachings of Jesus by saying that we cannot "know how many ostensibly devout people were secretly unbelievers,"[178] and that even "as late as the eighteenth and nineteenth centuries, in relatively free societies such as Britain and the United States, unbelievers as secure and prosperous as James Mill and Benjamin Franklin felt it advisable to keep their opinions private."[179] He doesn't offer any evidence of this persecution, but the implication is that "Ben Franklin is secretly one of ours."

Franklin, Voltaire, Jefferson, and Paine were not atheists. They were antireligionists. In this they were closer to the Narrow Way than to the atheist way. Although they shunned "revelation" and the idea of a personal God, they didn't necessarily shun the Bible. Most of them quoted it at length in their writings. They knew its content. But they were products of their age, not perfect. Hitchens says they were the *children* of *his* "species." I would respectfully disagree and say that they were children of *my* "species"—those on the Narrow Way. While Hitchens claims that Darwinism may have lured them to the atheistic perspective, we must remember that they were also historians, and with the benefit of hindsight they may have seen the wreckage caused by Darwinian nihilism and perhaps accepted a way that embraces biblical faith yet rejects arrogant and useless religion. Indeed, many of their words reflect this desire.

Why Was America Successful?

Along with this attempt to wrap the Founders in the robes of atheism, there's a parallel effort to claim that the Revolution was successful, not because of the faithful, but because of the wisdom of the "skeptics." There's been a tit for tat conflict playing out in the public arena over whether America was founded as a Christian nation with biblical roots or as a "skeptical" nation based merely on empiricism and reason.

This is where the crux of my argument lies. To whom do we owe America's great success? Is it, as the skeptics would insist, due only to the Founders' (implied) atheistic insights, or is it because of the Christian faith? I would argue that credit can be given to both deists and Christians, but I reject the prospect of giving any credit to atheists in this case. America is, at the least, a nation founded upon godly principles. To this the Founders, who used the name of God unashamedly (as in Jefferson's "Declaration of Independence," Franklin's request for prayer during the Constitutional Convention, and Washington's designation of Thanksgiving as a national holiday), would willingly submit.

Although the Constitution was "Godless" as authors Isaac Kramnick and R. Laurence Moore claim, this was obviously not in antagonism to faith, but an attempt to protect the Roger Williams of the world. Rhode Island and Pennsylvania were both founded upon the principle of religious freedom and toleration. One of these founders was a Quaker, and one was a Baptist. They weren't accepted in the Calvinistic church-state "city on a hill" Puritan communities, so they began their own places of refuge, tolerating all faiths.

America: The Religious Refuge

It's important to understand the mindset of the colonists regarding religion in the time period leading up to the Revolution in order to understand why people were so committed to the cause that they were willing to give up "their life, their fortunes, and their sacred honor." While there were some economic motivations for the Revolution, as the Boston Tea Party would reveal, the main motive for the Revolution was the desire to be involved in a grand experiment in freedom. Thomas Paine would put this motivation into eloquent words when he declared:

> O ye that love mankind! Ye that dare oppose, not only the tyranny, but the tyrant, stand forth! Every spot of the old world is over-run with oppression. Freedom hath been hunted round the globe. Asia, and Africa, have long expelled her. Europe regards her like a stranger, and England hath given her warning to depart. O! receive the fugitive, and prepare in time an asylum for mankind.[180]

The main part of this great experiment, according to Paine, was for America to become a place of religious tolerance. This is an important part of his vision for America in "Common Sense":

> For myself I fully and conscientiously believe, that it is the will of the Almighty, that there should be diversity of religious opinions among us: It affords a larger field for our Christian kindness. Were we all of one way of thinking, our religious dispositions would want matter for probation; and on this liberal principle, I look on the various denominations among us, to be like children of the same family, differing only, in what is called their Christian names.[181]

This vision was in direct contrast with those New England societies founded as denominational strongholds.

The Great Awakening

So how was it that Paine's dream was embraced by so many colonists? I would argue that one of the main reasons America would accept the Founding Father's revolutionary proposition was because of the Great Awakening. As many historians have recognized, this spiritual revival would "challenge old sources of authority and produce patterns of thought and behavior that helped fuel a revolutionary movement in the next generation."[182] This spiritual movement would lead to the disintegration of the established religious order of Puritanical New England and would help make the colonies more receptive to the American Revolution. It led to the colonists' reception of the concept of individual rights, religious freedom, democratization, and nationalism.

The Great Awakening was characterized by an emphasis on inner experience rather than outward duties. Because Puritan religious leaders were being influenced by "dry" European rationalism and deism, the common man became very receptive to the emotional, heartfelt message of the revivalist preacher.

Theodore Frelinghuysen

The Awakening Revival can be traced back to German pietism, a Lutheran movement of the seventeenth and eighteenth centuries that "emphasized heartfelt religious devotion, ethical purity, charitable activity, and pastoral theology rather than sacramental or dogmatic precision."[183] (They were on the Narrow Way!) According to William Warren Sweet, author of *Religion in Colonial America*,[184] Theodore Frelinghuysen, a German who was educated under pietistic influences, was called to America by three Dutch congregations in New Jersey in 1720. Sweet describes these Dutch communities as "rough and boorish"[185] saying they had "little desire beyond the outward conformity to accepted religious rites."[186] They merely wanted "to preserve the Dutch church as a symbol of their Dutch nationality."[187] Sweet says "the last thing they wanted was to have a religion that would stir the emotions and set up high standards of personal conduct. This was just the kind of religion, however, that Domine Frelinghuysen now began to preach."[188] He had an "impassioned manner of preaching"[189] and advocated inner religion and conversion rather than the performance of outward religious duties.

This caused a split in the Dutch congregations. Those who were well off (and usually held leadership positions in the church) were upset, while the poor and the young supported Frelinghuysen's enthusiasm. This was to be a common theme of revivalism and one of the traits that caused it to be a catalyst for democratic principles. By emphasizing a religion that appealed to the common man, revivalism would lay the foundation for the belief that government could be "of the people." It shattered the viewpoint that the educated clerical class and aristocracy needed to serve as a type of vanguard for the uneducated.

The Frelinghuysen revival prepared the way for the next stage of the revival, which occurred among the Scotch-Irish Presbyterians in the Middle Colonies.

William Tennent, a powerful preacher who was very evangelical for his day, felt called to educate young men for the ministry. He began the Log College at Neshaminy in Pennsylvania and in the course of twenty years educated sixteen to eighteen men for ministry, many of them his own sons. These young men were to achieve distinction for their scholarly achievements, but according to Sweet, "their principal distinction, however, was due to their flaming evangelical zeal."[190]

Most of these young men settled into churches in the New Jersey area and because Frelinghuysen had already paved the way for their message, Sweet says that "a militant revivalism swept the whole region."[191] Frelinghuysen himself recognized that one of Tennent's sons, Gilbert, had a "kindred spirit" and warmly welcomed him to the work in New Jersey.

Although there was great success, there was also opposition to the revival by many, especially older ministers. In an attempt to keep the revival from spreading, they tried to control the ordination of ministers by requiring candidates to present diplomas from New England or European colleges, a tactic obviously targeted toward shutting down Log College graduates.

Jonathan Edwards

Eight years after the Frelinghuysen revivals, in the fall of 1734, the Great New England Awakening began. Jonathan Edwards began to work with young people in his community, encouraging them to "assemble in several parts of the town and spend the evening in prayer and other duties of social religion. Their example was soon followed by their elders."[192]

Jonathan Edwards, taking advantage of this rising religiosity, began to preach on "Awakening" themes. He stopped reading his sermon notes from the pulpit and began to preach in an extemporaneous style more common to the Log College preachers. One of his most famous sermons, "Sinners in the Hands of an Angry God," led to outbursts of emotion in the usually stoic congregations of Puritanical New England. Sweet describes the reaction of the people to Edward's preaching:

> It seemed as though he were walking up and down the village street, pointing his accusing finger at "one house after another, unearthing secret sins and holding them up for all to see." Thus the revival of 1734 and 1735 began, and for three months excitement gripped the

town. The number of converts grew to more than three hundred and the meetinghouse could not contain the throngs who came to witness the receiving of a hundred new members on a certain Sunday morning. Night and day the parsonage was thronged with agonized sinners seeking the pastor's help so that they too might join the company of the saved and rejoicing.[193]

This was the situation in the colonies when the most famous of all revival preachers came onto the scene. The Frelinghuysen/Tennent/New England revivals merely laid a foundation for the work of the itinerant preacher, George Whitefield, whose message and style would lead to the crystallization of the revivals occurring in isolation into a great revival that would cross the continent.

George Whitefield

Whitefield was an Anglican from England. He had been influenced by the Wesley brothers (founders of Methodism) and came to America, where he began preaching in 1739. He landed in Lewes, Delaware, and began preaching in "the very region where Domine Frelinghuysen and the Log College evangelists had been preparing the soil for his seed."[194]

Whitefield was supported wholeheartedly by the Log College preachers and Presbyterians (more than his own Anglicans) and also gained support from "many educated and sober-minded men in the Middle Colonies such as Benjamin Franklin."[195] Writing about Whitefield, Franklin said: "In 1739 arriv'd among us from England the Rev. Mr. Whitefield, who had made himself remarkable there as an itinerant Preacher. He was at first permitted to preach in some of our Churches; but the Clergy taking a Dislike to him, soon refus'd him their Pulpits and he was obliged to preach in the Fields."[196]

Franklin would print Whitefield's sermons and pamphlets. He had a working relationship with Whitefield, but he also respected him and enjoyed his company as a friend. He says that even though Whitefield would "pray for [his] conversion,"[197] theirs was "a mere civil Friendship, sincere on both Sides, and lasted to his Death."[198]

Whitefield had visited Georgia in 1738 and saw the plight of the children of settlers who had gone there to find refuge from debtor prison. Franklin said that they didn't have the skills or industry necessary to endure the hardships of a new settlement. Because of this many died, "leaving behind many helpless Children unprovided for. The Sight of their miserable Situation inspired the benevolent Heart of Mr. Whitefield with the Idea of building an Orphan House there."[199]

According to Franklin, even he couldn't resist the charms of George Whitefield. Franklin thought that Whitefield's orphanage should be built in the north and the children should be brought to it, but Whitefield remained resolute in his position that the house be built in Georgia, so Franklin decided not to give money to the cause. He says that he was attending one of Whitefield's sermons and mention was made of the collection for the orphanage and he "silently resolved he should get nothing from me."[200] Franklin admits he had in his pocket "a handful of Copper Money, three or four silver Dollars, and five Pistoles in Gold."[201] But as Whitefield spoke, he "began to soften, and concluded to give the Coppers. Another stroke of his oratory made me asham'd of that, and determin'd me to give the Silver; and he finished so admirably, that I empty'd my Pocket wholly into the Collector's Dish, Gold and all."[202]

Nathan Cole, a farmer and carpenter of Connecticut, describes the excitement he and his wife felt when they found out that Whitefield was going to be in town. They dropped everything, got on a horse—they both shared one horse—and drove as fast as they could for twenty miles just to catch a glimpse of Whitefield. They weren't disappointed. According to Cole:

> When I see Mr. Whitfeld come upon the Scaffold, he looked almost angellical—a young, slim, slender youth before some thousands of people, and with a bold, undaunted countenance. And my hearing how God was with him everywhere as he came along, it solomnized my mind, and put me in trembling fear before he began to preach, for he looked as if he was Cloathed with authority from the great God. And a sweet, solomn Solemnity sat upon his brow, and my hearing him preach gave me a heart wound, by God's blessing. My old foundation was broken up and I saw that my righteousness would not save me.[203]

Whitefield traveled up and down the eastern seaboard preaching the Reformation principle of "justification by grace through faith." His message was simple: you must be born again. He believed in instant conversion. Nathan Cole, the farmer who was mentioned previously, experienced the "new birth" preached by Whitefield:

> Now I had for some years a bitter prejudice against three scornful men that had wronged me, but now all that was gone away Clear, and my Soul longed for them and loved them; there was nothing that was sinful that could any wise abide the presence of God; And all the air was love, now I saw that every thing that was sin fled from the presence of God. As far as darkness is gone from light or beams of the Sun for where ever the Sun can be seen clear there is no Darkness... Now I saw with new eyes, all things became new, A new God; new thoughts and new heart.[204]

It was this simple, heartfelt message of the Good News that spread like wildfire throughout the colonies and gave hope to common men like Nathan. But in the same way that the common man rejoiced, many of the clergy rejected Whitefield. He was invited, for example, to the Bishop of London's Commissary in South Carolina to answer questions, and while there he was immediately accused of "Enthusiasm and Pride, for speaking against the Generality of the Clergy."[205] Whitefield had charged them with preaching something other than justification by faith alone. The Commissary was so offended by his encounter with Whitefield that he kicked him out of his house. Whitefield went to the Commissary's church a couple of days later because it was arranged beforehand that he should speak, and his popularity would have made it difficult for the Commisary to uninvite him. The Commissary, still angry, introduced him "under the character of the Pharisee, who came to the temple saying, 'God, I thank thee that I am not as other Men are.'"[206]

Far and away the biggest controversy caused by the Great Awakening was the emotional response of the people to the message. Sweet says that "too much of their preaching was of a character to terrify the people, resulting in faintings, cries, and bodily agitations."[207] He says that Whitefield was "much less given to this kind of preaching than were the Scottish-Irish revivalists"[208] of the Log College and that Whitefield opposed these kinds of manifestations and didn't "consider them to have any relationship to true conversion."[209]

Old Lights vs. New Lights

The immediate impact of the revival was a division in the Presbyterian Church. The "Old Lights" who rejected the work of the Great Awakening expelled the "New Lights." So the New Lights formed the New York Synod, which was composed of "twenty-two ministers, with the leadership shared between the Log College men and the Yale graduates... members were generally young men, enthusiastically devoted to the revival, which they regarded as a blessed work of God."[210] The Philadelphia Synod, on the other hand, was "composed of ministers trained in the European universities, who had entered the ministry without experiencing any spiritual crisis in their own lives, and were not concerned in furthering revivalistic religion."[211] These clergy of the Philadelphia Synod were to become the "Old Lights" who became more and more immersed in European rationalism and would later become known as the 'latitudinarians.'"[212]

Laying the Groundwork for Freedom

Harvard professor Alan Heimert writes in his essay "Toward a Republic" [213] that the Great Awakening was in some ways an early Declaration of Independence from Europe. It had produced a uniquely American religious experience, which had broken away from the influence of European rationalism and philosophies. Instead of being dry and lifeless, as many thought the churches of New England had become, the Awakening emphasized the potency of the spoken word. Sweet describes this contrast:

> The novelty of Whitefield's extemporaneous preaching; his impassioned utterances; his marvelous voice and vivid dramatic power must have been a welcome relief to people accustomed to sermons read from closely written manuscripts held in the hand of the preacher, and upon themes as dreary as the droning voice in which they were uttered. It is easily understood why the crowds paid him such extravagant honor, for he "substituted human interest stories for logic and gave churchgoing America its first taste of the theatre under the flag of salvation.[214]

Although most "tended to agree with Ben Franklin that 'Modern Political Oratory' was chiefly, and most properly, 'performed by the Pen and Press,'"[215] evangelicalism "can be said to have inaugurated a new era in the history of American public address."[216] According to J.M. Bumsted, this new experience with gathering to hear a speaker was a natural aspect of colonialism brought about by revivalism. He says when "Bostonians gathered on the Boston Common in 1773 to listen to an oration 'on the Beauties of Liberty,' the mass meeting they attended was a form that was made respectable by George Whitefield in 1740."[217]

Even the complex arguments over the Great Awakening that were printed in newspapers and pamphlets laid the groundwork for the complex arguments over revolution. J. M. Bumstead says that "it was the revival which had first involved colonial Americans on a grand scale in confrontational politics, sloganeering, and ideological name-calling and labelling. The Great Awakening produced a general political polarization in matters of intellectual principle. Its great debates prefigured the great debates over the meaning of Empire."[218]

Unifying the People

Another impact of the Great Awakening on American life was its impact on national unity. Dr. Edwin Gaustad, a leading authority on the history of American religion, describes the lack of unity in America:

> Communication among the colonies was infrequent if not totally absent, transportation on north-south roads was agonizingly slow, so much so that journeys down river were infinitely to be preferred to any other mode of travel.... No coastal canals, few port roads, no common newspaper, no common assembly, no free trade, no common faith, no common loyalty, and for a significant minority not even a common heritage or a common language. What could bind this scattered, fractured, two million souls into a national community, into a social whole.[219]

Gaustad says that "economic grievances, political deprivations, and ideological assertions" played a part, but he believes that the revival played a great part in developing the sense of community needed to wage a war and win. He says that "the wave of religious enthusiasm known as the Great Awakening transcended denominational barriers, ignored colonial boundaries, melted divisions between rich and poor, male and female, black and white."[220] It brought people out of their homes, businesses, farms, and studies "to hear and rejoice in a gospel open to all."[221]

In the 1740s and 1750s, says Gaustad, nearly everyone came, thus finding themselves "part of a larger community, larger, closer than any they'd previously known in America."²²² Consequently, the Great Awakening with her itinerant circuit preachers was one of the nation's first unifying forces, causing an organic unity that heretofore was nonexistent.

Christianity or Enlightened Rationalism?

Although many modern day conservatives say that America is a "Christian nation," pointing to quotes from the Founding Fathers to prove their point, and liberals point to secularism as being truer to the Founders' ideology, the truth is that both viewpoints existed during the formative years of pre-colonial America. What may not be understood is that the beliefs of revivalist evangelical Christianity produced some of the same political principles as those of Enlightenment rationalism.

This alignment of ideals (a type of "alignment of the planets" if you will) helped to produce a revolution whose political leaders could write eloquently from a somewhat secular perspective and yet align perfectly with the newly formed religious ideals formed by the Great Awakening. It took both perspectives to produce the fervor that would be needed for the American Revolution to occur. The Founders provided the intellectual wisdom that was needed to form a government, borrowing ideas from Montesquieu and Locke, while evangelicals got their wisdom from the scriptural imperatives, which were more accessible to the common man and produced a passion and commitment that was needed by the masses to do the sacrificial work of fighting a war.

For example, two key Enlightenment principles were the dignity of the individual and the right to individual liberty or freedom. To promote these principles to evangelicals was in a sense "preaching to the choir." They could easily find a home in the churches of the Great Awakening. Because revival preachers emphasized the Reformation principle of "the priesthood of the believer," that is, the ability of the *individual* to gain access to God without the clergy, evangelicals had already begun to believe in the dignity and worth of the individual. So when the Founders spoke of "natural rights" being given to the individual, the evangelical could wholeheartedly concur. When Thomas Jefferson, a deist, wrote of men being equal and endowed by their Creator with certain inalienable rights (life, liberty, and the pursuit of happiness) the evangelical could easily receive this language. They believed in a Creator and were grateful for the protection of life (in contrast to being burnt at the stake for holding alternative religious viewpoints) and liberty, which to them implied religious freedom in particular.

Religious freedom and toleration were important principles to Enlightenment thinkers such as John Locke and Thomas Paine who wrote that it is the "indispensable duty of all government, to protect all conscientious professors thereof" and that he "fully and conscientiously believe[s], that it is the will of the Almighty, that there should be diversity of religious opinions among us."[223] For evangelicals, many who had "converted" and come out of Puritanism, this wouldn't have been an alien concept. In fact, since most colonies, other than Pennsylvania and Rhode Island, had some form of church establishment, numerous battles were fought over religious control.

One of the greatest battles occurred when Massachusetts attempted to collect taxes (tithes) for its Congregational Churches from Baptist and Separatist Churches. The movement for tax (or tithe) exemption was led by Isaac Backus, a Middleborough Baptist pastor. He wrote two works on religious tolerance: "Appeal to the Public for Religious Liberty Against the Oppressions of the Present Day" (1775) and "History of New England with Particular Reference to the Denomination Called Baptists." According to Bumstead:

> The "History" was a careful indictment of the religious persecutions of the Puritans and made a hero out of Roger Williams. The writings of Backus were a constant source of dismay to New England's revolutionary leaders [those "Old Light" Christians who were promoting the revolution based on their rationalistic beliefs], for the Baptist leader insisted on gaining the same rights and liberties for his denomination others were demanding from England. In 1744 Backus went to the Continental Congress to plead for religious liberty in New England—to the delight of the opponents of the rebellion and the embarrassment of Puritan revolutionaries like Sam and John Adams.[224]

In Virginia a similar campaign for religious toleration was led by Sam Davies, making religious toleration not only an Enlightenment principle, but a rallying cry for evangelicals, too.

The beliefs of evangelicals and Enlightenment thinkers aligned again when it came to Montesquieu's concept of "checks and balances." Because evangelicals believed in the theological principle of "original sin" or the corrupt condition of human nature, they could easily embrace the thought that it was necessary for government to have a system of accountability that would hold corrupt human authority in check.

Also, when Thomas Paine wrote in "Common Sense" about his opposition to monarchies and the necessity of separating from England, he quoted 1 Samuel where God was upset with Israel for wanting a king. This was the language of the evangelical. The Enlightenment belief that "natural" freedom was more orderly for society than hierarchical structure would have been agreeable to the evangelical simply because of this principle found in 2 Samuel, that God would rather have his people trust in and be led by him than by an earthly king. Even though Paine says his ideas were based on common sense and reason, the revivalist evangelical could embrace them based on scriptural truth and personal experience.

Another place where the Enlightenment thinkers and the evangelical aligned in their thought was in their anticlerical attitude. Voltaire and Locke, who railed against the established Catholic Church of Europe because of the corruption and hypocrisy of its clergy and promoted religious toleration in their writings, were easily understood by the rebels of the Great Awakening. They believed that the established churches of America had lost their life and were leading people astray. They didn't trust the clergy and believed they were more interested in maintaining power and control than in caring for the people. The evangelical understood that anticlericalism didn't mean anti-God; it just meant that they didn't want to subject themselves to what they believed were hypocritical religious leaders—and they didn't have to anymore because they could get to God individually, without clergy.

This anticlerical attitude also led to a democratization in religion. Because of the Great Awakening, people could believe individually before God, which put all humans on level ground. Hierarchy in religion was no longer necessary. All were created equal! This belief naturally led to a democratization in politics. If all were equal before God, aristocratic systems of government were no longer legitimate. So when Locke said that there shouldn't be "government without the consent of the governed," the evangelical who was now equal in his eyes with both the clergy and the aristocracy could wholeheartedly agree.

A Special Mission for America

As said before, the other belief that was promoted by Thomas Paine in "Common Sense" was that of a special mission for America. This cause was sensed from the earliest days of the colonies. For example, John Winthrop, leader of the Massachusetts Bay Colony said in 1630: "Wee must Consider that wee shall be as a Citty upon a Hill, the eies of all people are uppon us; soe that if wee shall deale falsely with our god in this worke wee have undertaken and soe cause him to withdraw his present help from us, wee shall be made a story and a by-word through the world."[225]

Jonathan Edwards agreed with this idea of a special mission, also. He wrote that "this new world... was probably discovered that God might in it begin a new world in a spiritual respect, when he creates the new heavens and the new earth."[226]

All of our religious and philosophical traditions aligned in the belief that America had a special mission from God. It's difficult to understand American politics without understanding this long held religious tradition. America was to be a "light to the nations." Deist, Puritan, or evangelical, all Americans "came to believe that the new nation came into being for 'the illumination of the ignorant and the emancipation of the slavish part of mankind over the earth.' America would be the new chosen people, the promised land."[227]

As a result, almost all American wars had a missionary aspect, not as crusades to conquer, but as battles over vital, fundamental concepts—to take on the role of guardian of the free world. From the wars fought against slavery, fascism, communism, and now terrorism, American commitment to this belief is so strong that we've repeatedly offered to die for it.

Populism

Although Great Awakening evangelicals were committed to certain causes in the political arena, they were mostly concerned with religion. The only time they would become active in the political world was when they saw humanitarian abuses or oppression. The great social reforms of the nineteenth century, such as concern for the poor, abolishing slavery, women's suffrage, and child labor laws would be directly connected to evangelicals such as Charles Finney and William Booth of the Salvation Army. The result of this was a type of "populism" (the rejection of hard politics), a desire to be active only on certain issues of moral concern. According to Heimert, populism was assumed to be a child of the Age of Reason, but it was really a child of the "New Light" Awakenings.

Liberal clergy "Old Lights" like Jonathan Mayhew used "pulpit politics" to promote the Revolution while the itinerant revivalist preacher only preached religion from the pulpit, but the attitudes planted in the hearts of people by the "Awakening" doctrines contributed to and advanced revolutionary principles in the common man, making him prepared to be the foot soldier needed to fight for freedom.

Calvinist "Election" Cast Aside

The equivocation of revival with rebellion (against the corrupt established church) and the consequential blessings that many experienced led to an attitude that rebellion was acceptable. Unlike Calvinistic "election," men were no longer "pre-determined" in their lot in life. They could choose their destiny. If this was true for individuals, then why not for nations? The Great Awakening's emphasis on "choosing" to receive Christ had an impact on attitudes toward national destiny. If a man could choose to be free from the tyrannical power of Satan, couldn't nations choose to be free from the tyrannical power of a corrupt king?

The Great Awakening and its leaders may not have been a political movement, but its political implications were undeniable. Its emphasis on individualism and anti-authoritarianism shook the established religious communities of New England, crushing their power and leading to religious freedom. The moral fervor produced by the Great Awakening would impact many humanitarian causes in the future and would inspire many to give their lives for what they considered to be the cause of freedom. This fervor has continued for many generations and is felt even today as the "battle for the hearts and minds" of the Iraqi people is fought—that America has a special mission in the world for the cause of freedom.

The French Revolution

It needs to be pointed out that another revolution of freedom, inspired by the Enlightenment thinkers, was going on at the same time in France. But this revolution would be characterized by mobs and a guillotine. Why was this? What was the difference? Why did one revolution succeed and one fail when they were both inspired by the same ideas? And why, if Enlightenment deism was so profound, does it no longer exist as a force to be reckoned with?

One way in which those on the Narrow Way differed with those philosophes of the French Revolution was in the Scriptural understanding of the nature of man. Diderot and the Encyclopedists believed in the "alluring doctrine that the primitive state of man was one of virtue and happiness" and this state of happiness could only be corrupted by the presence of "priests, kings, lawyers, and the like,"[228] while the Christian view of human nature is that man is a fallen creature and capable of abject wickedness. Therefore freedom without the cords of faith leads to depravity in one form or another. The Founders decided to align themselves with Montesquieu's insistence on the necessity of checks and balances to hold corrupt human nature accountable, rather than with Diderot's belief in man's goodness.

This Christian perspective on human nature was to be proven true again during the Reign of Terror. The sweeping away of the *ancien regime* (the Catholic Church and the royal monarchy) in France, as Edmund Burke forewarned, without anything to replace it, could only lead to anarchy. As Jesus said, "When an evil spirit comes out of a man, it goes through arid places seeking rest and does not find it. Then it says, 'I will return to the house I left.' When it arrives, it finds the house swept clean and put in order. Then it goes and takes seven other spirits more wicked than itself, and they go in and live there. And the final condition of that man is worse than the first (Luke 11:24-26)." H.G. Wells would sum up the condition of France in similar terms, saying that Locke and Montesquieu deserve "credit for clearing away many of the false ideas that had hitherto prevented deliberate and conscious attempts to reconstruct human society. It was not [their] fault if at first some extremely unsound and impertinent shanties were run up on the vacant site."[229]

Enlightenment freedom to the French meant freedom from God and his laws. The Jacobins would get rid of the seven-day work week and replace it with a ten-day one. They would throw off the bonds of sexual propriety, making divorce as easy as marriage and not allowing any difference between legitimate and illegitimate children. They would also change the names of the months, turn the Royal Palace into Equality Palace, and set up a holiday for "Lady Reason."

Because the French population had only been subjected to the "fat shepherds" of monarchy and priesthood, they were unprepared to handle the responsibility of freedom. Therefore they would submit themselves to Robespierre who was "inspired by a new order of human life."[230] After all, as Hobbes would argue in his *Leviathan*, order is always preferable to chaos. So, Wells tells us, Robespierre began to "construct." Part of constructing that "new order" would include chopping off the heads of anyone who disagreed.

Contrast this revolution with the American Revolution. In America, the Great Awakening had "filled their houses with good things" (Job 22:18). The population had a proper view of freedom. They understood the biblical foundation for democracy and equality. Their anti-clerical attitude wasn't birthed out of bitterness and rebellion, leading to mob justice against clergy and royalty, but their attitude was birthed out of an understanding that their individual rights were the result of the doctrine of the priesthood of the believer. They would protect and defend these rights, not with animal ferocity, but with reason and calmness, because, as the little farmer Nathan who accepted Whitefield's gospel message, the grace of God had filled their hearts with love.

The established New England churches would not have been able to create this fervor in the hearts of so many people. While fighting for their own religious freedom against the Church of England, they were still unable to see that they didn't offer the same freedom to others. These were the same Puritanical communities that had produced the witch trials. They were so wrapped up in their own religious importance, believing that they had a special calling in the New World to construct "a city on a hill," (their Eden) and that that made them a special target for attacks from the devil, that they neglected justice and compassion. They were deluded and became poison. They wouldn't accept the message of grace brought by the revival preachers. Whitefield was even forced to preach on a box in the city square or in a cornfield in their communities. Religion always hates and persecutes the bearers of Life and grace.

But the message of grace was preached throughout the thirteen colonies. It was received with open arms by the common people, and as a result it produced Life. Alexis DeTocqueville, the political philosopher, wanted to understand why America was succeeding. What made her so great? He traveled from city to city and town to town, talking to people and trying to understand. He went to her schools, to governmental meetings, businesses, and could find nothing unique about them. But then he visited her churches, "aflame with righteousness," and returned to France with this summary:

> There is no country in the whole world in which the Christian religion retains a greater influence over the souls of men than in America; and there can be no greater proof of its utility, and of its conformity to human nature, than that its influence is most powerfully felt over the most enlightened and free nation of the earth.... The Americans combine the notions of Christianity and of liberty so intimately in their minds, that it is impossible to make them conceive the one without the other.[231]

Christians would even spread their faith within the United States in order to ensure the continuation of liberty. De Tocqueville explains further:

> I have known of societies formed by the Americans to send out ministers of the Gospel into the new Western States to found schools and churches there, lest religion should be suffered to die away in those remote settlements, and the rising States be less fitted to enjoy free institutions than the people from which they emanated.[232]

He also noted the difference between the French and American revolutions:

> In France I had almost always seen the spirit of religion and the spirit of freedom pursuing courses diametrically opposed to each other; but in America I found that they were intimately united, and that they reigned in common over the same country.[233]

The gospel message isn't a danger to a nation; it's a blessing.

Deism died out because Darwin and Kant "proved" that it was unnecessary to have a "first cause," so it was no longer on the cutting edge, scientifically speaking; and because of the failure of the French Revolution, it was also thought to be a political disappointment. It was a religion that was merely formed by certain men who molded it to fit the culture of their time. Since it rejected parts of the Word, it would pass away in time, only to be added to the other failed ideals of history. But (just as in Calvinism) the part of it that lived on is the part that aligned with the Scriptures and is lived out by those on the Narrow Way.

For modern day skeptics to try to pervert and twist this part of America's heritage is a cheap shot. It's actually an injustice and a form of revisionist history. As it turns out, those who are the most reasonable, rational, and capable of handling liberty are the same people the skeptics would like to shut out and shut up for the *sake* of reason, rationality, and liberty.

It could be argued that both France and America were religious attempts to restore paradise. But the difference is that France did it her own way, while America tried to do it God's way. America followed the Narrow Way—the way of grace and love… and it's the closest the world has ever come to paradise. Even now millions flock to her shores in search of the freedom and prosperity that she has to offer.

Just as Nero falsely accused Christians of setting Rome on fire, there's another all-out attack to paint Christians as though they are the enemy of liberty. They are often portrayed as right-wing fascists, but the truth is that those on the Narrow Way, who trusted in the Word, blessed the world and stood on the right side of history again. Just like Jesus said, they are the salt and the light. They preserve society. They light the pathway of goodness. And wherever they are, a little bit of Eden is restored.

CHAPTER EIGHT
The Narrow Way Abolishes Slavery

"Ah me, what wish can prosper, or what prayer
For merchants rich in cargoes of despair!
Who drive a loathsome traffic, gauge and span,
And buy the muscles and the bones of man." —William Cowper

"There is a fountain filled with blood drawn from Immanuel's veins,
And sinners plunged beneath the flood lose all their guilty stains."
—William Cowper

Those on the Narrow Way had already abolished slavery once before in the Roman Empire. They did it without even firing a shot or leading a rebellion. It was accomplished through sheer moral force brought about by the words and teachings of Jesus and the apostles. But as the Word became buried in tradition and blended in with worldly philosophy, it began to lose its power. The world became a dark, superstitious place where the Scriptures were obscured and all pursuit of truth was subject to the priesthood. On the other hand, the restoration of those Words as a result of the work of Wycliffe, Luther, Erasmus, Tyndale, and others brought forth light, life, and freedom. Advances in knowledge, science, and human rights can be directly associated with the spread of the Gospel. The success of the American experiment can be attributed to those on the Narrow Way, and contrary to what many skeptics say, the abolition of slavery can also be directly associated with the work of Christians who were on the Narrow Way.

THE NARROW WAY

There's no doubt that parts of Christianity failed regarding Southern slavery, but there's also no doubt that slavery was eliminated primarily through the efforts of committed believers. Christianity has always been at war with itself. Jesus warned us that the wheat would grow up with the tares. We have to remember that *not all Christianity is true Christianity!* Let me say again, true Christianity is characterized by grace and love. When we receive God's grace, the way is opened for his Spirit to come to us and produce his love. Those who insist on turning Christianity into a religion with rituals and man-made laws, and who revert to the Old Testament Law as a source for doctrine, rather than understanding that it was a type and shadow that pointed us to Jesus, will only develop a false, poisonous, religious Christianity.

The Southern slaveholder proclaimed Christ, but then he also blended it in with Old Testament teachings,[234] forgetting that the new wine must be poured into new wineskins and the ax has been put to the root of the old tree. That old religious system was merely a vehicle to point us to Christ! We're under a new covenant now and mustn't go back and forth between the old and new.

As I hope to show in this chapter, neither deism, atheism, science, reason, nor poisonous religion could reveal the right way to go during this challenging time. All of these paths failed when there was need for a great moral force. Only the Word of God, correctly divided, can lead us to the right way. Only the Word is "a lamp to my feet and a light for my path" (Psalm 119:105).

Since wrong doctrine is the source of much evil, the abolitionists got out the Word of God, (also known as the Sword of the Spirit), and began brandishing it in an attempt to restore right doctrine. As early as 1675, author after author began writing attacks on the institution of slavery. Samuel Sewall, author of the tract *The Selling of Joseph*,[235] was one of the first, but he would be joined by many other Christian writers, including Thomas Clarkson (*Thoughts*), David Lee Child (*Despotism of Freedom*), Charles Stuart (*West India Question*), George Stroud (*Laws Relating to Slavery*), John Rankin (*Letters*),[236] Lydia Marie Child (*Appeal*), John Paxton (*Letters*), Benjamin Lundy (*Genius of Universal Emancipation*), and many, many more.

Just as the church had gone astray during the Dark Ages, and it had taken those on the Narrow Way to battle the wrong teachings and restore the Truth, the church had gone astray concerning slavery. Unfortunately, just as the Protestant/Catholic division resulted in the Thirty Years War, the American Civil

THE NARROW WAY ABOLISHES SLAVERY

War would be a result of the church's split over slavery. Methodist against Methodist, Baptist against Baptist, Presbyterian against Presbyterian. There was no consensus. The church was divided.[237] Stephen S. Foster, a pioneer in the antislavery movement, would criticize this division in the church in his book *The Brotherhood of Thieves: or, A True Picture of the American Church and Clergy*. He had spoken out at a Methodist Episcopal Church convention and accused the attendees—clergy and congregants—of supporting slavery, something he felt it was his duty to expose and hold them accountable for:

> The remarks which I made at your Convention were of a most grave and startling character. They strike at the very foundation of all our ecclesiastical institutions, and exhibit them to the world as the apologists and supporters of the most atrocious system of oppression and wrong, beneath which humanity has ever groaned. They reflect on the church the deepest possible odium, by disclosing to public view the chains and handcuffs, the whips and branding-irons, the rifles and bloodhounds, with which her ministers and deacons bind the limbs and lacerate the flesh of innocent men and defenceless women.[238]

Foster wasn't a skeptic. He insisted: "I am a firm believer in the Christian religion, and in Jesus, as a divine being, who is to be our final Judge. I was born and nurtured in the bosom of the church, and for twelve years was among its most active members." He even studied for the ministry at Union Theological Seminary[239] (after graduating from Dartmouth) but then felt it necessary to renounce "the priesthood and an organized church," and said he left them because of "an unresistable conviction, in spite of my early prejudices, that they are a 'hold of every foul spirit,' and the devices of men to gain influence and power."[240]

Foster was on the Narrow Way. He trusted in Jesus and lived a life of love for others. And he opposed poisonous religion. Just as others in the past had experienced, his efforts to speak out against the corruption in the church were met by violent mobs. To this he responded:

> If our clergy and church were the ministers of Christ, would their reputation be defended by drunken and murderous mobs? Are brickbats and rotten eggs the weapons of truth and Christianity? Did

Jesus say to his disciples, "Blessed are ye when the *mob* shall speak well of you, and shall defend you? The church, slavery, and the mob are a queer trinity! And yet that they are a trinity—that they all "agree in one"—cannot be denied. Every assault which we have made on the bloody slave system, as I shall hereafter show, has been promptly met and repelled by the church, which is herself the claimant of several hundred thousand slaves; and whenever we have attempted to expose the guilt and hypocrisy of the church, the mob has uniformly been first and foremost in her defence.[241]

William Lloyd Garrison

The greatest of all American abolitionists was William Lloyd Garrison, and he had a similar problem with irrational responses to his efforts. Unknown to Garrison, "fearing that he might be waylaid by enemies," as he walked three miles home each night, "negroes sought to protect Garrison from bodily harm" by following behind him, "armed with cudgels."[242] Perhaps they were willing to watch over him because he spoke so humbly and kindly to them. In an address to "the oppressed" he delivered these words:

> I never rise to address a colored audience, without feeling ashamed of my own color; ashamed of being identified with a race of men, who have done you so much injustice, and who yet retain so large a portion of your brethren in servile chains. To make atonement, in part, for this conduct, I have solemnly dedicated my health, and strength, and life, to your service. I love to plan and to work for your social, intellectual, and spiritual advancement. My happiness is augmented with yours; in your sufferings I participate.[243]

Garrison then went on to say that he was not a follower of any man—not Luther, not Calvin, nor "His Holiness the Pope." He says his only "discharge; as a lover of my fellow-man, I ought not to shun; as a lover of Jesus Christ, and of his equalizing, republican and benevolent precepts, I rejoice to perform."[244] Garrison loved God, trusted in Jesus, and loved his neighbor. He understood that Christianity didn't consist in church attendance or rituals, it consisted in identifying with the "least of these" and caring for them. Garrison went on and tried to encourage those at the meeting by announcing good news from England:

Why should this not be an occasion of joy, instead of sorrow? Listen to those trumpet tones which come swelling on the winds of the Atlantic, and which shall bring an echo from every harp in heaven! If there is joy in that blissful abode over one sinner that repenteth, how mighty and thrilling must it be over a repentant nation! Her people are humbling themselves before God, and before those whom they have so long held in bondage. Their voices are breaking, in peals of thunder, upon the ear of Parliament, demanding the immediate and utter overthrow of slavery in all the colonies; and in obedience to their will, the mandate is about being issued by Parliament, which shall sever at a blow the chains of eight hundred thousand slaves! What heart can conceive, what pen or tongue describe, the happiness which must flow from the consummation of this act?

Garrison was referring to the abolition of slavery in the British Empire, an act that was accomplished as a result of the untiring efforts of William Wilberforce.

William Wilberforce

William Wilberforce is buried in Westminster Abbey and is considered to be a national hero for his efforts to get rid of slavery in the British Empire. Influenced by the revival preacher George Whitefield, whom he met as a child, and John Newton, the former slave trader who repented and penned the words to the song, "Amazing Grace," Wilberforce would be a man of faith… but not of religion. He recognized the damage that religion had caused and wanted to differentiate true faith in God through trusting in Jesus, from religion that takes the form of ritual and produces abusive behavior. Answering the accusing skeptic, he would explain:

> Have not these doctrines been ever perverted to purposes the most disgraceful to the religion of Jesus? If you want an instance, look to the standard of the inquisition, and behold the pious Dominicans torturing their miserable victims for the love of Christ. Or would you rather see the effects of your principles on a larger scale, and by wholesale, if the phrase may be pardoned, cast your eyes across the Atlantic, and let your zeal be edified by the holy activity of Cortez and Pizarro, and their apostles of the western hemisphere? To what

else have been owing the extensive ravages of national persecutions, and religious wars and crusades, whereby rapacity, and pride, and cruelty, sheltering themselves under the mask of this specious principle, have so often afflicted the world? The Prince of Peace has been made to assume the port of a ferocious conqueror, and, forgetting the message of good will to men, has issued forth, like a second Scourge of the Earth, to plague and desolate the human species. That the sacred name of Religion, has been too often prostituted to the most detestable of purposes; that furious bigots and bloody persecutors, and self-interested hypocrites, of all qualities and dimensions, from the rapacious leader of an army, to the canting oracle of a congregation, have falsely called themselves Christians, are melancholy and humiliating truths, which (as none can so deeply lament them) none will more readily admit than those who best understand the nature of Christianity, and are most concerned for her honor.[245]

Wilberforce would admit that religion can be poisonous, yet he still embraced Jesus with "affection," saying that each person should:

[S]olemnly ask ourselves, whether we have fled for refuge to our appointed hope? And whether we are only looking to it as the only source of consolation? Other foundation no man can lay: there is no other ground for dependence, no other plea for pardon; but here there is hope, even to the uttermost. Let us labor then to affect our hearts with a deep conviction of our need of a Redeemer, and of the value of his offered mediation. Let us fall down humbly before the throne of God, imploring pity and pardon in the name of the Son of his love. Let us beseech him to give us a true spirit of repentance, and of hearty undivided faith in the Lord Jesus.[246]

Wilberforce was on the Narrow Way of grace and love. He found rest in the blood of the Lamb; he didn't rely on self-effort, and it produced a life of great love. Wilberforce faced scathing humiliation and scorn as he presented resolution after resolution in Parliament, but he persevered, and working with members of the Clapham Sect (evangelical members of the Anglican Church who had been influenced by the Great Awakening) in 1807 the Slave Trade Act was passed, which outlawed slave trading in the Empire. And in 1833, the Slavery Abolition Act would be passed, which completely abolished slavery in the British Empire. It was this momentous occasion that William Lloyd Garrison was referring to when he was trying to encourage his black listeners.

Wilberforce also worked for animal rights, education for poor children, improvement of working conditions, prison reform, and the spread of Christianity to India, where he supported those who worked to overcome the Hindu practices of infanticide, widow burning (suttee), the caste system, and polygamy. He was also very generous with his wealth, giving away money to the poor, getting people out of debt, and always being hospitable. Wilberforce's faith produced the fruit of love.

Enlightenment Thought Inadequate

It was this great love, for his God and for his neighbor, which enabled Wilberforce to work for the abolition of slavery with a single-minded surety of purpose that blazed in his heart. All other belief systems were inadequate for this purpose. For example, deists weren't able to abolish slavery because of their belief that God was the grand watchmaker in the sky, who wound up the clock and then let it go without interference. He was Newton's "First Cause," the Great Designer, but he didn't interject himself into the affairs of men. Therefore, the deist could only believe that slavery would gradually be abolished over time.

For example, Thomas Jefferson opposed slavery, even though he had slaves. He thought it was wrong to let his slaves go, though, because they were unprepared to care for themselves and were like children. Therefore, the only solution to the slavery problem was to provide for them and wait for a gradual emancipation that would be accomplished through the "march of time":

> My opinion has ever been that until more can be done for them, we should endeavor with those whom fortune has thrown on our hands to feed and clothe them well, protect them from all ill usage, require such reasonable labor only as is performed voluntarily by freemen, and be led by no repugnancies to abdicate them and our duties to them.[247]

There are debates over whether Jefferson failed to take a stronger stand against slavery because he was a politician who feared losing re-election, whether he believed a strong stance would lead to war, or whether he was concerned that any bold actions he took would hinder slavery from finally being conquered in a rational, orderly way. There are many debates on what his views were, but one aspect of Jefferson's views that isn't as well known is his attitude toward race. Jefferson desired to be on the cutting edge of scientific knowledge, and one popular theory of the early nineteenth century was known as "scientific racism."

Jefferson was an Enlightenment scholar who was eager to learn more about chemistry, astronomy, geology, and natural history. He was a great collector of seeds, plants, and specimens of animals and birds. His *Notes on Virginia* included observations on mountains, rivers, plants, and animals. He also included observations on the "aborigines" (the Native Americans) and on the black race. Unfortunately, Jefferson's willingness to abandon parts of the Word and follow the man-made religious formulation of deism would allow him to slide into a belief system we now look upon as bankrupt and immoral.

Jefferson thought that blacks were inferior to whites because of the way they looked and smelled, and mentioned that they had no ability to plan or give forethought to their actions, were easily aroused sexually, and had no reasoning skills. All of this was described in scientific language (reticular membrane, symmetry, transpiration, secretion, pulmonary apparatus, principal regulator, etc.):

> To these objections, which are political, may be added others, which are physical and moral. The first difference which strikes us is that of colour. Whether the black of the negro resides in the reticular membrane between the skin and scarf-skin, or in the scarf-skin itself; whether it proceeds from the colour of the blood, the colour of the bile, or from that of some other secretion, the difference is fixed in nature, and is as real as if its seat and cause were better known to us. And is this difference of no importance? Is it not the foundation of a greater or less share of beauty in the two races? Are not the fine mixtures of red and white, the expressions of every passion by greater or less suffusions of colour in the one, preferable to that eternal monotony, which reigns in the countenances, that immoveable veil of black which covers all the emotions of the other race? Add to these, flowing hair, a more elegant symmetry of form, their own judgment in favour of the whites, declared by their preference of them, as uniformly as is the preference

of the Orangutan for the black women over those of his own species. The circumstance of superior beauty, is thought worthy attention in the propagation of our horses, dogs, and other domestic animals; why not in that of man? Besides those of colour, figure, and hair, there are other physical distinctions proving a difference of race. They have less hair on the face and body. They secrete less by the kidneys, and more by the glands of the skin, which gives them a very strong and disagreeable odour. This greater degree of transpiration renders them more tolerant of heat, and less so of cold, than the whites. Perhaps too a difference of structure in the pulmonary apparatus, which a late ingenious experimentalist has discovered to be the principal regulator of animal heat, may have disabled them from extricating, in the act of inspiration, so much of that fluid from the outer air, or obliged them in expiration, to part with more of it. They seem to require less sleep. A black, after hard labour through the day, will be induced by the slightest amusements to sit up till midnight, or later, though knowing he must be out with the first dawn of the morning. They are at least as brave, and more adventuresome. But this may perhaps proceed from a want of forethought, which prevents their seeing a danger till it be present. When present, they do not go through it with more coolness or steadiness than the whites. They are more ardent after their female: but love seems with them to be more an eager desire, than a tender delicate mixture of sentiment and sensation. Their griefs are transient. Those numberless afflictions, which render it doubtful whether heaven has given life to us in mercy or in wrath, are less felt, and sooner forgotten with them. In general, their existence appears to participate more of sensation than reflection. To this must be ascribed their disposition to sleep when abstracted from their diversions, and unemployed in labour. An animal whose body is at rest, and who does not reflect, must be disposed to sleep of course. Comparing them by their faculties of memory, reason, and imagination, it appears to me, that in memory they are equal to the whites; in reason much inferior, as I think one could scarcely be found capable of tracing and comprehending the investigations of Euclid; and that in imagination they are dull, tasteless, and anomalous.[248]

Jefferson was a scientific racist. He believed the blacks were inferior merely because of the color of their skin. While this may seem archaic to us, Jefferson thought that he was merely using empirical methodology, and scientific observation. He was joined by a chorus of Enlightened persons.

While the Scientific Revolution was initially caused by Christians who were trying to find evidence for the existence of God in nature, the rational scientist would attempt to wrestle science away from revelation. Since there was no need for the Scriptures as a source of truth, science was free! And one of its first contributions would be that of scientific racism. It was popular to subscribe to this belief, and many of the greatest Enlightenment thinkers gave their assent to its contents. For example, David Hume rejected faith and relied only on reason for his knowledge, ascribing a lofty role to the purposes of science: "The sweetest and most inoffensive path of life leads through the avenues of science and learning; and whoever can either remove any obstruction in this way, or open up any new prospect, ought, so far, to be esteemed a benefactor to mankind."[249]

Yet, Hume, unwilling to submit to any standard of Truth, used his "science and learning" to conclude:

> I am apt to suspect the Negroes, and in general all other species of men to be naturally inferior to the whites. There never was any civilized nation of any other complection than white, nor even any individual eminent in action or speculation. No ingenious manufactures among them, no arts, no sciences… such a uniform and constant difference could not happen, in so many countries and ages, if nature had not made an original distinction between these breeds of men.[250]

And Immanuel Kant, who, in part, defined Enlightenment thought as simply the freedom to think for oneself, would make this scientific observation in agreement with Hume:

> The Negroes of Africa have received from nature no intelligence that rises above the foolish. Hume invites anyone to quote a single example of a Negro who has exhibited talents. He asserts that among the hundred thousands of blacks who have been seduced away from their own countries, although very many of them have been set free,

yet not a single one has ever been found that has performed anything great whether in art or science or in any other laudable subject; but among the whites, people constantly rise up from the lowest rabble and acquire esteem through their superior gifts. [251]

The Enlightenment emphasis on reason and science, rather than revelation, would be exemplified in the person of Voltaire and he had this to say about the black race:

> Their round eyes, their flat nose, their lips which are always thick, their differently shaped ears, the wool on their head, the measure even of their intelligence establishes between them and other species of men prodigious differences. If their understanding is not of a different nature from ours, it is at least greatly inferior. They are not capable of any great application of ideas, and seemed formed neither in the advantages nor the abuses of our philosophy.[252]

Thomas Jefferson was in a quandary over the issue of slavery and held many positions, unable to settle any of them with finality. His scientific beliefs led him to dabble in racism, and his deist beliefs led him to embrace gradual emancipation, yet there was a moral side to him that was plagued by the Christian position which led him to make this pronouncement: "Indeed I tremble for my country when I reflect that God is just." Not willing to make any final judgment on the issue, he merely maintained the status quo and continued owning slaves, not even letting them go at his death, as George Washington had done.

Science Inadequate

One of the major arguments of the abolitionists was that all races came from a single source, therefore they were all equal. This position is known as monogenism and is supported by Acts 17:26, which declares: "From one man he made every nation of men, that they should inhabit the whole earth." It's a New Testament confirmation of the Genesis story of Adam and Eve.

Evangelicals would find themselves battling the racism brought about by so-called scientific advances. In an attempt to defend the "aborigines" from the abuse of British colonizers, Christians set up the Aborigines Protection Society. William Howitt, a Quaker who wrote an expose called *Colonisation and Chris-*

tianity, lamented the treatment that the tribal peoples received under European colonization,[253] saying their previous cruelties hindered missionary work. His title page contains the words of the prophet Malachi: "Have we not all one father?—Hath not one God created us? Why do we deal treacherously one man against his brother? (2:10)" Out of this group, another organization known as the Ethnological Society of London would form for the express purpose of battling scientific racism. Their motto, "*ab uno sanguire*" (from one blood) would counter polygenistic theories on the origin of man.

Its members would include Thomas Hodgkin, Thomas Fowell Buxton (who would have a great influence on the African missionary, David Livingstone, and would carry on William Wilberforce's anti-slavery efforts), Joseph Lister (the founder of anti-septic surgery), Thomas Clarkson, Joseph Sturge, Henry Christy, and William Allen.

Together they would battle against the pseudo-science popularized by Samuel George Morton, a believer in phrenology,[254] and *president* of the National Academy of Science, who attempted to develop a racial theory based on the measurement of skull size. He collected skulls from around the world and, in his opinion, the skulls found near the Caucasus Mountains in the Near East were the most perfect. These were the skulls of white people, and Europeans would eventually get lumped together with the Caucasians, which led to the term "Caucasian" being used in reference to the white race. His *Crania Americana* would describe the black man in a way similar to other Enlightened persons:

> Characterized by a black complexion, and black, woolly hair; the eyes are large and prominent, the nose broad and flat, the lips thick, and the mouth wide; the head is long and narrow, the forehead low, the cheekbones prominent, the jaws protruding, and the chin small.[255]

Morton's disciples, George Gliddon and Josiah Nott, would write *Types of Mankind* (or *Ethnological Research*), which was used by Southern slaveholders as a scientific justification for slavery. And even Louis Aggasiz, the renowned glacial scientist and Harvard professor of natural history, would abandon the Word and become a follower of Morton's scientific racism, immersing a whole generation of students (who would later become professors) into Morton's racial theories.

Polygenism was a scientific theory that supposed that the ancestral lineages of the different races were separate, therefore making them unequal. Perhaps other races weren't completely human, but sub-human. Hence, much time was spent by the skeptical scientist and philosopher in contrasting the physical attributes and mental capabilities of various races with those of the white race.

In 1833, Richard H. Colfax would write a pamphlet, *Evidence Against the Views of the Abolitionists*, which would cite Jefferson, Voltaire, Gibbon, and others as asserting the polygenistic viewpoint that the black race was inferior. The *Charleston Medical Journal* published a debate between Dr. Morton, who held a polygenist view, and Rev. John Bachman, who held a monogenist view. The *Southern Presbyterian Review* held a monogenist view, while *De-Bow's Review* and *Southern Quarterly Review* held a polygenist view.

Frederick Douglass

Battling against this madness (which would eventually blossom into the full-fledged eugenic racism of Hitler) were the abolitionists. John Bird Sumner would argue against polygenism in *A Treatise on the Records of the Creation*, but would end up being ridiculed as an evangelical whose trust in the Scriptures made him blind to scientific facts. Frederick Douglass would also battle scientific racism and mockingly referred to Morton, Gliddon, Nott, and Aggasiz as a "phalanx of learned men."[256] In a speech given at Western Reserve College in 1854, entitled, "The Claims of the Negro Ethnologically Considered," Douglass would attempt to refute polygenism. He was a monogenist who asked that the truthfulness of a scientific theory be judged by its fruit, by what it produced in society and whether it brought glory to God:

> Which of these answers [yes or no to monogeny] is most in accordance with the facts, with reason, with the welfare of the world, and reflects most glory upon the wisdom, power, and goodness of the Author of all existence, is the question for consideration with us. On which side is the weight of the argument, rather than which side is absolutely proved. It must be admitted… that, viewed apart from the authority of the Bible, neither the unity nor diversity of origin of the human family, can be demonstrated. To use the terse expression of the Rev. Dr. Anderson [President of the University of Rochester]… "It is impossible to get far enough back for that." This much, however, can be done. The evidence on both sides, can be accurately weighed and the truth arrived at with almost absolute certainty.[257]

In other words, Frederick Douglass was using the wisdom of Jesus, who said "by their fruit you will recognize them." (Matt. 7:20). If polygenism was keeping blacks in the bondage of slavery, it couldn't be true.

Douglass would also demand that the United States live up to the language found in the Declaration of Independence which asserted that "all men are created equal," realizing fully that the latest scientific knowledge had allowed Jefferson and others to justify slavery by declaring that the African wasn't really a man but a sub-species.

Douglass would also struggle with Christian hypocrisy. Even though he was committed to Christ and, as so many other slaves, would find a message of freedom in the Bible, he would lash out at Christian hypocrisy:

All this prejudice sinks into insignificance in my mind, when compared with the enormous iniquity of the system which is its cause—the system that sold my four sisters and my brothers into bondage—and which calls in its priests to defend it even from the Bible! The slaveholding ministers preach up the divine right of the slaveholders to property in their fellow- men. The southern preachers say to the poor slave, "Oh! if you wish to be happy in time, happy in eternity, you must be obedient to your masters; their interest is yours. God made one portion of men to do the working, and another to do the thinking; how good God is! Now, you have no trouble or anxiety; but ah! you can't imagine how perplexing it is to your masters and mistresses to have so much thinking to do in your behalf! You cannot appreciate your blessings; you know not how happy a thing it is for you, that you were born of that portion of the human family which has the working, instead of the thinking to do! Oh! how grateful and obedient you ought to be to your masters! How beautiful are the arrangements of Providence! Look at your hard, horny hands—see how nicely they are adapted to the labor you have to perform! Look at our delicate fingers, so exactly fitted for our station, and see how manifest it is that God designed us to be his thinkers, and you the workers—Oh! the wisdom of God!"—I used to attend a Methodist church, in which my master was a class leader; he would talk most sanctimoniously about the dear Redeemer, who was sent "to preach deliverance to the captives, and set at liberty them that are bruised"—

he could pray at morning, pray at noon, and pray at night; yet he could lash up my poor cousin by his two thumbs, and inflict stripes and blows upon his bare back, till the blood streamed to the ground! all the time quoting scripture, for his authority, and appealing to that passage of the Holy Bible which says, "He that knoweth his master's will, and doeth it not, shall be beaten with many stripes!"[258] Such was the amount of this good Methodist's piety.[259]

Notice the scientific racism he encountered in his relationships with the slaveholders!

Thomas Paine

Hitchens points to the "freethinker"[260] Thomas Paine as one of the earliest persons to speak out against slavery. Paine was an Enlightenment philosopher and a deist (therefore he supported gradual emancipation, as he declared when he, as the Assembly clerk, wrote the "Pennsylvania Act for the Gradual Abolition of Slavery" in 1780), but his writings in opposition to slavery were based upon Scriptural admonitions. (Just as his call for revolution in "Common Sense" was based on the scripture that demeaned the Israelites for wanting a king.) In his pamphlet, written in 1775, entitled "American Slavery in America," he referred to God as being the Lord of *all* (a reference to Acts 17:26) and called on Americans to obey the admonition of Jesus to love our neighbor. He also said that there shouldn't be a return to Old Testament Law. Even though Paine would point to common sense and reason for much of his life, it was understood that the Bible didn't conflict with either and he used its Words liberally:

> Most shocking of all is edging the Sacred Scriptures to favour this wicked practice. One would have thought none but infidel cavillers would endeavour to make them appear contrary to the plain dictates of natural light, and the Conscience, in a matter of common Justice and Humanity; which they cannot be. Such worthy men, as referred to before, judged other ways; Mr. BAXTER declared, the Slave-Traders should be called Devils, rather than Christian; and that it is a heinous crime to buy them. But some say, the practice was permitted to the Jews. To which may be replied,

1. The example of the Jews, in many things, may not be imitated by us; they had not only orders to cut off several nations altogether, but if they were obliged to war with others, and conquered them, to cut off every male; they were suffered to use polygamy and divorces, and other things utterly unlawful to us under clearer light.

2. The plea is, in a great measure, false; they had no permission to catch and enslave people who never injured them.

3. Such arguments ill become us, since the time of Reformation came, under Gospel light. All distinctions of nations and privileges of one above others are ceased; Christians are taught to account all men their neighbours; and love their neighbours as themselves; and do to all men as they would be done by; to do good to all men; and Man-stealing is ranked with enormous crimes. Is the barbarous enslaving of inoffensive neighbours, and treating them like wild beasts subdued by force, reconcilable with the Divine precepts! Is this doing to them as we would desire they should do to us? If they could carry off and enslave some thousands of us, would we think it just? One would almost wish they could for once, it might convince more than Reason, or the Bible. As much in vain, perhaps, will they search ancient history for examples of the modern Slave-Trade. Too many nations enslaved the prisoners they took in war. But to go to nations with whom there is no war, who have no way provoked, without farther design of conquest, purely to catch inoffensive people, like wild beasts, for slaves, is an height of outrage against Humanity and Justice, that seems left by Heathen nations to be practised by pretended Christians. How shameful are all attempts to colour and excuse it! [261]

Therefore, even the "freethinker" Thomas Paine's anti-slavery position was birthed out his understanding of the will of God as revealed in the Scriptures, rather than from rational, Enlightened thought.

Reason Inadequate

Pulitzer Prize-winning author, Merle Curti, in his immense historical synthesis, *The Growth of American Thought*, explains that many arguments were put forward by the South in their justification of slavery. He says that "at least fourteen pro-slavery novels appeared shortly after *Uncle Tom's Cabin*, and each made use of one or more of the arguments from the Bible, from expediency, from ethnology, and from example."[262] A list of some of these reasons would include:

1. Slaves are better off than the Northern employees of the industrialist capitalists.
2. The Haitian uprising could happen here, therefore, we need to keep them under control.
3. The Southern climate necessitates using blacks.
4. Blacks are incapable of being educated. (This was part of the polygenist argument.)
5. Slavery existed in great civilizations of the past (especially Greece and Rome).
6. The slaves are not unhappy.
7. Until they are prepared for freedom, we need to care for them (George Fitzhugh's argument).
8. They're better off here than they were in Africa. At least here they can hear the Gospel.
9. Slavery is a "necessary evil."
10. The U.S. Constitution didn't outlaw slavery.
11. The overseas slave trade has been protected by the U.S. government for decades.
12. The "fugitive slave law" mandates that slaves be returned over state lines.
13. The "3/5 clause" of the Constitution agrees that blacks are sub-human.
14. Letting slaves go could mean the South would be ravaged by African savages.
15. The slave system domesticates and civilizes the black heathens.
16. The government is the one who enslaved the Africans, not individuals.
17. The laws of slaveholding states prohibit the liberation of slaves.
18. Some slaves have cruel masters, therefore its best to buy and hold them as a benevolent act.

Senator John C. Calhoun

Finally, Senator John C. Calhoun would develop an intricate argument that Curti said "represents a high level of analysis, reflection, and synthesis."

[It] borrowed from Jefferson the doctrine of states' rights and from the Federalists the concept of a balance of interests, rights, and powers. These he put together, along with a Hobbesian conception of human nature and, as he understood it, the Greek idea of a democracy of free citizens in which the degree of liberty any citizen enjoyed was related to his own competence. That the free citizens might devote themselves to the public well-being, they, like the ancient Athenians, were freed from physical toil by the slaves who in turn profited from the intelligent guardianship of masters stronger and wiser than they.[263]

Calhoun's attempt to use Enlightenment thought (which put a high value on freedom and equality) to justify slavery is not unlike the Southern attempt to use the Bible to justify slavery. It was a perversion of those ideals that were meant to give individuals dignity and set men free.

Science wasn't capable of producing the truth necessary to stand against evil, religion wasn't capable of standing against evil, and "reason" wasn't capable of standing against evil either, but those on the Narrow Way of grace and love were at the forefront of opposing the wicked institution of slavery.

The Second Great Awakening

It's probable that the popular support necessary for the abolition of slavery would have never developed if it hadn't been for Charles Finney and the Second Great Awakening. Although Calvinism and the Reformed tradition had a stronghold in New England, through the Great Awakenings, America would abandon the doctrine of predestination and embrace the doctrine of free will. Finney would only have contempt for the Calvinist clergy, saying they tangled "election, predestination, free-agency, inability, and duty in one promiscuous jumble," and confounded the sinner "with you can and you can't, you shall and you shan't, you will and you won't, you'll be damned if you do, and you'll be damned if you don't." While he was preparing for ordination he flatly refused to attend Princeton, telling his ministerial advisers that he had no desire to subject himself to such influences as had made them what they were. He deplored the "mouthing… lofty style of preaching" popular in his day, and talked in the pulpit "as the lawyer does when he wants to make a jury understand him perfectly… the language of common life."[264]

THE NARROW WAY ABOLISHES SLAVERY

Finney was not impressed with religious showmanship or theological bondage. Starting in the "burned over district" of upstate New York, the Second Great Awakening would spread across the United States, reaching into small villages, farmlands, forests, frontiers, and cities. Circuit riders would go from place to place preaching in tents and cornfields. As a result of the preaching of the gospel of grace, the United States would become an "evangelical empire."

The break away from Calvinism would change the entire conversion experience away from salvation due to the fear of hell, to salvation in order to live a new life of love, or "benevolence," as Finney called it. Believers were now called to live for the "interests of God's kingdom." Gilbert Hobbes Barnes, author of *The Anti-slavery Impulse: 1830-1844*, says that "among Finney's converts this gospel released a mighty impulse toward social reform."

Robert William Fogel, in his book, *Without Consent or Contract: The Rise and Fall of American Slavery*, explains the impact of Finney and his "holy band" on the abolition of slavery:

> If religious radicalism had been as widespread in the second decade of the century as it was by the middle of the fourth decade, the [immediate emancipation] appeals of [George] Bourne and [Rufus] King might have had a different effect. The emergence of the abolitionist crusade required not just an idea, and not just a corps of missionaries ready to spread the idea, but a public ready to receive it. By the mid-1830s such a public existed in the evangelical churches of New England.[265]

According to historian Dwight Lowell Dumond, "evangelism and the anti-slavery movement were inseparable."[266] He says that the "evangelistic movement, particularly Finney's revival, provided a host of young men dedicated to preaching the Gospel… and gave the anti-slavery movement "an unprecedented number of devoted apostles" who, as intellectuals, would be "the greatest combination of moral and intellectual power ever assembled in support of any cause before or since." To help them in this endeavor, Dumond says:

> They had the Bible. They had the great charters of Western liberalism. They had the writings of Woolman, Benezet, Rush, Hopkins, Cooper, Rice, Branagan, Barrow, Duncan, Rankin, and a host of British liberals such as Sharp, Clarkson, and Wilberforce. They

needed all of this and more to beat down and destroy the doctrine of racial inequality, enshrined in slavery, and upheld by the courts, the churches, and the political parties.[267]

One of Finney's greatest converts was Theodore Dwight Weld, who would become an articulate and passionate abolitionist alongside William Lloyd Garrison. After he encouraged and convinced students at Lane Seminary to work to abolish slavery, the faculty rebuked him, and he, along with many other students, moved to an unknown little school known as Oberlin College. It would become a base for the anti-slavery movement. After training seventy students in the abolitionist cause, he would send them out and "few, if any, escaped continuing insults and danger."[268] Indeed, "the records of all the anti-slavery evangelists are strewn with their shattered meetings, tar-and-feathering incidents, and fearless appeals to civil rights which held completed tragedies to a minimum."[269]

Immediate or Gradual Emancipation?

Weld, like Garrison, would also be a supporter of immediate emancipation. The revivalist plea to receive Christ because "today is the day of salvation,"[270] would translate into the abolitionist plea for "immediate emancipation." Martin Luther King, Jr., would later echo this concern over "time" in his "Letter from a Birmingham Jail":

> For years now I have heard the word "wait!" It rings in the ear of every Negro with piercing familiarity. This "Wait" has almost always meant "Never." We must come to see, with one of our distinguished jurists, that "justice too long delayed is justice denied." We have waited for more than 340 years for our constitutional and God given rights. The nations of Asia and Africa are moving with jetlike speed toward gaining political independence, but we still creep at horse-and-buggy pace toward gaining a cup of coffee at a lunch counter.[271]

Martin Luther King, Jr., would battle against Jim Crow, and he would also battle against religion. Even though he loved the church and said he was nurtured in her bosom and would remain true to her until his death, he still had to fight against poisonous religion:

THE NARROW WAY ABOLISHES SLAVERY

When I was suddenly catapulted into the leadership of the bus protest in Montgomery, Alabama, a few years ago, I felt we would be supported by the white church. I felt that the ministers, priests, and rabbis of the South would be among our strongest allies. Instead, some have been outright opponents, refusing to understand the freedom movement and misrepresenting its leaders; all too many others have been more cautious than courageous and have remained silent behind the anesthetizing security of stained-glass windows.[272]

King was on the Narrow Way. He loved Jesus and loved his neighbor, but like so many before him, this would bring him into a direct conflict with poisonous religion. King was very disappointed with the "laxity of the church." He expected more support, but said he always ran into religious leaders who would "stand on the sideline and mouth pious irrelevancies and sanctimonious trivialities." Instead he realized that the only church he could trust was "the inner spiritual church, the church within the church, as the true ekklesia and the hope of the world." He said he was grateful that "some noble souls from the ranks of organized religion have broken loose from the paralyzing chains of conformity and joined us in the active struggle for freedom." Some of them, he said, were "dismissed from their churches, have lost the support of their bishops and fellow ministers," but their "witness has been the spiritual salt that has preserved the true meaning of the gospel."[273]

Redeeming Slaves

Just as in the early church, there was a movement to purchase (or redeem) slaves from their bondage, Richard Allen, founder of the African Methodist Episcopal Church, redeemed slaves. Levi Coffin, one of the main conductors on the Underground Railroad said "that in the face of such appeals, it was hard to refuse, almost impossible if one brought the case home to himself."[274] James Russell Lowe would also admit in a letter written in 1849 that even though he didn't have much money, still "if a man comes and asks us to help him buy a wife or child what are we to do?"[275] He couldn't refuse. Harriet Beecher Stowe would take Milly Edmundson on a tour of New England churches, which resulted in enough money to redeem her two children. And Garrison would print notices in the *Liberator*, such as this one, which appeared in January of 1837:

George Potter and Rosella, his wife, would take this opportunity to express their gratitude to God, and under him, to the benevolent individuals, who generously contributed to aiding them to redeem their two children from Slavery. They have the unspeakable happiness of informing the generous donors that, on the 12th... they received their children, aged eleven and seven years, raised from the degradation of Slavery to the rank of Freemen.[276]

Civil Disobedience

Also, just as Paul and Peter would question the justice of a law and break it because they would rather obey God's Higher Law,[277] Charles Beecher would implore Christians to disobey the Fugitive Slave Law. He appealed to the teachings of Jesus and asked:

Suppose... a fugitive mother and child should come knocking at your door on a winter night pleading for aid. What does the law require of you? What must you do, to obey the law? What is obedience to law? You must shut your door in her face, or you must take her captive, and shut her up until the hounds of officers can come up. This is obedience, and if you do not do this you are a law-breaker. If you give her a crust of bread, you break the law. If you give her a shawl, a cloak; if you let her warm herself by your fire an hour, and depart, you break the law. If you give her a night's rest, and let her go, you break the law. If you show her any kindness, any mercy, if you treat her as Christ treated you, if you do to her as you would wish to be done by, you have broken the law.[278]

Beecher went on to explain that he could not obey the Fugitive Slave Law because it "commands me, when fully obeyed, to deny Christ, to renounce and abjure Christ's law, to trample under foot Christ's spirit, and to remand Christ's flesh and blood into cruel bondage." He also said that blind obedience to the law would strike at the "throne of God" and would shipwreck "every principle of religious liberty for which our fathers ever contended; it is a bare-faced dereliction of every position of the Reformation, and a giving up of everything which as Protestants and as republicans we have ever held dear. If this law is to be obeyed merely because it is law, no matter how diabolical its spirit, then farewell to liberty, farewell to religion."[279]

Frederick Douglass would also claim to be a law-breaker when he opened his speech at a meeting of the Massachusetts Society in January of 1842 with these words: "I appear before the immense assembly this evening as a thief and a robber. I stole this head, these limbs, this body from my master, and I ran off with them."[280] And Harriet Tubman, the escaped slave who became a conductor on the Underground Railroad, also appealed to the Higher Law of God when she asserted, "God willed us free. Men willed us slaves. We will do as God wills."[281]

An Appeal to the Heart

In his book, *Narrative of the Life of Frederick Douglass*, Douglass told of abuses suffered as a slave. This method would be effective in persuading readers to oppose slavery. Lewis Tappan's wife would be one of his fans. She would read it over and over again and, as Tappan wrote in a letter to Douglass, "Its contents will be laid up in our hearts."[282]

While the Southern slaveholder always used the Bible as a justification for his own "rights," the abolitionist would always appeal to the Higher Law, the Royal Law of Love, and to the tenderness in a person's heart. It was this appeal to tenderness and mercy that made Harriet Beecher Stowe's best-selling book, *Uncle Tom's Cabin*, such an overwhelming success. She would share the horrors of slavery with the masses, and consequently, shift the heart of the nation. This method was so effective that President Abraham Lincoln would invite her to the Oval Office with the greeting, "So you're the little woman who made this big war."[283]

Reform Movements

The heartfelt enthusiasm that was so appealing to the masses in the revivals, would now be turned to abolition, temperance, poverty, and women's rights. (Abolitionism would, in some sense, give birth to the suffrage movement, as women who were working in the anti-slavery movement wouldn't be allowed to sit in on the conventions. This led to the Elizabeth Cady Stanton's "Declaration of Sentiments" which she read at the Seneca Falls Convention on women's rights. The abolitionist movement would give many women, such as Lydia Marie Child and Angela Grimke, an outlet for their intellect. As women worked to elevate blacks, they became elevated themselves.)

In Great Britain, evangelicals would not only overthrow slavery, but they would also work to counter the social conditions brought about by the industrial revolution. The Clapham Sect (associated with Wilberforce) and William Booth's Salvation Army would labor to bring Christianity to the poor. The evangelicals would begin "ragged schools" to help poor children learn how to read (the parliamentarian Lord Shaftesbury would found a Union to promote them), open safer factories that paid double the wages of other factories, open hostels for homeless children, help the children of miners, care for and feed the poor, set up houses to help prostitutes get out of their profession, and become part of the temperance movement, because in their experience, they saw that drinking led men to "squander what money they had on drink, leading to hungry and often brutalized families."[284]

Merle Curti admits that the inspiration for many reformers was Jesus. He says, "No one can read widely in the reform literature without being profoundly impressed by the religious character of the arguments that filled the tracts, periodicals, lectures, and private correspondence of the crusaders."[285]

With so many societal strongholds lined up against the abolitionists, how was it that they were able to see the light of truth in the midst of so much darkness? The atheist, Hume, wasn't able to discern evil. The scientist, Morton, wasn't able to discern. The Southern slaveholder, relying on his perverted understanding of Old Testament Law, wasn't able to discern. But those who trusted in the grace of God, were washed in the blood of the Lamb, and as a result, loved their neighbor as themselves, had the ability to discern good from evil, even when every hardship hounded them because of their position. They formed a bulwark the slave could run to for safety and help. They were determined to "correctly divide the Word of Truth," and as a result of their efforts, slavery would rightly be reviled in Western society, hopefully never to return again.

CHAPTER NINE
The Narrow Way on a Mission

> *"Human progress never rolls in on wheels of inevitability; it comes through the tireless efforts of men willing to be co-workers with God."*
> —Martin Luther King, Jr., *"Letter from a Birmingham Jail"*

> *"Blister the meddlesome missionaries! They write tons of these things. They seem to be always around, always spying, always eye-witnessing the happenings; and everything they see they commit to paper. They are always prowling from place to place; the natives consider them their only friends; they go to them with their sorrows; they show them their scars and their wounds, inflicted by my soldier police; they hold up the stumps of their arms and lament because their hands have been chopped off, as punishment for not bringing in enough rubber, and as proof to be laid before my officers that the required punishment was well and truly carried out. One of these missionaries saw eighty-one of these hands drying over a fire for transmission to my officials—and of course he must go and set it down and print it. They travel and travel, they spy and spy! And nothing is too trivial for them to print."* —Mark Twain, *"King Leopold's Soliloquy"*

The Second Great Awakening unleashed the greatest force for good the world has ever seen! The fruit of this revival was similar to that produced by the early church. Christians shared the love of Jesus to the uttermost parts of the Earth, and wherever they went societies changed for the better.

Hospitals, orphanages, schools, and universities were established. Infanticide, which was widely practiced in China, India, and the Pacific Islands, was abolished. Murder of the elderly was stopped. Cannibalism ended. Widow burning was abandoned. Painful foot-binding was opposed. Human sacrifice is no longer a common cultural practice. The worship of pagan deities declined and their powerful priesthoods were dismantled. It took those on the Narrow Way to accomplish this. They spread the Good News of God's grace and love wherever they went, and the world was radically changed.

Unfortunately, the history of the missions movement has gotten jumbled up with other strands of thought and activity that were occurring simultaneously. This has led to accusations such as this, found at the web site *The Rejection of Pascal's Wager: A Skeptic's Guide to Christianity*: "Missionaries have always held a heroic and romantic place within the Christian imagination. Even today churches regularly collect contributions for the mission field. The reality, of course, is very different. From its very beginnings, Christian missionaries have inflicted tremendous harm on the people they 'witnessed' to."[286]

While it's very true that natives around the world went through tremendous abuse, it wasn't at the hands of evangelical missionaries. In fact, in almost every case, it was the evangelical missionaries who were standing up to *oppose* the abuse.

There were four main groups who were actively going out into the world at this time:

1. The Catholic conquerors and explorers. These were searching for gold (as Cortez and Pizarro) or attempting to win souls for the Catholic Church.
2. The secular explorers, traders, and settlers. They were usually documenting their discoveries and developing maps (Captain Cook, for example) or they were developing trade routes and stations (as the Dutch East India Company in South Africa).
3. The Liberal Protestants who blended evolutionary science with Christianity and accepted the case for biblical criticism. They were proponents of social Darwinism and "the white man's burden" to civilize or lift up the heathen.
4. The evangelical missionaries who were sent out by voluntary affiliations such as the London Missionary Society. They opposed social Darwinism and abusive Western imperialism, believing instead in the "brotherhood" of the races and that men shouldn't be used for another's gain.

The fruit of each of these groups isn't that difficult to assess once they are separated and sifted.

The Catholics

The Spanish conquistadors, "motivated by religion, pride of nation, and dreams of personal enrichment,"[287] explored and conquered most of South America. Using horses and firearms, they defeated the local natives and established the joint rule of Spanish monarchy and Catholicism. The Spanish ships would carry precious metals and sugars to Europe and slaves, settlers, and supplies back to South America.

The effect of diseases carried by the Spanish explorers and their animals and suffered by the South Americans, who were previously isolated from "lethal microbes," was catastrophic:

> The Spanish priest Bartolome de las Casas recorded that "of that immensity of people that was on this island and which we have seen with our own eyes" only about one thousand were spared among a population of between 1 and 3 million that had existed when Columbus arrived in 1493. Of some 15 million inhabitants in central Mexico before Cortes' arrival, nearly half perished within 15 years. In the Valley of Mexico… the estimated population was 1.5 to 3 million before the conquistadors arrived. Eighty years later, in 1600, only 70,000 native people could be counted.[288]

Catholics, especially in South America, would use conquest as a means of conversion. After the spectacular conquest of Mexico's Aztec empire by Hernan Cortes and the Peruvian Incas by Francisco Pizarro, "the Spanish enslaved thousands of native people and assigned them work regimens that severely weakened their resistance to disease. Some priests, like Bartolome de las Casas waged life-long campaigns to reduce exploitation of the Indians, but they had only limited power to control the actions of their colonizing compatriots."[289]

Las Casas was an exception to this attitude, and he wrote to the King of Spain to complain of the hypocrisy of those claiming to be followers of Christ:

> Your Majesty will also now perceive that here there are no Christians but only devils; no servants of God and the Crown but only traitors to His laws and Yours. It is my considered opinion that the greatest obstacle that stands in the way of the pacification of the New World, and with it the conversion of the people to Christ, is the harshness and cruelty of the treatment meted out by Christians to

those who surrender. This has been so harsh and so brutal that nothing is more odious nor more terrifying to the people than the name Christian, a word for which they use in their language the term yares, which means demons. And such a usage is amply justified, for what has been done to them by the Spanish commanders and by their men has been neither Christian nor indeed the work of devils; and so, when the locals find themselves on the receiving end of such merciless butchery, they assume that such actions are standard among Christians and that they derive ultimately from a Christian God and a Christian King.[290]

The Jesuits had set up communities called *reductiones* throughout South America, instructing the natives in how to read and write, teaching them practical skills, and even producing enough products to trade, but these communities were short-lived because Charles III of Spain cast out the Jesuits in 1769. Unfortunately, the Spanish conquistadors had carried the cross into their battles and harshly abused the natives under the banner of Christianity.

The Traders, Explorers, and Settlers

The earliest groups to venture out into the New World were the explorers and traders. Marco Polo had whetted European appetites with stories of silk, spices, jewels, gold, and perfumes that could be found in the Orient, and consequently the explorers were determined to find a way to go eastward without going overland through the Muslim world. Columbus was looking for this shorter trade route, but ended up discovering an unknown continent instead. The Portuguese explorer, Vasco da Gama, traveled around the Cape of Africa and actually found Polo's gold. He also wrestled the African gold trade away from Muslim control.

In North America, the Virginia Company of London sent England's original settlers to the New World under the king's charter to bring the Christian religion to native people who "as yet live in darkness and miserable ignorance of the true knowledge of God." But even Captain John Smith, leader of the Jamestown colony, acknowledged the hypocrisy of the charter, saying, "We did admire how it was possible such wise men could so torment themselves with such absurdities, making religion their colour, when all their aim was profit."[291]

THE NARROW WAY ON A MISSION

Other traders such as the British East India Company or the Hudson Bay Company were also looking for resources. They weren't motivated by their faith and didn't act like it either. In their attempts to make lucrative trade deals, they often took advantage of the natives for their own gain. Disease spread throughout the native populations as they came into contact with Europeans.

In 1616, visiting English fishermen triggered a ferocious outbreak of respiratory viruses and smallpox that wiped out three-quarters of some 125,000 Indians. Five years later, an Englishman exploring the area described walking through a forest where human skeletons covered the ground.[292]

Even the Puritans, under the auspices of the Massachusetts Bay Colony, who came to America to find religious freedom, were not innocent in the way they treated the Native Americans. Their attempt to build a Christian commonwealth, a "city on a hill," would cause them to conflict with the "heathens" in an attempt to get more land to fulfill their vision, and it would also cause them to try to "Christianize" the Indian population in order to accomplish their ideal society. But other than the work done by John Eliot, who helped to set up fourteen Indian villages, the Puritans warred in their relationships with native tribes.

In contrast, the Quaker, William Penn, established Pennsylvania as a refuge for Indians. Writing to the Delaware chiefs who lived in Pennsylvania, he said, "The king of the Country where I live, hath given me a great Province, but I desire to enjoy it with your Love and Consent, that we may always live together as neighbors and friends."[293]

According to the historians who wrote the college textbook *The American People: Creating a Nation and Society*, "In this single statement Penn dissociated himself from the entire history of European colonization in the New World and from the widely held negative view of Indians. Recognizing the Indians as the rightful owners of the land included in his grant, Penn pledged not to sell one acre until he had first purchased it from local chiefs."[294] In this, Voltaire would agree, saying, "It was the only treaty made by the settlers with the Indians that was never sworn to, and the only one that was never broken."[295]

The European explorers would also travel to faraway places such as Tahiti and Hawaii, places that had never been exposed to white men, and bring disease and corruption with them. For example, Captain Bligh, of the infamous

HMS Bounty (whose men would lead a mutiny against him) would record in his journals that venereal diseases were spread through the ranks of his sailors:

> References to venereal infections now appeared more or less regularly, one man received twelve lashes for "having connection with a Woman while he was infected... " and suspecting that some of the men were not reporting their symptoms, Bligh had the ship's company again undergo an examination by the surgeon. The boatswain and an unnamed midshipman were found to be among the infected.[296]

Again, the explorers and traders who brought disease and suffering to the natives, *preceded* evangelical missionaries.[297] The European church/state unions that were supporting the trade expeditions caused the name of Christ to be associated with such efforts, but at this, men such as William Howitt would become indignant. As one of the first persons to speak out against colonial abuses in his book *Colonisation and Christianity* (1838), Howitt, another Quaker, laments "the blood-stained history of European contacts with aboriginal races" and rejects the notion that these abuses were perpetrated by true Christians:

> The barbarities and outrages of the so-called Christian race, throughout every region of the world, and upon every people that they have been able to subdue, are as to be paralleled by those of any other race, however fierce, however untaught, and however reckless of mercy and of shame, in any age of the earth. Is it fit that this horrible blending of the names of Christianity and outrage should continue?... If foul deeds are to be done, let them be done in their own foul name; and let robbery of lands, seizure of cattle, violence committed on the liberties or the lives of men be branded as the deeds of devils and not of Christians.[298]

The Aborigines Protection Society (mentioned in the last chapter) also spoke out against the abuses it saw in colonization. Thomas Fowell Buxton, a member of the evangelical Clapham Sect that helped abolish slavery in the British Empire, and successor to Wilberforce in the Parliament, had been told by missionaries of colonial abuses and urged the appointment of a Select Committee of the House of Commons "to consider what measures ought to be adopted with regard to the native inhabitants of countries where British settlements are made, and to the neighboring tribes, in order to secure them the due observance of justice and protection of their rights."[299]

As a result of this request, made in 1835, a two-year investigation was made and a summary was issued in 1837 entitled *Report of the Parliamentary Select Committee on Aboriginal Tribes, (British Settlements)*. In it, the greed of the colonizers was exposed:

> The national honor has been tarnished; common honesty has been thrown aside; life itself has again and again been sacrificed for the mere convenience of trade... Men calling themselves Christians, subjects of a Christian government, professors of the Christian faith, have stooped, for the attainment of selfish ends, to practice upon the confiding ignorance of these simple and untutored children of the desert.[300]

For this information, the *Report* gives thanks to missionaries who were crying out against the evils perpetrated by British colonialists:

> For the greater part of the information we now possess, we are indebted to the Christian Missionaries sent out from this country. To the labours of these invaluable men the cause of humanity is unspeakably indebted. Amid persecution and scorn, obloquy, ridicule, and contempt, they have steadily persevered in their work of faith and labour of love, until to them, in an especial degree, belongs the honor of having first exposed the evil workings of our colonial policy.[301]

Social Darwinism and the "White Man's Burden"

The accusation that missionaries were guilty of colonial abuse flies in the face of the facts. The missionaries were always in conflict with those who abused native peoples. For example, John Mackenzie, of the London Missionary Society, appointed to Tswana territory, clashed with Cecil Rhodes. According to the University of Botswana's History Department:

> On the one hand there was the Reverend John Mackenzie, one of the most articulate spokesmen among Christian missionaries of the later 19th century and prime exponent of ideas of protection of "native" interests. On the other hand there was Cecil John Rhodes, the diamond magnate whose name has becomes synonymous with

monopoly capitalism and territorial expansion in later 19th century Africa, who stood for colonization, development, and exploitation of African lands by European settlers.[302]

Mackenzie would go back to London in 1882 to campaign for "British protection of Bechuanaland from the depredations of Boer 'filibusters' from the Transvaal republic. He became the leading voice of a humanitarian lobby appealing to parliament for justice for the Bechuana (Tswana)...."[303] Mackenzie attempted to establish a British protectorate in Bechuanaland in order to protect the Africans from the abuse of Cecil Rhodes, who was a social Darwinist. Rhodes' dream was to spread the British Empire, led by the Anglo-Saxon race, around the world. He thought that there could only be world peace if the white race was in power. In his last will and testament, Rhodes said of the British, "I contend that we are the finest race in the world and that the more of the world we inhabit the better it is for the human race."[304]

The missionaries, on the other hand, disagreed with the notion of social Darwinism, arguing instead that the darker races were less advanced because they hadn't heard about Jesus. The reason that the "Anglo-Saxon" race had become more highly developed, they argued, was simply because they were the first recipients of the Gospel.

As explained in the previous chapter, scientific racism was the belief that each of the races had different parents (polygenism). This was a popular belief of those who embraced Enlightenment views. Instead of all races having a common ancestor in Adam and Eve (monogenism), the darker races were considered to be sub-human, like a lower form of animal. This allowed the white race to subjugate the darker races without concern for treating them equally, as was provided for "all men" in the Declaration of Independence. It would be used by Southern slaveholders to justify slavery. But paradoxically, Darwinism would cause polygenism to become outmoded and monogenism would prevail because of evolutionary claims that all life evolved from a common ancestor.

So, like sheep, the whole scientific community flocked back to monogenism. But now, instead of the degradation of the darker races being justified because they were subhuman, abuse would be excused merely because the darker races were less evolved. The lighter the skin, the more evolved the race, was the thinking.

THE NARROW WAY ON A MISSION

An example of the prevalence of this ideology could be found at the Columbian Exposition, the World's Fair in Chicago, in 1893. Along the Midway Plaisance, a type of human zoo was set up, which allowed those who attended the fair to walk through the evolutionary history of man. Beginning with the African race and moving forward through the red and yellow races, villages were set up and people of color put on display. The exhibit ended with European villages and culminated with the glorious "White City" which was the final goal that mankind was moving toward. This wasn't a sideshow; it was a scientific endeavor! The best minds were put to the task, since the goal of the Columbian Exposition was to showcase humanity's progress.

To lend anthropological legitimacy to their enterprise, Chicago's exposition directors placed the Midway under the nominal direction of Harvard's Frederic Ward Putnam, who had already been chosen to organize an Anthropology Building at the fair. Putnam envisioned the Midway as a living outdoor museum of "primitive" human beings that would afford visitors the opportunity to measure the progress of humanity toward the ideal of civilization presented in the White City.[305]

Putnam was a student of Louis Agassiz, the influential Harvard professor who embraced scientific racism and immersed a whole generation of students in the doctrine. Putnam was influential as a museum builder. He traveled around the world to find material for the Columbian Exposition and then donated it to begin the Field Museum in Chicago. Later he would be active at the University of California at Berkeley.

The impact of social Darwinism, although rarely heard of today (perhaps due to the embarrassment felt by the scientific and intellectual community for supporting it), was widespread. In 1864, the *Atlantic Monthly* declared that Herbert Spencer (who coined the phrase "survival of the fittest" and is considered to be the founder of social Darwinism) was a "power in the world" and that he represented the "scientific spirit of the age."[306] His influence would continue in the intellectual community until World War II, when the logical outcome of his ideology would be revealed in all its horror in the Nazi camps. Until then, adherents of social Darwinism read like a "Who's Who" of money, power, and intellect of the Victorian era.

Virtually every major Euro-American thinker of the latter portion of the nineteenth century was profoundly influenced by Spencer: William James [psychology], Josiah Royce [philosophy], John Dewey [education], Borden Browne [theologian], Paul Harris [lawyer], George Howison [philosophy], James McCosh [theology], and the founders of American sociology, Lester Ward, Charles Cooley, Franklin Giddings, Albion Small, and William Graham Sumner....[307]

Spencer also had a profound influence on "Henry Cabot Lodge, Calvin Coolidge, Teddy Roosevelt, Woodrow Wilson, Winston Churchill, John D. Rockefeller, and Andrew Carnegie."[308]

Evolutionary theory would be applied to history, psychology, theology, law, architecture, art, education, economics, political science, anthropology, and sociology. Three events would make social Darwinism...

... seductive to late nineteenth century intellectuals. First, the emergence of huge industrial enterprises deeply divided labor and capital, forcing some to justify increasing social divisions. Second, biblical criticism dislodged Christianity as the central scheme by which people understood their world. And third, the social sciences emerged as an academic discipline proposing to use the lessons of natural science to explain developments in society. Social Darwinism could respond to the needs created by each of these developments.[309]

The liberal Christian, as a result of aligning themselves with the latest scientific theory or societal trend, would have a patronizing attitude toward other races. The authors of *Unto a Good Land: A History of the American People* explain: "Echoing such purpose were advocates of the 'white man's burden' who drew on social Darwinism to argue that the Anglo-Saxon 'race,' as the finest product of natural selection, had a duty to bring order and uplift to the benighted 'darker' peoples everywhere."[310]

Under the cloak of Christianity they advocated a form of racism that they adopted from the scientific and intellectual community:

As popularized by such writers as the Episcopal clergyman and professor William Graham Sumner of Yale University, Darwinian laws also ruled the social order. Such thinking justified the ruthless competition of the marketplace, they argued, but paradoxically it also demanded imperial conquest as a way to lift the savages from their own misery and barbarism."[311]

The most popular advocate of social Darwinism was the Congregationalist minister, Josiah Strong. In his hands, "such ideas became a command for expansionism" and in his "hugely popular book, *Our Country* (1885), Strong insisted that the Anglo-Saxon was 'divinely commissioned' to be, in a peculiar sense, his 'brother's keeper' and that God was thus 'training the Anglo-Saxon for its mission' of Christianizing and civilizing 'the weaker races.'"[312]

To the social Darwinist/imperialist, the word "civilize" could be a euphemism for the word "work." The lower evolutionary status of the dark races meant that they were incapable of producing anything that required advanced knowledge, so the best that whites could do for them was to put them to work, house them, and re-dress them in European clothing.[313]

The social Darwinists aligned themselves with those who proposed a type of "social gospel" in the belief that it was necessary to bring civilization to the natives first and Christianity later, saying that it was better to be a hypocrite than a heathen. Sir Henry H. Johnston, writing in the forward to the book *Christus Liberator*, admits as much: "The promulgation of the new religion [Christianity] has often bred a distasteful hypocrisy; but after all, hypocrisy is the homage which vice pays to virtue, and it is doubtful whether the hypocrite is worse under his mask than he was before the preaching of a better religion taught him, at any rate, the decency of disguising sin."[314]

Although Johnston claimed to be a Christian, he would also be an evolutionist and a racist. He spoke of the African in evolutionary terms: "If he was to remain in the conditions in which he was found by the first Caucasian invaders of Africa, twenty-thousand, ten-thousand, five thousand years ago, he would have become permanently embedded in a brutishness from which eventually he could no more be stirred than can the anthropoid apes of Malaysia and West Africa."[315]

In 1920, Johnston authored the book *The Backward Peoples and Our Relationship With Them*. His attitude would be a perfect example of the Christian imperialism that was typical of the time.

Evangelical Missionaries

In response to this overwhelming rush of "intellect" the Bible-believing church stood alone. Refusing to go along with higher criticism (the attempt to look at the Bible as if it were the same as any other book and hold it up to the scrutiny of current science and history) and holding on to the Word of God as the Truth, even when every reason appeared to exist to doubt it, the only people that went into the world in order to bless it rather than take from it and serve it rather than dominate and abuse it were the missionaries.

Benjamin Harrison, the former president of the United States, was Honorary Chairman of the "Ecumenical Missionary Conference" at Carnegie Hall in 1901, and would give its opening address. In it, he counters racial imperialism and speaks of the giving attitude that the Christian should have:

> The highest conception that has ever entered the mind of man is that of God as the father of all men—the one blood—the universal brotherhood. It was not evolved, but revealed. The natural man lives to be ministered unto—he lays his imposts on others. He buys slaves that they may fan him to sleep, bring him the jeweled cup, dance before him, and die in the arena for his sport. Into such a world there came a King, not to be ministered unto, but to minister.[316]

This was a strong stand, considering that others would be at the gathering who held racist views. Being a huge ecumenical gathering of many denominations, 162 mission agencies, and nearly 200,000 people, the attendees would not all hold the same viewpoints on science and race. Politicians would take advantage of the large audience and give special honor to the work of the missionaries. The New York Times gave special coverage of the event.

Jon Bonk, author of *Between Past and Future: Evangelical Mission Entering the Twenty-First Century*, acknowledged that there was a "growing theological bifurcation in American Protestantism"[317] at the time, but the "evangelical consensus" still remained intact and the conference was imbued with an optimism about the new century and the role missionaries could play. Yet there was a division in the church over the role of science and its impact on society.

Is it merely coincidence that the scientifically leaning "Christians" (those Old Light liberals who went the way of Enlightenment rationalism, scientific racism, and now biblical criticism and Social Darwinism, and who had embraced the idea of church/state Christendom) believed that it was necessary to *impose* civilization on native populations and that Bible-believing Christians thought it was best to serve and love the native populations in an attempt to win their hearts and minds for Christ? The evangelical missionary believed that civilization would proceed from knowing Christ, not that knowing Christ would proceed from civilization.

In fact, many Christians would argue that the "civilizing" influences of the white man had turned the natives *away* from Jesus. William Howitt made this point explicitly:

> People have wondered at the slow progress, and in many countries, the almost hopeless labors of the missionaries;—why should they wonder? The missionaries had Christianity to teach—and their countrymen had been there before them and called themselves Christians! That was enough: what recommendations could a religion have, to men who had seen its professors for generations in the sole character of thieves, murderers, and oppressors? The missionaries told them that in Christianity lay their salvation;—they shook their heads, they had already found it their destruction! They told them they had come to comfort and enlighten them; they had already been comforted by the seizure of their lands, the violation of their ancient rights, the kidnapping of their persons; and the midnight flames of their own dwellings. Is there any mystery in the difficulties of the missionaries?[318]

Speaking of the abuse that natives on the Pacific Islands experienced at the hands of white "Christians," Helen Barrett Montgomery argued that:

> The indictment against so-called Christian nations becomes heavy indeed. Their lands stolen, their fisheries depleted, their freedom taken away, their men sold into virtual slavery as contract laborers in distant lands, their strength enfeebled by the importation of foul diseases, the islanders of the Pacific might well question the blessing brought them by contact with the whites.[319]

And yet Montgomery insisted that missions are necessary. Seeing all that Western imperialism had done to harm indigenous peoples, she made the case that removing the missionaries would be cruel and unjust.

> To withdraw the missionaries would not stop a single trader, nor a gallon of rum, nor one cruel exploitation; it would simply leave to run riot the forces of evil. The strongest reason why the conscience of Europe and America ought to continue and immensely to strengthen its missionary forces in the island world is to make the largest, most costly and statesmanlike reparation for the ills inflicted on them by unwourthy representatives of our race, and by our still unchristianized governments.[320]

She said that the missionary was the only person who had shown himself to be selfless and giving, and hearkened back to the argument of race—insisting in the brotherhood of man:

> To take away the missionary would be to take away the one man who is in the islands, not for what he can get of them, but for what he can give to them; the one man who gives the natives books in their own tongue, schools, hospitals, churches; nurses their sick, teaches their children, resents their wrongs, protects them against imposition and fraud, teaches them new arts of practical life—in short, who is their brother.[321]

Missionaries Battle Social Darwinism

The missionary movement was a response to the commandment of Jesus to "go into all the world and make disciples," (Matt. 28: 19)," but it also became a conscious attempt to counter scientific racism and/or social Darwinism. For example, William Knibb, the heroic missionary to Jamaica, would beg for black equality saying: "All I ask is, that my African brother may stand in the same family of man; that my African sister shall, while she clasps her tender infant to her breast, be allowed to call it her own; that they both shall be allowed to bow their knees in prayer to that God who has made of one blood all nations as one flesh."[322]

Knibb would be hated by traders, planters, and merchants who relied on slavery for a living, and would even end up in jail under false accusations, but he didn't care. His heart was broken by the brutality he saw:

> I call upon children, by the cries of the infant slave who I saw flogged on the Macclesfield Estate, in Westmoreland.... I call upon

parents, by the blood streaming back of Catherine Williams, who, with a heroism England has seldom known, preferred a dungeon to the surrender of her honour. I call upon Christians by the lacerated back of William Black of King's Valley, whose back, a month after flogging, was not healed. I call upon you all, by the sympathies of Jesus.[323]

William Knibb would start schools, train teachers, start a newspaper to give blacks a voice, found a seminary, buy land for emancipated slaves with his own money, and baptize 3,000 blacks who were "each spiritually readied for the event—he would not baptise anybody merely to swell the numbers."[324]

William Knibb was recognized as one of Jamaica's greatest heroes: "In 1988, on the 150th anniversary of the abolition of slavery in the British Empire, William Knibb was granted Jamaica's highest civil honour, *The Order of Merit*. Only one other non-Jamaican and no white man shared this honour at the time." His award would read as follows:

For Knibb's work as Liberator of the slaves;
For his work in laying the foundation of Nationhood;
For his support of black people and things indigenous;
For his display of great courage against tremendous odds;
For being an inspiration then and now.[326]

Knibb was a hero of history, and he was on the Narrow Way. He trusted in the work of Jesus and loved his fellow man. He wasn't caught up in the latest trends of the day, but held to the plumb line of the Word of Truth. And because he was faithful, one little corner of the world was brought closer to Eden.

The evangelical missionaries were committed to the belief that all races were equal and just needed to hear the Gospel in order for their societies to advance. Because of this they didn't assign the natives to menial labor, but instead made education the priority. One motive for education was to give them the ability to read the Bible, but it was also to counter the claims of social Darwinists. It was a grand experiment, which put high hopes and expectations on the Declaration's premise that *all men are created equal.*

For example, the Australian La Trobe Collection contains "the visitors (or visitors') books of two nineteenth-century Gippsland mission stations,

Ramahyuck (or Lake Wellington) and Lake Tyers. These 'visitors books' were created by a decision of the Board for the Protection of the Aborigines [of London, as mentioned previously] in September 1878."327 The mission was under fire for "segregating" the Aborigines on to mission compounds, so the visitor books were kept as an open record or testimony of activities on the mission, to counter claims of abuse. Interestingly enough, the books became a record of the two conflicting worldviews that prevailed at the time, each side writing from their own perspective. Bain Atwood, commented on what the books revealed:

> The responses of many of these visitors, I would argue, occurred within what J. G. A. Pocock would call "a certain paradigmatic situation," one which was shaped by the modes of colonial racial thought. There were two easily distinguishable racial idioms concerning Aborigines apparent in the second half of the nineteenth century: a humanitarian one shaped by the Enlightenment, and evangelical Christianity which held that Aborigines were capable [the word "capable" is the key here, rather than being forced or used for personal gain] of being "civilised and christianised" and that Europeans were morally obliged to compensate and care for the dispossessed—and a more secular one, increasingly expressed in the language of social Darwinism, which held that Aborigines were "a dying race" and that Europeans either should (or could) not alter "the laws of nature." These "visitors books" provide evidence of both, although particularly the former.328

One visitor could see the advancement of the Aborigines since his visit fifteen years earlier, but he still held that "before the advance of civilisation, the race may doubtless become extinct. It is gratifying, however, to see the last days of the Aboriginal inhabitants of this colony are made as happy as possible."329 As a social Darwinist, he believed that the Aborigines, as the "weaker race," wouldn't survive. This was precisely the attitude that missionaries were battling against.

Isaac Taylor Headland, a missionary to China, writes of an encounter with social Darwinist attitudes in his book, *By-products of Missions*. He says he met a young shoe salesman on a train and began a conversation with him. When the young man found out he was a missionary, he declares to Headland that he didn't believe in foreign missions and that the money should be spent on home missions (but he admitted he didn't give). The conversation continued:

"Don't you suppose" I went on, "that there was just as much need of men and money in Jerusalem and Judea and Samaria when Jesus Christ was preaching to his disciples as there is in Topeka and Kansas and the United States to-day?"

"Oh, yes, I suppose so," he admitted.

"Well, why do you suppose, when he only had a dozen trained men, and they did not have any money, his last words to them, in Acts 1:8, were to go "to the uttermost part of the earth?"

He did not have any answer to that question, and I went on: "Let me ask you another question. Suppose those dozen disciples had believed just as you do, where would you and I have been to-day?"

"Oh," he exclaimed, "the white man would have gone up anyhow!"[330]

The conversation continued on in this manner, with Headland explaining how much more advanced the Chinese were than the Europeans at one time. The young man refused to believe it and ended the conversation by exclaiming, "I never did like preachers! They're a lazy lot."[331]

The Missionaries and Education

The first line of attack in the battle against social Darwinism and racism was education. As a result of the work of a handful of missionaries, most of the world's greatest universities were started. Christians had already founded every Ivy League college except Cornell University (Harvard, Yale, Princeton, Columbia, University of Pennsylvania, and Dartmouth), and the list of colleges, universities, and seminaries in the United States that were started by Christians is too numerous to list here, but how many know that most of China's universities were founded by missionaries? According to the official web site on Chinese culture, put out by the People's Republic of China:

In 1901, the Methodist Episcopal Church, South set up Soochow University, which was the first Western-style university—in China. Then Christian universities were set up in succession, including St. John's University in Shanghai, Hangzhou Christian College, West China Union University in Chengdu, Huazhong University in Wuchang,

Nanjing Ginling University, Huanan College of Arts and Science in Fuzhou, Xiangya University of Medicine in Changsha, Ginling College of Arts and Science for Girls, Shanghai Hujiang University, Canton Christian University in Guangzhou, Yanjing University in Beijing, Shandong Qilu University, Fujian Christian University, and some small colleges. These Western-styled colleges and universities contributed much to the training of modern personnel.[332]

In China, it's evident that the missionaries weren't only interested in converting the Chinese and giving them the Scriptures; they also fought against the social Darwinist belief that the darker races couldn't learn. They opened schools and printed materials. John Fryer played a pivotal role in translating, not only the Scriptures, but "in 28 years Fryer translated more than 170 titles, from textbooks in mathematics, physics, and chemistry, to popular books on history, political institutions, and other aspects of Western Civilization."[333] John Fryer would also translate textbooks on hydraulics, electricity, gases, heat, thermodynamics, chemistry, and math. Chinese libraries, which had been reserved for the higher classes, would also be democratized because of the influence of missionaries, who pushed to make them more accessible to the general population.

Roland Bainton, the great church historian, describes the impact that missionaries had on education:

> The missionaries have reduced hundreds of languages to writing and have provided these tongues with dictionaries and grammars. The immediate purpose, of course, was to translate the Scriptures… [but] native literature was not neglected. Of special significance was the introduction of the printing press. William Carey, at Serampore in Bengal, working in a Baptist mission under the Danish flag, established the first press in the land, which issued, by 1832, translations of portions of the Scripture in forty-four languages and dialects. He and his associates also translated into English a great Indian epic poem.[334]

The work of translation went on around the world. If the languages were scattered as a result of the "religious" effort at the Tower of Babel, the effort of those on the Narrow Way to translate all languages would be the greatest restoration of linguistic understanding since the scattering had occurred.[335] On the day of Pentecost, the disciples were sent out into the streets with power and there were no language barriers; everyone heard the Gospel in their own language. The missionaries would carry on this Pentecostal miracle by going into all the world and working tirelessly, usually under very difficult conditions, to bridge the gap between race, class, and tongue. The work of the missionary wasn't an effort to bring religion; it was an effort to display the kindness and love of God to the world, and to make up for the atrocities of hypocritical "Christendom" and science.

The missionaries were always accused of being radicals. Wherever they went they stirred up trouble. To South Africa, the London Missionary Society sent John Philip to direct their work. Leonard Thompson's classic, *A History of South Africa*, says that he was "committed to fighting for the liberation of the oppressed classes" and that he "wrote a long, passionate polemic, exposing the injustices experienced by the Khoikhoi." Thompson writes:

> I found them in the most oppressed condition of any people under any civilized government known to us upon earth.... The Hottentot has a right to a fair price for his labour; to an exemption from cruelty and oppression; to choose the place of his abode, and to enjoy the society of his children; and no one can deprive him of those rights without violating the laws of nature and of nations."[336]

The work of missionaries to translate and educate would eventually lead to the freedom movements of the twentieth century. As Bainton describes it: "The missionary movement, by instilling ideals of dignity and equality of opportunity, has been indirectly responsible for the rise of self-government and nationhood."[337]

Nelson Mandela is an example of the influence of missionaries on the freedom movements. He attended the University College of Fort Hare, a Methodist missionary school, and says it was "the only residential center of higher education for blacks in South Africa. Fort Hare was more than that: it was a beacon for African scholars from all over Southern Central and Eastern Africa. For a young black South African like myself, it was Oxford and Cambridge, Harvard and Yale, all rolled into one."[338]

Mandela describes the education he received there in his autobiography *Long Walk to Freedom*:

> Fort Hare, like Clarkebury and Healdtown, was a missionary college. We were exhorted to obey God, respect the political authori-

ties, and be grateful for the educational opportunities afforded to us by the church and the government. These schools have often been criticized for being colonialist in their attitudes and practices. Yet, even with such attitudes, I believe their benefits outweighed their disadvantages. The missionaries built and ran schools when the government was unwilling or unable to do so. The learning environment of the missionary schools, while often morally rigid, was far more open than the racist principles underlying government schools.[339]

Mandela says that "Fort Hare was both home and incubator of some of the greatest African scholars the continent has ever known."[340] This was only possible because of the work of missionaries and their commitment to the belief in the brotherhood of the races.

Were Missionaries "Destroyers of Cultures?"

The other argument against missionaries is that they are guilty of destroying the cultures and religions of the native peoples. David Frawley, an American Hindu who is often quoted on web sites that are opposed to religion (paradoxically) such as www.religionislies.com, claims:

> Missionary activity always holds an implicit psychological violence, however discreetly it is conducted. It is aimed at turning the minds and hearts of people away from their native religion to one that is generally unsympathetic and hostile to it… missionary activity and conversion, therefore, is not about freedom of religion."[341]

Implicit in this argument is an understanding that the indigenous culture was good and that the savage was "noble" (as Rousseau liked to believe). But this was far from the reality. As Bainton explains:

> Unquestionably, the missionaries have sought to introduce whatever they deemed to be good in their own culture; medicine, sanitation, education, transportation, and technology, especially in agriculture. As for native customs, of course missionaries have opposed suttee, the burning of widows, in India. This the British government suppressed [with pressure from Wilberforce]. They have opposed child murder, prostitution, polygamy, cannibalism, and headhunting, but native liter-

ature, native drama, native music, native architecture, they have sought to learn, conserve and revive.[342]

Evidence to support this assertion is prolific in missionary testimonies. It wasn't until the missionaries, often through great suffering, went into "all the world" as Jesus commanded them, that these horrendous practices stopped. At a recent debate between Dinesh D'souza and Christopher Hitchens, a man from Tonga[343] stood up to say that he would have had Hitchens for supper if he had visited the island 100 years ago. It was the Gospel message that had changed the islanders' hearts and consequently their actions.

As mentioned before, Isaac Taylor Headland, a missionary who spent twenty years in China, explained that advances in science were a result of Christianity, and that medicine, in particular, was a consequence of the Gospel. He says that there were no dentists, no tooth-fillings, in the non-Christian world, and especially points to clean water as a by-product of the Gospel. Even now, Christians go to distant lands and dig wells to provide fresh, clean water for needy people. The introduction of wells was especially exciting to island peoples who had always had to collect rainwater in the past.

Bishop Selwyn, of the London Missionary Society, who went to the Melanesians in 1842, described the poisonous religious conditions that the natives were subject to:

> They have a vague dread of the powers of nature, and a defined one of their priests, who have such power over them that if they curse them, the victims will sometimes at once go home and die of terror. In some islands sharks, crocodiles, and serpents—fierce and destroying creatures—receive a species of worship; and a vague dread of ghosts seems to be the only idea in many islands bearing any resemblance to the belief in the immortality of the soul.[344]

It took those on the Narrow Way, bearing the Good News of grace, to set the Melanesian people free from their fears and give them peace.

The Missionaries: Lights in the Darkness

The missionary stories sound like movies!

In 1830, the first European missionary, John Williams, also of the London Missionary Society, arrived on the Samoan Islands. He was able to make Samoan converts and, as a result, the practice of polygamy and widow strangling stopped. These converts also spread the Gospel to other islands, including Anaiteum. In 1848, missionaries were able to settle there and build on the work of the Samoans. The London Missionary Society reported the dramatic change:

> In 1856, out of a population of 4,000 Samoans, only 200 or 300 remained heathens. Schools were established all over the island, under the management of native teachers; large chapels were erected at the two principal stations; and boarding houses were attached to the dwellings of the missionaries. The rapid improvement of the character of the people, their goodwill, their quickness in learning to read and write, and willingness to adopt the social habits of their instructors, are so many facts which call for thankfulness in themselves, and give pledges of hope for the future of other islands which are now what Anaiteum was.[345]

Even the Samoans recognize the efforts of Williams, saying on the web site of the American Samoa Historic Preservation Office that "he and his followers had a profound impact on the Samoans and their culture."[346] Unfortunately, Williams would visit another island that wasn't converted (Erromango) and be eaten by cannibals.

The official web site of the country of Fiji (www.fijihighcommission.org) had this to say about the influence of missionaries: "Cannibalism practiced in Fiji at that time quickly disappeared as missionaries gained influence. When Ratu Serv Cakobau accepted Christianity in 1854, the rest of the country soon followed and tribal warfare came to an end."[347]

On the island of New Hebrides, Scottish missionary John G. Paton and his wife entered into very difficult circumstances. Surrounded by cannibals, the fear was almost overwhelming. Shortly after reaching the island, Paton's wife would die giving birth, and he had to bury her and the baby with his own hands. The grief and loneliness was almost too much to bear. His missionary partner also died of fear and stress shortly after reaching the island.

The island natives warred amongst themselves, and the victors would eat the losers and their families. Yet for some reason, the cannibals were unable to kill the lone missionary Paton. Many times they would threaten him, throw spears and axes at him, point muskets at him, or chase him through the jungle, to no avail. Paton explains how he survived:

THE NARROW WAY ON A MISSION

Life in such circumstances led me to cling very near to the Lord Jesus. With my trembling hand clasped in the hand once nailed on Calvary, and now swaying the scepter of the universe, calmness and peace abode in my soul. Trials and hairbreadth escapes strengthened my faith and seemed only to nerve me for more to follow. Without that abiding consciousness of the presence and power of my dear Lord and Saviour, nothing else in all the world could have preserved me from losing my reason and perishing miserably. His words, "*Lo, I am with you alway, even unto the end of the world*," became very real to me and I felt His supporting power. I had my nearest and dearest glimpses of the face and smile of my blessed Lord in those dread moments when musket, club, or spear was being leveled at my life.[348]

Paton was on the Narrow Way. Because of his efforts, there are no longer cannibals on New Hebrides.

The modern push for multiculturalism, as a response to Christian "imperialism", may seem sympathetic enough, but can only proceed on a somewhat dishonest basis. Just as it's easy enough to criticize the Israelites for their war on the Canaanites, even though we weren't there to experience the fear and horror as Baal worshipers practiced human sacrifice, it's also easy to forget that the native cultures really were wicked. They weren't "noble savages." They were savages. And while it is gratifying to celebrate their special dances, food, music, art, literature, and costumes, we can't forget that these cultural phenomena have been divorced from the brutal and bloody activities that characterized their people when they had no knowledge of Jesus. Is it wrong to thank the missionaries for the change they brought upon the world? Is it wrong to acknowledge that they did a mighty work and that they were right in their attempt to try to prove the brotherhood of men and that the Enlightenment principle of equality even applied to the darker races—even when the Enlightenment thinkers didn't think so?

Finally, I'd like to share the story of Mary Slessor, as found in the book *What if Jesus Had Never Been Born*:

> The work of William Carey is well known, as is that of David Livingstone and Hudson Taylor. But for every one of these famous missionaries of the last two centuries there are thousands of lesser-known lights who carried the Gospel to those who previously lived in darkness…. I will tell you of only one, Mary Slessor of Calabar

(1848-1915), who was from Scotland. She was converted in her teens, and after doing mission work in the slums of Dundee, she felt the call of God to serve as a missionary to Africa. In 1876, she left for Nigeria.

She learned that beyond Okoyong, deeper in the heart of Africa, around Calabar, was an area in which lived 4 million savages so ferocious, so fierce, that even the government soldiers feared to penetrate the land. These 4 million cannibals were so degraded, their customs so vile, that it stretches the imagination to consider the types of things they did.

Witchcraft and drunkenness were rampant. The savages worshiped fetishes; they murdered twins; they turned the mother of twins out into the jungle to be devoured by beasts, because they believed twins were brought about by a conjunction with a demon. Almost half of the population was slaves. When a man died, they would eat fifty slaves; twenty-five more would have their hands tied behind them and their heads would be cut off. Unmarried women were chattel. They could be raped, tortured, or murdered at will. It was an incredible degradation, especially for women. Children were considered to be no better than animals, often simply left to die.

Mary's heart was touched by the plight of twins always left to die or ground to pieces in a pot. She would snatch them up and take them in. At first the people were astonished, because they believed that anybody who touched a twin would die, but Mary didn't die. So she gathered around her over the years many of these young "bairns" as she called them, to nurture them.

In incredible ways, by her faith in God, in her prayer, her winning countenance, the love she demonstrated, she was accepted. People milled around her. They had never seen a white person before. They touched her skin.

She began to teach them about the Son of God who had loved them enough to die for their sins. Astonishingly, God opened up their hearts. They became very willing to hear. One after another, the chiefs of the various villages yielded their lives to Christ. One after another the tremendously horrible customs plaguing these people for years were abolished; the murder of twins, infanticide, the slaughter of wives and slaves, the trial by poison and boiling oil, and all other terrible customs.

Perpetual warfare among the different tribes had continued for innumerable centuries, but when she would hear of a tribe of warriors going out to attack another tribe, Mary would run barefoot through the jungle, where there were poisonous snakes and plants. She would head them off, standing in front of a whole host of armed cannibals with outstretched arms to demand that they stop. They did. Through her ministry, thousands from the Ibo tribe became Christians and abandoned their degrading ways. Without Jesus Christ, there would never have been a Mary Slessor of Calabar.[349]

Have Atheists Made the World Better?

Christopher Hitchens closes many of his debates with Christians by asking this question: Is there any moral or ethical act that a Christian can do that an atheist cannot?

My response would be this: No. All humans are capable of doing good (all can eat of the Tree of the Knowledge of Good and Evil), *but my complaint is that the atheist hasn't.* Repeatedly, the atheist drowns in the swamp of historical moral forgetfulness. He rarely ever rises up and acts valiantly. Nearly all of the great heroic feats, the advances, the leaps forward, have been accomplished by Christians (or those who knew and wielded the Bible—as the Enlightenment philosophers). Where are the atheist Mary Slessors? How have the atheists ever confronted poisonous religion? They may have been victimized, but they never had the power to overcome. They never had any Light to overcome the darkness of evil. The excuse used by atheists is that they could never accomplish much because they would be persecuted by the church/state monopoly, but that never stopped the Christian from having the courage to oppose the poisonous religions of the world. Aligning yourself with atheism is abandoning all the bravest, brightest, and kindest that humanity has to offer. You *can* do any moral act that a Christian can, but for some reason, your *species* (as you call yourself) *hasn't.*

And yet, I suppose you want humanity to ignore your track record and believe you when you say you'll do better in the future. How many abused wives have heard that one?

CHAPTER TEN
The Narrow Way Confronts Hitler

"See to it that no one takes you captive through hollow and deceptive philosophy, which depends on human tradition and the basic principles of this world rather than on Christ." —Colossians 2:8

"Many Christians gave their lives to protect their fellow creatures in this midnight of the century, but the chance that they did so on orders from any priesthood is statistically almost negligible. This is why we revere the memory of the very few believers, like Dietrich Bonhoeffer and Martin Niemoller, who acted in accordance only with the dictates of conscience."—Christopher Hitchens, God Is Not Great: How Religion Poisons Everything

"In Hitler's view, as long as Jews remained in Germany, they were a constant source of ideological infection and a threat to German racial purity. The racial theories Hitler adopted, like his nationalism, had deep roots in the German past and appealed strongly to many Germans." —Afterword, The Diary of Anne Frank

Christians and atheists have both played the blame game when it comes to ascribing guilt for one of the most horrifying realities of the twentieth century. Grisly human experimentation, foul air filled with the smell of baking men, women, and children, starving and bony people forced to work in freezing conditions, railroad cars filled with families rather than cattle, nail-scratched walls of gas chambers disguised as showers, were all part of the legacy of the Nazis. Who wants to be associated with this? So, just as Adam and Eve in the Garden, we point fingers. "Hitler was an atheist and an evolutionist!" say the Christians. "No! He was a Christian!" say the atheists. They both point to *Mein Kampf* as their proof. Christians point to quotes like this, which reveal an evolutionary "survival of the fittest" ethic:

> For as soon as the procreative faculty is thwarted and the number of births diminished, the natural struggle for existence which allows only healthy and strong individuals to survive is replaced by a sheer craze to "save" feeble and even diseased creatures at any cost. And thus the seeds are sown for a human progeny which will become more and more miserable from one generation to another, as long as Nature's will is scorned. But if that policy be carried out the final results must be that such a nation will eventually terminate its own existence on this earth; for though man may defy the eternal laws of procreation during a certain period, vengeance will follow sooner or later. A stronger race will oust that which has grown weak; for the vital urge, in its ultimate form, will burst asunder all the absurd chains of this so-called humane consideration for the individual and will replace it with the humanity of Nature, which wipes out what is weak in order to give place to the strong.[350]

And atheists point to quotes such as this one, which reveal Hitler's desire to do God's will:

> Everybody who has the right kind of feeling for his country is solemnly bound, each within his own denomination to see to it that he is not constantly talking about the Will of God, merely from the lips but that in actual fact he fulfills the Will of God and does not allow God's handiwork to be debased. For it was by the Will of God that men were made of a certain bodily shape, were given their natures and their faculties. Whoever destroys His work wages war against God's Creation and God's Will.[351]

They also show pictures of Catholic bishops, cardinals, and priests shaking hands with the Nazis and show pictures of church altars decorated with swastikas. Surely, they say, this proves that Hitler and the Nazis were Christians.

What is the truth?

I would argue that Hitler may have believed he was a Christian who was doing the will of God, but his ideas and beliefs weren't taken from the Bible. Rather, his was a mixture of philosophy, science, and theology gleaned from the popular ethos of his day. And the reason that most German people followed Hitler was not so much because they were somehow hypnotized by him into mass hysteria and madness, but because Hitler spoke their language. Like Hitler, they were also immersed in a particular culture and mindset that led them to embrace Nazism. So, what was this philosophy that 1930s Germany was familiar with?

Georg W. F. Hegel

It's impossible to understand the mindset of Hitler or the German people without understanding the German philosophers. The most important of these philosophers was Hegel. While studying Hegel can be an arduous task, I hope that the reader will bear with me as I try to simplify his teachings. It was out of the womb of Hegelianism that both Nazism and communism were birthed, so if a person has an understanding of Hegel's philosophy, they will have a much greater understanding of the twentieth century and why there was so much bloodshed. It's very difficult to understand Hegel. He said his goal was to attempt to develop a system of truth in scientific form. Here is a typical sample of his writing:

> We have thus to consider as to the object, whether in point of fact it does exist in sense-certainty itself as such an essential reality as that certainty gives it out to be; whether its meaning and notion which is to be essential reality, corresponds to the way it is present in that certainty. We have for that purpose not to reflect about it and ponder what might be in truth, but to deal with it merely as sense-certainty contains it.[352]

His language was the epitome of what George Orwell may have been talking about when he wrote his essay "Politics and the English Language." Although Hegel spoke German, the meaning of Orwell's essay remains applicable. Some of Hegel's most often used words are those that Orwell says are used to "dress up simple statements and give an air of scientific impartiality to biased judgments."[353] He says words like "phenomenon, element, individual (as noun), objective, categorical, effective" are all examples of words used by bad writers. Orwell thought that language should be used "as an instrument for expressing and not concealing… thought" and that "political chaos is connected with the decay of language."[354] How true in the case of Hegel.

Schopenhauer (no easy read either!) described the period when it was in vogue to speak with arrogant and fancy language. But he wasn't impressed:

> What was senseless and without meaning at once took refuge in obscure exposition and language. Fichte was the first to grasp and make vigorous use of this privilege; Schelling at least equaled him in this, and a host of hungry scribblers without intellect or honesty soon surpassed them both. But the greatest effrontery in serving up sheer nonsense, in scrabbling together senseless and maddening webs of words, such as had previously been heard only in madhouses, finally appeared in Hegel.[355]

Perhaps the difficulty of understanding Hegel explains why those who adopted his teaching never seemed to embrace it in its entirety. They cherry-picked what they wanted to use, but never fully applied all of it. But Hegel appealed to the pride of intellect, so it probably offered credibility to Hitler and Marx to make use of him. I'm sure Hegel would have been astounded that his philosophy was used in the way it was.

In light of Hegel's influence, I think it would be of help to have somewhat of a cursory understanding of his philosophy if we are to defend Christianity against the charge of Nazism. As Hitchens says, sometimes it's necessary to "know your enemy"[356] in order to defeat him.

Hegel was born in 1770, on the eve of the American and French Revolutions. When Hegel was nineteen, in 1789, the Bastille had fallen, and the French Revolution had begun. Hegel and his friends were so excited that they planted a "liberty tree" to commemorate the great event. Wordsworth wrote about this moment in time: "Bliss was it in that dawn to be alive, but to be young was very heaven!" Hegel was to write later that "the French Revolution was a 'glorious dawn' and that 'all thinking beings shared in the jubilation of this epoch.'"[358] But Hegel, like so many others, was to become greatly disappointed.

Hegel attended Tubingen Seminary and studied theology. From there he took a position as a tutor for a wealthy family in Switzerland. When his father died, he received a small inheritance, which allowed him to attend the University of Jena. While he was at Jena, he began to write and had some pamphlets published. But when his inheritance began to run out, he became somewhat desperate and began writing *Phenomenology of Mind*, which was published in 1807. The initial response to his work was respectful, but not enthusiastic.

In 1811, at the age of forty-one, Hegel married a younger woman, and they had two sons. He continued writing and eventually was invited to become Professor of Philosophy at the University of Heidelberg. His reputation grew, and in 1818 he was asked by the Prussian Minister of Education to take the chair of philosophy at the University of Berlin. He accepted this offer and taught there until he died in 1831. It was there that he wrote *Philosophy of Right* and lectured on the philosophy of history. He began to attract large audiences, and people came from all over the German-speaking world to hear him. He was even elected Rector of the University because of his great status. He had many students that he considered to be his disciples, and their notes from his lectures make up many of his other writings.

The world after the French Revolution (that Hegel was so excited about) was disillusioned by the Terror that had resulted in imprisonment and beheading, but according to Charles Taylor, author of *Hegel and Modern Society*, this didn't leave intellectuals of the 1790s hopeless. "On the contrary, there was a sense that a great transformation was both necessary and possible and this aroused hopes which at other times would have seemed extravagant. It was felt that a breakthrough was eminent."[359]

But what could the world look like? Who would have the idea that would lead to a happy society? In the French Revolution there was freedom, but there was no order. There was freedom from God and the church, but there was bondage to the guillotine. What could people learn from this, and how could they order the world to make a good society?

One popular response to this challenge was to try to blend or unify great thought. According to Taylor: "The terms of the synthesis were variously identified. For the young Friedrich Schlegel the task was to unite Goethe and Fichte, the former's poetry representing the highest in beauty and harmony, the latter's philosophy being the fullest statement of the freedom and sublimity of the self."[360] Others tried to unify Kant and Spinoza. Another idea that was popular was to unite the best of ancient and modern life; the Greeks representing the highest in "expressivist perfection."[361] Hegel attempted to unify Immanuel Kant's "categorical imperative" with Johann Gottfried Herder's "expressive theory."

Because Herder saw the society that was created by the Enlightenment philosophers in France and was disappointed, his work can be seen as "a protest against the Enlightenment view of man."[362] He rejected the idea that man was just a ball "of egoistic desires, for which nature and society provided merely the means to fulfillment… that it was utilitarian in its ethical outlook, atomistic… and… looked to a scientific social engineering to reorganize man and society."[363]

Instead Herder "developed an alternative notion of man."[364] Human life was seen as "having a unity rather analogous to a work of art, where every part or aspect only found its proper meaning in relationship to all the others. Human life unfolded from some central core—a guiding theme or inspiration—or should do so, if it were not so often blocked and distorted."[365] Herder believed that all men belonged to a culture, and the highest expression of that culture could only be found in community. Each community had a "'Volkgeist' or national spirit which provides its people with their inspiration or creative impulse."[366]

For example, the Athenian community produced the Parthenon, democracy, and great philosophers. The Egyptian community produced the pyramids, hieroglyphics, and mummification. Each society had a different personality or way of expressing themselves, which Herder would say was that community's expression of God in the physical realm. Herder believed that no other community could replace the other's contribution.

Hegel didn't think Herder's ideal state went far enough, though. He thought that Herder's "expressivism" could define the ancient world (such as Greek society), but that the modern world was different because it belonged to a different era that had Christianity and the Reformation as part of its intellectual heritage. The modern man was aware of his "capacity for freedom and [his] ability to make [his] own decisions in accordance with [his] conscience."[367] He wasn't able to be a part of a simple expressivist community that might take an irrational form. He had to be part of a rational society based on universal moral law.

This is why Hegel chose to blend Herder with Kant. The "categorical imperative" as described in Kant's second *Critique*, "describes morality as being separated from the motivation of happiness or pleasure."[368] This "categorical imperative" involves action based on reason alone. Kant believed that it was possible to make moral decisions without being influenced by desires. If we are acting from desire, then we aren't truly free. But how is it possible to act from reason alone? Kant's viewpoint was that "When we take away all desires, even the most basic ones, we are left with the bare, formal element of rationality, and this bare formal element is the universal form of the moral law itself."[369]

Kant believed that a rational mind developed moral laws. He believed that their source came from pure reason. Therefore, he believed that rational minds could accept moral law. They didn't have to reject it. It was reasonable. Therefore, it was possible for the purely rational mind to choose these absolutes without being influenced by outward concerns or sources such as temptations or emotions. When a person could use their reason to obey the moral law without being influenced by externals, then he was truly free and autonomous, not controlled by anything. Therefore, according to Kant, moral law was the highest authority. He believed that it was possible for a rational man to act right with the right motive... the right motive being respect for the universal law of reason and morality.

Accordingly, the Kantian ethic can actually be "summed up by the slogan 'Duty for duty's sake.'"[370] In other words, we're truly free when we do our duty for its own sake, and not otherwise. Therefore, to Hegel, pure freedom meant that a person could do their moral duty in the midst of a rationally organized community that was centered on moral absolutes. This is why Hegel called his Ideal State "concrete morality." But what does the state that blends Hegel's freedom with communal values look like? The British philosopher F.H. Bradley tried to describe this "organic community":

> The child... is born... into a living world... he does not even think of his separate self; he grows with his world, his mind fills and orders itself; and when he can separate himself from that world, and know himself apart from it, then by that time his self, the object of his self-consciousness, is penetrated, infected, characterized by the existence of others. Its content implies in every fiber relations of community. He learns or already perhaps has learnt, to speak, and here he appropriates the common heritage of his race, the tongue that he makes is his own in his country's language, it is... the same that others speak, and it carries into his mind the ideas and sentiments of the race... and stamps them indelibly. He grows up in an example

and general custom.... The soul within him is saturated, is filled, is qualified by, it has assimilated, has got its substance, has built itself up from, it is one and the same life with the universal life, and if he turns against this, he turns against himself.[371]

Hegel believed that our desires are shaped by community, and an organic community fosters desires that most benefit the community. Members of the community attain their identity by being part of a whole, therefore they won't even think of pursuing their own interests. This would be comparable to cutting off a person's arms to find something better to do with them than putting food in his mouth. The body needs the arms, and the arms need the body. The organic community can no more disregard the interests of its members than the body can ignore the loss of its arms.

If this organic community were organized around moral absolutes, freedom would no longer be limited. People would want to obey the law. There would be harmony between the rational man and the rational state, perfect freedom would be achieved, and the history of the world would have achieved its goal. The "end of history" would have occurred.

Hegel tried to prove his "end of history" theory by using actual history. He believed that the history of the world was "none other than the progress of the consciousness of freedom."[372] He was a student of history. In fact, his *Philosophy of History* is basically an outline of history. It starts with the early civilizations of China, India, and Persia, and proceeds through ancient Greece and Rome, and then follows the path of European history—from feudalism to the Reformation, to the Enlightenment and the French Revolution. But it wasn't just an outline of history. It was also an attempt to determine the meaning and significance of history.

Beginning with what Hegel called the Oriental World of China and India, he said that they seemed to reach a certain point in their development and then "somehow stuck fast."[373] As such, they were outside of his philosophy of history and not part of its process of development. In the Oriental world only one man—the emperor—was free. All others in society had to submit to an absolute ruler. In fact, they weren't free at all in the modern sense, because even their sense of right and wrong came from external regulation. Morality didn't come from an individual's conscience, but from outside sources. For example, the Chinese state was organized around "family." The emperor was the paternalistic manager of the state and all others were children of the state. In India, there was no concept of individual freedom, because the caste system wasn't a political institution but something natural and therefore unchangeable. Therefore, even though there were no human despots in India, there was a despotism of nature.

Hegel considered Persia to be the first empire of his philosophy, because Persia had a law that governed the ruler as well as the subject. Persia was a theocratic monarchy, which meant that society's rules were based on principles (the religion of Zoroaster) and even the ruler was subject to those principles, though he was an absolute ruler and the only free man in the empire. To Hegel, this was the first instance of Spirit ("Geist") in world history. Hegel thought that rule based on an intellectual or spiritual principle was the beginning of the "consciousness of freedom."

The next great step in history, according to Hegel, was the Battle at Salamis. When the Persian Empire came into contact with the Greek city-states, the emperor asked the Greeks to say that he was supreme, but they wouldn't, so he gathered his armies and they met a Salamis. This was a battle between an absolute emperor who wanted to rule the world and separate city-states who recognized free individuality. When the Greeks won, that meant that world history moved from absolute Oriental rule to the realm of the city-state.

Although history had progressed from despotism to a form of free individuality, Hegel didn't recognize the Greek world as being fully developed for two reasons. The first was that slavery existed, therefore some were free, not all; and secondly, the freedom they knew was incomplete. Hegel said the Chinese weren't free, because they had external laws and regulations, but they didn't have all-encompassing laws: they had habit. It was habit and upbringing that made them act in a certain way, not abstract principles or moral laws.

As in Herder's vision of community, they were so connected to the community and her customs that they knew no other lifestyle. Therefore, doing what was best for the community came from the development of habits and customs, not reason. For example, if a person does something from habit, he may not be doing it because he's reasoned it all out. Therefore his actions may still be governed by outside or external forces. Consulting the Oracle for guidance is an instance of relying on habit and upbringing rather than using reason to determine what to do. Hegel thought that true freedom involved critical thought and reflection. So instead of being the victim of an oracle or a despot, free individuals have the capacity to reason and think. Thus Socrates was one of the first individuals to question and reason. This is why he was such a threat to the Athenian city-state. The people of the community had accepted the customs and habits that had developed over time, but then Socrates began to think and reflect upon these customs. Hegel believed that the death sentence bestowed on Socrates was correct, because Socrates was a threat to the customary morality on which the community's existence was based.

Rome was seen differently by Hegel. Instead of the customary morality that was experienced by the Greeks, he saw the Roman Empire as a collection of very different people groups held together by force. This was comparable to the despotism of the Orients, except that the gains made by the Greeks weren't entirely lost. Rome had a political constitution and a legal system that honored individual rights. Whereas law existed in the Persian Empire, it hadn't developed the idea of individual rights. In the Roman Empire there was a constant tension between the rights of the individual and the absolute power of the state. Hegel thought that the Roman Empire was oppressive and that the demands that it made upon individuals to conform made individual freedom impossible to obtain except by retreating into oneself. Thus, the philosophies of Stoicism, Epicureanism, and Scepticism evolved out of the Roman Empire. But he thought that these philosophies were inadequate solutions to the problem of freedom and were just a concession that people were really helpless.

Hegel saw the need for a more positive solution to the yearning for freedom and said that Christianity was that answer. He believed that human beings weren't just animals, but they were spiritual beings. The Christian religion was special, according to Hegel, because Jesus Christ was both a human being and the Son of God. This taught humans that they were made in the image of God and that they, like Jesus, had an infinite value and eternal destiny. This encouraged them to break the hold that the natural world had on them and hope for a spiritual world where their true home would be made. Hegel also believed that this inner freedom could transform the outer world. He said that the first thing Christianity did was oppose slavery in the Roman Empire. The second was to get rid of the Oracles. And thirdly, Christianity established a morality based on love, rather than the customary morality of the Greeks.

Christianity became the official religion of the Roman Empire under Constantine, and even though the Western half of the Empire fell to the barbarian invasions, the Byzantine Empire remained in power for more than 1,000 years. But, according to Hegel, this Eastern Orthodox form of Christianity was decadent, because it was only a veneer over structures that were totally corrupt.

Hegel then began to refer to the period of history from the time of the fall of the Roman Empire up to his day as "The Germanic World." The reason he did this was that he believed that the Reformation, which occurred in Germany, was the single most important event of history since Roman times. He believed that the Middle Ages were a "long, eventful and terrible night,"[374] and he referred to the Renaissance as "that blush of dawn which after long storms first betokens the return of a bright and glorious day."[375] But it was the Reformation, not the Renaissance, which Hegel described as "the all-enlightening Sun."[376] Hegel believed that the Catholic Church was corrupt, and instead of treating the Deity as a purely spiritual thing, they attempted to embody it in the material world through ceremonies, rituals, and other outward expressions. Therefore, a person's spirituality was tied to the material world rather than the spiritual world. This is why, he thought, the church could justify the selling of indulgences.

Hegel saw the Reformation as an achievement of the German people "arising from 'the honest truth and simplicity of its heart.'"[377] He believed that the Reformation did away with the "pomp and circumstance of the Roman Catholic Church and to substitute the idea that each individual human being has, in his own heart, a direct spiritual relationship to Christ."[378] But Hegel's view of history requires that the Reformation not only impact the church, but society also. The Reformation was that point in history when individuals realized that they had the ability to relate to God without an outside authority. Hegel thought that the "individual conscience is the ultimate judge of truth and goodness. In asserting this, the Reformation unfurls 'the banner of Free Spirit' and proclaims as its essential principle: 'Man is in his very nature destined to be free.'"[379] And Hegel believed that since the Reformation, the world was being transformed in accordance with this principle.

This is why he thought an Ideal State could be accomplished. He thought that if individuals were free to use their reasoning abilities to judge truth and goodness, then rational and good governments would be welcomed as a result.

Therefore, all social institutions such as law, government, and constitutions could be designed in a way that rational man could accept. This would lead to Hegel's view of perfect freedom.

But how does this fit in with the reality of what actually happened as the next big event in human history? How is it that mankind, using its freedom, instead created the French Revolution? Hegel himself thought that the French Revolution was "a glorious mental dawn"[380] and even joined in the jubilation of freedom. But he was to see the "dawn" become terror instead. How did this fit in with Hegel's philosophy of history, which was supposed to be the "progress of the consciousness of freedom"?

Hegel developed a theory called the "spiral view of history." In this theory, he developed the position that history is trying to attain an ever-expanding freedom and yet is always in constant conflict. In this viewpoint, he explained the constant conflict as being a "dialectical method." This is explained in detail in his *Philosophy of Logic*. Basically the dialectical (contradicting) method is a process of change whereby a "thesis" is transformed into its opposite, the "antithesis," and is therefore preserved by it. The combination of the two then takes on a higher form of truth known as the "synthesis." Edward H. Carr defines it as a doctrine in which:

> The world moves forward through a continuous interplay and conflict of ideas: one idea, or thesis, is contradicted and assailed by its antithesis; and of this struggle comes, not the victory either of thesis or of antithesis, but a new synthesis; the synthesis is thus established as a thesis, and the process of contradiction begins once more. This state of flux, or historical process, is the ultimate reality: it is also rational, since it is moving forward along certain lines which can be determined by rational investigation.[381]

In this viewpoint, the conflict of ideas on the world stage is necessary for the next great leap in freedom to occur. So, although the French Revolution led to the terror, it also led to many changes in Germany. It helped establish freedom for persons and freedom of property. It led to a code of rights. It led to more civil service jobs for the most talented citizens. It abolished feudal obligations. And even though the Prussian state was ruled by a monarchy, Hegel thought that the system of laws and organization of the government kept the ruler in check. He said that the decision of the monarch was "in point of substance, no great matter."[382]

Since Hegel believed that the history of the world was the progress of the consciousness of freedom and that this freedom was always expanding, his philosophy of history was "that in past Oriental civilizations *one* was free; in classical antiquity, Greece and Rome, *some* were free; and in modern Germanic and Anglo-Saxon civilization, *all* are free."[383]

This march of freedom through history, according to Hegel, is actually the working of Spirit (Geist) in the material world. Hegel believed that Spirit couldn't exist independently of men. According to Charles Taylor, Hegel's "Spirit" was "a spirit who lives as spirit only through men. They are vehicles... of his spiritual existence."[384] Geist was the spiritual reality underlying the universe as a whole. Hegel believed that Spirit had purposes and realized ends, but could only do this through people. Therefore, "the realm of the Spirit consists only in what is produced by man."[385]

To Hegel, God wasn't everlasting or unchanging but was an essence that needed to manifest itself in the world in order to perfect itself. This viewpoint of God makes progress very important, because the onward movement of history is the path God must take to achieve perfection. Perhaps this belief was the reason that Hegel appealed to revolutionary and radical thinkers such as Marx and Hitler.

Karl Marx

After Hegel's death, his school of thought would split into two camps. One school remained true to Hegel's teachings and would be called the Right Hegelians, while the other school, the Young Hegelians or Left Hegelians, would become the home of Karl Marx. Marx would adopt parts of Hegel's teaching, especially that of "alienated labor," but he also thought that Hegel had failed to live out his ideas. He thought that there needed to be "a unity of theory and practice," so he wasn't interested in merely contemplating ideas, but rather putting those ideas into action. Perhaps this is why the Eleventh Thesis of Feuerbach, which says "the philosophers have only interpreted the world in various ways, the point, however, is to change it"[386] is engraved on Marx's tomb.

With this desire for change in mind, Marx truly believed he could design Hegel's Ideal State. He thought Hegel's "hero" was an engineer who could look at society in the same way that a master builder looked at a blueprint. He wanted to create a rationally organized state where there would be genuine freedom, but rejected Hegel's idea of the Zeitgeist. He joined with two other young Hegelians, Feuerbach and Strauss, who had written books that criticized Christianity.

German Historicism

This division of Hegel's thought was also reflected in German society during the latter half of the nineteenth century. The animosity toward secular Enlightenment rationalism, brought about by Napoleon's defeat of the Prussian state, led to the creation of the German Idealism of Goethe and Wagner. The German intelligentsia, just as Hegel, also attempted to translate the new scientific mindset onto their intellectual tradition by applying methodological standards of research to the study of the social sciences. Since science led to the discovery of empirical reality, if scientific methods could be applied to the study of history, for example, we would be more likely to discover the truth. Thus Leopold von Ranke and others were looking for "history as it really was"[387] in a scientific sense. Archaeology thrived, records were combed, and museums were created to house their discoveries.

This method of pursuing historical truth would even end up being applied to theology. Schleirmacher and others would employ scientific historical methods to try to determine the truthfulness of the Bible. Instead of believing everything the Bible said, they would expose it to the scrutiny of the new historical methods. This historicist concept of discovering "history as it was" would now be applied to the sacred texts, each verse being scrutinized in a way in which only that which could be proven historically would be accepted as truth. The quest was now on for the "Historical Jesus." This was the beginning of the modern liberal interpretation of Scriptures. No longer was the Bible an inerrant document that served as the plumb line for history; instead history was now the plumb line for the Scriptures. So if portions of the text couldn't be proven through archaeology or confirmed by other ancient texts, then the authenticity of that portion of the Bible would come into question.

Social Darwinism

At the same time the Bible was being discredited, Herbert Spencer's "social Darwinism" was becoming much more popular. According to Andrew Heywood, author of the text *Political Ideologies*, "The notion that human existence is based upon competition or struggle was particularly attractive in the period of intensifying international rivalry that eventually led to war in 1914. Social Darwinism had a considerable impact upon emerging fascism."[388] This evolutionary concept would be combined with a "science of race."[389] According to Heywood:

> The first attempt to develop a scientific theory of racialism was undertaken by the French social theorist Joseph-Arthur Gobineau, whose "Essay on the Inequality of the Human Races" claimed to be a "science of history." Gobineau argued that there is a hierarchy of the races, with very different qualities and characteristics. The most developed and creative race is the "white peoples" whose highest element Gobineau referred to as the "Aryans."[390]

These ideas were adopted by the composer Wagner and his English son-in-law, H.S. Chamberlain, "whose 'Foundations of the Nineteenth Century' had an enormous impact on Hitler and the Nazis,"[391] whereby history was merely the confrontation between the Jews and "Teutons" (the German people). This racial theory led to Hitler's formulation of a "master race." The Aryans, according to Hitler, were the "'founders of culture' and [he] literally believed them to be responsible for all creativity, whether in art, music, literature, philosophy, or political thought."[392] On the other hand, the Jews were "destroyers of culture."[393] Thus, good and evil were determined by whether or not the image of God was preserved through German culture.

Adolph Hitler

The biblical standard of right and wrong had been blended in with a scientific form of philosophy and a belief formed out of scientific racial theory. Consequently, aggressive war was justified, because all Hitler was doing was trying to obtain Lebensraum (living space) for the culturally superior Aryan race. Since they were the fittest, they had the right to survive. With this in mind, we can understand the culture that Adolph Hitler existed in and read Adolph Hitler's words in *Mein Kampf* and make sense out of them:

> In this part of the world, human culture and civilization are inextricably bound up with the presence of the Aryan element. If it died out or went under, the black veil of a cultureless period would once again descend upon this globe. To anyone who views the world

> through Nationalist eyes, any breach in the existence of human civilization, effected by the race which maintains it, would appear in the light of the most accursed of crimes. Whoever dares lay his hand on the most noble image of God is sinning against the kindly Creator of that marvel and is lending a hand in his own expulsion from paradise.[394]

Hitler thought that the Jews, who were dispersed around the world in 70 AD, were poisoning the bloodlines of the individual races and that this was hindering God from expressing himself in that culture. The image of God was being sinned against. An individual culture was a "marvel" according to Hitler, and anyone who tainted that culture was committing the worst of sins against their creator and deserved "expulsion from paradise." Hitler actually believed that by exterminating the Jews, he was serving God.

Hegel's "Ideal State" was also important to Hitler, but he thought it was more important to preserve culture first:

> Thus, if an attempt is to be made to realize the ideal of a national state, we shall have to ignore the forces now controlling the life of the public and seek for another force, determined and able to take up the struggle for that Ideal State. For there is a struggle ahead of us if our first task is not creation of a new conception of a State, but removal of the present Jewish conception.[395]

Hitler believed that the Jews were involved in an international banking conspiracy. They became the scapegoat, not only for the defeat of Germany in World War I, but for the humiliation at Versailles and even for the financial struggle that Germany found itself in. Paradoxically, even irrationally, Hitler "suggested that the Jews were responsible for an international conspiracy of capitalists *and* communists, whose prime objective was to overthrow the German nation."[396]

Hitler also adopted Hegel's viewpoint on the four persons in history—the citizen, person, hero, and victim. Even though Napoleon had crushed the armies of Prussia at Jena, and Hegel was living in Jena at the time, he wrote a letter the day after Jena was occupied by the French, "which shows only admiration for Napoleon: 'The Emperor—this world soul—I saw riding through the city to review his troops; it is indeed a wonderful feeling to see such an individual who, concentrated into a single point, sitting on a horse, reaches out over the world and dominates it.'" Hegel was enthralled by what he called the "hero" of history. This is similar to Nietzsche's "idea of 'ubermencsch'—the 'overman' or 'superman.'"[397] Hegel thought that since the hero was being propelled by Geist, he was above the law and was justified in "trampling down many an innocent flower."[398] God was working through the hero to bring about the furtherance of the progression of freedom either by being the thesis or the antithesis in any given situation.

Hitler's viewpoint on the popular vote was also adopted from Hegel. Although Hegel believed that the ultimate goal of history was freedom, he didn't believe in the right to vote. He thought that people were too easily manipulated. He didn't think that the mass of people were able to make rational decisions, and therefore, to "make the entire direction of the State dependent on such arbitrary choices would amount to handing over the destiny of the community to chance."[399] This view was reflected in Hitler's belief on the popular vote:

> While all human civilization is but the outcome of the creative force of personality, in the community as a whole and especially among its leaders, the principle of the dignity of the majority makes a pretence of being the deciding authority, and it is beginning gradually to poison all life below it—and in fact to break it up. The destructive workings of Judaism in the bodies of other nations can at bottom only be ascribed to the perpetual effort to undermine the importance of personality throughout the nations who are their hosts, and to substitute the will of the multitude.[400]

Hitler believed that the Jews were like parasites or leaches that sucked the life of God out of the nations of the world as they intermingled with and poisoned communities. He thought it was necessary and better to have strong leaders who could oppose the workings of Judaism than to subject the State to the will of the people, since they might have been corrupted by the Jews.

He also went along with Hegel's version of freedom. In this version, Hegel had emphasized that rationality was a necessary element in freedom, but then the question must be asked: who decides what is rational? If a ruler is armed with the doctrine that only rational choices are free, any ruler can then justify suppressing anybody who opposes his own rational plans for the State. For if a leader's plans are rational, those who oppose him must be irrational, and since their choices aren't based on reason, they aren't truly free in the Kantian sense. Therefore, to suppress newspapers and leaflets isn't interfering with the freedom of the press, and closing down their churches to set up more rational forms of worship isn't interfering with their religious freedom. In order to be truly free, they just have to fit in with their leaders' plans! This is the type of "Orwellian double-speak"[401] that Hegel provided through his definition of freedom and his tangled use of language.

There's no indication that anything Hitler did was the result of any Christian beliefs. His was a hodge-podge of ideas, not grounded in any traditional Christian doctrine. He may have believed he was a Christian because he embraced certain common cultural viewpoints about God, but Herder's expressivism was a human construct, not a biblical one. There's no teaching in the Bible that says cultures are the expression of God on earth.

Perhaps the genius of Hitler was his Hegelian-like attempt to unify science *and* romanticism. He was able to use German Idealism to appeal to the masses (perhaps because the German people wanted to believe the nationalistic assertion that the German culture, being the birthplace of the Reformation, was the very highest expression of God on earth) and at the same time present himself as an advocate of the latest scientific theories. The German intelligentsia had taken pride in their ability to apply scientific methods to the humanities (thus the *social* sciences) yet in the process, used their scientific methods to promote racism and discredit the Bible.

Neither Marx nor Hitler adopted Hegel's philosophy in its entirety. I believe Hegel would have rejected Nazism, because its attempt to exterminate millions of people obviously didn't square with Kant's "categorical imperative," which had its source in universal moral law, and he would have also rejected communism because Marx didn't acknowledge the presence of a Zeitgeist in history.

In my estimation, Hegel went wrong on two main counts in his attempt to blend Herder and Kant. In using Herder's nationalistic perspective as a foundation for his philosophy, he adopted an unbiblical teaching. He also made a mistake in adopting Kant's "categorical imperative" as the other foundation of his theory. The attempt to base morality on pure reason was the equivalent of leading people to eat of the wrong tree in the Garden. It was doomed to failure.

The Christian message isn't one of duty or obligation, especially to a particular human leader, but instead is a message of passion for Jesus who is called the "Desire of Nations" (Hag. 2:7). Hegel led Germany to wrong doctrine and religion, not to grace and love. And death was the result.

The Confessing Church

Is it any wonder then that the only leaders who were able to see through this bubbling, societal stew were those who had an understanding of sound doctrine? It was the evangelical church, those committed to the inerrancy of the Word, who had the insight to realize that Nazism was wrong and possessed the courage to oppose it. They hadn't abandoned the plumb line, like the liberal church, with their emphasis on "higher criticism,"[402] so they still had a standard they could uphold.

Members of the Confessing Church, led by Martin Niemoller (creator of the Pastors Emergency League), Dietrich Bonhoeffer, and Karl Barth, joined together to write the Theological Declaration of Barmen, which was "An appeal to the Evangelical Congregations and Christians in Germany." Written in May of 1934, they saw far ahead of time that Germany was heading toward disaster and tried to warn Christians to not be a part of it. They emphasized to the church that if they were taking their "stand upon Scripture, then let no fear or temptation keep you from treading with us the path of faith and obedience to the Word of God." They were on the Narrow Way.

They began by mentioning that they were birthed out of the Reformation, which implied the understanding that they were against religious effort and believers in the grace received through Jesus. They didn't forget this. They opposed the errors that they felt were being taught by the "'German Christians' of the present Reich government." They had to oppose the false religious system that was developing before their eyes. They didn't want to divide the German Church, but they knew they had to "come out of her" in order to remain faithful and true to Jesus. They declared that "Jesus was the way, the truth, and the life," and they rejected "the false doctrine, as though the church could and would have to acknowledge as a source of its proclamation, apart from and besides this one Word of God, still other events and powers, figures and truths, as God's revelation." Their source of revelation was the Scripture, not philosophy or men.

They also argued that the church was not an organ of the state, that they weren't willing to submit to anybody other than Jesus as their Lord, and that the church wasn't subject to any prevailing ideologies, but instead had a timeless message of "faith, hope, and love." They were good shepherds, who encouraged their congregations to remember these words of Jesus: "'I will never leave you, nor forsake you.' Therefore, 'Fear not, little flock, for it is your Father's good pleasure to give you the kingdom.'"[403] They were brave, because they were committed to something higher than themselves and they had a hope for a future beyond this world.

Karl Barth

Karl Barth, the primary author of the Barmen Declaration, was a critic of liberal theology, accusing its proponents of allowing Christianity to be accommodated to modern culture. He was a liberal theologian himself at one time until a "day in August 1914 when he read a manifesto signed by ninety-three German intellectuals, including all his theology professors, supporting the Kaiser's war efforts."[404] He believed that the ethical lapse of liberal theology in supporting a war of aggression was that they lost sight of God and the revelation of Scripture, instead talking about "man in a loud voice."[405]

Karl Barth taught theology at the university in Bonn, but was eventually arrested by the Nazis while teaching his students, and sent back to his home country of Switzerland. His final words to his students as he was being arrested by the Nazis were reportedly, "Remember: exegesis, exegesis, exegesis." In other words he was admonishing his students to practice sound doctrine, sound doctrine, sound doctrine.

For atheists to insist that Hitler was a Christian because he mentions Herder's conception of God or because liberal churches were infused with Nazi symbolism is a shallow understanding of history. There were some religious leaders who compromised and embraced Nazism, but the church that was on the Narrow Way didn't follow Hitler. In fact, Bonhoeffer was involved in a plot (called "Valkyrie") to overthrow Hitler. He had already been arrested by the Nazis for helping Jews, so he was no longer able to be active in the plot, and instead ended up in a concentration camp where he was hanged a few days before the Allied liberation.

Dietrich Bonhoeffer

Bonhoeffer was no great follower of religion, either. He was intrigued by another great theologian, Paul Tillich, and his attempt to rehabilitate the word "religion." Tillich would declare that the "Bible fights for God against religion. This fight is rather strong in the Old Testament, where it is most powerful in the attack of the prophets against the cult and the polytheistic implications of the popular religion." He also says this anti-religious fight is "evident in the New Testament… which is full of stories in which Jesus violates ritual laws in order to exercise love, and in Paul the whole ritual law is dispossessed by the appearance of the Christ."[406]

Bonhoeffer believed that the conflict between good and evil wasn't the basis of ethical decision-making in the New Testament. Rather, it was to choose Life or Law. Just as in the Garden, each of us must make the same decision as Adam and Eve. But as Paul explained, reconciliation with God could never come through Law (by always doing what is right), because that's impossible! Therefore, it could only come by choosing Life (Jesus) rather than Law. We must put our faith in what Christ did for us since we were unable to do it for ourselves. For those who choose Law, "the problem is for man to reach God by way of the integrity and constancy of his own decisions." For those who choose Life, "the challenge is for man to decide in the light of the fact that God has reached him."[407]

In a letter written from Tegel prison and dated April 30, 1944, Bonhoeffer reflects on the possibility of a "religion-less Christianity." He asks, "Are there religionless Christians? If religion is only a garment of Christianity—and even this garment has looked very different at different times—then what is a religionless Christianity?"[408] Bonhoeffer understood that:

> Our relationship to God is not a "religious" relationship to the highest, most powerful, and best Being imaginable—that is not authentic transcendence—but our relationship to God is a new LIFE in "existence for others," through participation in the being of Jesus. The transcendental is not infinite and unattainable tasks, but the neighbor who is within reach in any given situation.[409]

Bonhoeffer had discovered the non-religious Narrow Way and realized that God's desire for him was not a life filled with sermons, liturgies, church, or even

Christian "community." But it was a life that lived out the will of God through love. Bonhoeffer thought hard about who was able to successfully oppose evil when confronted with it. He asked:

> Who stands fast? Only the man whose final standard is not his reason, his principles, his conscience, his freedom, or his virtue, but who is ready to sacrifice all this when he is called to obedient and responsible action in faith and in exclusive allegiance to God—the responsible man, who tries to make his whole life an answer to the question and call of God. Where are these responsible people?[410]

To Bonhoeffer it wasn't "enough for him to seek justice, truth, honesty and goodness for their own sake and patiently to suffer for them." He understood that we must have "loyal obedience to him who is the source and spring of all goodness, justice and truth and on whom he felt absolutely dependent."[411]

Bonhoeffer was eating from the Tree of Life. He wasn't religious. He was passionate about his God to the point that he was willing to die, not in some sort of suicidal quest for a heavenly paradise, but in a way that caused him to want to identify with Christ through the suffering world: "When did we see you hungry? When did we see you naked? When did we see you sick? When did we see you in prison? ... When you did it to the least of these, you did it unto me." (Matt. 25)."

Heroes of the Holocaust

This willingness to identify with the least in society was seen in heroic ways during the carnage of the Holocaust. Corrie ten Boom and her family hid Jews in their home and ended up in Ravensbruck prison camp because of it. Pastor Von Bodelschwing, head of the charitable community at Bethel-Bielefeld "barred with his body the efforts of the Nazis to remove deformed children from his institution in order to exterminate them."[412] Hans and Sophie Scholl, calling themselves the "White Rose," opposed the Nazi regime in Munich. Brother and sister, one a medical student and the other a philosophy student, they were inspired by their faith to oppose tyranny. They distributed leaflets, which read:

> Everywhere and at all times of greatest trial men have appeared, prophets and saints who cherished their freedom, who preached the

one true God and who with His help brought the people to a reversal of their downward course. Man is free, to be sure, but without the true God he is defenseless against the principle of evil.... We must attack evil where it is strongest, and it is strongest in the power of Hitler... we will not be silent. We are your bad conscience. The White Rose will not leave you in peace.[413]

They were arrested, interrogated, and beheaded for their disobedience to the Nazis. But they were faithful to God... as were countless other believers. Even non-religious persons such as Raoul Wallenberg and Oskar Schindler were heroic in their opposition to Hitler, but most of the religious community failed. For whatever reason, there was no major response to Nazism by Pope Pius XII. The bulk of the Christian community went along with the Nazis. They had no defense. They were drowning in the quicksand of wrong doctrine with nothing solid to stand on.

Martin Luther

Martin Luther also contributed to the German justification of disgust for the Jews.[414] He thought that it was the abusive Roman Catholic religious system that caused the Jews to reject the Gospel, but when they wouldn't receive it even from the Protestants, he got upset with them.[415] He wasn't an anti-Semite who was racially motivated, but he *was* spiritually motivated. He went way too far in his plan to rid Germany of the Jewish population. But Luther lived nearly 400 years before Hitler. The church could have discredited Luther's teaching on the Jews if they had taken the time or shown the interest. But they didn't. They let it stand.

In all fairness to Luther, it must have been difficult to be doctrinally sound on all issues that faced the church, especially when the church barely even understood the doctrine of justification by grace. He was blazing a new trail (or restoring the old one), and the bulk of his work was in opposing false religion. To Luther, the Jews represented a religious system that was as corrupt as the Roman Church. He was wrong, though, especially in his willingness to use coercive tactics to oppose "Judaism."

In spite of Luther's position on the Jews, the Confessing Church still embraced the Reformation (they didn't throw the baby out with the bath water) and remained a faithful community of believers. Over 1,000 pastors were a part of the Confessing Church, and almost all of them were killed in Nazi concentration camps.

For skeptics or liberals to constantly imply that fundamentalist Christians are purveyors of fascism and Nazism, as Sam Harris or even Chris Hedges (author of the book *American Fascists: The Christian Right and the War on America*) do, is an absolute perversion of the truth. Nazism was brought about by leaving sound doctrine. It was a mixture of utopianism, liberal interpretation of the Scriptures, social Darwinism, and man-made philosophies. None of this could in any way be associated with the Christian "Right." In fact most of these causes are in direct opposition to a fundamentalist interpretation of Christianity. To attempt to smear evangelical Christianity with the charge of fascism is a cheap shot and a deception. In fact it was the Allied forces, led by those countries that had large populations of those on the Narrow Way (those stupid American creationists)[416] who finally defeated Hitler.

Hitler wasn't a Christian who embraced the doctrines of the church. Instead he was immersed in German Idealism. At one point he even served as a "cultural officer"[417] in the army. This is why the people loved him. He spoke their language. Nazism was an example of what happens when men neglect the Truth for their own ideas. It was also another example of men attempting to get back to Eden their own way. Hitler and his German followers were caught up in a romantic pursuit of "Blood and Soil," an ideal world where peasants were at one with nature. They were looking for Eden. And because they chose not to do it God's way, they ended up with Auschwitz—hell on earth

CHAPTER ELEVEN
The Narrow Way Confronts Communism

"'Not by might, nor by power, but by my spirit,' says the Lord Almighty." —Zechariah 4:6

"My kingdom is not of this world." —John 18:36

"For if the willingness is there, the gift is acceptable according to what one has, not according to what he does not have. Our desire is not that that others might be relieved while you are hard pressed, but that there might be equality. At the present time your plenty will supply what they need, so that in turn their plenty will supply what you need. Then there will be equality, as it is written: 'He who gathered much did not have too much, and he who gathered little did not have too little.' —2 Corinthians 8:12-15

Marxist communism was the ultimate religious experiment. Since I define religion as mankind's attempt to get back to Eden without doing it God's way, utopian communism was a perfect example of rebellious religious effort. It was an attempt to restore Eden without doing it God's way, to create the Kingdom without the King.

While the West shuddered and lamented over the "Evil Empire," it may be good to consider how communism was able to gain such a strong foothold. In some sense "Christendom" created the Marxist monster. It did this in four ways:

1. It was guilty of greedy imperialistic abuses.
2. The liberal church embraced historical criticism.

3. The Orthodox Church was entirely inadequate in its ability to oppose totalitarianism.
4. Many Western churches were tempted by the idea of bringing about the kingdom of God on earth.

Western Imperialist Abuses

All of these causes were brought about by wrong doctrine. As seen in the last chapter, Western imperialism was, first of all, motivated by greed, and it found in social Darwinism, which had its roots in scientific beliefs, a justification for abuse. Industrialists could rationalize their harsh "survival of the fittest" tactics by saying that they were merely part of the natural order. (They could also point to Adam Smith's "invisible hand" and claim that it made laissez-faire[418] economics necessary.) According to Merle Curti:

> The Spencerian conceptions of laissez faire, progress, and the survival of the fittest were frankly appealed to as a rationale for the operations of the titans of industry.... Andrew Carnegie... welcomed the conditions inspired by nature herself, great inequality of environment, "the concentration of business, industrial and commercial, in the hands of the few, and the law of competition between these, as being not only beneficial, but essential to the progress of the race." However hard competition might be for the individual, it was necessary, continued the great steel magnate, because it is "best for the race, because it insures the survival of the fittest in every department."[419]

When the church blended this latest social science in with the Gospel, it was particularly easy to justify using others for personal gain. Reverend Josiah Strong was a proponent of the Darwinian gospel of the W.A.S.P industrialist. He promoted expansion and imperialism in the name of God:

> Then will the world enter upon a new stage of its history—*the final competition of races for which the Anglo-Saxon is being schooled.* If I do not read amiss, this powerful race will move down upon Mexico, down into Central and South America, out upon the islands of the sea, over upon Africa and beyond. And can anyone doubt the result of this competition of races will be the "survival of the fittest"?[420]

Instead of adhering to the teachings of Jesus, the latest wind of doctrine was held up as a greater authority than the pure Gospel, which was considered outmoded and stale. Implicit in these ideas was White Anglo-Saxon Protestant superiority. Senator A.J. Beveridge expressed this doctrine in a speech to Congress:

> It is elemental. It is racial. God has not been preparing the English-speaking and Teutonic peoples for a thousand years for nothing but vain and idle self-contemplation and self-admiration. No! He has made us the master organizers of the world to establish system where chaos reigns. He has given us the spirit of progress to overwhelm the forces of reaction throughout the earth. He has made us adept in government that we may administer government among savage and senile peoples. Were it not for such a force as this the world would relapse into barbarism and night. And of all our race he has marked the American people as his chosen nation to finally lead in the regeneration of the world. This is the divine mission of America, and it holds for us all the profit, all the glory, all the happiness possible to man. We are trustees of the world's progress, guardians of its righteous peace.[421]

This doctrinal mish-mash emboldened the robber baron industrialists. Consequently, because of the huge gap that developed between the "haves" and the "have-nots," Karl Marx would develop antipathy toward the capitalistic system. Thus we read in the *Communist Manifesto*:

> The bourgeoisie... has resolved personal worth into exchange value, and in place of the numberless indefeasible chartered freedoms, has set up that single, unconscionable freedom—Free Trade. In one word, for exploitation, veiled by religious and political illusions, it has substituted naked, shameless, direct, brutal exploitation.[422]

Marx could see the greed of industrialists carried on under the banner of "Christianity." This is why he said exploitation by the bourgeoisie was "veiled by religious... illusions."

Liberal Christianity

The atheist aspect of Marx's belief came about as a result of the effect of liberal Christianity. Influencing Marx to doubt the Scriptures were Ludwig

Feuerbach and David F. Strauss. Feuerbach was, like Marx, a student of Hegel. He rejected Hegel's conception of God as the "Absolute Spirit" (Geist) which can only be expressed in history, and instead says that God is merely an expression of the mind of man. In other words, *we created God* out of our own desires, wants, dreams and wishes of what we want him to be.

Strauss would claim in his book, *Life of Jesus*, that the supernatural elements of Christianity were merely myths and that Jesus was just a good teacher. The attempts at historical criticism by F.C. Bauer, Friedrich Schleiermacher, Julius Wellhausen, H.S. Reimarus, J.E. Renan, and J.R. Seely effectively cast doubt on the reliability of the Word. They held the Word up to the standard of known history, archaeology, and science, rather than vice versa. This caused many, such as the author George Eliot, to lose their faith. Although the work of men such as B.F.Westcott, F.J.A. Hort, and J.B. Lightfoot of Cambridge would counter the claims of historical criticism, and the work of archaeologists such as Sir William Ramsay (once a skeptic who set out to disprove the Bible) would further confirm the truth of the Bible, Marx was still taken in by the claims of biblical critics and therefore would reject Christianity and claim that its true purpose was merely to serve as the "opium of the people" which dulled their worldly pain and made them satisfied with obtaining a just world in the "by and by," rather than rising up to rebel and create it now. (I guess he wasn't aware of the American Revolution.) It was the wrong doctrine of liberal historicism that led Marx to reject Christianity.

Future Marxists would use these beliefs to discredit and persecute believers in the communist world. Indeed, Reverend Richard Wurmbrand, a Lutheran minister and founder of the Voice of the Martyrs ministry, describes these precise arguments being used against him while he was in a communist prison. Describing attempts to brainwash him, he says that a prison official "began to attack religion. Christ, he said, was a fantasy invented by the Apostles to delude slaves into hopes of freedom in paradise."[423] This could be Feuerbach speaking.

The liberal Christian, who was merely trying to "bridge the gap between Christian faith and modern knowledge,"[424] was complicit in ushering in revolutionary Marxist communism. Alistair McGrath explains how they abandoned the Word:

> Liberalism's program required a significant degree of flexibility in relation to traditional Christian theology. Its leading writers ar-

gued that reconstruction of belief was essential if Christianity were to remain a serious intellectual option in the modern world. For this reason, they demanded a degree of freedom in relation to the doctrinal inheritance of Christianity on the one hand, and traditional methods of biblical interpretation on the other. Where traditional ways of interpreting Scripture, or traditional beliefs, seemed to be compromised by developments in human knowledge, it was imperative that they should be discarded or reinterpreted to bring them into line with what was now known about the world.[425]

Instead of the Word being the source for truth, now science became the source for truth, and the liberal church attempted to adapt and evolve in order to accommodate the latest theories or discoveries. In the process, it took its eyes off Jesus as the Way and the Truth, and looked to the material world as its source for truth. It's easy to understand why the liberal church would begin placing its hope in the "things of this world" rather than in the Gospel. McGrath continues:

Liberalism was inspired by the vision of a humanity which was ascending upward into new realms of progress and prosperity. The doctrine of evolution gave new vitality to this belief, which was nurtured by strong evidence of cultural stability in Western Europe in the late nineteenth century. Religion came increasingly to be seen as relating to the spiritual needs of modern humanity, and giving ethical guidance to society.[426]

The liberal Christian wants to appear intelligent and reasonable in the face of so-called "scientific evidence," but he can't go so far as abandoning the faith (perhaps he earns a living from it!) and he wants to appear "rational," so he considers that the creation story was just allegorical and the resurrection was a myth created by the first-century church, and so on, yet the *teachings* of Jesus were sublime, he reasons, therefore, he doesn't want to completely abandon the Word; he just wants to determine which parts are valid or invalid, according to material standards or societal trends, rather than through proper biblical interpretation (exegesis). He wants to be accepted by his fellow man, but, of course, thought of as separate and above the lowly fundamentalist. Sadly, though, he is a compromiser who, in his attempt to appear rational, becomes *irrational.*

Sam Harris, in his book, *Letter to a Christian Nation*, recognizes the untenable position of liberal Christians. He begins by describing their beliefs:

> Of course, there are Christians who do not agree with either of us [fundamentalist Christians or atheists]. There are Christians who consider other faiths to be equally valid paths to salvation. There are Christians who have no fear of hell and who do not believe in the physical resurrection of Jesus. These Christians often describe themselves as "religious liberals" or "religious moderates." From their point of view, you and I have both misunderstood what it means to be a person of faith. There is, we are assured, a vast and beautiful terrain between atheism and religious fundamentalism that generations of thoughtful Christians have quietly explored. According to liberals and moderates, faith is about mystery, and meaning, and community, and love. People make religion out of the full fabric of their lives, not out of mere beliefs.[427]

He also gives a concise explanation of his true enemy: "The 'Christian' I address throughout is a Christian in a narrow sense of the term. Such a person believes, at a minimum, that the Bible is the inspired word of God and that only those who accept the divinity of Jesus Christ will experience salvation after death."[428]

This, of course, is the description that I've given all through this book of those who were on the Narrow Way. They trust in the work of Jesus (God, who came as the sacrificial Lamb) and trust in the Word. As a result, the Holy Spirit comes and lives a life of love through them. (I hope I've been able to reveal their good works.) According to this atheist, these "narrow" Christians on the "Right" (perhaps a veiled reference to fascism) are "troubling," "eerie," and need to be opposed, but Harris also tries to expose the illusion that liberals are living under. Echoing the teaching of Jesus ("He who is not with me, is against me" (Matt. 12:30), he explains:

> The issue is both simpler and more urgent than liberals and moderates generally admit. Either the Bible is just an ordinary book, written by mortals, or it isn't. Either Christ was divine, or he was not. If the Bible is an ordinary book, and Christ an ordinary man, the basic doctrine of Christianity is false. If the Bible is an ordinary book, and Christ an ordinary man, the history of Christian theology is the

story of bookish men parsing a collective delusion. If the basic tenets of Christianity are true, then there are some very grim surprises in store for nonbelievers like myself. You understand this. At least half of the American population understands this. So let us be honest with ourselves: in the fullness of time, one side is really going to win this argument, and the other side is really going to lose.[429]

In other words, stop trying to straddle the fence. There is no middle ground.
The damage done to society every time the Word is blended with, added to, taken away from, or misinterpreted, is immeasurable. The German historicist movement, which blended current (rather than scriptural) knowledge of ancient world history (discovered through archaeology and other "scientific methods") in with Darwinism and a form of ethical Christianity, would actually lead to Marx's loss of faith and the destruction of millions of people. By abandoning the Word, they abandoned truth, and consequently, abandoned humanity.

Leo Tolstoy

Pastor Basil Malof, in his book, *Sentenced to Siberia*, illustrated the effect of historicism on the Christian faith. He told of an encounter he had with Leo Tolstoy and how the great author had rejected the authority of the Bible:

> This led the conversation to the subject of personal religion. Under the influence of the writings of some German "New Theology" or modernistic writers of the Fifties and Sixties of the nineteenth century, Tolstoy had come to reject the doctrine of atonement by the sacrifice of the Lord Jesus Christ, inspiration of the Bible and other fundamental evangelical doctrines, and when Pastor Malof referred to the New Testament the novelist said, "My New Testament is much shorter than yours. I reject a great deal of that which you accept." In fact he had compiled a New Testament of his own, cutting out all the miracles and the resurrection of Christ. "By what authority?" demanded Pastor Malof. "Ah!" replied Tolstoy, "by the authority of my own reason."[430]

In *The Gospel in Brief*, Tolstoy explained that the only words in the Bible that he could truly trust were the words of Jesus. All the other words in the

Bible had had a pall of doubt cast over their authenticity. Malof described the connection between biblical doctrine and society. When humanity rejects God and his Word, invariably society becomes destructive rather than constructive. There's a link between sound doctrine and sound society:

> Here was noticeable the destructive results of the poison of the early German modernistic teachings upon the Russian mind which later with such terrible results spread in the theological schools and universities of Great Britain and America. The New Theology... like a terrible octopus of hell spread its poisonous tentacles over the thinking of... students and professors and preachers. Modernism in religion is the same revolutionary process as bolshevism and anarchy in politics. No more does the infallible and holy God decide, but the fallible human reason. Modernism, just as communism, is an uprising against authority.[431]

Malof continued to challenge Tolstoy until "looking at the Pastor with his penetrating, grey, mystical eyes, in his deep bass voice, as if speaking to himself, [Tolstoy] solemnly said: "Ya yesh-cho ish-chu." ("I still seek.")[432] To this, Malof commented that Tolstoy's answer expressed "the true spiritual face of the whole Russian nation—people who are still seeking, who have church, but not Christ."[433]

This searching attitude would be reflected in Tolstoy's *Confession*, in which he described in great detail, his search for God. He said he dabbled in all the latest philosophy. He had studied all the great thoughts of men and determined, as Solomon, that they were all vanity. He studied all the world's religions (even all forms of Christianity) and concluded that they weren't true because of their hypocrisy. They didn't live out the morality that they espoused.

But this made him feel hopeless and suicidal. What was the meaning in life? Why did he exist? So then Tolstoy turned to poor laborers to understand the faith that sustained them in their hardship and realized he may have been hasty in rejecting faith because of the hypocrites:

> And remembering how those very beliefs had repelled me and had seemed meaningless when professed by people whose lives conflicted with them, and how these same beliefs attracted me and seemed reasonable when I saw that people lived in accord with them,

I understood why I had then rejected those beliefs and found them meaningless, yet now accepted them and found them full of meaning.[434]

He described the condition of the intelligentsia who questioned the commandments of God, rather than accepting them as the uneducated peasants did:

If a naked, hungry beggar has been taken from the cross-roads, brought into a building belonging to a beautiful establishment, fed, supplied with drink, and obliged to move a handle up and down, evidently, before discussing why he was taken, why he should move the handle, and whether the whole establishment is reasonably arranged—the beggar should first of all move the handle. If he moves the handle he will understand that it works a pump, that the pump draws water and that the water irrigates the garden beds; then he will be taken from the pumping station to another place where he will gather fruits and will enter into the joy of his master, and, passing from lower to higher work, will understand more and more of the arrangements of the establishment, and taking part in it will never think of asking why he is there, and will certainly not reproach the master.

So those who do his will, the simple, unlearned working folk, whom we regard as cattle, do not reproach the master; but we, the wise, eat the master's food but do not do what the master wishes, and instead of doing it sit in a circle and discuss: "Why should that handle be moved? Isn't it stupid?" So we have decided. We have decided that the master is stupid, or does not exist, and that we are wise, only we feel that we are quite useless and that we must somehow do away with ourselves.[435]

Tolstoy said that he couldn't agree with Schopenhauer and Kant. He believed that God couldn't be found in the material world through sensory experience. He must be found in a realm outside of time and space, therefore their dismissal of God as the Cause didn't impress him. Instead, Tolstoy sensed the presence of love in the universe. He said this love was like the love of a mother:

But again and again, from various sides, I returned to the same conclusion that I could not have come into the world without any cause or reason or meaning; I could not be such a fledgling fallen from its nest as I felt myself to be. Or, granting that I be such, lying on my back crying in the high grass, even then I cry because I know that a mother has borne me within her, has hatched me, warmed me, fed me, and loved me. Where is she—that mother? If I have been deserted, who has deserted me? I cannot hide from myself that someone bored me, loving me. Who was that someone? Again "God"? He knows and sees my searching, my despair, and my struggle.

"He exists," said I to myself. And I had only for an instant to admit that, and at once life rose within me, and I felt the possibility and joy of being.[436]

Immediately after this burst of hope and joy, Tolstoy recalled what he had learned from liberal theologians:

Not twice or three times, but tens and hundreds of times, I reached those conditions, first of joy and animation, and then of despair and consciousness of the impossibility of living.

I remember that it was in early spring: I was alone in the wood listening to its sounds. I listened and thought ever of the same thing, as I had constantly done during those last three years. I was again seeking God.

"Very well, there is no God," said I to myself; "there is no one who is not my imagination but a reality like my whole life. He does not exist, and no miracles can prove his existence, because the miracles would be my imagination, besides being irrational.

"But my perception of God, of him whom I seek," I asked myself, "where has that perception come from?" And again at this thought the glad waves of life rose within me. All that was around me came to life and received a meaning. But my joy did not last long. My mind continued its work.

"The conception of God is not God," said I to myself. "The conception is what takes place within me. The conception of God is something I can evoke or can refrain from evoking in myself. That is not what I seek. I seek that without which there can be no life." And again all around me and within me began to die, and again I wished to kill myself.[437]

It was at this time, because of the simple faith he saw in the peasants, that Tolstoy decided to attend the Orthodox Church and join in their religious rituals. He thought that if he submitted, in due time, he would understand their meaning and find joy and peace in the life of the "community" as they became one with their forefathers by following the same traditions. But the opposite happened. If he just went to church and practiced the rituals, he would experience inexplicable pain in his heart. He was able to ignore it or blame it on his own sin, yet as he studied the "truths" he could no longer close his eyes to the faults of the Orthodox religion:

> How often I envied the peasants their illiteracy and lack of learning! Those statements in the creeds which to me were evident absurdities, for them contained nothing false; they could accept them and could believe in the truth—the truth I believed in. Only to me, unhappy man, was it clear that with truth falsehood was interwoven by finest threads, and that I could not accept it in that form.[438]

The Orthodox Church's insistence that truth resided in the performance of rituals caused Tolstoy pain in his conscience. Then he considered the existence of so many sects and divisions in Christianity and concluded:

> They emphasize the fact that they have a differently shaped cross and different alleluias and a different procession round the altar. We reply: You believe in the Nicene Creed, in the seven sacraments, and so do we. Let us hold to that, and in other matters do as you please. We have united with them by placing the essentials of faith above the unessentials. Now with the Catholics can we not say: You believe in so and so and in so and so, which are the chief things, and as for the Filioque clause and the Pope—do as you please. Can we not say the same to the Protestants, uniting with them in what is most important?
>
> My interlocutor agreed with my thoughts, but told me that such conceptions would bring reproach to the spiritual authorities for deserting the faith of our forefathers, and this would produce a schism;

and the vocation of the spiritual authorities is to safeguard in all its purity the Greco-Russian Orthodox faith inherited from our forefathers.

And I understood it all. I am seeking a faith, the power of life; and they are seeking the best way to fulfill in the eyes of men certain human obligations. And fulfilling these human affairs they fulfill them in a human way.[439]

The emphasis of the Russian Church on rituals, rather than simple love for God and neighbor, would confound Tolstoy. As the author of such beautiful Christian stories as "Where Love Is, There God Is Also," he would explain the Gospel message to his fellow Russians, but his own pursuit of God would be clouded by doubt under the influence of liberal Christianity, philosophy, and most sadly, the Russian Orthodox Church.

The Russian Orthodox Church

The Russian Church had remained in the same state since the Middle Ages—steeped in monastic mysticism (see Chapter 5). She never went through a period of true reformation and therefore remained entrenched in religious rituals and mystical pursuits that made her entirely inadequate to meet the challenges of atheist Marxism. Instead of creating religious leaders who tended the flock, orthodoxy created leaders who abandoned the flock. The attempt to achieve "divine union" through transcendental ecstasy had developed into a mark of spiritual maturity and exclusiveness, but that was a standard they had erected; it wasn't erected by the Word.

The Russian Church was at a crossroad in the 1500s when Nil Sorsky "called on the church to minister to society from a position of poverty, independent of secular, political concerns."[441] But Joseph of Volokolamsk "wanted church and state united, with the rich church supporting, and supported by, the ruler."[442] Sorsky's "Non-Possessors" would be persecuted by Joseph's "Possessors," leading to their withdrawal from society, and the Possessors would "become a wealthy landowner, holding as much as one-third of all property in Russia."[443]

In an attempt to become the "Third Rome," Moscow crowned Ivan the Terrible as the first Czar (Caesar) of the Russians. The Possessors also believed that Moscow deserved a patriarch just as Jerusalem, Constantinople, Antioch, and Alexandria, and made the patriarch the head of the Russian Orthodox

Church. These patriarchs would help Russia endure the "Time of Troubles" between the reign of the Ivan IV and the election of Michael Romanov, when there was a power dispute and terrible famine.

Michael was the young son of Filaret, the Roman patriarch at the time, who "completely dominated his weak son. The patriarch called himself 'The Great Sovereign' and sat on the throne beside his son, signing all state papers jointly with the Czar. Thus the Russian church and state became one."[444]

Several "Zealots of Faith" would eventually rise up around Michael's son, Czar Alexis, and travel across Russia, calling people back to spiritual devotion, rather than going the way of the state church toward a material emphasis. When Alexis became Czar, he appointed his fellow Zealot, Nikon, as patriarch, but the changes that Nikon made were silly, consisting of a declaration that the "sign of the cross must be made with three fingers raised, not two, as had been the Russian practice; [and] the three-fold *Alleluia* was to be sung in worship, not the two-fold."[445]

In response to this pettiness, Avvakum, the archpriest, began his call for reform against immorality and changes in the church. Avvakum and his followers (called "Old Believers") would be persecuted because Nikon had the power of the state to enforce the liturgical changes. A division would develop in the Orthodox Church, and Nikon would burn Avvakum and thousands of Old Believers at the stake, effectively squelching any attempts at reform.

Nikon then declared himself to be "The Great Sovereign," forcing Czar Alexis to remove him from office, due to fears that the state would become subservient to the church. Alexis' son, Peter the Great, would get rid of the patriarch altogether, appointing instead a synod of bishops, which would be overseen by the state. This "Ecclesiastical Regulation" effectively turned the Russian Orthodox Church into a "department of state,"[446] forcing priests to turn over plans of treason that might be heard in confession, and that would be harmful to the government, to the police.

A division between the state priests and the lower clergy continued to grow under Catherine the Great, and she even furthered the schism by confiscating all church and monastery lands, leaving the uneducated lower level priests and monks in destitution.

As a result, the Orthodox Church became less and less influential in the lives of common people, but spiritual hunger continues in the human heart, and if the church can't meet this need, people will resort to anything and everything to satisfy it. The Russians tried asceticism in the form of "*Khlysty* ('Flagellants'), *Skoptsy* ('Castrates'), *Dukhobors* ('Spirit Wrestlers'), [and] *Molokany* ('Milk Drinkers')."[447]

It wasn't until the eighteenth century that Czar Alexander I would sponsor the translation of the Scriptures into the common language under the leadership of the Russian Bible Society, but because the next Czar, Nicholas I, prohibited the distribution of the Scriptures, the Bible wasn't available to the average Russian until 1863! By that time Karl Marx had already written his *Communist Manifesto* (1848).

While there were periods of "reform" in the Russian Orthodox Church, they weren't biblical reforms; they were disputes over rituals and traditions. Unlike the reform in the Western church, where the Bible was translated into the languages of common readers in the 1500s and the doctrine of grace would be restored, it would take 300 more years for Russians to read the true Word. (Unbelievably, the Russian Bible Society completed the translation thirty years earlier, but the Orthodox Church [the Synod] demanded that the translation process cease, and they even confiscated any copy that may have gotten out into society!) Consequently, the Russian people weren't spiritually prepared at all for the battle that was coming their way. All they had was Christianity in the form of ritualistic religion.

Basil Malof

In the late nineteenth century, Russia would finally be discipled in the Word, as they became a beneficiary of the great missions movement discussed in Chapter 9 of this book. Pastor Basil Malof, referred to as "Russia's Luther and Wesley" rolled into one man (and who had met with Tolstoy) was part of this effort. He was supported by Reverend E.A. Carter's Pioneer Mission in England and the congregation of Oswald J. Smith of the Toronto People's Church. Trained in London at Charles Spurgeon's Pastor's School, Malof, a Latvian, was an answer to prayer for the mission societies who were hoping to get into Russia. At school, he read the stories of the great missionaries. By the time Malof graduated, Nicholas II had passed the religious freedom act that gave foreign mission societies a window of time, before the Bolshevik Revolution, to spread the Gospel in Russia. Carter and Smith gave financial support to

Malof for large meetings in St. Petersburg and Moscow. Thousands of Russians who were spiritually destitute came to these meetings to hear the Word and receive Jesus as their Savior. Malof also led meetings to reach university students. He described the situation that encountered the young people of Russia:

> Materialism, agnosticism and atheism were sadly prevalent among the students. The deadness and formalism of ancient churches, and the indifference of most of the priests as to conditions, vice and misery in which people lived, had reacted unfavorably on the minds of these young men and women, and for the most part they were rather revolutionary than religious… many of the students were full of revolutionary dreams of a sudden millennium through approaching violent political changes, dreams that filled their hearts with rosy hopes. To others such dreams had already been shattered by the slow process of events, and they were falling a ready prey to a coarse, atheistic quasi-philosophy such as that which St. Paul alluded to in the expression, "Let us eat and drink, for tomorrow we die."[448]

The students found no hope in the Orthodox Church, and their communist dreams were also being dashed, leaving them in a condition of despair. Malof offered them another way, a Narrow Way, and they responded with joy: "Sometimes as many as three hundred of these students would attend and, with visible tokens of strong emotion, many would surrender themselves to the Lord Jesus Christ. Among the young students kneeling and praying you could sometimes see a fine looking military officer or an army doctor, or a member of the Russian nobility."[449] These new converts to Christ would give all for their Savior, because their King had given all for them. Pastor Malof records their thankful attitude:

> Many heroic disciples of Christ in the subsequent post-revolution persecution of Christians have been enlisted from among these converted students. The young Russian convert flings himself unreservedly upon the altar of faith. He asks, "Lord, what will you have me to do? What may I sacrifice for the Master's cause? I am ready to do or to suffer for that which fills my heart—the joy of my salvation?"[450]

Those who came to Christ as a result of the short burst of evangelical activity at the turn of the twentieth century would provide a strong, pure internal opposition to communism, while the Orthodox Church compromised and became a part of the communist system. The Orthodox Church also opposed Malof, running a front-page warning in one of the newspapers that "the city of Moscow was being attacked by the arch-heretic, chief of demons, Basil Malof"[451] and forbade any member of the Orthodox Church to go to his meetings. The whole Russian clergy had declared him to be a dangerous heretic. (The declaration that Malof was a "devil" had the opposite effect on the superstitious Russian people, who turned out in droves to gaze upon the hoofed and horned demon! They brought their icons and avoided getting too close to Malof lest the "fiery breath of the devil" might breathe on them.) Instead, they heard the Gospel for the first time, and many began weeping and crying out to God. Malof pointed them to the Lamb as he closed the service with William Cowper's beautiful words:

There is a fountain filled with blood
Drawn from Immanuel's veins
And sinners plunged beneath the flood
Lose all their guilty stains.

As more and more people began to flock to the 2,000-seat Dom Evangelia (Gospel House), the Orthodox leaders became more and more hostile toward Malof. Here are some quotes from a Moscow newspaper:

"Orthodox Christians, what is being done in our holy Russia? What is happening to our mother Moscow, the whitestone City? From far-off lands, from seas of the enemy, an unseen army has come upon us—to make war against our holy faith."

"Ah! It is not faith that Malof is after. He wants to break in pieces, in the Orthodox people, their faith in Christ in order that after that he may destroy the Russian land itself... wake up, then O ye Orthodox, from your perilous dream. Quench these diabolical arrows of these Malofs and Perks [Malof's assistant]. Think well into what an abyss you are being drawn by these servants of the antichrist."[452]

The meetings continued, so the Orthodox Church tried another tactic. They called Malof to their office and offered to make him a bishop in the state church, providing him a large income. Pastor Malof rejected the offer, and consequently, "The Most Holy Synod" accused him of being "an international agent in the service of Great Britain, working in order to help England make of Russia an English colony." They accused him of this because he was being supported by the English Pioneer Mission society. In response, Malof decided to cut himself off from English support. But this wasn't enough, and he was still brought to the Kremlin and sentenced to Siberia.

Malof's ministry would extend into the Eastern Block countries, where he would start churches, a Bible college, Christian magazines, and author books. When he was released from Siberia, he was exiled from Russia. This wasn't the end of Malof's ministry, though. He found himself in Germany, where two million Russian soldiers were being held as prisoners of war (from World War I), and he led a campaign into the prison camps, where spiritually hungry soldiers consumed gospel tracts provided as a "gift from American friends." Spurgeon, Moody, Torrey, Haldeman, F.B. Meyer, and others wrote tracts that Malof translated for the cause. The effort to reach the Russian soldiers with the Good News of Jesus was also supported by Dr. R.S. McArthur, Reverend C.I. Scofield, Reverend J. Ross Stevenson, Dr. J.H. Jowett, Dr. W.I. Haven, Dr. James Gray, Dr. Sandison, Reverend John MacNeill, Dr. Jesse W. Brooks, and many, many more believers.

It was a huge interdenominational effort in which Pastor Malof would see the hand of God, saying that "it was worthwhile for one preacher of the Gospel to have been banished from Russia, so as to make it possible for much larger results to take place."[453] The converted Russian soldiers now returned to thousands of little towns and villages, equipped with New Testaments and tracts, ready to share the Gospel with their families and friends.

Malof, who kept a plaque of his motto, "OTHERS" on his desk as a constant reminder, also helped care for the poor and sick, at one time turning the Dom Evangelia into a hospital for wounded soldiers. He was on the Narrow Way and because of it was opposed by poisonous religion and atheism. Just as Jesus was convicted by both secular and religious authorities, Malof was also despised by both. The new Christians would enter into the same battle.

Pastor Malof described the attitude of the revolutionaries toward Christianity by quoting Anatoly Lunacharsky, the Commissar of Education and Enlightenment:

Christian love is a hindrance to the development of the revolution. Down with love for one's neighbor. What we want is hatred. We must know how to hate, for only at this price can we conquer the universe. We have done with the kings of the earth; let us deal now with the kings of the skies. All religions are poison.... A fight to death must be declared upon religion. Our task is to destroy all kinds of religion, all kinds of morality.[454]

This sounds comparable, of course, to several statements made by Christopher Hitchens. Even the title of his book, *God Is Not Great: How Religion Poisons Everything*, could have been taken from this quote. Indeed, the last paragraphs of his book make the same declarations as Lunacharski. Hitchens says that sexuality must be divorced from religious morality and that "it has become necessary to know the enemy [religion], and to prepare to fight it."[455] As stated before, he also declared in a debate with Alistair McGrath that it was immoral to love our enemies, rather we needed to have a "cold, steady dislike of them and a determination to encompass their destruction."[456] Certainly, Hitchens doesn't truly want to align himself with this kind of thinking, does he? Or maybe he thinks that what he's promoting is a new thing... a horse of a different color? Yet he sounds very similar to Lunacharsky ("There is nothing new under the sun [Eccles. 1:9].")

Christian Opposition to Communism

After the revolution, because of Lenin's commitment to religious liberty and the guarantee of "separation of church and state," there would be a period of relative freedom, where the Gospel could spread throughout the Soviet Union, but starting in the 1930s, Stalin's Purges began. As in other times, a madness began to grip those who rejected faith in God. Communist atheists began to mock and persecute those who believed in Jesus. Christians were called mentally ill and, as Anna Chertokova, were sent to an insane asylum to be "cured." They were arrested and sent to prison camps where they endured unbearable cold, hunger, and workloads. There Christians were beaten and tortured. Their testimonies are too numerous to share here, but they could include Reverend Richard Wurmbrand, Aida Skripnova, Alexander Solzhenitsyn, Vera Yakovlena, Joana Mindrutz, Shenia Komarov, Nikolai Khamara (whose eyes were gouged out and tongue cut off for praising Jesus), Dr. Margareta Pescaru (who smuggled medicine to patients that had been through "re-education efforts"), Louise Klassen Matson, Georgi Vins, Pavel Zakharov, Ivan Moiseyev, and so many, many more.

Christians in other countries would suffer persecution also, as the "Revolution" spread to places such as China, Korea, Vietnam, Cambodia, Laos, Thailand, Africa, Central America (through "Liberation Theology"), Cuba, and South America. Watchman Nee, the famous Chinese pastor, was a victim of communist aggression. He was sentenced to fifteen years in prison for preaching the Gospel and died in his cell. The last words he wrote were, "In my sickness, I still remain joyful at heart." Missionaries from the China Inland Mission, such as Arthur and Wilda Mathews, had to flee for their lives or be slowly starved (on purpose) in the Chinese prison camps.

Brother Andrew

Brother Andrew, the Bible smuggler, worked tirelessly to bring the Word of God to those trapped behind, not only the Iron Curtain, but the Bamboo Curtain also. He also tried to awaken the West to the fact that communists persecuted the church. He agreed that communism was a religion:

> Wherever it spreads, it takes the place of other ideologies and religious beliefs. It has its own counterfeit for almost every Christian doctrine and practice. It has several Messiahs—Marx, Lenin, and Mao. It has a doctrine of conversion—the repentance for sins "against the people" and commitment to the cause of Revolution. It has a body of "scripture"—Mao's *Red Book* and the writings of Marx and Lenin. It has a tradition of evangelism—the drive for worldwide Revolution that has Russian, Chinese, and Cuban young people all around the world working for it.[457]

Brother Andrew reiterated that communism was "an extremely intolerant religion" and was distraught that the West didn't care more about the plight of the underground church:

> I am appalled at the trend in America and Western Europe to dismiss the Revolution as a tame, toothless adversary. The politics of detente has lulled us to sleep. It is no longer fashionable to oppose

the communistic menace. Even in our churches we are assured that "things are better" behind the Iron Curtain, that Christians are not suffering so much anymore.[458]

The Social Gospel

As stated before, because of historical criticism, portions of the church embraced Darwinism and rejected the miraculous. Again, the deity of Christ was brought into question, leading many theologians to emphasize the ethical teachings of Jesus, rather than redemption. As a type of "Red-letter Christians," they promoted the "Social Gospel" that they believed Jesus emphasized in the Sermon on the Mount. Their views on evolution had changed because the Russian anarchist, Peter Kropotkin, "suggested that the principal reason why the human species had survived and prospered was because of its capacity for 'mutual aid.'"[459] Saying that "the vast majority of species live in societies" and that those that don't are "doomed to decay,"[460] they soon could embrace Marxism, not as "dialectical materialism," which entailed an earthly, rather than spiritual, version of Hegel's dialectic of "thesis-antithesis-synthesis," (and would manifest as revolutionary class warfare), but as a kinder, gentler, evolutionary process, or to put it sociologically, a *progressivism.*

Harry F. Ward authored the *1908 Social Creed of the Churches*, which was a very reasonable response to the abuses of industrialism and advocated:

1. For the protection of the worker from dangerous machinery, occupational diseases, injuries and mortality.
2. For the abolition of child labor.
3. For such regulation of the conditions of labor for women as shall safeguard the physical and moral health of the community.
4. For a release for [from] employment one day in seven.
5. For a living wage in every industry.
6. For the recognition of the Golden Rule and the mind of Christ as the supreme law of society and the sure remedy for all social ills.
7. [For] the toilers of America and [for] those who by organized effort are seeking to lift the crushing burdens of the poor, and to reduce the hard ships and uphold the dignity of labor.

Yet over time, Ward, a professor at Union Theological Seminary, would become an outspoken communist. His hope was that through socialism, the kingdom of God would be brought to the earth. He wasn't a revolutionary, but an evolutionary (or progressive) socialist. He would join other Fabian socialists (those who believed that redistribution of wealth could be accomplished by a slow, but sure, infiltration of society rather than through revolution) such as Sidney Webb and Beatrice Potter Webb. The Society would grow to include Bertrand Russell, H.G. Wells, George Bernard Shaw, Sinclair Lewis, Annie Besant, and Harry Dexter White. In 1918, Ward gave a speech at the Race Street Meeting House in Philadelphia, entitled *The Christian Demand for Social Reconstruction,* which explained the Darwinist/progressive, socialist, Christian position:

> Christianity seeks a revolutionary goal, but it proceeds by the evolutionary method, step by step. For twenty centuries it has been spreading through our Western civilization the great teaching that men and not things is the goal of living; that love and not force is the organizing principle of society. These teachings have controlled many individual lives. They have been partially expressed in many social movements. They have never yet become the dominant principle of government and industry. The great change which is now to be made is to put them into their rightful place as the controlling principles of social organization.
>
> This means a change in the thinking of men concerning the dynamic of the social order. This generation has been taught to look upon social living as strife and conflict. It talks glibly about the survival of the fittest. The phrase represents the popular understanding of evolutionary development, but the dominant teaching of science is that the development of life, both animal and human, is very much more a process of co-operation than of conflict. Not strife, but mutual aid, is the law of development. In the animal world those individuals survive which belong to the most cooperative groups; and those groups which can best cooperate are the survivors in the struggle against nature to get food.[461]

Ward and Walter Rauschenbusch, known as the "Father of the Social Gospel," helped establish the Federal Council of Churches (which would later become the National Council of Churches) and later would found the American

League Against War and Facism, a well-known communist front group. Ward was also the chairman of the American Civil Liberties Union.

Soviet communists were gleeful for the help of liberal churches. They had discovered that the most successful way to shut down a church in Russia was through infiltrating congregations with spies, therefore they considered that the best way to advance communism in America was through infiltrating universities, seminaries, and churches. Get the leaders—the shepherds—and the flocks would follow.

The Soviet Union used liberal Christian organizations in America to discourage opposition. The *Manifesto* of the American League Against War and Fascism, adopted at the first U.S. Congress Against War, opens with the words: "The black cloud of imperialist war hangs over the world."[462] It then goes on to explain that there's no group in the Soviet Union that can benefit from war, unlike the military/industrial complex in the United States:

> Only in the Soviet Union has this basic cause for war been removed. There are no classes or groups which can benefit from war or war preparations. Therefore the Soviet Union pursues a positive and vigorous peace policy and alone among the governments proposes total disarmament. Serious struggle against war involves rallying all forces around this peace policy and opposing all attempts to weaken or destroy the Soviet Union.[463]

The World Council of Churches vs. the Voice of the Martyrs

Because the Sermon on the Mount, which contained the phrase "Blessed are the peacemakers," was the ultimate biblical teaching to the Liberal Left (rather than rightly dividing the entire Word), they were easily deceived by the communists. Reverend Wurmbrand describes the temptation faced by churches that based their beliefs on mixtures of Christianity with ritual, tradition, or science:

> Once the Communists came to power, they skillfully used the means of seduction toward the church. The language of love and the language of seduction are the same. The one who wishes a girl for a wife and the one who wishes her for only a night both say the words, "I love you." Jesus has told us to discern between the language of

seduction and the language of love, and to know the wolves clad in sheepskin from the real sheep. Unfortunately, when the Communists came to power, thousands of priests, pastors, and ministers did not know how to discern between the two voices.[464]

Wurmbrand says he attended a meeting where the communists brought together 4,000 leaders of all Christian denominations in the Parliament Building and that these pastors, priests, and ministers chose Joseph Stalin, then the current president of the "World Movement of the Godless" as the honorary president of that congress. He says that "one after another, bishops and pastors arose and declared that communism and Christianity are fundamentally the same." The speeches at the meeting were broadcast across the Soviet Union.

Wurmbrand described the consequences of that meeting:

> Orthodox and Protestant church leaders competed with each other in yielding to communism. An Orthodox Bishop put the hammer and sickle on his robes and asked his priests to no longer call him "Your Grace," but "Comrade Bishop." Priests like Patrascoiu and Rosianu were more direct. They became officers in the secret police. Rapp, deputy bishop of the Lutheran church in Romania began to teach that God had given three revelations: one through Moses, one through Jesus, and the third through Stalin, the last superseding the one before.[465]

The World Council of Churches would also buy into this ideology. Even today, after the fall of the Soviet Union, the dream remains. The Soviets didn't get it right because they left out religion, they reason, but through Christ the world can achieve utopia. Perhaps forgetting that Jesus said that his kingdom is not of this world, they still believe that humanity must order and construct a new Eden. The General Secretary of the World Council of Churches, Dr. Philip Potter, put out a Directive explaining the beliefs of the organization:

> The participation of the church in the creation of a new society is not a secondary or derivative dimension of its existence. It begins at the very centre in the celebration of the sacraments as an anticipation of what the world is to become.... We call upon the churches to move beyond charity, grants and traditional programming to rele-

vant and sacrificial action leading to new relationships of dignity and justice among all men and to become THE AGENTS FOR THE RADICAL RECONSTRUCTION OF SOCIETY (sic).[466]

Reverend Wurmbrand explains that he left the Soviet Union, because he was saddened by the persecution of the underground church and frustrated by the role the World Council of Churches was playing in covering up the suffering of so many Christians. As a consequence, he decided to come out and tell the world himself. He determined to become "the voice of the martyrs" because "some Western church leaders don't care about" those believers who were suffering under communism. Instead, "while they were being tortured and sentenced, the Russian Baptist and Orthodox official leaders who had denounced and betrayed them were received with great honor at New Delhi, at Geneva, and at other conferences. There they assured everyone that in Russia there is full religious liberty."

Alexander Solzhenitsyn

In Alexander Solzhenitsyn's book, *One Day in the Life of Ivan Denisovich*, the Baptist character Alyosha tries to share his faith with Shukov (Ivan). But Shukov tries to point out the hypocrisy of Christians:

"Listen to me. At our church in Polomnya we had a priest…"

"Don't talk to me about your priest," Alyosha said imploringly, his brow furrowed with distress.

"No, listen." Shukov propped himself up on an elbow. "In Polomnya, our parish, there isn't a man richer than the priest. Take roofing, for instance. We charge thirty-five rubles a day to ordinary people for mending a roof, but the priest a hundred. And he forks up without a whimper. He pays alimony to three women in three different towns, and he's living with a fourth. And he keeps that bishop of his on a hook, I can tell you. Oh yes, he gives his fat hand to the bishop, all right. And he's thrown out every other priest they've sent there. Wouldn't share a thing with 'em."

"Why are you talking to me about priests? The Orthodox Church has departed from Scripture. It's because their faith is unstable that they're not in prison."[467]

THE NARROW WAY CONFRONTS COMMUNISM

Fyodor Dostoyevsky

Dostoyevsky also realized the hypocrisy of some religious leaders since he chose to make the "Grand Inquisitor" from his book, *The Brothers Karamazov*, not an atheist but a cardinal in the Catholic Church who oversaw the "*auto da fe* of a hundred burnt heretics" in one day of the Spanish Inquisition. Even Ivan, the atheist who is telling the story, can see the contrast between the cardinal and Jesus. The Grand Inquisitor blames Jesus for making faith too hard (only a few ascetics who live on locusts and roots were strong enough to accomplish it, while the weak merely languished [of course, this is an Orthodox view of spirituality, not the view of Jesus, whose sacrifice gives rest from spiritual works]) and says that the religious leaders devised a better way. While Jesus, at the time of his temptation by the devil in the wilderness, rejected "miracle, mystery, and authority," the church "corrected your deed and based it on miracle, mystery, and authority. And mankind rejoiced that they were once more led like sheep."[468]

It's at this point that Ivan describes the tendency of men like the Inquisitor to develop a vanguard "for the sake of humanity." He says the presence of Jesus only hindered the work of those Caesars, Tamerlanes, Genghis Khans, and Popes. By scorning the gift of "the kingdoms of this world" offered by Satan, he says Jesus neglected humanity and their needs!

> Why did you reject that last gift? Had you accepted that third counsel of the mighty spirit, you would have furnished all that man seeks on earth, that is: someone to bow down to, someone to take over his conscience, and a means of uniting everyone at last into a common, concordant, and incontestable anthill—for the need of universal union is the third and last torment of men. Mankind in its entirety has always yearned to arrange things so that they must be universal.[469]

Then, the Grand Inquisitor says that the world will go through a stage of freedom, but it would only lead to a time of confusion, which he says only religious leaders will be able to offer a way out of:

> For they will remember to what horrors of slavery and confusion your freedom led them. Freedom, free reason, and science will lead them into such a maze, and confront them with such miracles

and insoluble mysteries, that some of them, unruly and ferocious, will exterminate themselves; others, unruly but feeble, will exterminate each other; and the remaining third, feeble and wretched, will crawl to our feet and cry out to us: "Yes, you were right, you alone possess his mystery, and we are coming back to you—save us from ourselves."[470]

The desire to bring peace and contentment to the masses would be given as an excuse for the necessity of burning the "heretics." Because of this, the Grand Inquisitor dares Jesus to judge him:

Judge us if you can and dare. Know that I am not afraid of you. I, too, blessed freedom, with which you have blessed mankind, and I, too, was preparing to enter the number of your chosen ones, the number of the strong and mighty, with a thirst "that the number be complete." But I awoke and did not want to serve madness. I returned and joined the host of those who have corrected your deed. I left the proud and returned to the humble, for the happiness of the humble. What I am telling you will come true, and our kingdom will be established. Tomorrow, I repeat, you will see this obedient flock, which at my first gesture will rush to heap hot coals around your stake, at which I shall burn you for having come to interfere with us. For if anyone has ever deserved our stake, it is you. Tomorrow I shall burn you.[471]

There is always somebody who thinks they can correct the work of Christ! Ivan agrees that there may be many (like Shukov's priest in *One Day in the Life of Ivan Denisovich*) who did what they did merely for "vile material gain," but then asks:

Why can't there happen to be among them at least one sufferer who is tormented by great sadness and loves mankind? Look, suppose that one among all those who desire only material and filthy lucre, that one of them, at least, is like my old Inquisitor, who himself ate roots in the desert and raved, overcoming his flesh, in order to make himself free and perfect, but who still loved mankind all his life, and suddenly opened his eyes and saw that there is no great moral blessedness in achieving perfection of the will only to become convinced,

THE NARROW WAY CONFRONTS COMMUNISM

at the same time, that millions of the rest of God's creatures have been set up only for mockery, that they will never be strong enough to manage their freedom, that from such pitiful rebels will never come giants to complete the tower, that it was not for such geese that the great idealist had his dream of harmony. Having understood all that, he returned and joined... the intelligent people. Couldn't this have happened?... In his declining years he comes to the clear conviction that only the counsels of the great and dread spirit could at least somehow organize the feeble rebels, "the unfinished, trial creatures created in mockery," in a tolerable way. And so, convinced of that, he sees that one must follow directives of the intelligent spirit, the dread spirit of death and destruction, and to that end accept lies and deceit, and lead people, consciously now, to death and destruction, deceiving them, moreover, all along the way, so that they somehow do not notice where they are being led, so that at least on the way these pitiful, blind men consider themselves happy. And deceive them, notice, in the name of him in whose ideal the old man believed so passionately all his life! Is that not a misfortune?[472]

While skeptics often point to Dostoyevsky's chapter on the Grand Inquisitor as some sort of great indictment against Christ, I think Alyosha had it right when he said, "Your poem is in praise of Jesus, not in blame of him—as you meant it to be." Dostoyevsky is trying to indict "religion," not Jesus! Just as Solzhenitsyn's Alyosha demands that he not be lumped in with the priest, Dosteyevsky's Alyosha separates Christ from the Grand Inquisitor.

The tragedy of all religion is that it is tyranny inflicted in the name of God. Dostoyevsky was revealing, perhaps prophetically, the tactic of the "great and dread spirit." This wasn't an accusation against Christ; it was an accusation against the devil, who tries to copy those things that only Jesus can truly offer: unity, brotherhood, material provision ("bread"), true peace, love, and joy. The communist revolution was an attempt to bring all of this to needy humanity, but without submitting to Christ... instead blatantly rejecting Christ, torturing and beating him again, as has happened over and over since Cain killed Abel. And yet, there will always be those, like Marx, Hitler, or perhaps even Hitchens, who want to "build the tower" without Christ. They want to bring about Eden for "the sake of humanity," but in order to do this, they're left in the sadistic position of killing Christ again.

It's those on the Narrow Way, who have received the Lamb and allowed his Spirit to live through them, who are consistently sacrificed in the most horrifying ways so that mankind can accomplish something noble. Willing to kill to maintain doctrine, to battle the devil, to rid the world of poverty, to keep pure the "expression of God on Earth," to save the planet from global warming, to form a religious peace through toleration… there will always be another good cause. As J.R.R. Tolkien would say, the use of the Ring of Power always has a righteous justification, yet those who place the ring on their finger, as Frodo, Bilbo Baggins, and Gollum did, in some ways are consumed with a madness. It can descend on an entire population as they try to build the Kingdom without the King. The end will justify any means.

Communism has been opposed internally by the true church, but externally it has been opposed mostly by the United States. Again, the cause of freedom has been carried out by a nation in which a large part of the population believes in creationism. Americans defended Korea and preserved the southern portion of the country from a madman. They also defended Vietnam, and although they lost (in part due to the antiwar crowd), many of the Hmong freedom fighters found a home in the United States, while millions of others suffered horrible deaths under Pol Pot's Khmer Rouge in the "killing fields" because we pulled out of Phnom Penh. According to Chuck Colson's Prison Fellowship ministries:

> Interestingly, in the city of Pailin, Cambodia, where some of the worst criminals of the Pol Pot regime lived, the light of Christ has pierced the darkness [through the showing of *The Jesus Film*] and thousands of former Khmer Rouge have given their hearts to Jesus, finding forgiveness and new life! Now, instead of blaring communist propaganda through loud speakers, they're sharing the Gospel of grace and love on the radio. It's a beautiful testimony of the triumph of Christianity. [473]

Ronald Reagan

Ronald Reagan also took a strong stance against communism, refusing to forget those behind the Iron Curtain. Reagan grew up in Dixon, Illinois, and attended the First Christian Church. Reagan biographer Paul Kengor says that Reagan believed God had a plan for his life and that this confidence gave him the strength to pursue a Cold War victory "when few put stock in the possibility." He was influenced by Whitaker Chambers' book *Witness*, which is the story of a former communist spy who becomes a Christian.

Reagan's policies were controversial, but he was willing to defend Christians such as Prudencio Baltodano, who was persecuted by the Sandinistas (his ears were cut off) merely because he was a Christian pastor. The speech in which he implored "Mr. Gorbachev, tear down this wall" was a burst of hope for those still imprisoned in East Berlin. In 1989, the wall came down—despite the fact that Reagan was constantly derided for his comments on the "Evil Empire" and his attempt pass the Strategic Defense Initiative (mockingly known as "Star Wars"). Yet, under his watch, the Soviet Union disintegrated, and religious freedom was made possible there (at least for a time).

While those who blended the Word with other ideologies became stooges and compromisers with evil, ending up on the wrong side of history again, those on the Narrow Way would stand for the truth of the Word and Jesus, and, of course, pay a great consequence. But opposition to the evil of communism didn't mean that they lost their humanity. In fact, it enhanced it. Take the example of Liuba Ganevskaya of Russia and judge whether her faith in Christ made her poisonous:

> Liuba Ganevskaya had been beaten repeatedly in the Russian prison. But when she looked up at her torturer, holding the whip above her back, she smiled.
>
> "Why do you smile?" he asked, stunned.
>
> "I don't see you as a mirror would reveal you right now," Liuba said. "I see you as you surely have been—a beautiful, innocent child. We are the same age. We might have been playmates."
>
> God opened Liuba's eyes to see the man differently. She saw his exhaustion; he was as tired of beating her as she was of being beaten. He was frustrated that he wasn't able to make her reveal the activities of other believers.
>
> "He is so much like you," God said into Liuba's heart. "You are both caught in the same drama of life. You and your torturers pass through the same veil of tears."

"Seeing the man through God's eyes, Liuba's attitude changed. She continued talking to him. "I see you too, as I hope you will be. A persecutor worse than you once lived—Saul of Tarsus—and he became an apostle and a saint." She asked the calmed man what burden weighed on him so much that it drove him to the madness of beating a person who had not harmed him.

Through her loving concern, Liuba ushered her torturer into Christ's kingdom.[474]

Paradise isn't paradise because it has streets of gold and many mansions. It's paradise because its people love one another. And through Christ, as Bonhoeffer has said, we have the greatest power of all—the ability to love our enemies. And because of this power, a little bit of Eden was restored in that Russian prison cell.

CHAPTER TWELVE
The Narrow Way Confronts Terrorism

"Greater love has no one than this: that he lay down his life for his friends." —John 15:13

"Love your neighbor as yourself." —Leviticus 19:18, Matthew 22:39

"Mercy to the guilty is cruelty to the innocent." —Adam Smith

It's a dangerous thing to do a historical analysis of an event without substantial time elapsing for the benefit of hindsight to truly develop. Obviously, this is the treacherous situation I find myself in as I write about the War on Terror. But I also find that I cannot ignore this most recent part of world history, because it's another example of those on the Narrow Way being a blessing to humanity.

While most of the religious world opposed the war in Iraq and categorized it as unjust, those who believe most fervently in the Word, those dumb creationists, supported both the war in Iraq and Afghanistan and, as a result, fifty million people have been set free from murderous dictatorships.

It's impossible to know how many people around the world have hoped for American invasions of their country. As I was writing this book, over and over, I read of oppressed and persecuted people in prison cells or hiding from tyrants, whose greatest hope was the American military. All over the globe, in the most obscure places, victims have longed for the presence of an American GI. I'm not sure if the liberal church understands this aspect of force. Not only can force be abused and used to dominate; it can also be used to love, protect, and liberate. Even Jesus, who came first as the suffering servant, will come again as the conquering king. He will be a warrior who opposes evil.

The understanding that those in positions of power are not able to help others by wielding the sword is a misreading of Scripture. Again, the Word must be divided correctly. While Jesus did say that "all who draw the sword will die by the sword" (Matt. 26:52b), Romans 13:4 also says that the government is "God's servant to do you good. But if you do wrong, be afraid, for he does not bear the sword for nothing. He is God's servant, an agent of wrath to bring punishment on the wrongdoer." This does not mean that governments can be cruel and tyrannical with their power, but that they are there to assist victims of abuse, making sure that justice is meted out and not ignored. This is the role of a criminal justice system.

The police department also plays an important role. In some sense, they are a pre-emptive force. They're armed in case they need to go to battle to rescue somebody in trouble. Would anybody dispute the necessity of attacking a murderer in the process of strangling a little girl? Of course not. Pure pacifism is unjust. While it's true that Jesus said, "Blessed are the peacemakers" (Matt. 5:9), it needs to be pointed out that he didn't say "peacekeepers." Martin Luther King, Jr., distinguished between the two kinds of peace in his "Letter from a Birmingham Jail": "I had hoped that the white moderate would understand that the present tension in the South is a necessary phase of the transition from an obnoxious negative peace, in which the Negro passively accepted his unjust plight, to a substantive and positive peace, in which all men will respect the dignity and worth of human personality."[475]

In other words, peace without justice is a false, tyrannical peace. There comes a time when it can no longer be endured. Peacekeepers promote a "negative" peace at all costs, even ignoring the cries of victims, while peacemakers try to bring about a "positive," lasting peace that's based on justice and gives relief to victims.

While King advocated non-violent resistance and civil disobedience to bring about social change, it must be noted that King and his civil rights marchers were not government entities. They only appealed to public opinion and hoped to move the hearts of those in authority. This was consistent with the teachings of Jesus.

Political Bondage

Unfortunately, history has shown that those societies that blend church and state are more likely to become abusive. Islamic societies are no exception. Those who don't agree with the religious authorities are consistently persecuted. The Taliban in Afghanistan was an example of a tyrannical church/state entity. They wouldn't let men trim their beards. Little girls were publicly executed if caught attending underground schools. They wouldn't allow women to earn money. They banned music. They whipped people for sexual violations. They had no regard for human life and would kill at will. Saira Shah, an independent reporter, whose videos of Taliban abuse were used in the CNN program *Beneath the Veil*, says that she traveled back to her childhood home of Afghanistan in order to see what it was like since the Taliban takeover in 1996.

As she passed from village to village, Shah says, there was a terrible sameness to the stories. The death, cruelty, and abuse were everywhere. A little girl wearing white shoes was beaten by Taliban officials, because the color of her shoes was the color of their flag—which the culture police declared shows disrespect. Another girl—perhaps only twelve years old—hid in a bread oven, watching in horror as the Taliban killed her father for his wristwatch and waistcoat. Little boys also were targets. One who was deemed to have a Western-style haircut was hunted down with dogs and beaten.[476]

The people of Afghanistan were desperate. They were war-weary after so many years of fighting against the Soviet Union, and now they were controlled by religious fanatics. The last thing you would think that they wanted was another war, yet Shah reported that the "women continue to resist the oppression with the hope that a U.S. invasion might liberate them."[477]

While Saddam Hussein was more secular than religious, Iraq still had a type of religious tyranny. The country was Shiite in the south and Kurdish in the north, but was still ruled by a Sunni minority. Unfortunately, none of the sects could appropriately respond to the treachery of the Ba'ath Party. David

Brooks, a columnist for the New York Times, conveyed this story about the brutality of Saddam Hussein's regime:

> Um Haydar was a 25-year-old Iraqi woman whose husband displeased Saddam Hussein's government. After Haydar's husband fled the country in 2000, some members of Fedayeen Saddam grabbed her from her home and took her into the street. There, as two men grabbed her arms while another pulled her head back, Haydar was beheaded, in front of her children and mother-in-law. Ba'ath Party officials watched the murder, put her head in a plastic bag and took away her children.[478]

Saddam and his sons not only terrorized their own people with torture, murder, rape, and chemical weapons, they led an invasion of Kuwait in an attempt to capture their oil fields, tried to develop weapons of mass destruction, and evaded United Nations resolutions for years.

Iraqi People Plea for Help

Iraqi dissidents begged for U.S. help. George Packer, writing about "The Liberal Quandary Over Iraq" tells of a panel discussion leading up to the war in Iraq:

> One chilly evening in late November, a panel discussion on Iraq was convened at New York University. The participants were liberal intellectuals, and one by one they framed reasonable arguments against a war in Iraq: inspections need time to work; the Bush doctrine has a dangerous agenda; the history of U.S. involvement in the Middle East is not encouraging. The audience of 150 New Yorkers seemed persuaded.
>
> Then the last panelist spoke. He was an Iraqi dissident named Kanan Makiya, and he said, "I'm afraid I'm going to strike a discordant note." He pointed out that Iraqis, who will pay the highest price in the event of an invasion, "overwhelmingly want this war." He outlined a vision of postwar Iraq as a secular democracy with equal rights for all of its citizens. This vision would be new to the Arab world. "It can be encouraged, or it can be crushed just like that. But think about what you're doing if you crush it." Makiya's voice rose as he

came to an end. "I rest my moral case on the following: if there's a sliver of a chance of it happening, a 5 to 10 percent chance, you have a moral obligation, I say, to do it."

The effect was electrifying. The room, which just minutes earlier had settled into a sober and comfortable rejection of war, exploded in applause. The other panelists looked startled, and their reasonable arguments suddenly lay deflated on the table before them.

Michael Walzer, who was on the panel, smiled wanly. "It's very hard to respond," he said.[479]

Dr. B. Khalaf, an Iraqi doctor living in London, wrote a letter to *The Guardian*, protesting the London antiwar protests leading up to the Iraq war:

I am so frustrated by the appalling views of most of the British people, media and politicians. I want to say to all these people who are against the possible war, that if you think by doing so you are serving the interests of Iraqi people or saving them, you are not. You are effectively saving Saddam. You are depriving the Iraqi people of probably their last real chance to get rid of him and to get out of this dark era in their history.

My family and almost all Iraqi families will feel hurt and anger when Saddam's media shows on the TV, with great happiness, parts of Saturday's demonstration in London. But where were you when thousands of Iraqi people were killed by Saddam's forces at the end of the Gulf war to crush the uprising? Only now when the war is to reach Saddam has everybody become so concerned about the human life in Iraq.[480]

Another Iraqi dissident, nineteen-year-old Rania Kashi, penned an open letter asking where the antiwar movement was during Saddam's war against Iran in the 1980s, which caused the death of one million Iraqis and Iranians, or during his attack on the people of Halabja, when thousands of Iraqi Kurds were gassed to death. She explains:

Saddam rules Iraq using fear; he regularly imprisons, executes, and tortures large numbers of people for no reason whatsoever. Believe me, you will be hard-pressed to find a single family in Iraq which has not had a son/father/brother killed, imprisoned, tortured, and/or "disappeared" due to Saddam's regime. What then has been stopping you from taking to the streets to protest against such blatant crimes against humanity in the past?... I have attended the permanent rally against Saddam that has been held every Saturday in Trafalgar Square for the past five years. The Iraqi people have been protesting for years against the war—the war that Saddam has waged against them. Where have you been?[481]

The inability to discern right from wrong again plagues those who abandon the Word or blend it with other ideologies. Instead of reacting to the evil of Saddam Hussein, liberals instead painted George W. Bush as the evil person. Robert Scheer of the Los Angeles Times questioned American willingness to "trade the lives of U.S. troops and Iraqis for the obsession of Empire."[482] But dissidents kept asking, "Where are the Iraqis in these protests?"

If the suffering of Iraq's people meant anything to the protesters, such cries from the heart might have prompted twinges of shame, or at least some second thoughts. But there is little evidence that the antiwar campaign cares at all about those whom Saddam has hurt. Countless demonstrators carried signs reading "Don't Attack Iraq," "Not In My Name," and "No Blood For Oil." Others toted posters defaming Bush and British Prime Minister Tony Blair—portraying them with swastikas or Hitler moustaches, for example. For those who failed to grasp the point, a large sign in Rome spelled it out: "Bush is the new Hitler."[483]

Abd al-Majid al-Khoei, another Iraqi dissident, who would be assassinated in Najaf the day after the Iraqi dictatorship was overthrown, discussed the morality of a war in Iraq. Speaking of the Iraqi people and their position on the war, he said:

They see the issue as being essentially one of ethics and humanity, and furthermore believe that the task of freeing them of this tyranny is an obligation enjoined by every sacred code of law and supported by every secular ethical system. Anyone, therefore, who can perform this task will win their gratitude. To them it is entirely unacceptable that someone who is able to bring about—or help bring about—the collapse of this regime should, nonetheless, do nothing.[484]

Most of the World's Religious Leaders Oppose the Iraq War

And yet, even with the pleas for help and the descriptions of torture, people being placed in wood chippers, eaten by dogs, beheaded, and gassed, the religious leaders of the world could find no justification for the war. Instead they chose to align themselves with United Nations Security Council members, giving precedence to "international law" rather than any higher law. China, Russia, Germany, and France, all opposed the war, causing the United States to appear to act "unilaterally" (although sixty nations actually joined the U.S., including Great Britain and Australia). This alignment caused Charles Krauthammer, journalist for the Washington Post, to "question the logic by which the approval of the Security Council confers moral legitimacy on this or any other enterprise. How does the blessing of the butchers of Tiananmen Square... lend moral authority to anything?"[485]

Pope John Paul II "declared that there was nothing in the catechism that supports the notion of a pre-emptive war,"[486] and after the successful invasion of Iraq and capture of Saddam Hussein, Cardinal Renato R. Martino, head of the Pontifical Council for Justice and Peace would still claim that "the war was useless, and served no purpose."[487]

The Archbishop of Canterbury, Dr. George Carey of the Anglican Church, believed that "military action to disarm Saddam Hussein does not meet the criteria of a just war"[488] and that "there were 'no grounds whatsoever' for war against Iraq at the present time, and it would be shocking if the West attacked without the support of the United Nations."[489]

The World Council of Churches also joined the chorus in opposition to the war, saying that it was "immoral, ill-advised and in breach of the principles of the United Nations Charter."[490]

The United Church of Christ (Barak Obama's denomination) spoke out against the war in Iraq, also. John Thomas, president and "principal spokesperson" of the liberal denomination, claimed that the war was a moral compromise and that America was an occupying force in Iraq similar to the Israelis who are occupying Palestine.[491]

The New York Times ran a full-page ad in December of 2002 by "Religious Leaders for Sensible Priorities," which claimed that President Bush was violating the teachings of Christ. Its signatories included:

Bishop Melvin G. Talbert, Ecumenical Officer, Council of Bishops, The United Methodist Church. Bishop Thomas J. Gumbleton, Auxiliary Bishop, Archdiocese of Detroit. Pat Clark, National Coordinator, Fellowship of Reconciliation. Dave Robinson, National Coordinator, Pax Christi USA. Kathy Thornton, RSM, National Coordinator, NETWORK, National Catholic Social Justice Lobby. Rev. Michael E. Livingston, Exec. Dir., International Council of Community Churches. Bishop Bennett J. Sims, Founder, Institute for Servant Leadership. Bishop Paul Moore Jr., Episcopal Bishop of New York (ret.). Jim Walis, Exec. Dir., Sojourners. Michael S. Kendal, Archdeacon, Episcopal Diocese of New York. Rev. George M. Houser, fmr. Exec. Dir., American Committe on Africa. Frederick Buechner, Minister. Sister Gail Worcelo, President, Green Mountain Monastery. Rabbi Steven B. Jacobs, Temple Kol Tikva. The Reverend Jeri R. Dexheimer-Dowle, The Evangelical Lutheran Church in America. The Reverend John M. Fischer, American Baptist Churches, USA. The Reverend Mary Navarré Moore, Episcopal Diocese of East Tennessee. Morad Abou-Sabé, President, Arab American League of Voters of NJ. Rev. Robert Moore, Pastor, East Brunswick Congregational Church & Livingston Ave. United Church of Christ, NJ. Rev. Roy Bourgeois, MM, Founder, SOA Watch. Rev. Peter Laarman, Senior Minister, Judson Memorial Church. Rev. Kathleen S. Wiliams, International Ministerial Felowship. Very Rev. James Parks Morton, Dean Emeritus.Frank McNeirney, National Coordinator, Catholics Against Capital Punishment. Rev. Patricia L. Bruger, Executive Director, CUMAC/ECHO. Rev. James E. Flynn, St. Lawrence Church, Heber City, UT. Sister Mary Landon, fsp, Franciscan Sisters of Peace. Marilyn Katz, Chicagoans Against War in Iraq. Rev. Richard Deats, Editor, Fellowship, Fellowship of Reconciliation. Rev. Wiliam A. Richard, Pastor, Our Lady of the Lake Catholic Church, Rockwal, TX. Rev. Stacy Pever, Bering Memorial United Methodist Church, Houston, TX. Rev. Dr. Mark Rutledge, Campus Minister, Duke University. Rev. Dr. George Regas. Reverend Robert E. Nee, LICSW, Catholic Priest, Chaplain, Children's Hospital Boston. Sister Helene O.Sulivan, M.M., Maryknol Sisters Congregational Leadership Team. David Selzer, Chair, Janet Chisolm, Vice Chair & Jackie Lynn, Executive Director, Episcopal Peace

Felowship. Rev. Gary Cox, Senior Minister, University Congregational Church, Wichita KS. Rev. Sam A. Sirianni, Pastor, Holy Angels Church, Trenton NJ. Prof. James R. Kely, Fordham U. Jeanne Derer, fsm, & Irma Kennebeck, fsm, Franciscan Sisters of Mary, St. Louis, MO. Pax Christi New Jersey. Eric M. LeCompte, National Council Chair, Pax Christi USA. Debra W. Haffner, M. Div., Director, Religious Institute for Sexual Morality, Justice, and Healing, Norwalk, CT. Eunice Hyer, Coordinator, Pax Christi, Middle Peninsula VA. Redwood City Franciscan Sisters, Srs. Of St. Francis of Penance and Christian Charity. Margaret Hoffman, SND, J/P Coordinator, Sisters of Notre Dame de Namur of California. The Rev. Dr. Wiliam A. Greenlaw, Rector, Church of the Holy Apostles (Episcopal); Exec.Dir., Holy Apostles Soup Kitchen, NY City. Veronica Felerath, Regional Coordinator Pax Christi Long Island. Tom Rothschild, Clerk, Brooklyn Monthly Meeting Religious Society of Friends (Quakers). Rev. Thomas C. Gibbons, Presbyterian Minister, Riichardson, TX. Rev. Dr. Theodore W. Loder, Author, United Methodist Minister, (ret.). Stephanie Mertens, ASC, Coordinator of Justice & Peace Office, US Adorers of the Blood of Christ, Red Bud, IL. The Reverend Saly K. Brown, St. Andrew.s Episcopal Church, Denver, CO. The Rev. Ron Sala, Minister, Universalist Unitarian Society in Stamford, CT. Robert C. Broker, Retired, US/DHHS, former CEO/ Serve New England, Inc. The Rev. Robert Edwards, Episcopal Church, Diocese of New Jersey. The Rev. Rob & Sylvia McCann. Fr. Richard Creason, Pastor, Holy Trinity Catholic Church, St.Louis, MO. Ray & Barbara Shiffer, West Side Moravian Church, Green Bay, WI. Phil Runkel, Archivist, Marquette University. Patty Gaines, Coordinator, Pax Christi Weavers. Patricia Krommer C.S.J., Co-Director, Pax Christi, Los Angeles Chapter. Magister Monika Galuccio, Pax Christi, Austria. Michele Anton, St. Mary's Church (Catholic), Mansfield, A. Megan Castelan. Maureen Dorney O'Connel, Regional Coordinator, Pax C. Madeline C. Labriola, Pax Christi USA. The Rev. Dr. M. Douglas Borko, Conference Minister, Florida Conference, United Church of Christ. Rev. Dr. Lyle G. Miler, D.D., ECLA Pastor and Bishop Emeritus, Sierra Pacific Synod. Lorraine Soukup, SSND. Lilia Langreck, SSND, School Sisters of Notre Dame (ret.). Fr. Kevin M. Quealy, TOR, Franciscan Priest, Pax Christi USA. The Rev. John A. Nelson, Dover, MA. Rev. John Dear, S.J. Joan Chittister, Osb, Benedictine Sisters of Erie. Sister Joan Kirby. Jim O. Hanlon, Pastor, ELCA. Jerry Carpenter, Minister United Methodist. The Rev. Jeff Gil, The

Parish of Christ Church (Episcopal), Andover, MA. James F. Powers, Spiritual Director, Pax Christi, Atlanta. Rev. George J. Kuhn, Pastor, St. Joseph's RC Church, Yonkers NY. The Rev. Frank J. Alagna, Ph.D., Episcopal Priest, The Diocese of New York. Frank Galuccio, M.D., Pax Christi. Frank Ostrowski, Ph.D., Fellowship of Reconciliation; Psychologists for Social Responsibility. Dr. Frank Fromherz, Director, Catholic Archdiocese of Portland (Oregon) Office of Justice & Peace. Francis J. Skeith, Coordinator, Pax Christi Texas. The Rev. Elizabeth G. Maxwel, Church of the Holy Apostles, NYC. Eleanor Frankenberg, SSND. The Rev. Ed Bacon, Rector, Al Saints Episcopal Church, Pasadena. Dorothy Olinger, SSND, School Sister of Notre Dame, St. Paul, MN. Diana Oleskevic csj/a, Justice Coordinator, Sisters of St. Joseph of Carondelet, St. Louis Province. The Rev. Dr. Dennis B. Calhoun, United Church of Christ, Middlebury, CT. Dennis Teal-Fleming, Director of Faith Formation, The Catholic Church of Mary, Queen of Apostles, Belmont, NC. Rev. Dr. Charles McColough, United Church of Christ. Reverend Carolyn Bulard, Christian Church (Disciples of Christ). Sister Carol Bialock, RSCJ. Rev. Bryan Travis Hooper, Pastor, Washington Square United Methodist Church. Rev. Bruce N. Teague, Amherst College. The Rev. Bruce H. Davidson, Director, Lutheran Office of Governmental Ministry in NJ. Bil & Mary Carry. Ambassadors of Peace, Pax Christi USA. Father Bernard Survil, Roman Catholic Priest, Diocese of Greensburg. The Rev. Arthur R. Lee, III. Rector St. David's Episcopal Church; The Episcopal Diocese of Southwest Florida. Anne O. Calaghan, Catholic Peace Felowship, St. Malachy Philadelphia, PA. The Rev. Alfred Krass, Co-Chair, Peacemaking Committee Metropolitan Christian Council of Philadelphia. Pax Christi Minnesota. Catholic Action Network/Center for Theology & Social Analysis of St. Louis, MO. Pax Christi Metro. Presentation Sisters Social Justice Team, Aberdeen, SD. Mary C. Daly, RSM. Janet M. Weber, RSC. Ann Welch, RSM. Suzanne Lavoie. Judith Anderson, RSM. Paula Marie Koplar, RSM. Marceline Janisse. Maureen Marr, SND. Pauline Bridegroom, PHSC. Virginia Keleker, CSJ. Katherine Chazotte, SBS. Celeste Marie Nuttman, RSM. Susan Harvey, BM. Catherine M. Dowling, RSM. Roberta Silbert. Audrey B. DeLucia. April Shuman. Alayne Reed. Elizabeth J. Canilo. Jennifer Eisensmith. Natalie M. Cappielo. Elizabeth Baldwin. Jim Madura. Mary Groncheski. Carl Florence Trahan, RSM. Angelita Heinrich, RSM. Maryann Malasics, RSM. Mary C. Bilderback, RSM. Jaele Dragomir. Educator. Eugeniea Clark. Broker, Clark & Co Real Estate. Elizabeth B. Mulford, Attorney at Law. Louisa D. Kirchner, Prof. Emerita of Modern Languages, Uconn, Pax Romana USA. Patricia & Peter Ladley, Pax Christi USA. Terry & George Molina. Mike Sharp. Carri Nelson. Kely Epstein, Pax Christi. Peter Thompson, Minneapolis, MN. Jeanne Fischer Zylstra. Michael DeGregory, anthrax displaced postal worker. Frank & Mary Herzel. Judy Johnson. Elizabeth McDermott, R Catholic. Rita Wels Clark, Dallas Peace Center. Phil Tephan, Bus Station Terminal Manager. Sharyn DuPuy. Sheila K. Dixon. Donna Estabrook, Library Supervisor, University of Michigan. June Foran. Joseph G. and Sneha Jacob. Joyce Klava, concerned citizen, Roman Catholic. Barney & Marjorye Heeney. Joan & Iris Starr, members, First Congregational Church of Berkeley, CA. Jennifer Angyal, Pax Christi USA. Rosemary Hobson, Pax Christi USA. Elizabeth B. Mulford, Attorney at Law. Joe Hovel, President, County Line Wood Prod. Richard R. Rivard. Debbie Parsons, Universalist Unitarian Church. Deborah Michalewicz, Water Valey, TX. Jim Newberry, Peace Advocate. Ann Crites, Minister, U.C.C. Prof. Stephen Crites (ret.)[492]

In order to go to war in Iraq, Bush even had to go against the leaders of his own Methodist denomination.

A Few Religious Leaders Support the Iraq War

Defying nearly all the other religious leaders of the world, one small group of Christian leaders supported the War in Iraq. Dubbed the "Land Letter" because it was drafted by Richard Land, the president of the Ethics and Religious Liberty Commission of the Southern Baptist Convention, the letter would be addressed to President George W. Bush and begin with these words:

> In this decisive hour of our nation's history we are writing to express our deep appreciation for your bold, courageous, and visionary leadership. Americans everywhere have been inspired by your eloquent and clear articulation of our nation's highest ideals of freedom and of our resolve to defend that freedom both here and across the globe.
>
> We believe that your policies concerning the ongoing international terrorist campaign against America are both right and just. Specifically, we believe that your stated policies concerning Saddam Hussein and his headlong pursuit and development of biochemical and nuclear

weapons of mass destruction are prudent and fall well within the time-honored criteria of just war theory as developed by Christian theologians in the late fourth and early fifth centuries A.D.[493]

The letter would be signed by Richard Land, Bill Bright, president of Campus Crusade for Christ, Dr. James Kennedy, President of Coral Ridge Ministries, Chuck Colson, former Watergate convict and founder of Prison Fellowship Ministries, and Dr. Carl D. Herbster, President of the American Association of Christian Schools.

They acknowledged that ridding Iraq of Saddam would be defending "freedom and freedom-loving people from state-sponsored terrorism and death," and also agreed with a quote from President Bush in a speech he gave to the United Nations General Assembly:

> The United States has no quarrel with the Iraqi people.... Liberty for the Iraqi people is a great moral cause, and a great strategic goal. The people of Iraq deserve it; the security of all nations requires it. Free societies do not intimidate through cruelty and conquest, and open societies do not threaten the world with mass murder. The United States supports political and economic liberty in a unified Iraq.[494]

In response to these words of President Bush, the signers of the "Land Letter" would declare: "This is clearly a just and noble intent."

These religious leaders stood out in the crowd as they, like the signers of the Barmen Declaration, were able to see clearly in the midst of a muddy societal stew. Each of them is an evangelical/fundamentalist that believes in the grace of God through Jesus (just as Barth, Niemoller, and Bonhoeffer) and embraces a literal interpretation of the Word. I would even venture to say that most of them are creationists.

According to Paul Kengor, author of the biography *God and George W. Bush: A Spiritual Life*, Bush's theology also "seems to mix all three of those primacies—Scripture, God's grace, and God's love—but with special emphasis on the third."[495] Bush also admits he's a creationist. While campaigning for the presidency, he was asked about the teaching of evolution in schools. He responded that he thought that there were different opinions on how the world began and that he believed it was alright for children to learn all viewpoints.

Then he declared, "Here's what I believe: I believe God did create the world. And I think we're finding out more and more and more as to how it actually happened."[496]

The World Hates President Bush

Of course, this language is maddening to liberals such as Eric Alterman, who says in his book, *Why We're Liberals: A Political Handbook to Post-Bush America*, (and who refers to the "scientifically based theory of evolution" in contrast to the "religious myth of intelligent design,")[497] that many historians consider the Bush era as "the single most destructive presidency in our nation's history."[498] Bush has been called Hitler, Stupid, President Evil, cowboy, moron, names that refer to his middle initial "W." such as W-rong, W-armonger, W-easel, W-anker, and W-itless. He's also been accused of lying about the weapons of mass destruction[499] in Iraq and bumper stickers and t-shirts that say "Bush is a lying sack of shit" and "Bush lied, people died" are sold at internet shops such as CafePress. There are also continual cries to impeach Bush for "war crimes." As recently as this week, Joe Biden, the Democratic Vice Presidential candidate, talked about impeaching the president. Hugo Chavez, the president of Venezuela, called Bush "the Devil" at a speech given to the United Nations, and the newest bumper sticker/t-shirt says: "Embarrassed to be a Bush-era American."

The Iraqi and Afghan People Thank Bush

The vitriol against Bush coming from the Left is profuse, and yet the people of Iraq and Afghanistan are free and he is considered to be a national hero by many citizens of both countries. His picture can still be found in Iraqi homes. Bush was mocked for believing that U.S. troops would be considered liberators. But on April 9, 2003, the American Marines entered Baghdad, not knowing what to expect, and slowly but surely, the Iraqi people began to respond.

Within half an hour, the battle-weary soldiers were out of crouch position to pose for snapshots with smiling Iraqi families. One troop was tugged aside by an Iraqi mother and father who wanted a picture of him holding their two daughters. Another was pulled away by an Iraqi man who insisted on frying him an egg. Women held up babies for soldiers to kiss. Some adult men were so swept up by the emotion of the moment that they rushed into the streets wearing only their underwear, awkwardly embracing Marines in full combat gear. "We were nearly mobbed by people trying to shake our hands," said Major Andy Milburn of the Seventh Marines.[500]

Juad Amir Sayed, an Iraqi Shiite Muslim, emoted, "I believe that Allah worked through Mr. Bush to make this happen. If I met Mr. Bush, I would say, 'thank you, thank you, you are a good human, you returned me from the dead.'"[501]

Cameras from around the world were pointed at Saddam Hussein's statue as the Iraqi people tried to express their disdain for the dictator by pulling it down. At first they just beat on it, but then they tried to topple it. They weren't able to do it by themselves, so they enlisted the help of American soldiers who were watching nearby. Corporal Edward Chin of New York City placed a chain around the neck of the statue and pulled it down with an American tank. The Iraqi people went wild with excitement and joy. Little boys began to ride the head through the streets of Baghdad.

Henry Payne, the editorial cartoonist for *The Detroit News*, recorded the responses of the Iraqis who had been exiled and now lived in Dearborn, Michigan. Henry Choulagh, a Baghdad native cried out: "President Bush has made our dreams come true!"[502]

An Iraqi poet exiled to London, Awad Nasir, wrote a piece called "Thank you" to express his gratitude to America for setting the Iraqi people free. Noting that it wasn't "the mullahs of Tehran and their Islamic Revolutionary Guards who liberated Iraq Shiites, nor was it Turkey's army, the Arab League, or the European Left."[503] Instead, he says: "Believe it or not, Iraqis of all faiths, ethnic backgrounds and political persuasions were liberated by young men and women who came from the other side of the world—from California and Wyoming, from New York, Glasgow, Sydney, and Gdansk to risk their lives, and for some to die, so that my people can live in dignity... they have gained an eternal place in our hearts."[504] Dominique Moisi echos this sentiment as he tells of a fellow French citizen who:

> ...expressed a sense of diminishment that his country had sat out this stirring story of political liberation. A society like France with a revolutionary history should have had a hand in toppling the tyranny in Baghdad. Instead, a cable attached to a U.S. tank had pulled down the statue, to the delirium of the crowd. It was soldiers

from Burlington, Vermont, and Linden, New Jersey, and Bon Aqua, Tennessee who raced through the desert making this new history and paying for it.[505]

Ironically, David Shater of ITN television told of a twelve-year-old boy who said he "finally felt safe"[506] as the American tanks rolled into the city. All across Iraq, pictures of George W. Bush were held up and kissed. He was called their hero, and Iraqis chanted "George Bush! George Bush! George Bush!" in the streets while women put on their best dresses and danced. The same rejoicing went on in American cities where Iraqi citizens lived as exiles. They couldn't believe it was really true.

In the same way that the Iraqi people disdained Saddam Hussein, CNN captured Iraqi men carrying signs that said, "Go Home Human Shields: You U.S. Wankers!"[507] There was no patience on the part of the Iraqis for those who opposed their liberation. Steve Centanni, of *Fox News* says that the Iraqis chased an Al Jazeera news crew out of Iraq and into Kuwait because they had opposed the war.

On YouTube there are films dedicated to everything imaginable, but one film, entitled "An Open Message to America from Iraqi Citizen" posted by Iraqtube on April 27, 2007, details why the Iraq people are so grateful.

1. The U.S. and Coalition forces removed an evil dictator, Saddam Hussein, from power.
2. Iraq held free elections and more than seventy percent of the Iraqi people participated.
3. Iraq is free!
4. Forty satellite stations and over 100 new periodicals are now available to the Iraqi people.
5. Internet, fax, and mobile phones are now allowed to all, not just Sadda mists.
6. The Iraqi people can buy cars.
7. The Iraqis can import any product.
8. Iraqi oil profits will go to build Iraq rather than to fund Saddam's war machine.
9. Iraqis can now travel; before they were essentially prisoners.
10. The Iraqi economy is growing at six percent per annum.

Finally, says the computer enhanced voice and image, the Iraqis will conquer even though Iran, Syria, Saddamists, and Al Qaeda terrorists are continuing to hinder their progress. Most of all, the poster just wanted to say thank you to America, to the Republicans, to the military, and especially George W. Bush.[508]

Many of the freedoms mentioned, such as that of a free press and elections, are advocated by Enlightenment ideology, wherein the Left supposedly finds its roots, but they still rejected the liberation of Iraq. The Bush administration, on the other hand, looked at the liberation as an opportunity to make a friend and establish an outpost of democracy in the Middle East. What better way to get rid of an enemy than to make him into a friend? So when American soldiers went to Iraq, it was to battle against Saddam Hussein, but it was also to make and lift up a friend.

There was bad news out of Iraq, as the enemies of freedom tried to rise up and rule over the beaten down Iraqi people, but there was also good news. Coalition forces began to stabilize the country, restoring power, reestablishing trash pick-up, strengthening medical facilities, bringing fresh water, repairing oil facilities, opening schools, feeding the hungry, and showing kindness, especially to little children. They also began the process of training men to serve in the army and as police officers. The Iraqis also had to be taught how to run a democracy and establish elections that weren't corrupt. It was this effort that produced the purple-dyed thumbs of those who risked their lives in order to vote.

The Kurds in the north were particularly grateful for their freedom, and were the most self-sufficient of the Iraqi ethnic groups. They began a publicity campaign called "The Other Iraq" to show how happy and prosperous they had become since the liberating invasion. They had suffered so much under Saddam's regime—he actually used poison gas to murder thousands of their people—and they were longing for the day when they would be free from oppression. When that day came, they embraced it with vigor.[509]

What is Love?

Elie Wiesel, author of *Night*, the autobiography of how he suffered during the Holocaust, said that the opposite of love wasn't hate, it was indifference. Was the bulk of the religious community complicit in their indifference to the suffering of the Iraqi people?

Could it really be possible that the entire religious world was wrong again and that one man, a born-again Christian who believes in the Bible and has received God's grace, could be one of the most loving and heroic men of our time? Could it be that again one little band of believers, standing on the Word of God and supporting him, could impact the world in such a beautiful way?

And as the world rages against George W. Bush and the "Christian Right" (called the "Christian Reich" by some) have they missed the fact that he's a hero on another continent also? Chris McGreal wrote an article in *The Guardian* entitled "George Bush: A Good Man in Africa?" which tells about the American AIDS initiative in Africa:

> They may not be George Bush's natural constituency but Rwanda's prostitutes have good things to say about him. So do poor South Africans abandoned by their quixotic government, and doctors across Africa who otherwise regard the American president as a walking crime against humanity.
>
> As Bush arrives in Africa today at the start of a five-country tour he will be welcomed chiefly for an initiative which has gone largely unnoticed outside the continent but which has saved the lives of more than a million people with HIV.
>
> The $15bn (£7.6bn) President's Emergency Plan for Aids Relief (Pepfar) is in its fifth year and has been hailed as a "revolution" that is transforming healthcare in Africa and has been praised as the most significant aid programme since the end of colonialism.... Bush's primary contribution will be greatly extending millions of lives even though the programme has been criticised for emphasising abstinence in Aids education and using religious organisations to deliver care.
>
> "This is the best thing that ever happened to the poor people I work with," said Edward Phillips, a Catholic priest overseeing the distribution of life-saving antiretroviral drugs (ARVs) in Nairobi, Kenya. "It's one of the few times I've seen US government money really reach down to the poorest of the poor. It's kept a hell of a lot of people alive."
>
> Dr Francois Venter, head of the HIV Clinicians Society in South Africa, where Pepfar is providing 200,000 people with ARVs, is one of a number of Aids doctors almost disbelieving in praise of Bush.

"I look at all the blood this man has on his hands in Iraq and I can't quite believe myself but I would say it's a bold experiment from the last people in the world I would expect to do it, and it is saving a lot of lives. To intervene on such a scale and make such a difference is huge," he said.[510]

While Colin Powell played a part in urging President Bush to go forward with the initiative, Bush was also lobbied by American Christian evangelicals who ministered in Africa. Again, Bush was loving his neighbor, and as Bob Geldorf, the anti-poverty organizer, said in a *Telegraph* article by David Blair entitled "Analysis: How George W. Bush Became an African Hero," even though "this side of the president's legacy has earned him few votes and precious little international credit, Mr. Bush did it anyway."[511]

Spiritual Freedom

In the same way that a Christian (George W. Bush) helped deliver the Iraqis and Afghanis from political oppression, spiritual freedom is also growing in the Muslim world as more and more people hear about Jesus. Muslim religious leaders used to have complete control over their subjects for centuries, but technology has been able to breach through those barriers. Television, satellite dishes, internet, and radio have given Muslims access to other ways of believing and thinking. There's an underground movement throughout the Islamic world that is spreading both the Gospel and democratic freedom.

In the book, *Iran: Desperate for God*, an Iranian woman (she must remain anonymous for fear of reprisals) described how watching a video led her to Christ:

> During this time of my life, one of my sisters came back from college to our small town and brought a movie with her. It was the life of Christ according to Luke. I went to a room of our house and sat on the carpet where we all watch TV. I just happened to be alone and put the movie in. While watching how Jesus loved people, I began to cry. At the end of the film, there was the prayer of repentance. I prayed it six times. I rewound the tape to the prayer, backwards, forwards, backwards and forwards. I don't think I realized what repentance meant, but I wanted to be near to God.[512]

After this, she was hungry for the Word. She wanted to know more about this Jesus who was so kind and good, but the Iranian Bible Society was closed when Iran became an Islamic Republic in 1979, so now Christians in Iran must often travel hundreds of miles just to find a New Testament. It's risky to possess any Christian materials in most Muslim countries, but efforts at distribution continue.

One of the most popular methods of spreading the Gospel around the world is through the "JESUS Film Project." The movie about the life of Christ has been translated into 1,000 languages and is hauled by young missionaries all over the world, into the most remote villages, to share the love of Jesus with those who, in some cases, are seeing a movie for the first time. This is a story about what happened when the film went into a Pakistani village:

> Now everyone wanted to see the movie. They whispered about it in the market and even in the mosque. "What is it about?" "Is it really that bad, that people should get arrested for having it?"
>
> In Jacobadad, Pakistan, two men were arrested for distributing the film and other Christian materials. Both men were beaten, and local mullahs, Muslim religious leaders, urged that charges be filed against them and others who had been involved in distributing the materials. They went one step beyond, encouraging Muslims in the city to take action against all Christians. Soon, a local pastor's possessions were stolen, and shots were fired near a Christian school. The town seemed on the verge of outright violence. However, things soon began to change. Instead of boycotting the movie, everyone in the town wanted to see the "sinful" film. They wanted to know about all the fuss firsthand. Black-marketed copies began making rounds, and eventually the *JESUS* film was even shown on local television. The city judge watched the movie, and he declared that it was not anti-Islam.[513]

There are also Muslims who have discovered Christ through internet chat rooms. In fact, some former Muslims are sharing the Gospel with seekers in the West! Those who have found Jesus are anxious to share their faith with others. They've been set free, and they're rejoicing!

Islam is a very ritualistic religion. Rather than simply receiving the Lamb, Jesus, as the Way to God, they attempt to get to God their own way. There are Five Pillars of Faith that every Muslim must do:

1. Recite the phrase "There is no God but Allah, and Mohammed is his messenger."
2. Pray five times a day.
3. Give alms to the poor.
4. Keep the fast of Ramadan.
5. Make the pilgrimage to Mecca at least once in a lifetime.

Some Muslims believe in a Sixth Pillar—jihad (struggle), which can refer to either personal internal struggle or external struggle against the enemies of Islam.

While these are the necessary practices of Islam, some (just as Martin Luther) try to prove their spiritual commitment by going much further. "Padina" (another false name) describes her attempt to please Allah by joining "Zeinabiyeh" (the House of Zeinab), a place where women can study the Koran. She attended this school for seven years, waking up at 1 a.m. every morning to pray on a cloth on the floor until 5 a.m. After attending school all day, she would pray again. The women at the school would wear black in order to grieve for the dead prophets. She also describes the public rituals:

> Some very dark celebrations included large parades in the streets. The mourners, all men, marched in long lines and beat themselves with chains. Women couldn't walk in these parades or even watch. We couldn't even see the men out the door. We performed the same rituals as the men behind the walls of our homes. We women formed circles and began grieving. In the middle of the circles, women would fall down and tear at their faces. Others would bang their heads on the floor and pull out their hair. On one particular holiday, we would beat our chests so hard that we'd be painfully black and blue.[514]

And yet, all this effort didn't lead to peace with God. Rather, it led to fear, since Padina was never sure she was doing enough:

> I feared that if any of my hair stuck out of my scarf, Allah would hang me from my hair in heaven forever. We wore stockings on our hands to prevent our hands from being exposed, even a little bit. They told us that we would be hung by our hands in heaven. Heavy black socks covered my legs. If I accidentally revealed my ankles to

anyone, Allah would drop me repeatedly into hell to burn my legs. I wore all this stuff and cried all the time."[515]

Because of these fears, Padina had nightmares all the time. She says she was taught that "when a dead person went underground all the dead spirits attacked him if he didn't believe in the twelve imams and pray to them, or if he wasn't good enough."[516] This led to depression and hopelessness.

Padina was in religious bondage.

But again, right in the middle of her depression, it was a television program that told Padina about Jesus. She saw a televised church service, and the pastors were *singing*! They were happy! She had been taught that music (other than funeral music) was bad and says, "Imam Khomeini never cracked a smile."[517] Why were these people so happy? Why were their children jumping up and down, singing and clapping? Why did the old people even raise their hands in joy? She wanted to know more about this God of joy and happiness. Padina's heart would long for more of Jesus. She would devote herself to this God who took away her sin and filled her heart with peace and love.

Just as the Russians never had the Word until the nineteenth century, the Muslim world has also been cut off from the Gospel. After so many years of darkness, Muslims are hearing the Good News, and when they see the goodness of Jesus and the beauty in what he did, they begin to love him; and when they see he died for them, they weep. Their hearts are tender. Finally, when they realize that he sets them free from their *religious* bondage, they rejoice and rivers of living water come out of them, causing them to risk all in order to tell others the Good News!

Only Jesus offers hope to those in religious bondage. There is no other source of freedom, no other light in the darkness.

Heroes for Christ

History documents that over and over Christianity produces heroes who oppose poisonous religion. In the book *Extreme Devotion*, produced by "The Voice of the Martyrs," are the stories of Christians all over the world who are facing persecution for their beliefs. Pastor Jeremiah Logara, of the Sudan, is one of those who remained courageous against the madness of poisonous religion. The Muslim soldiers had arrested six boys from his church and falsely accused them of being spies. When Jeremiah, their pastor, tried explaining that the boys were Christians, not spies, the soldiers decided to arrest him, too.

The Islamic soldiers tied Pastor Logara's arms and legs together and hung him four feet in the air with a rope. They whipped him and dripped hot melted wax on his chest. He recalled the prayer of Jesus in the Garden. He prayed, "Oh God, if it is your will for me to die today, let it be done." He could not bear that he might give in to the tortures of the Northern Sudanese Arabs as he stood before the young, impressionable boys.

But God's will was that he live on as a testimony for these boys. He was released. But the boys were retained… probably being forced to train as soldiers.

When the pastor reflected upon that incident, he recalled, "I thought of Jesus' death, that Jesus died to save the whole world. I thought my death could be part of the salvation of these boys as I followed in the footsteps of my Lord. I pray my example of suffering for them will encourage them to remain faithful to God."[518]

Pastor Logara wasn't able to defeat the soldiers through force, but he may have saved the boys through his suffering. Will they ever forget his courage and stamina as he was being tortured for trying to rescue them? Perhaps this beautiful act will be tenderly preserved in their memory as their kidnappers try to do everything to erase Christianity from their minds. Perhaps love will prevail over hatred and cruelty.

The Sons of Ishmael

In the introduction to the book, *Into the Den of the Infidels: Our Search for Truth*, the writer conveys the heart of the Sons of Ishmael, the first son of Abraham. I share it here because I found it so touching:

As the prodigal son returned to his father after a time of being lost, going astray, and wandering aimlessly, so Ishmael goes back nowadays to the bosom of his father Abraham, even to the bosom of Christ who existed before Father Abraham. He existed before the foundation of the world.

Ishmael goes back to the One who came from heaven and was incarnated for him. Yes, my God and my Savior, You came to preach the

THE NARROW WAY CONFRONTS TERRORISM

Good News to the poor, to bind the brokenhearted, to proclaim freedom for the captives and release from darkness the prisoners, to bestow on them a crown of beauty instead of ashes, the oil of gladness instead of mourning, and a garment of praise instead of a spirit of despair.

You came to rebuild the ancient ruins and restore the places long devastated; to renew the ruined cities that have been devastated for generations, and proclaim freedom, peace, healing, and love. Oh my God and Savior, You came to save all nations.

We, the Sons of Ishmael, have lived so many years unaware of You, knowing nothing about You, and many times we not only denied You and fought against You, but also were hostile to You. But your love that is beyond all minds, all imagination, and beyond all enmity found us, guided us, had mercy on us and purified us.

Your love, my Savior, brought us back to You as the prodigal to the bosom of his father, as a fondling returns to his mother's bosom, as a drowning person brought back to the ship of rescue.

My God and my Savior, here we are, we sought You and You found us; we asked You and You answered us; we prayed to You and You have heard our prayers. You have loved us first.

Now we have become sons not slaves, free not captives. We became righteous instead of being wicked; we became like You in loving whole nations.

We are the children of Ishmael, the sons of our father Abraham, who was called "the friend of God." We decided on the coming few pages to proclaim to all nations our love, admiration, submission, and loyalty to you. We are the branches and You are the vine; we are the bride and You are the groom; we are Your city and you are our God, Savior, and King.

Yours,
The Children of Ishmael[519]

The same book ends with these words, which I think sums up the message of my book well:

My dear brothers and sisters, I want you to know that our Lord and Savior Jesus Christ is not forcing us to follow him as slaves. He does not want us to pray in public squares or on street corners. He does not want us to fast and change our faces to be known to others as people who fast.

Our Lord and Savior Jesus Christ is against all sorts of pride, deceit, fake mannerisms, and hypocrisy. He is the God who sees the secret desires of the heart and the inner reality of yourself. He requests that your faith be from the heart and that you fast and pray secretly. Your relationship with him is a personal fellowship and is far from being just a hollow, fake motto.[520]

Islamic terrorism must be fought on two levels. George W. Bush opposed it in the material realm, by setting Muslim nations free from evil dictatorships, but we must also oppose terrorism on a spiritual level, realizing that getting rid of corrupt political and religious leadership is useless (as in the overthrow of France's *ancien regime*) without having something good to replace it with. Without Christ, one terror only produced another terror.

As the public activity of nation-building is occurring in Iraq and Afghanistan, the underground work of the Gospel is also spreading like a fire in the Islamic world. Bruce Russett may believe that the key to peace is democracy, but I say that the key to democracy is the gospel of love. Only sacrificial acts of love and kindness will win the hearts and minds—and souls—of the Muslim people. This started with Jesus and continues with us. These are the gentle words of the gospel of peace:

Love must be sincere. Hate what is evil; cling to what is good. Be devoted to one another in brotherly love. Honor one another above yourselves. Never be lacking in zeal, but keep your spiritual fervor, serving the Lord. Be joyful in hope, patient in affliction, faithful in prayer. Share with God's people who are in need. Practice hospitality. Bless those who persecute you; bless and do not curse. Rejoice with those who rejoice; mourn with those who mourn. Live in harmony with one another. Do not be proud., but be willing to associate with people of low position. Do not be conceited. Do not repay anyone evil for evil. Be careful to do what is right in the eyes of everybody. If it is possible, as far as it depends on you, live at peace with everyone. Do not take revenge.... Do not be overcome by evil, but overcome evil with good. (Romans 12:9-21)

THE NARROW WAY CONFRONTS TERRORISM

How can terrorism thrive in this atmosphere?

As a Gentile, I've been grafted into the vine, I'm adopted, but I'm still a part of Abraham's family and a sister to the sons of Ishmael. One day we will all become one large family, and peace and love will prevail. Even now, if I met an Iranian or a Saudi or an Egyptian who loved Jesus, we would all rejoice together in love. This is the unity the world longs for. This is Eden. But only those on the Narrow Way have discovered it.

CHAPTER THIRTEEN
The Narrow Way Cannot Go Astray

My hope is built on nothing less than Jesus' blood and righteousness.
I dare not trust the sweetest frame, but wholly lean on Jesus' name.
On Christ the solid rock I stand, all other ground is sinking sand,
All other ground is sinking sand. —Edward Mote, "The Solid Rock"

Batter my heart, three-personed God; for you
As yet but knock, breathe, shine, and seek to mend;
That I may rise and stand, o'erthrow me, and bend
Your force, to break, blow, burn, and make me new.
I, like an usurped town, to another due,
Labor to admit you, but oh, to no end,
Reason, your viceroy in me, me should defend,
But is captived, and proves weak or untrue.
Yet dearly I love you, and would be loved fain,
But am betrothed to your enemy:
Divorce me, untie, or break that knot again,
Take me to you, imprison me, for I
Except you enthrall me, never shall be free,
Nor ever chaste, except you ravish me. —John Donne, "Holy Sonnet XIV"

The church has a charge to keep.

Paul said, "In the presence of God and of Christ Jesus, who will judge the living and the dead, and in view of his appearing and his kingdom, I give you this charge: Preach the Word, be prepared in season and out of season; correct, rebuke and encourage—with great patience and careful instruction" (2 Tim. 4:1-2).

Why?

Because "the time will come when men will not put up with sound doctrine. Instead, to suit their own desires, they will gather around them a great number of teachers to say what their itching ears want to hear. They will turn their ears away from the truth and turn aside to myths" (2 Tim. 4:3-4).

For 2,000 years the charge to preach and teach the sound doctrine of the Word has been in force. Paul took it so seriously that he warned the Church at Ephesus for three years, weeping over the possibility that "savage wolves will come in among you and will not spare the flock" (Acts 20:29b). He knew that false apostles, appearing as angels of light, would distort the truth and seduce the virgin bride away from the bridegroom (2 Cor. 11:1-15).

As an apostle of love, who said, "If I speak in the tongues of men and of angels, but have not love, . . . I gain nothing" (1 Cor. 13:1a,3b), and "the only thing that counts is faith expressing itself through love" (Gal. 5:6b). Paul knew that teaching the Word would restore goodness, freedom, and justice to the world, but when we abandoned the sound teaching of the doctrine of grace and love, and instead, resorted to dead religious works, we abandoned humanity, allowing arrogance, cruelty, and tyranny to prevail.

As I hope I've shown in the chapters of this book, every time that the church was seduced and led astray from the pure Word, the world was plunged into darkness. Conversely, every time the Word was restored and "correctly divided," the world was blessed.

God's grace and love are the main teachings of the Word. Jesus was the Lamb whose sacrifice would give grace to all who were willing to receive it. As a result of this experience of grace, recipients would be filled with love and joy. New life would flow from them, and the world would become more beautiful.

Evidence for this has been borne out by history.

The early church, under the pristine teachings of the disciples, changed the ancient world, blessing it with the love of Jesus. Infanticide, blood sport, and slavery were abolished. The sick and the poor were cared for. Widows and orphans were taken in. Love and compassion grew in the human heart.

But then the church went astray, blending the Word with man-made traditions and Greek philosophy. The result was a thousand-year period of darkness, leaving the world in scientific and educational backwaters, characterized by religious tyranny, poverty, filth, disease, cruelty, and superstition.

The Reformation restored sound doctrine. Luther's insistence that we are justified by grace through faith changed the world. Coupled with the printing press, which gave the average person access to the Word, light would burst throughout society. It would lead to the Scientific Revolution, religious tolerance, political freedom, educational advances, the abolition of slavery—again, charitable societies, women's rights, medical insights, and prosperity. It would also get rid of cannibalism, infanticide, superstitious pagan deity worship, and widow burning.

But then, the church abandoned the Word, going astray in the nineteenth century under the banner of historical criticism. It blended the Word with evolution and socialism, believing that the truth of the Bible had to be a myth because it didn't seem to hold up under the intense scrutiny of archaeologists, scientists, and historians. In the process, though, both communism and Nazism were birthed, leading to the rule of totalitarian dictators, world wars, and massive genocide.

Church! We have a charge to keep!

We have to stop playing around with the teachings of Christianity as though our actions were inconsequential. Jesus said we were the salt of the earth, the preserver of society, and when we fail, the world suffers.

And yet, we dabble in theology as though we were merely creating a new recipe. (Let's blend a little Aristotle in here, a little Marx there, and then serve it up with a little Darwin. No, maybe we should try a little mysticism for good measure. Returning to the ancient practices could be very tasty.) In each era, the ingredients change, but the outcome is the same—an impure, defiled, and perverted Christianity, which has now become corrupted, spoiled, and even poisonous. One rotten egg will ruin a whole omelet, and as Jesus said, "Be on your guard against the yeast of the Pharisees… a little yeast works through the whole batch of dough (Matt. 16:6, Gal. 5:9)."

Paul said in his letter to the Ephesians that the ministry of the church, through the apostles, prophets, evangelists, pastors, and teachers was to prepare and strengthen the body of Christ so that it wouldn't be tossed about by "every wind of teaching and by the cunning and craftiness of men in their deceitful scheming. (Eph. 4:14b)." But everywhere I turn to look, the pastors, prophets, apostles, evangelists, and teachers are weakening the body of Christ and casting their flocks into the wind to be tossed about!

On the Right, the church has gone astray into the prosperity movement, the Latter Rain movement, the shepherding movement, the manifest sons of God movement, Toronto laughter, the Brownsville revival, the Kansas City prophets and revival, dominion theology, the Third Wave, Joel's Army, the Lakeland revival, and recently soaking prayer and contemplative practices have been added.

The Left has also gone astray into environmentalism, historicism, evolution, socialism, contemplative prayer, and recently they've entered into a neo-Gnosticism, setting aside the Word for a new revelation from God.

Trying to straddle both the Left and the Right is the emergent church. Brian McLaren, in his book *A Generous Orthodoxy: Why I Am a Missional, Evangelical, Post/Protestant, Liberal/Conservative, Mystical/Poetic, Biblical, Charismatic/Contemplative, Fundamentalist/Calvinist, Anabaptist/Anglican, Methodist, Catholic, Green, Incarnational, Depressed-yet-Hopeful, Emergent, Unfinished Christian*[521] claims to be an evangelical, while forgetting the Good News that Jesus alone came to conquer religious struggle. His newest book, called *Finding Our Way Again: A Return to the Ancient Practices*,[522] doesn't lead to freedom, but rather to the bondage of religious practices that characterized the Dark Ages! He also challenges the authority of the Word, questioning whether Jesus is the only Way.

This trend away from the Word is more than troubling. On both the Left and the Right there has been a willingness to embrace special revelation. It manifests on the Right in the form of dreams, visions, and prophecies (Kenneth Hagin called it a "rhema word"), and on the Left in the form of new revelation taking place in the context of "community."

The Religious Right gives a lot of credence to "the vision." One of the most popular visions is that of Rick Joyner's *Final Quest*. This is an experience that Joyner had in which an angel showed him a future civil war within the church. In this vision he climbed a mountain and battled against those trying to hinder the move of God. This is simply a new form of Gnosticism! Paul warned that Christians shouldn't "go beyond what is written" (1 Cor. 4:6). It leads to false doctrine.

How can we, who were not eyewitnesses of the Exodus, the life of Christ, or any other biblical event, expect our *spiritual* revelation to have any authority? We weren't there when the Red Sea parted or the Israelites were led by pillars of fire and clouds. We didn't see the risen Christ. But the entire Jewish nation claims to have experienced God's presence in their corporate life in such a powerful way that thousands of years later they still commemorate the event. Christians were so convinced of the historical reality of the resurrection that they gave their lives for it. Dreams and visions, used for the purpose of developing new doctrinal positions, on the other hand, are subjective experiences, not historical events. This Gnostic mystical emphasis is dangerous! It turns the ground the Christian is standing on into shifting sand, rather than solid rock.

An example of Gnosticism on the Left is the "God is Still Speaking" campaign of the United Church of Christ. Claiming that the early church changed Old Testament laws, such as eating unclean foods, they believe *they* can also revise biblical revelation, especially concerning homosexual relationships.

Of course, I believe God is still speaking also, but not in a way that conflicts with sound doctrine. He speaks to us in our hearts about intimate personal matters, but this doesn't conflict with his Word. Jesus didn't conflict with the Word, either. He fulfilled the Law and covered it with his blood so that grace could prevail. Even when the church received permission to eat unclean foods through Peter's vision, they were merely fulfilling the Covenant promise that through Abraham that *all* nations would be blessed, opening the door for Gentiles to come into the body of Christ.

The United Church of Christ also points to Paul's admonition in Ephesians, "slaves, obey your earthly master (Eph. 6:5) " as evidence that the New Testament supports slavery, claiming this proves the Christian church must have a progressive revelation, but as I've shown in other parts of this book, that's not a correct interpretation of that Scripture, and it shouldn't be used to justify abandoning the Word for new revelation. The abolitionists stood on the Word; they didn't abandon it for science or reason. Their source was the Scripture. The Southern slaveholder, on the other hand, made the same mistake as the United Church of Christ, believing that the Bible endorsed slavery and reverting to reason or science to justify keeping others in bondage. But abandoning the Scriptures always leads to suffering. For example, illicit sexual activity has been particularly devastating to innocent children in Africa who have been ravaged by poverty, loneliness, and disease because of the AIDS virus.

Regarding homosexuality, where is the Scripture that prophesies its acceptance as a new lifestyle, as the acceptance of the Gentiles was foretold? Instead both the Old and the New Testament forbid it. The Word must confirm the Word. New doctrine cannot be interjected without Scriptural justification.

Of course Jude warned us about this kind of Gnostic false teaching. He said that he felt he had to write and urge the church to "contend for the faith that was *once for all* entrusted to the saints. For certain men whose condemnation was written about long ago have secretly slipped in among you. They are godless men, who change the grace of our God into a license for immorality and deny Jesus Christ our only Sovereign and Lord. (Jude 3b-4)." It continues: "In a similar way, Sodom and Gomorrah and the surrounding towns gave themselves up to sexual immorality and perversion.... (Jude 7)."

The United Church of Christ is willing to put more faith in their "interpretive process of discernment" than in the Word of God itself. They trust more in *their* subjective conversations with God, than in the *disciples'* historical conversations with Jesus.

Remember, Christian: *We have a charge to keep!*

We cannot abandon the Word! The Church has battled against Gnosticism, Pelagianism, Docetism, Manicheeism, and all other manner of false teaching. And in the early Middle Ages even the attempt to maintain sound doctrine became a source for wrong doctrine! But the Word must be preserved in purity, because it alone can oppose poisonous religion. Only the Judeo-Christian Scriptures can set humanity free from religious bondage, revealing a gracious God who longs to be with us in an intimate way, rather than a demanding, tyrannical God who can never be pleased with any amount of ascetic or ritualistic activity.

The Scriptures say the entrance of the Word brings forth light. And throughout history it did just this. For example, if the world had only heard the first sentence of the Bible, it would have been enough to bring countless blessings to humanity!

"In the beginning God created the heavens and the earth" (Gen. 1:1).

Isaac Newton based his work on the belief that there was a Creator. He also determined that he was going to look for truth, rather than rely on philosophy, saying that "Plato is my friend—Aristotle is my friend—but my greatest friend is truth." The Scientific Revolution was birthed out of a commitment to God as the intelligent designer who created everything and revealed his mind through the order of creation. The rejection of Greek philosophy led to Newton's laws of motion and gravitation. These would be developed further by Johannes Kepler, giving us the laws of planetary motion.

Spontaneous generation was one of the beliefs of the ancient Greeks. Aristotle hypothesized that the spontaneous action of nature could turn decaying matter into living animals. (This is a necessity for the belief in evolution, also.) But when it was cast aside as false, blessings were discovered. For example, Louis Pasteur challenged Aristotle's belief. This led to his discovery of pasteurization. He believed that life could only come from life (the law of biogenesis) and therefore devised a way for no other life to enter into a bottle of milk that was sterilized. This has led to countless blessings as we can now drink clean, bacteria-free milk and not become sick.

Joseph Lister also set out to understand why infection occurred in wounds. Sterilization of medical equipment and covering wounds with bandages were advances brought about by the rejection of Aristotle's spontaneous generation. How many lives have been saved from the danger of infection because of this discovery?

Although discovered earlier than pasteurization, canned food could also be based on the concept of creation. Germ theory also functions with this belief in mind. John Snow, who traced London's cholera outbreak in 1854 back to a dirty water well, is now known as the father of epidemiology, and as a result clean water has been made a priority throughout the world. (He also went to Genesis as a justification for his development of anesthesia, saying that, after all, God caused Adam to sleep when he removed his rib.) Hygiene, cleanliness, and health owe much to the belief that God was the Creator.

Politically and philosophically speaking, Enlightenment thought was influenced by the belief in a Creator. Deism was a direct result of reflecting on the concept of Newton's First Cause. To them God was the "Grand Watchmaker" who set the universe in motion. They were creationists. One of their most famous documents begins with the phrase: "We hold these truths to be self-evident, that all men are *created* equal and are endowed by their *Creator* with certain inalienable rights." Thus began the American experiment. The Founders appealed to a higher law when presenting their Declaration of Independence. And though the government they created separated the church from the state (they were vehemently anticlerical, yet not anti-God), the authority they gave for justification to rebel against tyranny was the Creator, whom they saw as the source of life, liberty, and happiness. The government that they founded has offered the greatest freedoms and happiness of any government in the history of the world. Millions have flocked to the shores of America for refuge and hope. The belief that there was a Creator blessed America.

It was the message of Genesis that the abolitionists appealed to as they opposed scientific racism. Believing that God created the first two members of the human race (Adam and Eve) and out of them flowed all other races, the antislavery messengers appealed to the higher authority of the Word while others, who embraced a science which conflicted with the Scriptures, traveled around the world collecting skulls to measure and compare the brain size of the different races. Their belief in polygenism would be used by slaveholders and even Enlightenment thinkers to justify slavery.

It was also the message of Genesis that emboldened and equipped the missionaries to counter social Darwinism and abusive Western imperialism as they went forth with the belief that there was a brotherhood of man, making all races equal (as descendents of Adam and Eve) when exposed to the Gospel and given the benefit of education. They began universities, hospitals, orphanages, and schools. And everywhere they went the light of Christ broke through the darkness of poisonous religious bondage and set people free. Humans no longer eat other humans, expose babies to animals, heat, and cold, and burn the widows of dead men to stop them from becoming a burden to society.

On the other hand, what damage has been done by those who reject that simple statement in the beginning of Genesis?

The Aristotelian view insisted on spontaneous generation. Even so, the medieval church blended and adapted it to their theology. Believing that the Greeks offered the highest understanding of the material world, the Roman Church had a stranglehold on science until the advent of Luther's Reformation. Calvin's writings, in particular, would lead Christian scientists such as Francis Bacon, Isaac Newton, and Johannes Kepler to search for the mind of God in his creation. Until then, the Ptolemaic view of the universe prevailed, spontaneous generation was accepted as truth, and there was no need for empirical proof because the Greeks valued reason over sensory evidence. Therefore, science was stunted.

While the American experiment was rooted in accountability to a Creator, the French experiment (both were Enlightenment endeavors) was rooted in the *rejection* of the Creator. They weren't simply anti-clerical, they were anti-God. In particular, they defied him by rebelling against the Genesis concept of a seven-day week. Instead, they implemented a ten-day week and worshiped a female statue of the Goddess of Reason. In the end, their passions led to the Terror, and the guillotine was the only thing that held them accountable.

As mentioned before, slavery was justified by scientific racism. The words of Genesis were rejected again, and it led to the subjection of millions of Africans and a horrendous civil war that ripped apart the United States. (Wrong doctrine also led to this war as the slaveholders neglected the admonition of Paul that the Old Testament Law was fulfilled by Jesus and should now be set aside.)

The colonialism and imperialism of the Victorian era were also justified by the anti-Genesis concept of social Darwinism. The application of the evolutionary principles of "natural selection" and "survival of the fittest" were applied to many endeavors, including Christianity, and especially to business, resulting in industrial exploitation by those who embraced Spencer's social philosophy to justify their actions. The abuses spawned by social Darwinism would lead directly to the communist backlash.

Marx blended his economic vision in with the rejection of God. Obviously Marx was an evolutionist. Instead of believing that God was the Creator and Designer, he began to use his own blueprint to construct his Eden. How many millions of people were destroyed as a result?

Nazism was also a result of social Darwinism. Hitler, a product of his era, believed in the survival of the fittest. *Mein Kampf* is replete with examples of this anti-creationist ideology. How many millions perished as a result of this belief?

And yet, the arrogant attitude of atheists, such as Sam Harris, toward creationists is maddening. He argues in his little book, *Letter to a Christian Nation*, that "nature offers no compelling evidence for an intelligent designer." (Tell that to Isaac Newton!) He acts astounded that at the "dawn of the twenty-first century" a Gallup poll "revealed that 53 percent of Americans are *actually* creationists" and that:

> Among developed nations, America stands alone in these convictions. Our country now appears, as at no other time in her history, like a lumbering, bellicose, dim-witted giant. Anyone who cares about the fate of civilization would do well to recognize that the combination of great power and great stupidity is simply terrifying, even to one's friends.[524]

And yet, there are fifty million people around the world tonight who have been liberated in the last decade due to the support of those stupid creationists. What, other than those stupid creationists, stops the world from sliding into the darkness of poisonous religious regimes? Even the world's most infamous atheist, Christopher Hitchens, has proudly sought refuge on the stomping grounds of the stupid creationists.

In light of the case that I presented for believing in a Creator, rather than in evolutionary theory (which I might add, offers no compelling evidence for its truthfulness), I would question who the stupid person is.

Even Jesus recognized that there were some people who would never be convinced to put their faith in Him. He tells this parable of the Rich Man and Lazarus:

> There was a rich man who was dressed in purple and fine linen and lived in luxury every day. At his gate was laid a beggar named Lazarus, covered with sores and longing to eat what fell from the rich man's table. Even the dogs came and licked his sores.
>
> The time came when the beggar died and the angels carried him to Abraham's side. The rich man also died and was buried. In hell, where he was in torment, he looked up and saw Abraham far away, with Lazarus by his side. So he called to him, "Father Abraham, have pity on me and send Lazarus to dip the tip of his finger in water and cool my tongue, because I am in agony in this fire."
>
> But Abraham replied, "Son, remember that in your lifetime you received your good things, while Lazarus received bad things, but now he is comforted here and you are in agony. And besides all this, between us and you a great chasm has been fixed, so that those who want to go from here to you cannot, nor can anyone cross over from there to us."
>
> He answered, "Then I beg you, father, send Lazarus to my father's house, for I have five brothers. Let him warn them, so that they will not also come to this place of torment."
>
> Abraham replied, "They have Moses and the Prophets; let them listen to them."
>
> "No, father Abraham," he said, "but if someone from the dead goes to them, they will repent."

He said to him, "If they do not listen to Moses and the Prophets, they will not be convinced even if someone rises from the dead."
—Luke 16:19-31

In telling this story, Jesus was predicting his resurrection. And he acknowledged that there are some people who, regardless of the evidence, just won't believe. Even if he came back from the dead and *hundreds of people saw him, testified to it, and were even willing to die for it,* some people still wouldn't believe.

They won't believe even if an entire nation of millions of people testifies *that they saw* God. The Jewish nation corporately insists that they saw God in a pillar of fire and a pillar of clouds. They all testify that they were delivered from the bondage of Egypt through the parted Red Sea. They testify that God manifested himself in their midst over and over. Handed down, generation after generation, are feasts which help the Jewish people to remember that something special happened long ago that they never want to forget. Yet the world rejects their testimony. They not only reject it, over and over they've joined in a frenzy of madness to destroy the Jews, who were recipients of the visitation. And even worse, the world has to insist that the Jews were delusional, that they were mad, in order to reject their testimony.

The Jews are unlike every other religion in the world—they claim to have been visited by God himself, not just his prophet or wise man. The Christians, as an extension of the Jewish faith, also make this claim about Jesus. He was God incarnate, Immanuel: God with us.

Archaeology

The evidence of archaeology won't even be enough to convince those who want to believe that the Judeo-Christian faith is a myth, either. Some people are just determined to close their ears and eyes to evidence. For example, most skeptics point to the opinions of Kathleen Kenyon, concerning the excavation of Jericho, when trying to discount biblical archaeology. The existence of a city with the grain bins still full (meaning there was a short siege) and the walls pushed outward, rather than inward (as an invasion would indicate) was overlooked because Kenyon hadn't found a piece of pottery which was found at other sites that would have dated the occupation to a certain time. Certainly, skeptics asserted, this disproved the accuracy of the Bible. But later studies of

Kenyon's findings would indicate that there was no occupation gap after all and that she mishandled evidence.[525]

Another person that the skeptics point to is Israel Finkelstein, who in one case asserts that the Bible must be untrue because it says the patriarchs used camels, which he claims weren't domesticated until a later date. Somehow he knows that this is true, therefore, the Bible, as an inspired document, must be discredited.

Critics of biblical archaeology always point to the minute *absence* of archaeological confirmation for proof of their claims, yet they overlook the vast amount of evidence that supports the truthfulness of the Scriptures. A short list: references to the "House of David" and the "king of Israel" on the Mesha Stele; the Behistun Rock, which helped to translate Near-East inscriptions that over and over have confirmed the Bible; Hittite monuments and documents (historical critics had always pointed to the Hittites as biblical "myths"); the Lachish Ostraca, which confirmed the truth of the Babylonian captivity; 17,000 cuneiform tablets at Elba which confirm the existence of writing before the time of Moses (critics had said Moses couldn't have written the Pentateuch because writing wasn't in existence); razors found in Egyptian tombs that proved Joseph shaved (when critics scoffed at Genesis 41:14 saying that it wasn't possible for Joseph to shave because razors didn't exist); cuneiform records from the excavated libraries of Assyrian kings which confirm the biblical record of the thirty-nine kings of ancient Israel and Judah; a clay prism describing Sennacherib's campaign against Judah; the discovery of the Egyptian cities Pithom and Ramses (whose buildings have a layer of bricks that have less straw in them, just as Exodus 5 claims); four clay cylinders in the city of Ur which confirm the existence of King Belshazzar; the Black Obelisk of Shamaneser which confirms the existence of the Israeli King Jehu; the Siloam Tunnel Inscription which confirms the biblical story that a reservoir was constructed in anticipation of the siege of Assyria; the Cyrus Cylinder; the Dead Sea Scrolls; the excavation of Gezer; the historical accuracy of Luke; worldwide flood accounts and geological evidence that supports a worldwide flood. I could go on and on and on. The biblical record is not a myth.

In a courtroom, a person is determined to be guilty or innocent based upon evidence. None of the jury actually saw the crime. They are expected to make a calculated determination of guilt or innocence based upon the evidence that's presented. Society has determined that they can rely on certain types of proof: physical proof, eyewitness proof (testimonies), and confessions. In Christianity all types of proof for validation of the Scriptures exist. There is the physical proof of archaeology. There are eyewitnesses who were even willing to die horrendous deaths in order to remain faithful to the truth. There's also the confession of Christ, who claimed he was God.

Finally, there's the evidence of fruit. Jesus said that a tree would be known by its fruit. The fruits of the Spirit are "love, joy, peace, patience, kindness, goodness, faithfulness, gentleness, and self-control." " (Gal. 5:22). As I've tried to show throughout this book, those on the Narrow Way have the fruits of the Spirit. They loved the unlovable. They shared the Gospel in the face of suffering and death. They cared for the people around them. They stood for freedom. They had joy in the worst of circumstances. They were courageous.

The Christian can stand firm in the face of adversity. We have history on our side. We have nothing to fear. Even death holds no sting for us. Let the world do what they will to us.

But remember: *We have a charge to keep.*

As we enter into the twenty-first century, perhaps the church can finally get it right. Perhaps we will avoid *blending* the Word with other beliefs and keep the Gospel pure and undefiled. Perhaps we can avoid religious activity and be more concerned with loving our neighbor. Perhaps we can remain engaged with the world and not run off to monasteries and caves, putting our light under a bushel, and abandoning others. Perhaps we can try to rightly divide the Word of truth, learning from the apostles, who explained that preserving sound doctrine means setting aside the Old Testament Law and learning how Jesus fulfilled it. Perhaps we can avoid mystical pursuits, which place us on shifting sand. Perhaps we can forsake extra-biblical doctrinal revelations and decide to "not go beyond what is written" (1 Cor. 4:6a). Perhaps we can stop seeking signs, knowing that's what a wicked generation does. Perhaps we can stop trying to build the kingdom of God on earth, instead planting it in the hearts of men by showing sacrificial love, just as Jesus did.

Perhaps when we do this we will become the bride without spot or wrinkle prepared to meet the bridegroom.

Finally, we need to point to Jesus as the great God who laid down his life for us. Christopher Hitchens mocks the concept of Vicarious Atonement. He derides it as though there's something evil in the concept of sacrificial love. But can't he see beauty in this kind of heroism? Isn't there beauty in the soldier who places his own body over the grenade in order to save the lives of his platoon members? Was there any beauty in the firemen who sacrificed their lives to rescue others on September 11th? Can Hitchens not find beauty in Dickens' character, Sydney Carton, who, for the sake of love, took the place of Charles Darnay in *The Tale of Two Cities*? Jesus said, "Greater love has no one than this, that he lay down his life for his friends" (John 15:13). This is what He did for us.

How can we belittle this sacrifice by saying that there are other pathways to God—as though the atonement wasn't necessary? Yet this is what so many "Christians" are doing in the name of religious unity and tolerance. They reject his loving sacrifice! And by doing this they assert that they will try to get to God their own way and, consequently, now must resort to religious works and rituals to express their "faith."

Perhaps you don't know Jesus as the sacrificial Lamb who died for you to rescue you from religious bondage, sin, and judgment. If not, he stands at the door of your heart and knocks. He longs for you. He will leave the ninety-nine sheep, he says, just to search for the one that's lost. You are precious to him. He made it so simple for you to be restored. Just receive him. Just let his blood cover your sins. Just as you are. He'll make you new again. You just have to reach out and take the gift that he offers.

When this happens, new life can flow through you! Even the worst of criminals, slave traders, genocidal murderers, and cannibals have found new life in Christ. He can set you free, too! And you don't have to perform any religious ritual or sacrificial act in order to prove yourself to God. He just wants you to humbly receive. He'll do the rest. What Good News!

To those who have received, God was able to turn the weakest of them into champions. He was able to make them brave and strong even as they battled against the very gates of hell.

I'm asking everyone that will, to join that long scarlet thread of wise men and women who have lived their lives trusting in God's grace and living lives of love. They are the heroes of history. They are the ones who were truly able to discern good from evil. They have consistently opposed tyranny. They reflect the best that humanity has to offer.

None of them were perfect—they were humans in need of forgiveness—but their dogged adherence to the Word and to the Lamb of God helped them uphold a standard of truth when all around them, other visions of paradise were vying for their affections.

They weren't religious. In fact they almost all opposed the poisonous religion that existed in their era, but they never lost faith in the One who stood before them as a vision of splendor and beauty. Loving and serving Jesus was their sole desire in life. In this hall of the faithful are names like Abraham, King David, Jeremiah, Isaiah, John the Baptist, John the Beloved, Paul, Blandina, Polycarp, John Huss, Martin Luther, William Tyndale, John Wycliffe, Thomas Cranmer, William Lloyd Garrison, Dietrich Bonhoeffer, Reverend Wurmbrand, Basil Malof, George Whitefield, Watchman Nee, Martin Luther King, Jr., and countless others who "did not love their lives so much as to shrink from death" (Rev. 12:11b).

Their testimonies shine in the darkness of an evil, corrupt, and poisonous world as evidence that there may be something higher, purer, and nobler to adhere to in this vast universe. And this something bids us all to "*Come!*"

"Whoever is thirsty, let him come; and whoever wishes, let him take the free gift of the water of life" (Rev. 22:17).

There is no other Way to restore Eden.

Endnotes

1. Christopher Hitchens, *God Is Not Great: How Religion Poisons Everything* (New York: Twelve, 2007), 282.
2. Christopher Hitchens, *God Is Not Great: How Religion Poisons Everything* (New York: Twelve, 2007), 283.
3. Ibid.
4. For a discussion on this, see Hitchens' chapter "The Last Ditch Case Against Secularism" in *God Is Not Great.*
5. William Wilberforce, *A Practical View of the Prevailing Religious System of Professed Christians: In the Higher and Middle Classes in this Country, Contrasted with Real Christianity* (New York: Leavitt, Lord, and Co., 1835), 64.
6. John Tosh, *The Pursuit of History: Aims, Methods and New Directions in the Study of Modern History*, rev. 3rd ed. (London: Pearson Longman, 2002), 7.
7. Hitchens, *God Is Not Great*, 230.
8. Ibid., 176.
9. Ibid., 230.
10. M.R. De Haan, *God's House of Symbols: A Walk Through the Old Testament Tabernacle* (Grand Rapids, MI: Radio Bible Class, 1981).
11. C.S. Lewis, *The Lion, the Witch, and the Wardrobe* (New York: Collier Books, 1970), 138.
12. Oswald Chambers, *My Utmost for His Highest* (Ulrichsville, OH: Barbour and Co., 1991), 179.
13. Even now, this clash plays itself out. While the Jews, descendants of the younger brother Isaac, are content just to be left alone, they're hounded by the jealous and hateful descendants of the older brother Ishmael. Religion isn't righteous, it's self-righteous. It's haughty, demanding that it receive its proper recognition and honor. (How dare anyone mock it?) It's not reasonable; it's irrational, driven by primordial instincts, howling like a beast in the night.
14. Josh McDowell, *Evidence That Demands a Verdict, Volume 1: Historical Evidences for the Christian Faith* (San Bernardino, CA: Here's Life Publishers, 1992), 53.
15. According to Norman Geisler and William E. Nix, writing in *A General Introduction to the Bible* (Chicago: Moody Press, 1968), the oldest known manuscript of Isaiah was dated 916 A.D. The Dead Sea Scrolls, which were found in 1947 by a Bedouin shepherd boy, are dated 125 B.C. The text of Isaiah had been copied by Jewish scribes for over 1000 years and as one example of the book's accuracy, Isaiah 53 only had one word (three letters) in question after a thousand years of transmission. This one word does not significantly change the meaning of the passage (as discussed in McDowell, *Evidence That Demands a Verdict*, 58).
16. Here is a short list of Old Testament prophecies fulfilled by Jesus, as compiled by Dr. Stanley Horton and presented in the book *What You Should Know About Prophecy* by C.M. Ward (Springfield, MO: Gospel Publishing House, 1975), 44-45:
    1. Betrayed by a friend (Psalm 55:12-14, 41:9; Matthew 26:46-50; John 13:18).
    2. Sold for thirty pieces of silver (Zechariah 11:12; Matthew 26:14-15).

ENDNOTES

3. Money obtained to be cast to the potter (Zechariah 11:13; Matthew 27:3-10).
4. To be accused by false witnesses (Psalm 35:11, 109:2; Matthew 26:59-60).
5. Disciples to forsake Him (Zechariah 13:7; Matthew 26:56; Mark 14:27).
6. Smitten and spat upon the face (Isaiah 50:4-6; Luke 22:64; Matthew 26:67-68).
7. To be dumb before accusers (Isaiah 53:7; Matthew 27:12-14; 1 Peter 2:23).
8. To be wounded and bruised (Isaiah 53:5; Matthew 27:26-29).
9. To fall under the cross (Psalm 109:24; John 19:17; Luke 23:26).
10. Hands and feet to be pierced (Psalm 22:16; Luke 23:33; John 20:25-27).
11. To be crucified with thieves (Isaiah 53:12; Mark 15:27-28).
12. To pray for His persecutors (Isaiah 53:12; Mark 15:27-28).
13. People to shake their heads (Psalm 109:25, 22:7; Matthew 27:39).
14. People to ridicule Him (Psalm 22:8; Matthew 27:41-43).
15. People to stare astonished (Psalm 22:17; Isaiah 52:14; Luke 23:35).
16. Garments parted and lots cast (Psalm 22:18; John 19:23-24).
17. To cry, "My God, my God, why hast thou forsaken me?" (Psalm 22:1; Matthew 27:46).
18. To be offered gall and vinegar (Psalm 69:21; Matthew 27:34; John 19:28-29).
19. To commit himself to God (Psalm 31:5; Luke 23:46).
20. Friends to stand far off (Psalm 38:11; Luke 23:49).
21. Bones not to be broken (Psalm 34:20, noting that the Passover lamb was not to have its bones broken and Christ is our Passover Lamb; Exodus 12:46; 1 Corinthians 5:7).
22. His side to be pierced (Zechariah 12:10; John 19:34-37).
23. His heart to be broken (Psalm 22:14; John 19:34).
24. Darkness to cover the land (Amos 8:9; Matthew 27:45).
25. Buried in a rich man's tomb (Isaiah 53:9; Matthew 27:57-60).
For another list of messianic prophecies that were fulfilled by Jesus, see the article entitled "Messianic Prophecies" by J. Hampton Keathley, III at www.bible.org.

17. Christopher Hitchens and Alistair McGrath, "Poison or Cure?: Religious Belief in the Modern World," Debate, Michael Cromartie Berkely Center for Religion, Peace, and World Affairs, Washington, D.C., October 11, 2007, *Ethics and Public Policy*, http://www.eppc.org/publications/pageID.390/default.asp (accessed 9/25/2008).
18. An example of this is the "God Is Still Speaking" campaign by the United Church of Christ.
19. Marcus Borg, *The Heart of Christianity: Rediscovering a Life of Faith* (San Francisco, CA: HarperSanFrancisco, 2003), 198-199.
20. Ibid., 119.
21. Ibid., 189.
22. Ibid.
23. Ibid., 198.
24. Ibid., 189.
25. Joel Osteen, *Your Best Life Now: Seven Steps to Living at Your Full Potential* (New York: Warner Faith, 2004).
26. Hitchens, *God Is Not Great*, 283.
27. Ibid.
28. These are all chapter titles from *Your Best Life* Now by Joel Osteen.

ENDNOTES

29. Unfortunately, the church has made this mistake throughout much of its history, and this is the root of most of our failures. If we had stopped blending the old and the new, we wouldn't have killed witches (Leviticus) and we wouldn't have had southern slavery (the curse of Ham). These two sins, witch hunts and slavery, are some of the worst smears on the Christian record.

30. Joel Osteen takes this verse to mean that, "Jesus was saying that you cannot have a larger life with restricted attitudes. That lesson is still relevant today. We are set in our ways, bound by our perspectives, and stuck in our thinking. God is trying to do something new, but unless we're willing to change, unless we're willing to expand and enlarge our vision, we'll miss his opportunities for us. The fact that you are reading this book, however, says that you are ready to go to a higher level; you want to reach your full potential. The good news is, God wants to show you His incredible favor. He wants to fill your life with 'new wine,' but are you willing to get rid of your old wineskins? Will you start thinking bigger? Will you enlarge your vision and get rid of those old negative mindsets that hold you back?" (Joel Osteen, 6).

31. According to the footnotes to Matthew 15:2 in the *NIV Study Bible: New International Version* edited by Kenneth Barker (Grand Rapids, MI: Zondervan, 1985), 1464: "After the Babylonian captivity, the Jewish rabbis began to make meticulous rules and regulations governing the daily life of the people. These were interpretations and applications of the Law of Moses, handed down from generation to generation. It was not until c. A.D. 200 that it was put into writing in the Mishnah."

32. The admonition from Haggai 1:9-11, "Because of my house, which remains a ruin, while each of you is busy with his own house," applies to the covetousness and greed of the modern American church. While we are building huge cathedrals and homes, reveling in our own prosperity, the world church is languishing and dying in poverty and disease. We've overlooked the admonition in 2 Corinthians 8 to be generous to the point that "there might be equality." As the strong and vigorous were able to collect more manna in the wilderness and therefore were commanded to give their excess to the aged and weak, the church is also commanded to look out for people's needs. Paul says this is a *test* of the sincerity of the church's love (verse 8). While the rich can feel justified in their excess because they give tithes and offerings (something that is much more difficult for the poor to do) Paul makes it clear that this is no longer the standard. Instead he reminds us that the standard is that "he who gathered much did not have too much, and he who gathered little did not have too little (verse 15)." Religious laws only give a false sense of security, while the prophets always shook people out of their security and into compassion, justice, love, and righteousness. The early church took this leveling of economic provision seriously (Acts 4:32-36), and Jesus tells us it is more difficult for a rich man to enter the Kingdom than it is for a camel to go through the eye of a needle, even telling the rich young ruler that he needed to sell everything he had and give it to the poor (Matthew 19). And yet the modern church rushes headlong into the pursuit of riches and success, comfortably spending it on themselves and feeling justified because they still follow the Old Testament law of tithing. This is following the letter of the law, but neglecting its spirit. It's not motivated by love or compassion, but by self-justification.

33. In Matthew 19:28, Jesus tells the disciples there will be a "renewal of all things." This earth that has deteriorated and groans under the curse will be made new again!

34. "Why Jesus Never Existed," http://www.religionislies.com/whyjesusneverexisted.html (accessed 7/7/2008).

ENDNOTES

35. Christopher Hitchens, "Bah: Hanukkah: The Holiday Celebrates the Triumph of Tribal Jewish Backwardness, *Slate*, December 3, 2007, http://www.slate.com/id/2179045/ (accessed 2/14/2009).
36. H.G. Wells, *The Outline of History: Being a Plain History of Life and Mankind, Volume 1* (Garden City, NY: Garden City Books, 1949), 535.
37. Josh McDowell, *Evidence That Demands a Verdict*, 129.
38. Ken Humphreys, "Godman—Gestation of a Superhero," www.jesusneverexisted.com (accessed 2/14/2009).
39. Flavius Josephus, *The Works of Flavius Josephus, Volume II*, trans. William Whiston (New York: A.L. Burt, n.d.), 443.
40. Pliny the Younger, "Pliny's Epistle to Trajan About 112 CE," PBS Online, Frontline: *From Jesus to Christ: The First Christians*, http://www.pbs.org/wgbh/pages/frontline/shows/religion/ (accessed 2/14/2009).
41. P. Cornelius Tacitus, *The Annals and Histories*. trans. Alfred John Church, William Jackson Brodribb (Chicago: William Benton, 1952), 168.
42. Seutonius, *The Twelve Caesars*, trans. Robert Graves (Baltimore, MD: Penguin Books, 1960), 217.
43. Lucian, "Lucian of Samasota: The Passing of Peregrinus," The Tertullian Project, http://www.tertullian.org/rpearse/lucian/peregrinus.htm (accessed 2/9/2008).
44. McDowell, *Evidence*, 127.
45. Edward Vernon Arnold, *Roman Stoicism: Being Lectures on the History of the Stoic Philosophy with Special Reference to its Development Within the Roman Empire* (Cambridge, MA: Cambridge University Press, 1911), 286.
46. John Foxe, *Foxes' Book of Martyrs* (Pittsburgh, PA: Whitaker House, 1981), 7.
47. Ibid.
48. Ibid., 9.
49. Kenneth Humphreys, "Jesus—The Imaginary Friend," www.jesusneverexisted.com (accessed 2/14/2009).
50. Plato recognized the inadequacy of the Greek gods as a source of education for young people because they weren't heroic, but selfish, and therefore couldn't be used as role models for his "Republic." He said that the myths, which were filled with stories of greed and lust, were "likely to have a bad effect on those who hear them; for everybody will begin to excuse his own vices when he is convinced that similar wickednesses are always being perpetrated by" the gods. Therefore he thought it necessary to "put an end to such tales, lest they engender laxity of morals among the young." (*The Works of Plato, Four Volumes in One*. trans. B. Jowett [New York: J.J. Little and Ives Co., n.d.], 93.) Many in the early church, such as Justin Martyr, thought that Plato would have been a Christian if he had lived long enough to see Christ. It is particularly tempting to view *The Allegory of the Cave* as a search for Christ.
51. R.R. Palmer and Joel Colton, *A History of the Modern World*, 4th ed. (New York: Alfred A. Knopf, 1971),12-13.
52. Plato, *The Republic of Plato*, trans. Allan Bloom (New York: Basic Books, 1968), 88, 409e-410a.
53. Justin Martyr, "First Apology of Justin," *Early Christian Fathers: Volume I*, trans. Cyril C. Richardson (Philadelphia: The Westminster Press, 1952), 287.
54. Tertullian, "Apology 39," as quoted by Philip Schaff in *Latin Christianity: Its Founder, Tertullian, Ante-Nicene Fathers*, Vol. 3. (Grand Rapids, MI: Wm. B. Eerdman's Publishing Co., 1973). Christian Classics Ethereal Library, http://www.ccel.org/ccel/schaff/anf03.iv.iii.xxxix.html (accessed 1/25/2009).

ENDNOTES

55. Lucian, "Lucian of Samosata: The Passing of Peregrinus," The Tertullian Project, http://www.tertullian.org/rpearse/lucian/peregrinus.htm (accessed 2/9/2009).
56. Clement of Alexandria, *The Paedagogus*, New Advent, http://www.newadvent.org/fathers/02093.htm (accessed 1/15/2009).
57. Ignatius, "To the Smyrnaens," *Early Christian Fathers, Volume I*, trans. and ed. Cyril C. Richardson (Philadelphia: Westminster Press, 1953), 114.
58. Tertullian, "Apology 42," as quoted by Philip Schaff in *Latin Christianity: Its Founder, Tertullian*, Christian Classics Ethereal Library, http://www.ccel.org/ccel/schaff/anf03.iv.iii.xlii.html (accessed 1/25/2009).
59. Julian, "Letter to Arsacius." Based in part on the translation of Edward J. Chinnock, *A Few Notes on Julian and a Translation of His Public Letters* (London: David Nutt, 1901), 75-78, as quoted by D. Brendan Nagle and Stanley M. Burstein in *The Ancient World: Readings in Social and Cultural History* (Englewood Cliffs, NJ; Prentice Hall, 1995), 314-315. Then Again: Primary Source, http://www.thenagain.info/Classes/Sources/Julian.html (accessed 2/7/2009). Note: Julian the Apostate was in a type of spiritual war with Jesus. He went to his last battle trying to prove that the Greek and Roman gods were stronger than the Christian God, but then lost the battle. It's reported that he flung his blood toward God as he was dying and asked, "Are you happy?" His last words were, "You have won, Galilean."
60. Foxe, *Book of Martyrs*, 29-30.
61. Ibid., 30.
62. Dionysius, "Letter to Eusebius," as quoted by Arnold Harnack in *The Mission and Expansion of Christianity in the First Three Centuries*, trans. and ed. James Moffatt (Gloucester, MA: Peter Smith, 1972), 171.
63. Cyprian, "Letter to Demetrianus," as quoted by Arnold Harnack in *The Mission and Expansion of Christianity*, 172.
64. Eusebius, "The Ecclesiastical History," *The Essential Eusebius*. trans. Colm Luibheid (New York: The New American Library, 1966), 162-163.
65. Aristotle, "Politics," *The Basic Works of Aristotle*. ed. Richard McKeon (New York: Random House, 1941), 1131-1132.
66. "The Didache," *Early Christian Fathers, Volume I*, trans. and ed. Cyril C. Richardson (Philadelphia: The Westminster Press, 1953), 176.
67. Wells, *Outline of History*, 498.
68. Robert Ellsburg, *All Saints: Daily Reflections on Saints, Prophets, and Witnesses for Our Time* (New York: The Crossroad Publishing Co., 2005), 105.
69. Clement, "Letter to the Romans," *Early Christian Fathers: Volume I*, trans. Cyril C. Richardson (Philadelphia: The Westminster Press, 1952), 68.
70. William Barclay, *The Letter to the Hebrews* (Westminster: John Knox Press, 2002), 226.
71. "The Shepherd of Hermas," *Apostolic Fathers*, trans. J. B. Lightfoot and ed. J.R. Harner (Grand Rapids, MI: Baker House Books, 1967), Wesley Center Online, http://wesley.nnu.edu/biblical_studies/noncanon/fathers/ante-nic/hermas1.htm (accessed 2/23/2008).
72. Barclay, *Letter to the Hebrews*, 226-227.
73. Plutarch, "Of Superstition," *Plutarch's Moralia: Twenty Essays*, trans. Philemon Holland (London: J.M. Dent and Sons, 1911), 387-388.
74. Seneca, "De Ira," as quoted by Alvin J. Schmidt in *How Christianity Changed the World*, (Grand Rapids, MI: Zondervan, 2005), 49.
75. Allan K. Bowman, *The Cambridge Ancient History: XI, The High Empire, A.D. 70-192*, 2nd ed. (Cambridge: Cambridge University Press, 2000), 402.

ENDNOTES

76. Ibid.
77. Tacitus, "Histories," *The Complete Works of Tacitus*, trans. Alfred John Church and William Jackson Brodribb (New York: Random House, 1942), 659-660.
78. "The Epistle to Diognetus," *Early Christian Writings*, trans. Maxwell Staniforth, rev. trans. Andrew Louth (London: Penguin Books, 1987), 145.
79. "The Didache," *Early Christian Writings*, 191.
80. Barnabus, "The Epistle of Barnabus," *Early Christian Writings*, 180.
81. T.R. Glover, *The Conflict of Religions in the Early Roman Empire*, 10th ed. (London: Methuen and Co., Ltd., 1923), 116.
82. Foxe, *Book of Martyrs*, 18.
83. Ibid., 4-5.
84. Ibid., 22.
85. H.G. Wells, *The Outline of History*, 552-553.
86. Roland H. Bainton, *Christendom: A Short History of Christianity and Its Impact on Western Civilization* (New York: Harper Colophon Books, 1966), 65.
87. Ibid.
88. Ibid.
89. This teaching was called Docetism from the Greek word *dokeo*, which means "to seem." 1 John is referring to this Gnostic teaching when he tells us to "test the spirits" in chapter 4 verses 2-3: "This is how you can recognize the spirit of God: Every spirit that acknowledges that Jesus Christ has come in the flesh is from God, but every spirit that does not acknowledge Jesus is not from God. This is the spirit of the antichrist, which you have heard is coming and even now is already in the world."
90. Bainton, *Christendom*, 65.
91. Henry Chadwick, *The Early Church* (Baltimore, MD: Penguin Books, 1967), 36.
92. "The Gospel According to Mary Magdalene," *The Gnosis Archive*, The Gnostic Society Library, http:// www.gnosis.org/library/marygosp.html (accessed 1/9/2009).
93. 1 Timothy 4:1-3 discusses this strand of Gnostic teaching: "The Spirit clearly says that in later times some will abandon the faith and follow deceiving spirits and things taught by demons. Such teachings come through hypocritical liars, whose consciences have been seared as with a hot iron. They forbid people to marry and order them to abstain from certain foods, which God created to be received with thanksgiving by those who believe and who know the truth."
94. Jude warned against this strain of Gnosticism in Jude 1:3-4, saying that he had to write and urge the church "to contend for the faith that was once for all entrusted to the saints. For certain men whose condemnation was written about long ago have secretly slipped in among you. They are godless men, who change the grace of our God into a license for immorality and deny Jesus Christ our only Sovereign and Lord."
95. Chadwick, *The Early Church*, 36.
96. Bainton, *Christendom*, 64.
97. Shirley Jackson Case, *The Makers of Christianity: From Jesus to Charlemagne* (New York: Henry Holt and Co., 1934), 65.
98. Chadwick, *The Early Church*, 41.
99. Ignatius, "Letter to the Ephesians," *Early Christian Writings: The Apostolic Fathers*, trans. Maxwell Stanforth, rev. trans. Andrew Louth (New York: Penguin Books, 1968), 63.
100. Chadwick, *The Early Church*, 43.
101. Irenaeus, "Against Heresies," *Anti-Nicene Fathers, Volume I: The Apostolic Fathers, Justin Martyr, Ireneaus*, ed. Alexander Roberts and James Donaldson, rev. Cleveland Coxe (New

ENDNOTES

       York: Christian Literature Publishing Co., 1885), Christian Classics Ethereal Library, http://www.ccel.org/ccel/schaff/anf01.ix.ii.xi.html (accessed 2/13/2009).
102. Case, *Makers*, 96.
103. It was this lifestyle enshrined by Tolstoy's character Father Zosimov and revered by Alyosha in *The Brothers Karamazov*.
104. Robert Ellsburg, *All Saints: Daily Reflections on Saints, Prophets, and Witnesses for Our Time* (New York: The Crossroad Publishing Co., 2005), 22. Note that he believed prayer was the pathway to God. Instead of coming boldly to the throne room through the blood of Jesus, Evagrius thought that attaining a state of openness was how he could achieve union with God, while the Scriptures teach that Jesus is the way to God's presence.
105. Chadwick, *The Early Church*, 182.
106. Note the trend to restore contemplative prayer to the modern church through "Soaking In His Presence Weekends." Information on these events can be found at http://www.soakingprayer.net.
107. Foxe, *Book of Martyrs*, 48.
108. Case, *Makers*, 164.
109. Will Durant, *The Story of Philosophy: The Lives and Opinions of the Great Philosophers of the Western World* (New York: Simon and Schuster Paperbacks, 2005), 35.
110. Foxe, *Book of Martyrs*, 50.
111. Ibid., 50-51.
112. Walter Russell Bowie, *The Story of the Church* (New York: Abingdon Press, 1955), 80.
113. Ibid.
114. Ibid., 81-82.
115. Peter Waldo was convicted of heresy because he believed he had the right to preach without permission from the Roman Church. He gave up his riches to the poor and taught that salvation came through hearing the preaching of the Word rather than through receiving the Sacraments. He rejected the church teachings on purgatory and transubstantiation. The Waldensians would be persecuted by Pope Innocent III and would have to flee in the cold and snow to the Alps. Peter was on the Narrow Way of grace and love.
116. Bowie, *The Story of the Church*, 116.
117. A paraphrase from Foxe's *Book of Martyrs*, 57.
118. Jonathan Hill, *Zondervan Handbook to the History of Christianity* (Grand Rapids, MI: Zondervan, 2006), 217.
119. Tim Dowley, ed. *Eerdman's Handbook to the History of Christianity*, (Grand Rapids, MI: Wm. B. Eerdman's Publishing Co., 1978), 330. This would lay a foundation for the concept of civil disobedience.
120. Ibid.
121. Foxe, *Book of Martyrs*, 110.
122. Desiderius Erasmus, *In Praise of Folly*, cont. Horace Bridges (Whitefish, MT: Kessinger Publishing, 2004), 139.
123. A. T. Roberts, "What the Bible Has Done for Democracy: How We Got Our English Bible," *The Expositor* XXI, No. 241, 1919, 360.
124. Martin Luther, "Preface to the Complete Edition of Luther's Latin Works (1545)," trans. Brother Andrew Thornton, Internet Christian Library, http://www.iclnet.org/pub/resources/text/wittenberg/luther/pre-flat-eng.txt (accessed 2/10/2009).
125. Walter Russell Bowie, *The Story of the Church* (New York: Abingdon Press, 1950), 126.
126. Ibid.

ENDNOTES

127. Roland H. Bainton, *Here I Stand: A Life of Martin Luther* (Nashville, TN: Abingdon Press, 1978), 141.
128. Ibid., 144.
129. Ibid.
130. This is referring to the apostle John's exile on the island of Patmos.
131. Bainton, *Here I Stand*, 47.
132. Dowley, *Eerdman's Handbook*, 364.
133. Martin Luther, "A Mighty Fortress is Our God" *The Baptist Hymnal* (Nashville, TN: Convention Press, 1991), 8.
134. Bainton, *Here I Stand*, 204.
135. Pope Innocent X, in his papal bull *Zelo domus Dei* "would denounce its religious provisions as 'null and void, invalid, iniquitous, unjust, condemned, rejected, absurd, without force, or effect.'" *Documents of the Early Christian Church*, 2nd ed., ed. Henry Bettenson (London: Oxford University Press, 1963), 303-304.
136. Alistair McGrath, *Historical Theology: An Introduction to the History of Christian Thought* (Malden, MA: Blackwell Publishing, 1998), 215.
137. Ibid. (McGrath interestingly notes that "Locke's argument here is shaped by the Christian conception of salvation; a religion which demanded external conformity to a set of regulations would not fit in to his analysis.")
138. Foxe, *Book of Martyrs*, 100.
139. Jonathan Hill, *Zondervan Handbook to the History of Christianity* (Grand Rapids, MI: Zondervan, 2006), 254.
140. "Zwingli: The Reformer of Zurich." ReformationSA. Adapted from *The Greatest Century of Reformation*, Peter Hammond (Capetown, South Africa: The Reformation Society, 2006), http://www.reformationsa.org/articles/Zwingli.htm (accessed 8/8/2008).
141. Ibid.
142. Ibid.
143. Dowley, *Eerdman's Handbook*, 402.
144. Ibid., 401.
145. Unfortunately this would happen under the authority of the city council of Zurich while Zwingli was leader.
146. Bowie, *The Story of the Church*, 142.
147. Abraham Kuyper, *Calvinism: Six Lectures Delivered at the Theological Seminary at Princeton, 1898-1899* (New York: Fleming H. Revell, Co., n.d.), 11-12.
148. John Calvin, *Institutes*, Christian Classics Ethereal Library, http://www.ccel.org/ccel/calvin/institutes.html (accessed 2/8/2009).
149. *"For since the creation of the world God's invisible qualities--his eternal power and divine nature--have been clearly seen, being understood from what has been made, so that men are without excuse"* (Romans 1:21), and *"For by him all things were created: things in heaven and on earth, visible and invisible, whether thrones or powers or rulers or authorities; all things were created by him and for him. He is before all things, and in him all things hold together"* (Colossians 1:16-17).
150. Henry Morris, *Men of Science, Men of God* (San Diego, CA: Creation Life Publishers, 1982), 35.
151. J.H. Tiner, *Johannes Kepler: Giant of Faith and Science* (Milford, MI: Mott Media,1977), http://www.answersingenesis.org/creation/v15/i1/kepler.asp (accessed 2/2/2009).
152. Robert Boyle, *Selected Philosophical Papers of Robert Boyle*, ed. M.A. Stewart (Indianapolis: Hackett Publishing, 1991).

ENDNOTES

153. Charles Earle Raven, *John Ray, Naturalist*, 2nd ed., cont. S.M. Walters. (Cambridge: Cambridge University Press, 1986).
154. Ann Lamont, "John Ray: Founder of Biology and Devout Christian," *Answers in Genesis*, Dec. 1998, http://www.answersingenesis.org/creation/v21/ray.asp#f7 (accessed 2/12/2009), as found in J.G. Crowther's *Founders of British Science: John Wilkins, Robert Boyle, John Ray, Christopher Wren, Robert Hooke, Isaac Newton* (London: Cresset Press, 1960).
155. Allan L. Gillen and Frank J. Sherwin III, "Louis Pasteur's Views on Creation, Evolution, and the Genesis of Germs," *Answers Research Journal*, Vol. 1, 2008, 43-52, http://www.answersingenesis.org/articles/arj/v1/louis-pasteurs-views (accessed 2/13/2009).
156. Morris, *Men of Science*, 89.
157. Isaac Newton, "Original Letter from Isaac Newton to Richard Bentley," The Newton Project, Trinity College Library, Cambridge, UK, http://www.newtonproject.sussex.ac.uk/texts.
158. Isaac Newton, *Newton's Principia: The Mathematical Principles of Natural Philosophy*, trans. Andrew Motte (London: Benjamin Notte, 1729), 504.
159. John William Draper is an example of an author who tried to equate Christianity with scientific oppression. In his book *History of the Conflict between Religion and Science* he cast the Galileo incident "not as divisions between different scientists, but as theologians on the one side and scientists on the other, and they were made to typify all relations between the two groups" (Hill, *Zondervan Handbook*, 367). Andrew Dickson White also attempted to assert this "conflict theory" between religion and science in his book, *A History of the Warfare of Science with Theology in Christendom*, but Gary Ferngren, in his 2002 volume on the relationship between science and religion, dispels this myth: "While some historians had always regarded the Draper-White thesis as oversimplifying and distorting a complex relationship, in the late twentieth century it underwent a more systematic reevaluation. The result is the growing recognition among historians of science that the relationship of religion and science has been much more positive than is sometimes thought. Although popular images of controversy continue to exemplify the supposed hostility of Christianity to new scientific theories, studies have shown that Christianity has often nurtured and encouraged scientific endeavor, while at other times the two have co-existed without either tension or attempts at harmonization. If Galileo and the Scopes trial come to mind as examples of conflict, they were the exceptions rather than the rule" (Gary Ferngren, "Introduction," *Science & Religion: A Historical Introduction* [Baltimore: Johns Hopkins University Press, 2002], ix.)
160. Gale E. Christiansen, *In the Presence of the Creator—Newton and His Times* (London: The Free Press, 1984), 261.
161. Morris, *Men of Science*, 121-123.
162. Francis S. Collins, *The Language of God: A Scientist Presents Evidence for Belief* (New York: Free Press, 2006), 3.
163. http://www.brainyquote.com/quotes/quotes/i/isaacnewto395010.html (accessed 7/17/2008).
164. "Enlightenment Science and Its Consequences," http://royalsociety.org/publication.asp?id=3865 (accessed 7/19/2008). I'd like to note that the great advances in science by people of faith are glossed over and lumped in with Enlightenment Science. This makes it appear that the revolution in science was a result of skepticism, but the opposite is true! Newton's discoveries were adapted by the deists, who used his laws of motion as a foundation for the formulation of their religious belief—that of God the grand watchmaker. This was regardless of what the Scriptures revealed about the God

ENDNOTES

who interjected Himself in history through Jesus. Because of their belief in a distant God, the deists couldn't believe in the deity of Christ or his miraculous abilities. They could only look to him as a great ethical teacher.

165. N.K. Frankenberry, *The Faith of Scientists in Their Own Words* (Princeton, NJ: Princeton University Press, 2008), 38-39.
166. Isaac Kramnick and R. Laurence Moore, *The Godless Constitution: The Case Against Religious Correctness* (New York: W.W. Norton and Company, 1996), 12.
167. Christopher Hitchens, *The Portable Atheist: Essential Readings for the Nonbeliever* (Philadelphia: Da Capo Press, 2007).
168. Hitchens, *God Is Not Great*, 263.
169. Ibid, 254.
170. *Webster's New World Dictionary of the American Language*, 2nd ed., ed. David B. Guralink (Simon and Schuster, 1980).
171. A form of Micah 6:8. Thomas Paine, *The Age of Reason: Being an Investigation of True and Fabulous Theology* (New York: The Truth Seeker Co., 1898), 6.
172. Ibid.
173. Thomas Jefferson, "Letter to Dr. Benjamin Rush, With a Syllabus, April 4, 1803," http://www.positiveatheism.org/hist/jeff1122.htm (accessed 2/12/2009).
174. Will Durant, *The Story of Philosophy: The Lives and Opinions of the Great Philosophers of the Western World* (New York: Simon and Schuster Paperbacks, 2005), 185.
175. Ibid, 184.
176. Benjamin Franklin, *The Works of Benjamin Franklin, Volume VI*, ed. Jared Sparks (Boston: Hilliard, Gray, and Co., 1856), 93.
177. Ben Franklin, "Letter to John Huey, June 6, 1753," *Our Sacred Honor: Words of Advice from the Founders in Stories, Letters, Poems, and Speeches*, ed. William J. Bennett (New York: Simon and Schuster, 1997), 404-405.
178. Hitchens, *God Is Not Great*, 254.
179. Ibid.
180. Thomas Paine, *Common Sense* (London: Penguin Books, 1986), 100.
181. Ibid.
182. *The American People: Creating a Nation and Society, Volume One: To 1877*, 6th ed., Gary B. Nash and Julie Roy Jeffrey (New York: Pearson Longman, 2004), 149.
183. James D. Nelson, "Pietism," http://www.mb-soft.com/believe/txc/pietism.htm (accessed 12/5/2004)."
184. William Warren Sweet, *Religion in Colonial America* (New York: Charles Scribner's Sons, 1949).
185. Ibid., 274.
186. Ibid.
187. Ibid.
188. Ibid.
189. Ibid.
190. Ibid., 276.
191. Ibid.
192. Ibid., 286.
193. Ibid.
194. Ibid., 277.
195. Ibid.

196. *The Great Awakening: Event and Exegesis*, ed. Darret Rutman (New York: John Wiley and Sons, Inc. 1970), 36.
197. Ibid, 37.
198. Ibid.
199. Ibid, 37.
200. Ibid.
201. Ibid.
202. Ibid.
203. Ibid., 45.
204. J.M. Bumstead and John E. Van de Wetering, *What Must I Do To Be Saved? The Great Awakening in Colonial America* (Hinsdale, IL: The Dryden Press), 80.
205. Rutman, *The Great Awakening*, 40.
206. Ibid., 41.
207. Sweet, *Religion in Colonial America*, 279.
208. Ibid.
209. Ibid.
210. Ibid., 280.
211. Ibid.
212. Rutman, *The Great Awakening*, 288.
213. Ibid., 136.
214. Sweet, *Religion in Colonial America*, 287.
215. Rutman, *The Great Awakening*, 137.
216. Ibid., 138.
217. Bumstead, *What Must I Do to Be Saved?*, 160.
218. Ibid., 160-161.
219. Edwin Gaustad, "Sins of the Fathers: Religion and Revolution," http://www.american-revolution.org/gaustad.html (accessed 2/14/2009).
220. Ibid.
221. Ibid.
222. Ibid.
223. Paine, *Common Sense*, 109.
224. Bumstead, *What Must I Do to Be Saved?*, 157.
225. Rutman, *The Great Awakening*, 5.
226. Ibid., 6.
227. Gaustad, "Sins of the Fathers."
228. Wells, *The Outline of History*, 895.
229. Ibid., 894.
230. Ibid., 916.
231. Alexis De Tocqueville, *Democracy in America: Volume I*, trans. Henry Reeve (New York: D. Appleton and Country, 1904), 326-331.
232. Ibid.
233. Ibid.
234. As the abolitionists would prove, slaveholders *perverted* the Old Testament teachings on slavery and the sons of Noah, using them as justification for their own selfish purposes.
235. The United Church of Christ makes mention of Samuel Sewall in an attempt to show that they have always had spiritual foresight concerning societal reform (to support their acceptance of homosexual relationships), but they don't mention that Sewall also oversaw the Salem Witch Trials, although the story of his public repentance for this wrong is one of the most dramatic and touching in history.

236. This is my personal favorite, since it gives so many biblical defenses in such a clear way.
237. For a more detailed discussion on the battle over slavery in the American churches, see Dumond, *Antislavery*, 343-349.
238. Louis Ruchames, *The Abolitionists: A Collection of Their Writings* (New York: G.P. Putnam and Sons, 1963), 188.
239. Union Theological Seminary offered to pay for his final two years of school if he would "forego" speaking out on the slavery issue. According to his New York Times obituary (September 13, 1881) Foster "declined, on the ground that 'he could not be bought to hold his peace and refuse to open his mouth on a question so near his heart and conscience as 3,000,000 of his fellow beings in chains.'"
240. Ruchames, *The Abolitionists*, 187.
241. Ibid., 190.
242. Benjamin Quarles, *Black Abolitionists* (New York: Oxford University Press), 21.
243. Ibid., 38.
244. Ruchames, *The Abolitionists*, 40-41.
245. Wilberforce, *A Practical View*, 64.
246. Ibid., 104.
247. Thomas Jefferson, "Thomas Jefferson to Edward Coles, 1814," http://etext.virginia.edu/jefferson/quotations/jeff1290.htm (accessed 7/19/2008).
248. Thomas Jefferson, *Notes on the State of Virginia* (Richmond, VA: J.W. Randolph, 1853), 149-150.
249. David Hume, *An Enquiry Concerning Human Understanding: A Critical Edition*, ed. Tom L. Beauchamp (Oxford: Oxford University Press, 2000), 8-9.
250. David Hume, *The Philosophical Works of David Hume*, cont. Henry Maudsley (Boston: Little, Brown, and Co., 1854), 228.
251. Immanuel Kant, "Observations on the Feeling of the Beautiful and Sublime," quoted by David Brion in the book *Inhuman Bondage: The Rise and Fall of Slavery in the New World* (New York: Oxford University Press, USA, 2006), 75.
252. Voltaire, "Essai sur les mouers," quoted by David Brion in the book *Inhuman Bondage: The Rise and Fall of Slavery in the New World* (New York: Oxford University Press, USA, 2006), 75.
253. The first pages of William Howitt's book point out the hypocrisy of Christians when they shiver at the evil of the Huns and yet they don't look at their own wickedness as promoters of the Inquisition, wars, colonization, etc.
254. Phrenology is the attempt to chart the human skull and then read the lumps on persons' heads to determine their intellect and personality.
255. Samuel Morton, "The Debate Over Slavery: Excerpts from Samuel George Morton, Crania Americana," Center for History and New Media, George Mason University, http://chnm.gmu.edu/exploring/19thcentury/debateoverslavery/pop_morton.htm (accessed 2/7/2009).
256. Frederick Douglass, "The Claims of the Negro Ethnologically Considered," An Address Before the Literary Societies of Western Reserve College, At Commencement, July 12, 1854, *The Frederick Douglass Papers*, 10, The Library of Congress, http://memory.loc.gov (accessed 2/4/2009).
257. Ibid., 11.
258. Such a perverted use of this scripture (Luke 12:49)!
259. Frederick Douglass, "The Church and Prejudice," Plymouth County Anti-Slavery Society, November 4, 1841, http://www.frederickdouglass.org/speeches/#church (accessed 1/30/2009).

ENDNOTES

260. Hitchens, *God Is Not Great*, 178.
261. Thomas Paine, "American Slavery in America," http://www.cooperativeindividualism.org/paine_slavery.html (accessed 2/7/2009).
262. Curti, *The Growth of American Thought*, 435.
263. Ibid., 432.
264. Barnes, *Anti-slavery Impulse*, 9.
265. Robert William Fogel, *Without Consent or Contract: The Rise and Fall of American Slavery* (New York: W.W. Norton and Co., 1994), 269.
266. Dwight L. Dumond, *Antislavery: The Crusade for Freedom in America* (New York: W.W. Norton and Co. Inc., 1961), 158.
267. Ibid., 159.
268. Louis Filler, *Crusade Against Slavery: Friends, Foes, and Reforms, 1820-1860* (Algonac, MI: Reference Publications, 1986), 94.
269. Ibid.
270. Dumond, *Antislavery*, 310.
271. Martin Luther King, Jr., "Letter from a Birmingham Jail," African Studies Center, University of Pennsylvania, http://www.africa.upenn.edu/Articles_Gen/Letter_Birmingham.html (accessed 2/7/2009).
272. Ibid.
273. Ibid.
274. Herbert Aptheker, *Abolitionism: A Revolutionary Movement* (Boston: Twayne, 1989), 62.
275. Ibid.
276. Ibid.
277. To what higher law can the atheist appeal?
278. Dumond, *Antislavery*, 310.
279. Ibid.
280. Raymond Bial, *The Underground Railroad* (Boston: Houghton, Mifflin, Harcourt, 1999), 38.
281. Ibid.
282. Quarles, *Black Abolitionists*, 66. The Tappan Family was one of the major funding sources for the abolitionists.
283. Ibid., 67.
284. Hill, *Zondervan Handbook*, 352.
285. Curti, *Growth of American Thought*, 371.
286. Paul N. Tobin, "Christian Missionaries," *The Rejection of Pascal's Wager: A Skeptic's Guide to Christianity*, http://geocities.com/paulntobin/mission.html (accessed 2/7/2009).
287. Gary B. Nash and Julie Roy Jeffrey, *The American People: Creating a Nation and Society, Volume One: To 1877*, 6th ed. (New York: Pearson, Longman, 2004), 46-47.
288. Ibid., 49.
289. Ibid., 50.
290. *Bartolomé de las Casas—A Short Account of the Destruction of the Indies*, trans. and ed. Nigel Griffin (London: Penguin, 1992), 82.
291. Nash, 76.
292. Ibid., 93.
293. Ibid., 105.
294. Ibid.
295. "Treaty with the Indians at Shackamaxon," http://penntreatymuseum.org/treaty.php (accessed 1/28/2009).

ENDNOTES

296. Miriam Estenson, *The Life of Matthew Flinders: The Journeys of Matthew Flinders* (Sydney: Allen and Unwin, 2002), 19.
297. In fact, Charles Darwin, while traveling on the *HMS Beagle* to Tahiti, would comment on the work of the missionaries in a favorable manner.
298. William Howitt, *Christianity and Colonization: A Popular History of the Treatment of the Natives by the Europeans in All Their Colonies, 1838* (Whitefish, MT: Kessinger Publishers, 2004), 9-10.
299. *Report on the Parliamentary Select Committee, on Aboriginal Tribes, (British Settlements)* (London: William Ball, Aldine Chambers, Paternoster Row, and Hatchard and Son, Picadilly, 1837), xii.
300. Ibid., vii.
301. Ibid., viii.
302. Neil Parsons, "Colonial Administration Page 2: Charles Rey and Previous Commissioners of the Bechuanaland Protectorate," University of Botswana History Department, http://thuto.org/ubh/bw/colad2.htm (accessed 8/7/2008).
303. Ibid.
304. Cecil Rhodes, *The Last Will and Testament of Cecil John Rhodes: With Elucidatory Notes to which are Added Some Chapters Describing the Political and Religious Ideas of the Testator By Cecil Rhodes*, comp. William Thomas Stead (London: "Review of Reviews" Office, 1902).
305. Robert W. Rydell, "World's Columbian Exposition," *Encylopedia of Chicago* (Chicago Historical Society, 2006), http://www.encyclopedia.chicagohistory.org/pages/1386.html (accessed 8/11/2008).
306. Joseph L. Graves, *The Emperor's New Clothes: Biological Theories of Race at the Millennium* (New Brunswick, NJ: Rutgers University Press, 2002), 75.
307. Ibid.
308. Ibid., 76.
309. "Social Darwinism," *Encyclopedia of American History* (Answers Corporation, 2006), http://www.answers.com/topic/social-darwinism (accessed 1/19/2009).
310. David Harrell, Jr., et. al., *Unto a Good Land: A History of the American People, Volume I: to 1900* (Grand Rapids, MI: Wm. B. Eerdman's Publishing Co., 2005), 727.
311. Ibid., 727-728.
312. Ibid., 728.
313. Even clothing them would be done for ulterior motives—to expand the cotton market.
314. Henry H. Johnston, introduction to *Christus Liberator*, by Ellen C. Parsons (New York: Macmillan, 1905), 2.
315. Ibid.
316. Benjamin Harrison, "Speech Given at the Ecumenical Conference on Foreign Missions Held in Carnegie Hall and Neighboring Churches, April 21-May 1, 1900" (New York: American Tract Society, 1900).
317. Jon Bonk, *Between Past and Future: Evangelical Mission Entering the Twenty-First Century* (Pasadena, CA: William Carey Library, 2003), 67.
318. Howitt, *Colonisation and Christianity*, 9.
319. Dana Lee Robert, *American Women in Missions: A Social History of Their Thought and Practice* (Macon, GA: Mercer University Press, 1997), 265.
320. Ibid., 265-266.
321. Ibid., 266.
322. John Howard Hinton, *William Knibb: Missionary in Jamaica* (London: Houlston and Stoneman, 1847), 148.

ENDNOTES

323. Ibid.
324. Ibid.
325. Alan Jackson, "William Knibb, 1803-1845, Jamaican Missionary and Slaves' Friend," http://www.victorianweb.org/history/knibb/knibb.html (accessed 2/10/2009).
326. Ibid.
327. Bain Attwood, "Reading Sources in Aboriginal History: Mission Station Visitors Books," *La Trobe Journal* 43, 1989, http://calista.slv.vic.gov.au/latrobejournal/issue/latrobe-43/t1-g-t10.html (accessed 8/13/2008).
328. Ibid.
329. Ibid.
330. Issac Taylor Headland, *Some By-Products of Missions* (New York: Jennings and Graham, 1912), 58.
331. Ibid., 61.
332. "Christian Universities in China," http://www1.chinaculture.org/library/2008-02/04/content_26029.htm (accessed 2/3/2009).
333. Jing Liao, "The Contributions of Nineteenth Century Christian Missionaries to Chinese Library Reform," Project MUSE, University of Texas Press "Libraries and Culture," http://muse.jhu.edu/demo/libraries_and_culture/v041.3liao.html (accessed 2/8/2009).
334. Bainton, *Christendom*, 141.
335. This work continues through the heroic efforts of the Wycliffe translators. Their stories are too numerous to tell here, but they are dramatic and selfless.
336. Leonard Thompson, *A History of South Africa*, 3rd ed. (New Haven, CT: Yale University Press, 2000), 59-61.
337. Bainton, *Christendom*, 141.
338. Nelson Mandela, *Long Walk to Freedom: The Autobiography of Nelson Mandela* (New York: Little, Brown, and Co., 1995), 43.
339. Ibid., 44.
340. Ibid.
341. David Frawley, "Bush Sponsored Evangelism of India—II," *News Today*, February 7, 2007, http://www.newstodaynet.com/2007sud/Feb07/222207.htm (accessed 2/4/2009).
342. Bainton, *Christendom*, 140.
343. Christopher Hitchens and Dinesh D'Souza, "Is Christianity the Problem?" Debate, The King's College, October 27, 2007, http://www.youtube.com//watch?v=j3f8b1wdXkU (accessed 2/7/2007).
344. "The Island Mission: Being a History of the Melanesian Mission From Its Commencement" Project Canterbury, http://anglicanhistory.org/oceania/island_mission1869/01.html (accessed 2/8/2009).
345. Ibid.
346. "History," American Samoa Historic Preservation Office, http://www.ashpo.org/history.htm (accessed 2/8/2009). For an interesting view of the Samoan people, see how the Samoans are helping in the American "War on Terror" at "Our Troops," http://www.samoanews.com/our-troops.html, and visit one of their tourism web sites at http://www.visitsamoa.com, where they promote honeymoon suites, luxurious spas, surfing, golfing, fishing, waterfalls, trails through rainforests, etc. This wasn't the world that greeted the missionaries.
347. "About Fiji: History," Fiji High Commission to the United Kingdom of Great Britain and Northern Ireland, http://www.fijihighcommission.org.uk/about-1.htm (accessed 2/8/2009).

ENDNOTES

348. "John G. Paton: Apostle of Christ to the Cannibals," Wholesome Words, http://www.wholesomewords.org/missions/biopaton.html (accessed 2/8/2009).
349. James D. Kennedy, *What If Jesus Had Never Been Born?: The Positive Impact of Christianity in History* (Nashville, TN: Thomas Nelson, 2001), 167-169.
350. Adolph Hitler, *Mein Kampf*, Project Gutenberg Australia, http://gutenberg.net.au/ebooks02/0200601.txt (accessed 2/8/2009).
351. Ibid, Vol. 2, ch. 10.
352. G. W. F. Hegel, *Phenomonology of Mind, Volume I*, trans. J. B. Baillie (New York: Routledge Taylor & Francis Group, 1910), 93.
353. George Orwell, "Politics and the English Language," *The Informed Argument*, ed. Robert K. Miller (San Diego, CA: Harcourt, Brace, Jovanovich, 1986), 512.
354. Ibid., 519.
355. Kelley L. Ross, Ph.D., "G.W.F. Hegel: 1770-1831," http://www.friesan.com/hegel.htm (accessed 9/28/2003).
356. Christopher Hitchens, *God Is Not Great*, 283.
357. Peter Singer, *Hegel* (Oxford: Oxford University Press, 1983), 1.
358. Ibid.
359. Charles Taylor, *Hegel and Modern Society* (Cambridge: Cambridge University Press, 1983), 6.
360. Ibid, 7.
361. Ibid.
362. Ibid, 1.
363. Ibid.
364. Ibid.
365. Ibid.
366. Andrew Heywood, *Political Ideologies: An Introduction*, 2nd ed. (New York: Worth Publishers, 1998), 165.
367. Singer, *Hegel*, 55.
368. Taylor, *Hegel and Modern Society*, 4.
369. Singer, *Hegel*, 30.
370. Ibid., 31.
371. Ibid., 34.
372. Robert S. Hartman, *Hegel: Reason in History; A General Introduction to the Philosophy of History* (Indianapolis: Bobbs-Merrill Educational Publishing, 1953), xviii.
373. Singer, *Hegel*, 11.
374. Ibid., 19.
375. Ibid.
376. Ibid.
377. Ibid.
378. Ibid.
379. Ibid.
380. Ibid., 1.
381. Wilbur Smith, *World Crises and the Prophetic Scriptures* (Chicago: Moody Press, 1952), 277.
382. Singer, *Hegel*, 22.
383. Hartman, *Hegel: Reason in History*, xvii.
384. Taylor, *Hegel and Modern Society*, 11.
385. Hartman, *Hegel: Reason in History*, 20.
386. Singer, *Hegel*, 22.

ENDNOTES

387. He was especially interested in studying cultures without making ethnocentric judgments.
388. Heywood, *Political Ideologies*, 218.
389. Ibid., 230.
390. Ibid., De Tocqueville would have correspondence with Gobineau and disagree with him.
391. Ibid.
392. Ibid.
393. Ibid.
394. Adolph Hitler, *My Battle* (Boston: Houghton, Mifflin, Co., 1998), 154.
395. Ibid., 189.
396. Heywood, *Political Ideologies*, 231.
397. Ibid., 219.
398. Singer, *Hegel*, 12.
399. Ibid., 41.
400. Hitler, *My Battle*, 184.
401. Singer, *Hegel*, 42.
402. The attempt to look at the Bible as though it is just like any other book and subject it to tests of truthfulness in the realms of history, science, and archaeology.
403. Arthur C. Cochrane, "The Theological Declaration of Barmen," *The Church's Confession Under Hitler* (Philadelphia: Westminster Press, 1962), 237-242.
404. Robert Ellsburg, *All Saints: Daily Reflections on Saints, Prophets, and Witnesses for Our Time* (New York: The Crossroad Publishing Company, 2005), 205.
405. Ibid.
406. Paul Tillich, *Christianity and the Encounter of the World Religions* (New York: Columbia University Press, 1963), 90.
407. Benjamin Reist, *The Promise of Bonhoeffer* (Philadelphia: J.B. Lippincott Co., 1969), 65.
408. Dietrich Bonhoeffer, *Letters and Papers from Prison*, rev. ed. (New York: Touchstone, 1997), 280.
409. Reist, *The Promise of Bonhoeffer*, 120.
410. Note that, regardless of Hitchens' claims, Bonhoeffer didn't believe conscience alone was enough to cause a man to "stand fast." He says: "Then there is the man with a *conscience*, who fights single-handed against heavy odds in situations that call for a decision. But the scale of the conflicts in which he has to choose—with no advice or support except from his own conscience—tears him to pieces. Evil approaches him in so many respectable and seductive disguises that his conscience becomes nervous and vacillating, till at last he contents himself with a salved instead of a clear conscience, so that he lies to his own conscience in order to avoid despair; for a man whose only support is his conscience can never realize that a bad conscience may be stronger and more wholesome than a deluded one." Bonhoeffer realized that there needed to be a plumb line, something that remained as a solid standard for men to rely on. To him, the "responsible man" was the one "who tries to make his whole life an answer to the question and call of God." Neither reason, fanaticism, conscience, duty, freedom, or virtue are enough to cause a man to be courageous and not waiver. Only an allegiance to the God of the Bible can discern what is evil. He says that "the great masquerade of evil has played havoc with all our ethical concepts. For evil to appear disguised as light, charity, historical necessity, or social justice is quite bewildering to anyone brought up on our traditional ethical concepts, while for the

ENDNOTES

Christian who bases his life on the Bible it merely confirms the fundamental wickedness of evil." (*Letters and Papers*, 4-5)

411. Dietrich Bonhoeffer, *The Cost of Discipleship*, rev. ed. (New York: Collier Books, McMillan Publishing Company, 1963), 22.
412. Stewart Winfield Herman, *Report from Christian Europe* (New York: Friendship Press, 1953), 54.
413. Robert Ellsburg, *All Saints*, 88.
414. As a sidenote, in this anti-Semitism he would be joined by Voltaire and Diderot.
415. This is another example of wrong doctrine. If he had understood the teaching in Romans and Zechariah that the Jews would be saved collectively at the return of Christ, this German justification may have been averted.
416. Ibid., x-xi.
417. Peter Calvocoressi and Guy Wint, *Total War: Causes and Courses of the Second World War* (New York: Penguin Books, 1972), 7. According to these authors, Hitler who "was employed in the Press and News Section of the army headquarters in Munich, was appointed a *Bildungsoffizier* (a cultural instructor or ideological education officer)."
418. Laissez-fare economics is a term that comes from the French "to leave alone." It means allowing the marketplace to be unfettered by any regulations and rules. Adam Smith argued that the economy, if left alone, would adjust itself by an "invisible hand." Laissez-faire economics allowed economic competition to be brutal, contributing to the economic domination of industrialists, and social Darwinism gave them the justification for their actions—they were merely contributing to the strength and progress of mankind: the end justified the means—because they were ultimately contributing to the likelihood that the human race, particularly the white Anglo-Saxon Protestant race, would continue to exist.
419. Curti, *The Growth of American Thought*, 555-556.
420. Richard Hofstadter, *Social Darwinism in American Thought*, rev. ed. (Boston: Beacon Press, 1955), 179.
421. Senator A. J. Beveridge, speech given before the U.S. Senate, Jan 9, 1900, http://www.mtholyoke.edu/acad/intrel/ajb72.htm (accessed 2/9/2009).
422. Karl Marx and Frederick Engels, *Communist Manifesto*, Marxists Internet Archive, http://www.marxists.org/archive/marx/works/1848/communist-manifesto/ch01.htm (accessed 2/7/2009).
423. Richard Wurmbrand, *In God's Underground*, ed. Charles Foley (Greenwich, CT: Fawcett Publications, 1968), 239.
424. Alistair McGrath, *Historical Theology*, 232.
425. Ibid.
426. Ibid., 233.
427. Harris, *Letter to a Christian Nation*, 4-5.
428. Ibid., viii.
429. Harris, *Letter to a Christian Nation*, 5.
430. Oswald A. Blumit and Oswald J. Smith. *Sentenced to Siberia: The Story of the Ministry, Persecution, Imprisonment and God's Wonderful Deliverance of Pastor Basil A. Malof, Russian Missionary*, 6th ed. (Wheaton, IL: Mayflower Publishers, 1943), 73-74.
431. Ibid., 75.
432. Ibid.
433. Ibid.
434. Leo Tolstoy, *Confessions*, Christian Classics Ethereal Library, http://www.ccel.org/ccel/tolstoy/confession.ii.xi.html (accessed 2/8/2009).
435. Ibid.

436. Ibid., ch. 12.
437. Ibid.
438. Ibid., ch. 15.
439. Ibid.
440. Pastor Malof relates the story of how two years after his first encounter with Count Tolstoy, a wagon pulled up in front of the home of the son of Madame Tschertkoff (who was the Countess Chernicheff-Krouglikoff and friend of the Empress), while he was having a Bible study, and "from this carriage, to the surprise of everyone, stepped the Countess Sophie Tolstoy, wife of Count Leo." She had a message asking the pastor to pay a visit to her husband on that day. But Malof couldn't go because he had a train to catch. Pastor Malof says that this was the "greatest regret" of his life, because he later received a letter "stating that Count Tolstoy had anxiously awaited him the whole of that afternoon." (Blumit, *Sentenced to Siberia*, 71-81.) Right after this, Tolstoy left on his final search for God. The newspapers watched his every move as he traveled from monastery to monastery to speak with the "startsi" (aged saints). Deciding to never go home again, he wandered from place to place until finally dying at a railway station. Tolstoy was searching for the Narrow Way. He wanted a simple faith which would produce a relationship with God and produce love for others.
441. Dowley, *Eerdman's Handbook*, 456.
442. Ibid.
443. Ibid.
444. Ibid.
445. Ibid., 456-457.
446. Ibid., 458.
447. Ibid., 459.
448. Blumit, *Sentenced to Siberia*, 54.
449. Ibid., 54-55.
450. Ibid., 55.
451. Ibid., 61.
452. Ibid., 65-66.
453. Ibid., 129.
454. Ibid., 104. Interestingly, Lunacharsky wrote plays, one of which was described in an article in the January 21, 1929, issue of *TIME Magazine* entitled "Lunacharsky vs. Religion": "With the new Soviet anti-religious campaign now in full cry... Commissar of Education Anatole Lunacharsky released, last week, a cinema drama called *Salamander*. Heroine: Mme. Lunacharsky, strikingly beautiful, known to her intimates as "Natalia." Author: M. Lunacharsky. Plot: The pious folk of a Russian provincial town fiendishly conspire against a kindly atheist professor of zoology and his wife (Mme. Lunacharsky). The professor is expelled from his post, after the Christians 'frame' him in such fashion as to make it appear that he is a pervert. Reduced to penury, the professor's wife is seduced by the man who framed him; and this 'Holy Devil' then proceeds to poison her. Thenceforward the professor's misery grows more and more Tolstoyan until, as the grand climax, Commissar of Education Anatole Lunacharsky appears upon the film in his official capacity, raises up the professor from lowest depths, and places him in a Moscow laboratory where, among congenial atheists, he can complete his 'Great Experiment.'"
455. Hitchens, *God Is Not Great*, 283.
456. Christopher Hitchens and Alistair McGrath, "Poison or Cure?: Religious Belief in the

ENDNOTES

Modern World," Debate, Michael Cromartie Berkely Center for Religion, Peace, and World Affairs, Washington, D.C., October 11, 2007, *Ethics and Public Policy*, http://www.eppc.org/publications/pageID.390/default.asp (accessed 9/25/2008).
457. Brother Andrew and Charles Paul Conn, *Battle for Africa* (Old Tappan, NJ: Fleming H. Revell, 1977), 79-80.
458. Ibid.
459. Heywood, *Political Ideologies*, 108.
460. Peter Kropotkin, *Mutual Aid: A Factor of Evolution* (Boston: Extending Horizons Books, 1955), 293.
461. Harry F. Ward, *The Christian Demand for Social Reconstruction* (Philadelphia: W.H. Jenkins, 1918), 54.
462. "Manifesto and Program," *Daily Worker*, June 30, 1934, Vol. 11, No. 156, 54. U.S. Congress Against War and Fascism, http://www.marxists.org/history/usa/groups/alawf/1933/1001-alawf-manifestoprogram.pdf (accessed 1/22/2009).
463. Ibid.
464. Richard Wurmbrand, *Tortured for Christ* (Bartlesville, OK: Living Sacrifice Book Co., 1998), 15.
465. Ibid., 16.
466. "Manifesto and Program," *Daily Worker*, June 30, 1934. Vol. 11, No. 156, 4. U.S. Congress Against War and Fascism, http://www.marxists.org/history/usa/groups/alawf/1933/1001-alawf-manifestoprogram.pdf (accessed 1/22/2009).
467. Alexander Solzhenitsyn, *One Day in the Life of Ivan Denisovich* (New York: Dutton, 1963), 155.
468. Fyodor Dostoyevsky, *The Brothers Karamazov*, trans. Richard Pevear and Larissa Volokhonsky (New York: Farrar, Straus and Giroux, 1990), 257.
469. Ibid.
470. Ibid., 258.
471. Ibid., 260.
472. Ibid., 261.
473. Kristen Wright, "From the Killing Fields to the Cross," *Breakpoint*, November 14, 2006, http://www.breakpoint.org/listingarticle.asp?ID=5804 (accessed 1/22/2009).
474. The Voice of the Martyrs, *Extreme Devotion: Daily Devotional Stories of Ancient to Modern Day Believers Who Sacrificed Everything for Christ* (Nashville, TN: Thomas Nelson Publishers, 2001), 202.
475. Martin Luther King, Jr., "Letter from a Birmingham Jail."
476. Timothy W. Maier, "Taliban Demands Rigid Conformity," *Insight Magazine*, October 22, 2001, http://www.insightmag.com/archive/200110222.shtml (accessed 9/7/2008).
477. Ibid.
478. David Brooks, "We're In It For the Long Haul," *Milwaukee Journal Sentinel*, November 6, 2003.
479. George Packer, "The Liberal Quandary in Iraq," *The New York Times*, December 8, 2002.
480. Dr. B. Khalaf, "Letter to the Editor," *The Guardian*, February 14, 2003, http://www.guardian.co.uk/the guardian/2003/feb/14/ (accessed 2/14/2009).
481. Jeff Jacoby, "Where Are the Iraqi Peaceniks?" *Boston Globe*, February 21, 2003, http://www.frontpagemag.com/articles/Read.asp (accessed 2/7/2009).
482. Robert Scheer, "It's Time to Cut Our Losses," *Milwaukee Journal Sentinel*, November 6, 2003.
483. Jacoby, "Where Are the Iraqi Peaceniks?" *Boston Globe*, February 21, 2003, http://www.

ENDNOTES

frontpagemag.com/articles/Read.asp (accessed 2/7/2009).
484. Abd al-Majid al-Khoei, "Freedom: What Iraqis Want," *National Review Online*, February 21, 2003, http://www.nationalreview.com/comment/comment-al-khoei022103.asp (accessed 2/14/2009).
485. Charles Krauthammer, "American Unilateralism," *Imprimis*, https://www.hillsdale.edu/news/imprimis/archive/issue.asp?year=2003&month=01 (accessed 2/10/2009).
486. Bagehot, "The Moral Imperative," *The Economist*, February 27, 2003.
487. "Cardinal Criticises U.S. Treatment of Saddam," *The Tablet*, December 20, 2003, http://www.thetablet.co.uk/article/2878 (accessed 2/9/2009).
488. Bagehot, "The Moral Imperative," *The Economist*, February 27, 2003.
489. Jonathan Petre, "Carey Wary of Attack," *The Telegraph*, January 9, 2002, http://www.telegraph.co.uk/news/uknews/1408680/Carey-wary-of-attack-on-Iraq.html?mobile=true (accessed 2/9/2009).
490. "Statement on the War in Iraq," World Council of Churches, March 20, 2003, http://www.oikoumene.org/en/resources/documents/wcc-commissions/international-affairs/regional-concerns/middle-east/statement-on-the-war-in-iraq.html (accessed 2/9/2009).
491. This claim that Americans are "occupiers" of Iraq continues to this day. At John McCain's acceptance speech at the Republican Convention, a protester hung a sign asking, "How are Occupied People Free?"
492. "President Bush, Let Jesus Change Your Mind," advertisement by Religious Leaders for Sensible Priorities, *New York Times*, December 4, 2002.
493. Richard D. Land, "The Land Letter," *The Eleventh Hour*, October 3, 2002, http://www.11th-hour.info/Articles/Land_Letter.html (accessed 2/10/2009).
494. Ibid.
495. Paul Kengor, *George W. Bush: A Spiritual Life* (New York: Harper Collins, 2004), 41.
496. Ibid., 37.
497. Eric Alterman, *Why We're Liberals: A Political Handbook for Post-Bush America* (New York: Penguin Viking Group, 2008), 215.
498. Ibid., 333.
499. Obviously Saddam Hussein had biological and chemical weapons, since he used them against the Kurds, and it's no secret that he was hindered from getting nuclear weapons by the Israeli air strike on the reactor at Osirak. Whether he was still attempting to produce weapons of mass destruction is unknown. Much of the chemical, biological, or nuclear material is gone, although Iraqi General George Sada claims in his book *Saddam's Secrets* that the WMDs were sent to Syria. The top Israeli General, Moshe Yaalon, also claimed that the weapons were sent to Syria. (Perhaps Israel's 2007 bombing of a nuclear reactor in the Syrian desert may have had something to do with this transfer.) We know that Saddam was interested in nuclear weapons, because United Nations International Atomic Energy Agency inspectors discovered 550 metric tons of yellow cake (concentrated uranium) at the Tuwaitha Nuclear Research Facility in 1991. While the WMDs may have seemed to be "contained," there was no absolute proof that Saddam was no longer pursuing secret programs, as he had in the past. Because of this, nearly everyone, during the lead up to the 2003 Iraq war—Democrat, Republican, or even European, (all who had access to the same information as President Bush)—believed that Saddam Hussein could still be attempting to develop WMDs, yet George W. Bush is accused of being a liar who was purposely deceiving the public in order to go to war.
500. Kengor, *George W. Bush*, 253.
501. Ibid., 251.

ENDNOTES

502. Ibid., 255.
503. Ibid., 256.
504. Ibid.
505. Faoud Ajami, "The Falseness of Anti-Americanism," *Foreign Policy*, September/October 2003.
506. Kengor, *George W. Bush*, 256.
507. Ibid., 258.
508. "An Open Message to America from Iraqi Citizen," YouTube, http://www.youtube.com/watch?v=JRaQRbbu1jA&feature=related (accessed 2/9/2009).
509. "The Other Iraq," http://www.theotheriraq.com, (accessed 2/9/2009).
510. Chris McGreal, "George Bush: A Good Man in Africa," *The Guardian*, February 15, 2008, http://www.guardian.co.uk/world/2008/feb/15/georgebush.usa (accessed 2/9/2009).
511. David Blair, "Analysis: How George W. Bush Became An Africa Hero," *The Daily Telegraph*, July 7, 2008, http://www.telegraph.co.uk/news/worldnews/northamerica/usa/2262217/Analysis-How-George-W-Bush-became-an-African-hero (accessed 8/20/2008).
512. The Voice of the Martyrs, *Iran: Desperate for God* (Bartlesville, OK: Living Sacrifice Book Co. 2006), 130.
513. The Voice of the Martyrs, *Extreme Devotion*, 100.
514. The Voice of the Martyrs, *Iran: Desperate for God*, 34-35.
515. Ibid., 36-37.
516. Ibid., 36.
517. Ibid., 41.
518. The Voice of the Martyrs, *Extreme Devotion*, 62.
519. The Voice of the Martyrs, *Into the Den of the Infidels: Our Search for the Truth* (Bartlesville, OK: Living Sacrifice Book Co., 2003), 5-6.
520. Ibid., 174.
521. Brian McLaren, *A Generous Orthodoxy: Why I Am a Missional, Evangelical, Post/Protestant, Liberal/Conservative, Mystical/Poetic, Biblical, Charismatic/Contemplative, Fundamentalist/Calvinist, Anabaptist/Anglican, Methodist, Catholic, Green, Incarnational, Depressed-yet-Hopeful, Emergent, Unfinished Christian* (Grand Rapids, MI: Zondervan, 2004).
522. Brian McLaren, *Finding Our Way Again: The Return of the Ancient Practices* (Nashville, TN: Thomas Nelson, 2008).
523. J.E. McGuire, Martin Tammy, and Isaac Newton, *Certain Philosophical Questions: Newton's Trinity Notebook* (Cambridge: Cambridge University Press, 2003), 337.
524. Ibid.
525. Bryant Wood, "Did the Israelites Conquer Jericho?" *Biblical Archaeology Review*, March/April 1990, 50 (accessed 2/15/2009), updated at "Did the Israelites Conquer Jericho: A New Look at the Archaeological Evidence," *Associates for Biblical Research*, May 1, 2008, http://www.biblearchaeology.org/post/2008/05/Did-the-Israelites-Conquer-Jericho-A-New-Look-at-the-Archaeological-Evidence.aspx (accessed 2/15/2009).

Bibliography

"About Fiji: History." Fiji High Commission to the United Kingdom of Great Britain and Northern Ireland. http://www.fijihighcommission.org.uk/about-1.html.

A Few Notes on Julian and a Translation of His Public Letters, trans. Edward J. Chinnock. London: David Nutt, 1901.

Ajami, Faoud. "The Falseness of Anti-Americanism." *Foreign Policy*, Sept./Oct. 2003.

Al-Khoei, Abd al-Majid. "Freedom: What Iraqis Want." *National Review Online*, February 21, 2003. http://www.nationalreview.com/comment/comment-al-khoei022103.asp.

Alterman, Eric. *Why We're Liberals: A Political Handbook for Post-Bush America*. New York: Penguin Viking Group, 2008.

Aptheker, Herbert. *Abolitionism: A Revolutionary Movement*. Boston: Twayne, 1989.

Aristotle. "Politics." *The Basic Works of Aristotle*. edited by Richard McKeon. New York: Random House, 1941.

Arnold, Edward Vernon. *Roman Stoicism: Being Lectures on the History of the Stoic Philosophy with Special Reference to its Development within the Roman Empire*. Cambridge: Cambridge University Press, 1911.

Atkinson, James. "Reform." In Dowley, *Eerdman's Handbook to the History of Christianity*, 364.

Atwood, Bain. "Reading Sources in Aboriginal History: Mission Station Visitors' Books." *The Latrobe Journal*, No. 43, Autumn, 1989. http://calista.slv.vic.gov.au/latrobejournal/issue/latrobe-43/t1-g-t10.html.

Bagehot. "The Moral Imperative." *The Economist*. March 1, 2003.

Bainton, Roland H, *A Short History of Christianity and Its Impact on Western Civilization*, Vol. I and II. NewYork: Harper Colophon Books, 1949.

Barclay, William. *Letter to the Hebrews*. Westminster: John Knox Press, 1952.

Barnabus. "The Epistle of Barnabus." *Early Christian Writings*. translated by Maxwell Staniforth and Andrew Louth. London: Penguin Books, 1987.

Bennett, William. *Our Sacred Honor: Words of Advice from the Founders in Stories, Letters, Poems, and Speeches*. New York: Simon & Schuster, 1997.

Betteson, Henry. *Documents of the Early Church*, 2nd ed. London: Oxford University Press, 1963.

Beveridge, Senator A. J. Speech given before the U.S. Senate, Jan 9,1900. http://www.mtholyoke.edu/acad/intrel/ajb72.htm.

Bial, Raymond. *The Underground Railroad.* Boston: Houghton, Mifflin, Harcourt, 1999.

Blair, David. "Analysis: How George W. Bush Became An African Hero." *The Daily Telegraph.* http://www.telegraph.co.uk/news/worldnews/northamerica/usa/2262217/Analysis-How-George-W-Bush-became-an-African-hero.

Blumit, Rev. Oswald A., and Dr. Oswald J. Smith. *Sentenced to Siberia: The Story of the Ministry, Persecution, Imprisonment, and God's Wonderful Deliverance of Pastor Basil A. Malof, Russian Missionary.* 6th ed. Minneapolis, MN: Mayflower, 1943.

Bonhoeffer, Dietrich. *Letters and Papers from Prison.* New York: Touchstone, 1997.

Bonhoeffer, Dietrich. *The Cost of Discipleship.* revised ed. New York: Macmillan, 1963.

Bonk, Jon. *Between Past and Future: Evangelical Mission Entering the Twenty-First Century.* Pasadena, CA: William Carey Library, 2003.

Borg, Marcus J. *The Heart of Christianity: Rediscovering a Life of Faith.* San Francisco, CA: Harper, 2003.

Bowie, Walter Russell. *The Story of the Church.* New York: Abingdon Press, 1955.

Bowman, Allan K. *The Cambridge Ancient History: XI, The High Empire, A.D. 70-192.* 2nd ed. Cambridge: Cambridge University Press, 2000.

Boyle, Robert. *Selected Philosophical Papers of Robert Boyle.* edited by M. A. Stewart. Indianapolis, IN: Hackett, 1991.

Brion, David. *Inhuman Bondage: The Rise and Fall of Slavery in the New World.* Oxford: Oxford University Press, 2006.

Brooks, David. "We're In It for the Long Haul." *Milwaukee Journal Sentinel.* November 6, 2003.

Brother Andrew and Charles Paul Conn. *Battle for Africa.* Old Tappan, NJ: Fleming H. Revell, 1977.

Brown, Dan. *The Da Vinci Code.* New York: Anchor, 2006.

Bumstead, J. M., and John E. Van De Wetering. *What Must I Do to Be Saved?: The Great Awakening in Colonial America.* Hinsdale, IL: Dryden Press, 1976.

Calvin, John. "Institutes." Christian Classics Ethereal Library. http://www.ccel.org/ccel/calvin/institutes.html.

Calvocoressi, Peter, and Guy Wint. *Total War: Causes and Courses of the Second World War.* New York: Penguin, 1972.

Case, Shirley Jackson. *Makers of Christianity: From Jesus to Charlemagne.* New York: Henry Holt and Co., 1934.

Chadwick, Henry. *The Early Church.* Baltimore, MD: Penguin, 1967.

Chambers, Oswald. *My Utmost For His Highest.* Ulrichsville, OH: Barbour, 1991.

"Christian Universities in China." ChinaCulture.org. http://www1.chinaculture.org/library/2008-02/04/content_26029.htm.

BIBLIOGRAPHY

Clement. "Letter to the Romans." *Early Christian Fathers: Vol. I.* translated and edited by Cyril C. Richardson. Philadelphia: Westminster Press, 1952.

Clement of Alexandria. "Paedagogus." *New Advent.* http://www.newadvet.org/fathers/02093.htm.

Cochrane, Arthur C. *The Church's Confession Under Hitler.* Philadelphia: Westminster Press, 1962.

Collins, Francis S. *The Language of God: A Scientist Presents Evidence for Belief.* New York: Free Press, 2006.

Christiansen, Gale E. *In the Presence of the Creator—Newton and His Times.* London: The Free Press, 1984.

Curti, Merle. *The Growth of American Thought.* 3rd ed. New Brunswick: Transaction, 2003.

De Haan, M. R. *God's House of Symbols: A Walk Through the Old Testament Tabernacle.* Grand Rapids, MI: Radio Bible Class, 1981.

De Tocqueville, Alexis. *Democracy in America: Vol. I.* translated by Henry Reeve. New York: D Appleton and Country, 1904.

"The Didache." *Early Christian Fathers.* translated and edited by Cyril C. Richardson. Vol. I. Philadelphia: Westminster Press, 1953.

Dostoyevsky, Fyodor. *The Brothers Karamazov.* translated by Richard Pevear and Larissa Volokhonsky. New York: Straus and Giroux, 1990.

Douglass, Frederick. "The Church and Prejudice." Speech, Plymouth County Anti-Slavery Society, Nov. 4, 1841. http://www.frederickdouglass.org/speeches/#church.

Douglass, Frederick. "The Claims of the Negro Ethonologically Considered." Address Before the Literary Societies of Western Reserve College, Commencement, July 12,1854. *The Frederick Douglass Papers.* http://memory.loc.gov.

Draper, John William. *History of the Conflict Betwen Religion and Science.* Plain Label Books, 1910.

Dumond, Dwight L. *Antislavery: The Crusade for Freedom in America.* New York: W.W. Norton and Co., 1961.

Durant, Will. *The Story of Philosophy: The Lives and Opinions of the Great Philosophers.* New York: Simon and Schuster, 2005.

Eerdman's Handbook to the History of Christianity. edited by Tim Dowley. Grand Rapids, MI: Wm. B. Eerdman's, 1978.

Ellsburg, Robert. *All Saints: Daily Reflections on Saints, Prophets, and Witnesses for Our Time.* New York: Crossroad Co., 2005.

"Enlightenment Science and its Consequences." *The Royal Society.* http://royalsociety.org/publication.asp?id=3865.

"Epistle to Diognetus." *Early Christianity Writings.* translated by Maxwell Staniforth and Andrew Louth. London: Penguin Books, 1987.

BIBLIOGRAPHY

Erasmus, Desiderius. *In Praise of Folly.* edited by Horace Bridges. Whitefish, MT: Kessinger, 2004.

Estenson, Miriam. *The Life of Matthew Flinders: The Journeys of Matthew Flinders.* Sydney: Allen & Unwin, 2002.

Eusebius. "The Ecclesiastical History." *The Essential Eusebius.* translated by Colm Luibheid. New York: New American Library, 1966.

Ferngren, Gary. "Introduction." *Science and Religion: A Historical Introduction.* Baltimore: John Hopkins University Press, 2002.

Filler, Louis. *Crusade Against Slavery: Friends, Foes, and Reforms, 1820-1860.* Algonac, MI: Reference, 1986.

Fogel, Robert. *Wihout Consent or Contract: The Rise and Fall of American Slavery.* New York: W.W. Norton and Co., 1994.

Foxe, John. *Foxe's Book of Martyrs.* Pittsburgh, PA: Whitaker House, 1981.

Frank, Anne. *Anne Frank: The Diary of a Young Girl.* New York: Pocket Books, 1958.

Frankenberry, N. K. *The Faith of Scientists in Their Own Words.* Princeton: Princeton University Press, 2008.

Franklin, Benjamin. *The Works of Benjamin Franklin.* edited by Jared Sparks. Boston: Hilliard, Gray, and Co., 1856.

Frawley, David. "Bush Sponsored Evangelism of India—II." *News Today.* http://www.newstodaynet.com/2007sud/Feb07/222207.htm.

Fukuyama, Francis. *The End of History and the Last Man.* New York: Free Press, 2006.

Gaustad, Edwin. "Sins of the Fathers: Religion and Revolution." AmericanRevolution.org. http://www.americanrevolution.org/gaustad.html.

Geisler, Norman, and William E. Nix. *A General Introduction to the Bible.* Chicago: Moody Press, 1968.

Gillen, Allan L., and Frank J. Sherwin, III. "Louis Pasteur's Views on Creation, Evolution, and the Genesis of Gems." *Answers Research Journal* 1, 2008. http://www.answersingenesis.org/articles/arj/v1/louis-pasteurs-views.

Glover, T. R. *The Conflict of Religions in the Early Roman Empire.* Vol. 10. London: Methuen and Company, 1923.

Goethe, Johann Wolfgang Von. *Faust.* New York: Random House, 1950.

"The Gospel According to Mary Magdalene." The Gnosis Archive. http://www.gnosis.org/library/marygosp.html.

Graves, Joseph L. *The Emperor's New Clothes: Biological Theories of Race at the Millennium.* New Brunswick: Rutgers University Press, 2002.

BIBLIOGRAPHY

Griffin, Nigel. *Bartolome de las Casas: A Short Account of the Destruction of the Indies.* New York: Penguin Classics, 1992.

Guralink, David B. *Webster's New World Dictionary of the American Language.* 2nd ed. New York: Simon and Schuster, 1980.

Hammond, Peter. "Zwingli: The Reformer of Zurich." *The Greatest Century of Reformation.* Capetown, South Africa: The Reformation Society, 2006. http://www.reformationsa.org/articles/Zwingli.htm.

Harell, Jr., David. *Unto a Good Land: A History of the American People, Volume 1: to 1900.* Grand Rapids: MI: Wm. B. Eerdman's Co., 2005.

Harnack, Adolph. *The Mission and Expansion of Christianity in the First Three Centuries.* translated by James Moffat. Gloucester, MA: Peter Smith, 1972.

Harris, Sam. *Letter to A Christian Nation.* New York: Alfred A. Knopf, 2006.

Harrison, Benjamin. *Speech Given At the Ecumenical Conference on Foreign Missions Held in Carnegie Hall and Neighboring Churches, April 21-May 1, 1900.* New York: American Tract Society, 1900.

Harrison, Eugene Myers. "John G. Paton: Apostle of Christ to the Cannibals," *Heroes of Faith on Pioneer Trails.* Chicago: Moody Press, 1945. http://www.wholesomewords.org/missions/biopaton.html.

Hartman, Robert S. *Hegel, Reason in History: A General Introduction to the Philosophy of History.* New York: Bobbs-Merrill Educational Co., 1998.

Headland, Issac Taylor. *Some By-Products of Missions.* New York: Jennings and Graham, 1912.

Hegel, G. W. F. *Phenomonology of Mind.* translated by J. B. Baillie. Vol. I. New York: Routledge Taylor& Francis Group, 1910.

Herman, Stewart Winfield. *Report from Christian Europe.* New York: Friendship Press, 1953.

Heywood, Andrew. *Political Ideologies: An Introduction.* 2nd ed. New York: Worth, 1998.

Hill, Jonathan. *Zondervan Handbook to the History of Christianity.* Grand Rapids, MI: Zondervan, 2006.

Hinton, John Howard. *William Knibb: Missionary in Jamaica.* London: Houlston and Stoneman, 1847.

"History." American Samoa Historic Preservation Office. http://www.ashpo.org/history.htm.

Hitchens, Christopher, and Alistair McGrath. "Poison or Cure? Religious Belief in the Modern World." Debate, Michael Cromartie Berkely Center for Religion, Peace, and World Affairs, Washington, D.C., October 11, 2007. *Ethics and Public Policy.* http://www.eppc.org/publications/pageID.390/default.asp.

BIBLIOGRAPHY

Hitchens, Christopher, and Dinesh D'Souza. "Is Christianity the Problem?" Debate, King's College, October 27, 2007. http://www.youtube.com//watch?v=j3f8b1wdXkU.

Hitchens, Christopher. "Bah, Hanukkah: The Holiday Celebrates the Triumph of Tribal Jewish Backwardness." *Slate*, December 3, 2007. http://www.slate.com/id2179045/.

Hitchens, Christopher. *God Is Not Great: How Religion Poisons Everything*. New York: Twelve, 2007.

Hitchens, Christopher. *The Portable Atheist: Essential Readings for the Unbeliever*. Philadelphia: De Capo Press, 2007.

Hitler, Adolph. *Mein Kampf*. Project Gutenberg Australia. http://gutenberg.net.au/ebooks020200601.txt.

Hitler, Adolph. *My Battle*. Boston: Houghton Mifflin Co., 1998.

Hobbs, Gilbert. *Anti-Slavery Impulse:1830-1844*. Gloucester, MA: Peter Smith, 1957.

Hofstadter, Richard. *Social Darwinism in American Thought*. revised ed. Boston: The Beacon Press, 1955.

Howitt, William. *Colonisation and Christianity: A Popular History of the Treatment of the Natives by the Europeans in All Their Colonies, 1838*. Whitefish, MT: Kessinger Publishers, 2004.

Hume, David. *An Enquiry Concerning Human Understanding: A Critical Edition*. edited by Tom L. Beauchamp. Oxford: Oxford University Press, 2000.

Hume, David. *The Philosophical Works of David Hume*. edited by Henry Maudsley. Boston: Little, Brown, and Co., 1854.

Humphreys, Ken. "Godman—Gestation of a Superhero." JesusNeverExisted.com. http://www.jesusneverexisted.com.

Huntington, Samuel P. *The Clash of Civilizations and the Remaking of World Order*. New York: Simon & Schuster, 1998.

Ignatius. "To the Smyrnaens." *Early Christian Fathers*, edited and translated by Cyril C. Richardson. Vol. I. Philadelphia: Westminster Press, 1952.

"The Island Mission: Being a History of the Melanesian Mission from its Commencement (1869)." *Project Canterbury*. http://anglicanhistory.org/oceania/island_mission1869/01.html.

Jackson, Alan. "William Knibb, 1803-1845, Jamaican Missionary and Slaves' Friend." The Victorian Web. http://www.victorianweb.org/history/knibb/knibb.htm.

Jacoby, Jeff. "Where Are the Iraqi Peaceniks?" *Boston Globe*, February 21, 2003. *Front Page Magazine*. http://www.frontpagemag.com/articles/Read.asp.

Jefferson, Thomas. "Letter from Thomas Jefferson to Dr. Benjamin Rush, With a Syllabus: April 4, 1803." Positive Atheism.com. http://www.positiveatheism.org/hist/jeff1122.htm.

Jefferson, Thomas. "Letter to Edward Coles, 1814." University of Virginia Library. http://etext.virginia.edu/jefferson/quotations/jeff1290.htm.

BIBLIOGRAPHY

Jefferson, Thomas. *Notes on the State of Virginia.* Richmond, VA: J.W. Randolph, 1853.

Johnston, Henry H. Introduction to *Christus Liberator,* by Ellen C. Parsons. New York: Macmillan, 1905.

Josephus, Flavius. *The Works of Flavius Josephus.* translated by William Whiston. Vol. II. New York: A.L. Burt, n.d.

Joyner, Rick. *Final Quest.* New Kensington, PA: Whitaker House, 1996.

Kengor, Paul. *God and George W. Bush: A Spiritual Life.* New York: Harper Collins, 2004.

Kennedy, James D. *What If Jesus Had Never Been Born?: The Positive Impact of Chrisitianity in History.* Nashville, TN: Thomas Nelson, 2001.

Khalaf, B. "Letter to the Editor," *The Guardian,* February 14, 2003. http://www.guardian.co.uk/theguardian/2003/feb/14/.

King, Jr., Martin Luther. "Letter from a Birmingham Jail." African Studies Center, University of Pennsylvania. http://www.africa.upenn.edu/Articles_Gen/Letter_Birmingham.html.

Kramnick, Isaac, and R. Laurence Moore. *The Godless Constitution: The Case Against Religious Correctness.* New York: W.W.Norton and Co., 1996.

Krauthammer, Charles. "American Unilateralism." Speech given at the Mayflower Hotel, Washington, D.C., December 4, 2002. *Imprimis.* https://www.hillsdale.edu/news/imprimis/archive/issue.asp?year=2003&month=01.

Kropotkin, Peter. *Mutual Aid: A Factor of Evolution. Boston:* Extending Horizons Books, 1955.

"Kurdistan—The Other Iraq." http://www.theotheriraq.com.

Kuyper, Abraham. *Calvinism: Six Lectures Delivered at the Theological Seminary at Princeton, 1898-1899.* New York: Fleming H. Revell, n.d.

Lamont, Ann. "John Ray: Founder of Biology and Devout Christian." Answers in Genesis. http://www.answersingenesis.org/creation/v21/ray.asp#f7.

Land, Richard D., Chuck Colson, James Kennedy, Bill Bright, and Carl D. Herbster. "The Land Letter." Eleventh Hour. http://www.11thhour.info/Articles/Land_Letter.html.

Lewis, C.S. *The Lion, the Witch and the Wardrobe.* New York: Collier Books, 1970.

Liao, Jing. "The Contributions of Nineteenth Century Christian Missionaries to Chinese Library Reform." Project MUSE. http://muse.jhu.edu/demo/libraries_and_culture/v041.3liao.html.

Lucian. "Lucian of Samosata: The Passing of Peregrinus." The Tertullian Project. http://www.tertullian.org/rpearse/lucian/peregrinus.htm.

"Lunacharsky v. Religion." Time.com. http://www.time.com/time/magazine/article/0,9171,732175,00.html.

Luther, Martin. "A Mighty Fortress Is Our God." *The Hymnal for Worship & Celebration.* Waco, TX: Word Music, 1986.

BIBLIOGRAPHY

Luther, Martin, "Preface to the Complete Edition of Luther's Latin Works," translated by Brother Andrew Thornton. Internet Christian Library. http://www.iclnet.org/pub/resources/text/wittenberg/luther/pre-flat-eng.txt.

Maier, Timothy W. "Taliban Demands Rigid Conformity." *Insight Magazine*, October 21, 2001. http://www.insightmag.com/archive/200110222.shtml.

Mandela, Nelson. *Long Walk to Freedom: The Autobiography of Nelson Mandela*. New York: Little, Brown, and Co., 1995.

Marshall, Caroline T. "Jan Hus." In Dowley, *Eerdman's Handbook to the History of Christianity*, 330.

Martyr, Justin. "First Apology of Justin." *Early Christian Fathers*, translated by Cyril C. Richardson. Vol. I. Philadelphia: Westminster Press, 1952.

Marx, Karl, and Frederick Engels. *Communist Manifesto*. Marxists Internet Archive. http://www.marxists.org/archive/marx/works/1848/communist-manifesto/ch01.htm.

Maxwell, John C. *The 21 Irrefutable Laws of Leadership*. Nashville, TN: Thomas Nelson, 1998.

McDowell, Josh. *Evidence That Demands a Verdict, Volume I: Historical Evidences for the Christian Faith*. San Bernardino, CA: Here's Life, 1992.

McGrath, Alister E. *Historical Theology: An Introduction to the History of Christian Thought*. Malden, MA: Blackwell, 2003.

McGreal, Chris. "George Bush: A Good Man in Africa." *The Guardian*. http://www.guardian.co.uk/world/2008/feb/15/georgebush.usa.

McLaren, Brian. *A Generous Orthodoxy: Why I Am a Missional, Evangelical, Post/Protestant, Liberal/Conservative, Mystical/Poetic, Biblical, Charismatic/Contemplative, Fundamentalist/Calvinist, Anabaptist/Anglican, Methodist, Catholic, Green, Incarnational, Depressed-yet-Hopeful, Emergent, Unfinished Christian*. Grand Rapids, MI: Zondervan, 2004.

McLaren, Brian. *Finding Our Way Again: The Return of the Ancient Practices*. Nashville, TN: Thomas Nelson, 2008.

Melville, Herman. *Moby Dick*. New York: Signet Classics, 1998.

Morris, Henry. *Men of Science, Men of God*. San Diego, CA: Creation Life, 1982.

Morton, Samuel. "The Debate Over Slavery: Excerpts from Samuel George Morton, Crania Americana." Center for History and New Media. http://chnm.gmu.edu/exploring/19thcentury/debateoverslavery/pop_morton.htm.

Nagle, D. Brendan and Stanley M. Burstein in *The Ancient World: Readings in Social and Cultural History* (Englewood Cliffs, NJ; Prentice Hall, 1995).

Nash, Gary B. *The American People: Creating a Nation and Society, Volume I: to 1877*. 6th ed. New York: Pearson Longman, 2004.

Nelson, James D. "Pietism." http://www.mb-soft.com/believe/txc/pietism.htm.

---BIBLIOGRAPHY---

Newton, Isaac. *Newton's Principia: The Mathematical Principles of Natural Philosophy.* translated by Andrew Motte. London: Benjamin Notte, 1729.

Newton, Isaac. "Original Letter from Isaac Newton to Richard Bentley." *The Newton Project.* Cambridge, UK: Trinity College Library. http://newtonproject.sussex.ac.uk/texts.

"An Open Message to America from Iraqi Citizen," YouTube, http://www.youtube.com/watch?v=JRaQRbbu1jA&feature=related.

Orwell, George. "Politics and the English Language." *The Informed Argument,* edited by Robert K. Miller. San Diego, CA: Harcourt, Brace, Jovanovich, 1986.

Osteen, Joel. *Your Best Life Now: Seven Steps to Living at Your Full Potential.* New York, Warner Faith, 2004.

"Our Troops." http://www.samoanews.com/our-troops.html.

Packer, George. "The Liberal Quandary in Iraq." *The New York Times.* December 8, 2002.

Paine, Thomas. "American Slavery in America." The School of Cooperative Individualism. http://www.cooperativeindividualism.org/paine_slavery.html.

Paine, Thomas. *Common Sense.* London: Penguin Books, 1986.

Paine, Thomas. *The Age of Reason: Being an Investigation of True and Fabulous Theology.* New York: The Truth Seeker Company, 1898.

Palmer, R.R., and Joel Colton. *A History of the Modern World.* 4th ed. New York: Alfred A. Knopf, 1971.

Parsons, Neil. "Colonial Administration: Charles Rey and Previous Commissioners of the Bechuanaland Protectorate." http://thuto.org/ubh/bw/colad2.htm.

Petre, Jonathan. "Carey Wary of Attack." *The Telegraph.* January 9, 2002. http://www.telegraph.co.uk/news/uknews/1408680/Carey-wary-of-attack-on-Iraq.html?mobile=true.

Plato. *The Republic of Plato.* translated by Allan Bloom. New York: Basic Books, 1968.

Plato. *The Works of Plato, Four Volumes in One.* translated by B. Jowett. New York: J.J. Little & Ives Co., n.d.

Pliny the Younger. "Frontline: From Jesus to Christ: Primary Sources: Letters of Pliny the Younger and the Emperor Trajan." PBS. http://www.pbs.org/wgbh/pages/frontline/shows/religion/maps/primary/pliny.htm.

Plutarch. "Of Superstition." *In Plutarch's Moralia: Twenty Essays.* translated by Philemon Holland. London: J.M. Dent and Sons, 1911.

Reynolds, M. H. "The Truth About the World Council of Churches." http://www.cephasministry.com/world_council_of_churches.html.

Quarles, Benjamin. *Black Abolitionists.* New York: Oxford University Press, 1969.

BIBLIOGRAPHY

Raven, Charles Earle. *John Ray, Naturalist.* edited by S. M. Walters. 2nd ed. Cambridge: Cambridge University Press, 1986.

The Real Jesus in Picture Strip. Elgin, IL: David C. Cook, 1977.

Reist, Benjamin. *The Promise of Bonhoeffer.* Philadelphia: J.B. Lippincott Co., 1969.

Religious Leaders for Sensible Priorities. "President Bush, Let Jesus Change Your Mind." Advertisement. *New York Times.* December 4, 2002.

Report on the Parliamentary Select Committee, On Aboriginal Tribes, (British Settlements). London: William Ball, Aldine Chambers, Paternoster Row, and Hatchard and Son, Picadilly, 1837.

Rhodes, Cecil. *The Last Will and Testament of Cecil John Rhodes: With Elucidatory Notes to Which Are Added Some Chapters Describing the Political and Religious Ideas of the Testator.* edited by Thomas Stead. London: "Review of Reviews" Office, 1902.

Robert, Dana Lee. *American Women in Missions: A Social History of Their Thought and Practice.* Macon, GA: Mercer Press, 1997.

Roberts, A. T. "What the Bible Has Done for Democracy: How We Got Our English Bible." *The Expositor* XXI, 1919, 360.

Ross, Kelley L. "G.W.F. Hegel: 1770-1831." *Friesa.* http://friesa.com/hegel.htm.

Ruchames, Louis. *The Abolitionists: A Collection of Their Writings.* New York: G.P. Putnam, 1963.

Russett, Bruce. *Grasping the Democratic Peace.* Princeton, NJ: Princeton University Press, 1994.

Rutman, Darrett B. *The Great Awakening: Event and Exegesis.* New York: John Wiley & Sons, Inc., 1970.

Rydell, Robert W. "World's Columbian Exposition." Encyclopedia of Chicago, Chicago Historical Society. http://www.encyclopedia.chicagohistory.org/pages/1386.html.

Sagan, Carl. *Cosmos.* Chicago, IL: Ballantine Books, 1985.

Schaff, Philip. *Ante-Nicene Fathers, Volume 1: The Apostolic Fathers, Justin Martyr, Ireneaus.* edited by Alexander Roberts and James Donaldson, revised by Cleveland Coxe. New York: Christian Literature Publishing Co., 1885. Christian Classics Ethereal Library, http://www.ccel.org/ccel/schaff/anf01.ix.ii.xi.html.

Scheer, Robert. "It's Time to Cut Our Losses." *Milwaukee Journal Sentinel.* November 6, 2003.

Schmidt, Alvin J. *How Christianity Changed the World.* Grand Rapids, MI: Zondervan, 2005.

Seutonius. *The Twelve Ceasars.* translated by Robert Graves. Baltimore, MD: Penguin, 1960.

"The Shepherd of Hermas." *Apostolic Fathers,* translated by J. B. Lightfoot, edited by J. R. Harner. Grand Rapids, MI: Baker House Books, 1967. Wesley Center Online. http://wesley.nnu.edu/biblical_studies/noncanon/fathers/antenic/hermas1.htm.

Singer, Peter. *Hegel.* Oxford: Oxford University Press, 1983.

Smith, Wilbur. *World Crisis and the Prophetic Scriptures.* Chicago: Moody Press, 1952.

BIBLIOGRAPHY

"Social Darwinism." Answers.com. http://www.answers.com/topic/social-darwinism.

Solzhenitsyn, Alexander. *One Day in the Life of Ivan Denisovich.* New York: Dutton, 1963.

Sweet, William Warren. *Religion in Colonial American.* New York: Charles Scribner's Sons, 1949.

"Cardinal Criticises US Treatment of Saddam." *The Tablet.* December 20, 2003. http://www.thetablet.co.uk/article/2878.

Tacitus, P. Cornelius. "Histories." *The Complete Works of Tacitus,* translated by Alfred John Church and William Jackson Brodribb. New York: Random House, 1942.

Tacitus, P. Cornelius. *The Annals and Histories.* translated by Alfred John Church and William Jackson Brodribb. Chicago: William Benton, 1952.

Taylor, Charles. *Hegel and Modern Society.* Cambridge: Cambridge University Press, 1983.

Tenney, Tommy. *The God Chasers: My Soul Follows Hard After Thee.* Shippensburg, PA: Destiny Image, Inc., 1998.

Thompson, Leonard A. *A History of South Africa.* 3rd ed. New Haven, CT: Yale University Press, 2000.

Tillich, Paul. *Christianity and the Encounter of the World Religions.* New York: Columbia University Press, 1963.

Tobin, Paul N. "Christian Missionaries." *The Rejection of Pascal's Wager: A Skeptic's Guide to Christianity.* http://www.geocities.com/paulntobin/mission.html.

Tolstoy, Leo. "A Confession." Christian Classics Ethereal Library. http://www.ccel.org/ccel/tolstoy/confession.ii.x.html.

Tosh, John. *The Pursuit of History: Aims, Methods and New Directions in the Study of Modern History.* 3rd ed. London: Longman, 2002.

"Treaty with the Indians at Shackamaxon." Penn Treaty Museum. http://penntreatymuseum.org/treaty.php.

U.S. Congress Against War and Fascism. "Manifesto and Program." *Daily Worker,* June 30, 1934, Vol.11, No. 156. http://www.marxists.org/history/usa/groups/alawf/1933/1001-alawf-manifestoprogram.pdf.

VisitSamoa.com. http://www.visitsamoa.com.

The Voice of the Martyrs. *Extreme Devotion: Daily Devotional Stories of Ancient to Modern Day Believers Who Sacrificed Everything for Christ.* Nashville, TN: Thomas Nelson, 2001.

The Voice of the Martyrs. *Into the Den of Infidels.* Bartlesville, OK: Living Sacrifice Book Co., 2003.

The Voice of the Martyrs. *Iran: Desperate for God.* Bartlesville, OK: Living Sacrifice Book Co., 2006.

Ward, C. M. *What You Should Know About Prophecy.* Springfield, MO: Gospel House, 1975.

Ward, Harry F. *The Christian Demand for Social Reconstruction.* Philadelphia: W. H. Jenkins, 1918.

Wells, H. G. *The Outline of History: Being a Plain History of Life and Mankind*, Vol I. Garden City, NJ: Garden City Books, 1949.

What Ever Happened to Baby Jane?, VHS. Directed by Robert Aldrich. Los Angeles, CA: The Associates and Aldrich Co., 1962.

White, Andrew Dickson. *A History of the Warfare of Science with Theology in Christendom*. Buffalo, NY: Prometheus Books, 1993.

"Why Jesus Never Existed," Religion Is Lies. http://www.religionislies.com/whyjesusneverexisted.html.

Wilberforce, William. *A Practical View of the Prevailing Religious System of Professed Christians: In the Higher and Middle Classes in this Country, Contrasted with Real Christianity*. New York: Leavitt, Lord, and Co., 1835.

Wood, Bryant. "Did the Israelites Conquer Jericho?" *Biblical Archaeology Review*, 1990. http://www.ucgstp.org/llit/gn/gn039/jericho.html.

Wood, Bryant. "Did the Israelites Conquer Jericho: A New Look at the Archaeological Evidence," *Associates for Biblical Research*. 1 May 2008. http://www.biblearchaeology.org/post/2008/05/Did-the-Israelites-Conquer-Jericho-A-New-Look-at-the-Archaeological-Evidence.aspx.

World Council of Churches. "Statement on the War in Iraq." Press release, March 20, 2003. Oikoumene. http://www.oikoumene.org/en/resources/documents/wcc-commissions/international-affairs/regional-concerns/middle-east/statement-on-the-war-in-Iraq.html.

Wright, Kristen. "From the Killing Fields to the Cross." *Breakpoint*. November 14, 2006. http://www.breakpoint.org/listingarticle.asp?ID=5804.

Wurmbrand, Richard. *In God's Underground*. Greenwich, CT: Fawcett Publications, 1968.

Wurmbrand, Richard. *Tortured for Christ*. Bartlesville, OK: Living Sacrifice Book Company, 1998.

Index

9/11, 5
21 Irrefutable Laws of Leadership, The (Maxwell), 18
1908 Social Creed of the Churches (Ward), 256

Abel, 9-10, 18, 22, 29, 31, 91, 105, 112, 263
Aborigines Protection Society, 173, 192
Abraham, 24, 30-33, 56, 61-62, 288-89, 297, 302, 307
Abrahamic Covenant, 125
ad fontes, 113
Adam and Eve, 13, 21, 25-29, 33, 93, 173, 194, 213, 233, 300
Agassiz, Louis, 131, 195
Age of Reason, The (Paine), 141, 158
Al Qaeda, 282
Albigenses, 110
Alexander I, Czar, 250
Alexis, Czar, 249
Al-Khoei, Abd al-Majid, 272
Allah, 77, 280, 286-87
Allen, Richard, 183
Allen, William, 174
Alliance of Civilizations, 6
Alterman, Eric, 279
Amalekites, 35, 55
"Amazing Grace" (Newton), 167
American AIDS Initiative in Africa, 283
American Civil Liberties Union, 258
American League Against War and Fascism, 258
Amish, 124
Amos, 38-39, 48, 61
Anabaptists, 124
ancien regime, 159, 290
Andrew, the apostle, 77
Anglican Church, 122, 127, 168, 273
Anne Frank: The Diary of a Young Girl (Frank), 213
"An Open Message to America from Iraqi Citizen" (Iraqtube), 281
Anthony of Egypt, 102
Apostolic Constitutions, 87
Aquinas, Thomas, 107
archaeology, 226, 240, 243, 303-05
Aristides, 87
Aristotle, 83, 88, 129, 295, 298-99
asceticism, 46, 95, 97-98, 102-105, 115, 250, 261, 298
Athanasius, 102
Attila the Hun, 106
Augustine of Hippo, 102
Augustus, Emperor of Rome, 77
Averroes, 130
Avvakum, 249

INDEX

Ba'ath Party, 269-70,
Baal, 17, 35-37, 63, 90, 209
Babbage, Charles, 131
Backus, Isaac, 155
Backward Peoples and Our Relationship with Them, The (Johnston), 197
Bacon, Sir Francis, 122, 128, 300
Baltodano, Prudencio, 265
Bamboo Curtain, 255
Barmen Declaration, 232, 278
Barth, Karl, 231-33, 278
Bartholomew, the apostle, 77
Basilides, 99
Bauer, F. C., 240
Beatles, the, 4
Beecher, Charles, 184
Beneath the Veil, 269
Benedictine Rule, 103
Berlin Wall, 5, 7
Besant, Annie, 257
Beveridge, Senator A. J., 239
Biden, Joe, 279
Bilbo Baggins, 264
Biogenesis, 299
Blair, Tony, 272
Bligh, Captain, 191
blood sport, 9, 71, 78, 91, 294
Bolsec, Jerome, 126
Bolshevik Revolution, 250
Bonhoeffer, Dietrich, 1, 9, 45, 213, 231-34, 266, 278, 307
Book of Martyrs (Foxe), 76
Booth, William, 157, 186
Borg, Marcus, 48
Boyle, Robert, 129, 131
Brewster, David, 131
British East India Company, 191
Brother Andrew, 255-56
Brothers Karamazov, The (Dostoyevsky), 50, 261
Brownsville revival, 296
Brotherhood of Thieves, The (Foster), 165
Buddha, 76
Burke, Edmund, 159
Bush, George W., 281-83
Buxton, Thomas Fowell, 174, 192
By-Products of Missions (Headland), 202

Cain and Abel, 18, 29
Calhoun, Senator John C., 179-80
Callistus, bishop of Rome, 84
Calvin, John, Calvinism, 125-28, 133-34, 145, 158, 161, 166, 180-81, 296, 300,
Canaanites, 31, 35, 37, 125, 209
cannibalism, 80, 187, 206, 208-11, 295
Canon, the, 100, 102

INDEX

Cappadocian Fathers, 103
Carey, Dr. George, Archbishop of Canterbury, 273
Carey, William, 204, 209
Carter, Rev. E. A., 250
Carton, Sydney, 306
Cassian, John, 103
Castellio, Sebastian, 126
Cathars, 110
Cather, Willa, 4
Catherine the Great, 249
Chambers, Oswald, 15
Chambers, Whitaker, 265
Charles V, Emperor, 117
Chavez, Hugo, 279
checks and balances, 155, 159
Chertokova, Anna, 254
child sacrifice, 31, 55
Child, Lydia Marie, 164, 185
Chin, Corporal Edward, 280
Choulagh, Henry, 280
"Christian Demand for Social Reconstruction, The" (Ward), 257
Christ myth, the, 75
Christy, Henry, 174
Church of England, 127, 160
Cicero, 88
circumcision, 10, 18-19, 46, 58, 62, 64, 102
civil disobedience, 134, 184, 268
civil war, 120, 296, 301
"Claims of the Negro Ethnologically Considered" (Douglass), 175
Clapham Sect, 168, 186, 192
Clarkson, Thomas, 164, 74
clash of civilizations, 5
Clement, 77, 81, 86, 101, 106
CNN, 269, 281
Coffin, Levi, 183
Cold War, 4-5, 265
Cole, Nathan, 150-51, 160
Colfax, Richard, 175
Collins, Francis S., 132
Colonisation and Christianity (Howitt), 192
Colson, Chuck, 278
Columbian Exposition of 1893, 195
Common Sense (Paine), 141, 146, 156-57, 177
Communist Manifesto (Marx and Engels), 239, 250
Confessing Church, 231, 235-36
Confession (Tolstoy), 244
Constantine, Emperor, 89
Cook, Captain, 188
Copronyms, 89
Cortez, Hernan, 167, 188
Council of Constance, 111
Cowper, William, 163, 252

Crania Americana (Morton), 174
Cranmer, Thomas, 121, 307
Cuban Missile Crisis, 4
Cuvier, Georges, 131-32
Cyprian, 83, 102, 104

D'souza, Dinesh, 207
Da Vinci Code, The (Brown), 23, 115
Da Vinci, Leonardo, 131
Dark Ages, 105-10, 164, 296
Darnay, Charles, 306
Darwin, Charles; Darwinism, 6, 139, 145, 161, 194, 243, 256, 295
David, King of Israel, 33, 41-42, 61, 304, 307
Davies, Sam, 155
Davis, Bette, 2
Davy, Humphrey, 132
Dawkins, Richard, 6
Day of Atonement, 52
Day, Doris, 4
De Tocqueville, Alexis, 161
Dead Sea scrolls, 24, 304
Declaration of Independence, 140, 145, 152, 176, 192, 194, 299
"Declaration of Sentiments" (Stanton), 185
Demetrianus, 83
Democratic Peace Theory, 5
Dennett, Daniel, 6
Desert Fathers, 102
Desire of Nations, 68, 231
Dialogue Concerning the Two Chief World Systems (Galileo), 107
Dickens, Charles, 306
Didache, The, 84, 89
Diderot, Dennis, 159
Diet of Worms, 117
Dionysius, bishop of Alexandria, 83
Docetism, 96-97, 100, 298
Donne, John, 293
Dostoyevsky, Fyodor, 51, 261-63
Douglass, Frederick, 175-77, 185
Dutch East India Company, 188

Ecce Deus (Parker), 75
Edict of Worms, 118
Edmundson, Milly, 183
Edwards, Jonathan, 17, 148-49, 157
Eliot, George, 240
Elizabeth, Queen, 122, 124, 127
emergent church, 296
Encyclopedists, the, 159
end of history, 5, 220
Erasmus, Desiderius, 113-15, 119, 122, 134, 163
Esau, 22, 31
Ethnological Society of London, 174

Eucharist, the, 110, 122
Eusebius, 83
Evagrius, 103
Evidence Against the Views of the Abolitionists (Colfax), 175
Ezekiel, 39-40, 65

Fabian socialists, 257
Fabre, Henry, 131
Faraday, Michael, 131
Faust (Goethe), 1
Feasts of Israel, 52-53
Felicity and Perpetua, 86
Feuerbach, Ludwig, 3, 225-26, 240
Filaret, 249
Final Quest, The (Joyner), 296
Finkelstein, Israel, 304
Finney, Charles, 49, 157, 180-82
Five Pillars of Faith, 285
Flavius, Josephus, 73
Fleming, John Ambrose, 131
Fort Hare, University College of, 134, 205-06
Foster, Stephen S., 165
Foxe, John, 76-77, 82, 91-92, 105, 108, 111
Frankenstein (Shelley), 3
Franklin, Benjamin, 144, 152
Frawley, David, 206
Frelinghuysen, Theodore, 147-48
French Revolution, 8, 138, 141, 158-62, 216-17, 220, 224
Frodo, 264
Fryer, John, 204
Fugitive Slave Law, 179, 184
Fukuyama, Francis, 5

Galileo, 107, 130
Ganevskaya, Liuba, 265-66
Garrison, William Lloyd, 166-67, 169, 182, 307
Geist, 221, 225, 229, 240
Geldorf, Bob, 284
Generous Orthodoxy, A (McLaren), 296
Gentiles, 52, 53, 58, 73, 297
German historicism, 226, 243-44
germ theory, 299
Gliddon, George, 174-75
Gnostic, Gnosticism, 95-102, 104, 106, 128, 143, 251, 296-98
God Chasers, The (Tenney), 18, 63
"God is Still Speaking" campaign, 297
Goethe, Johann Wolfgang von, 1, 217, 226
Gollum, 264
Gorbachev, Mikhail, 265
Gospel of Mary, 96-97
Grand Inquisitor, the, 261-63
Great Awakening, the, 146-47, 151-54, 156-58, 160, 168, 180-81, 187

Great Society, 4
Greek Septuagint, 103
Gregory XI, Pope, 111
Grimke, Angela, 185

Harris, Sam, 137, 236, 242, 301
Harrison, Benjamin, 198
Hawkings, Stephen, 130
Haydar, Um, 270
Headland, Isaac Taylor, 202-03, 207
Heart of Christianity, The (Borg), 48
Hedges, Chris, 236
Hegel, Georg W. F., 3, 5, 215-31, 240, 256
Hemingway, Ernest, 4
Herbster, Dr. Carl D., 278
Herder, Johann Gottfried, 3, 218, 221, 230, 232
Herod, King, 77, 89
Herschel, Sir William, 131
Higher Law, 184-85, 273, 299
Hilarion, 88
Hindus, 6, 9, 79, 169, 206
Hircanus, King, 77
Hitchens, Christopher, 6-8, 10-11, 36-37, 45, 49-50, 55, 66, 72, 123, 138-42, 144-45, 177, 207, 211, 213, 216, 254, 263, 302, 305-06
Hitler, Adolph, 4, 175, 213-237, 263, 272, 279, 301
Hmongs, the, 264
Hobbes, Thomas, 160, 180
Holocaust, the, 2, 3, 234, 282
Holy Sonnet XIV (Donne), 293
Homer, 76
Hort, F. J. A., 240
Hosea, 37-38, 65
Howitt, William, 173, 192, 199
Hudson Bay Company, 191
Human Genome Project, 132
human sacrifice, 9, 35, 187, 209
Hume, David, 172, 186
Humphreys, Ken, 73
Huntington, Samuel P., 5
Huss, John, 111-12, 117, 307
Hussein, Saddam, 269-73, 277, 280-82

Ignatius of Antioch, 101
illuminism, 95
In Praise of Folly (Erasmus), 114
infanticide, 9, 71, 78, 88-89, 169, 187, 211, 294-95,
Inquisition, the, 106-11, 117, 121, 126, 140, 167, 261
intelligent design, 279, 298, 301
Iranian Bible Society, 285
Irenaeus, 102
Iron Curtain, 255-56, 264
Isaac, son of Abraham, 22, 31, 33

INDEX

Isaiah, viii, ix, 12-13, 23, 29, 33-35, 54, 307
Ishmael, son of Abraham, 22, 31, 288-91
Israel, 6, 32-41, 52-53, 58, 61, 65-66, 87, 89, 141, 156, 177, 209, 273, 296, 304
Ivan the Terrible, 248

Jacob, 22, 31, 33, 39, 62
Jagger, Mick, 3
James, the brother of Jesus, 17, 77, 80, 98-99
James, the brother of John, 76-77
Jefferson, Thomas, 138-45, 154, 169-76, 179
Jeremiah, ix, 21, 35-37, 61, 287-88, 307
Jericho, 32-33, 303
Jerome, 103, 105
Jesuit *reductiones,* 190
JESUS Film Project, 264, 285
jihad, 286
Jim Crow, 182
Joel, 38, 53
Joel's Army, 296
John Paul II, Pope, 273
John the Baptist, 8-9, 23, 33, 45, 59, 61, 80, 90, 307
John the Beloved, 307
Jonah, 40-41
Joseph, 22, 33, 304
Joseph of Volokolamsk, 248
Joshua, 54
Jovinian, 105
Joyner, Rick, 296
Julian the Apostate, 71, 82
Justin Martyr, 80

Kansas City prophets, 296
Kant, Immanuel, 3, 161, 172, 217-19, 230, 245
Kashi, Rania, 271
Kelvin, Lord, 131-32
Kennedy, Dr. James, 278
Kennedy, John F., 4
Kenyon, Kathleen, 303-04
Kepler, Johannes, 129, 131, 299-300
Khalaf, Dr. B., 271
Khamara, Nikolai, 254
Khmer Rouge, 264
King, Jr., Martin Luther, 4, 9, 10, 67, 71, 182, 187, 268, 307
King Leopold's Soliloquy (Twain), 187
Knibb, William, 200-01
Knox, John, 127
Komarov, Shenia, 254
Koresh, David, 24
Krauthammer, Charles, 273
Kropotkin, Peter, 256
Kruschev, Nikita, 4
Kurds, 271, 282

INDEX

La Trobe Collection, 201-02
Lakeland revival, 296
Land Letter, the, 277-78
Land, Richard, 277-78
Language of God, The (Collins), 132
las Casas, Bartolome, 189
Latimer, Bishop, 121
Latin Vulgate, 103
Latter Rain movement, 296
Lawrence, deacon of Rome, 82
League of Nations, 4
Leo the Great, 103, 106
Leo X, Pope, 116
Letter Concerning Toleration, A (Locke), 120, 141
"Letter from a Birmingham Jail" (King), 71, 182, 187, 268
Letter to a Christian Nation (Harris), 137, 242, 301
Letters and Papers from Prison (Bonhoeffer), 1
Leviathan (Hobbes), 160
Lewis, C. S., 13
Lewis, Sinclair, 257
Lex Rex (Rutherford), 134
Life of Jesus (Strauss), 240
Lightfoot, J. B., 240
Lincoln, Abraham, 185
Linnaeus, Carolus, 132
Linus, Bishop of Rome, 84
Lion, the Witch, and the Wardrobe, The (Lewis), 13
Lister, Joseph, 129, 131, 174, 299
Livingstone, David, 174, 209
Locke, John, 120, 141, 154-56, 159
Logara, Pastor Jeremiah, 287-88
Lollards, 111
London Missionary Society, 188, 193, 205, 207-08
Long Walk to Freedom (Mandela), 205
Lowe, James Russell, 183
Lucian, the playwright, 75, 81
Lucifer, 26-28, 42-43, 51
Lunacharsky, Anatoly, 253
Luther, Martin, 22, 118, 235-36, 286, 307

Mackenzie, John, 193-94
Makiya, Kanan, 270
Malleus Maleficarum, 108
Malof, Basil, 243-44, 250-54, 307
Mandela, Nelson, 134, 205-06
Manicheans, the, 298
Manicheeism, 298
Manifest Sons of God movement, 296
Manz, Felix, 125
Mao Tse Tung, 255
Marcionism, 99
Mark, 73, 77

INDEX

Martino, Cardinal Renato R., 273
Marx, Karl, 239-40, 243, 248, 250, 255, 263, 295, 301
Mary, Queen, 121-122, 127
Mary, the mother of Jesus, 23, 102, 105, 110, 123
Massachusetts Bay Colony, 157, 191
Arthur and Wilda Matthews, 255
Matson, Louise Klassen, 255
Matthew, the apostle, vi, ix, 9, 16, 33, 45, 61, 73, 77, 79, 84, 267
Maury, Matthew, 131
Maximinius, Daza, 83
Maxwell, James Clerk, 131-32
Maxwell, John C., 18
Mayflower, the, 127
Mayhew, Jonathan, 158
McGrath, Alistair (Alister), 37, 240-41, 254
McGreal, Chris, 283
McLaren, Brian, 296
Mein Kampf (Hitler), 214, 227, 301
Melania, 87
Melville, Herman, 1
Mendel, Gregor, 131
Mennonites, 124
Micah, 39, 141
Michal, the wife of King David, 42
Middle Ages, 93, 108, 110, 223, 248, 298
Milburn, Major Andy, 280
Mindrutz, Joana, 254
Moby Dick (Melville), 1
Moiseyev, Ivan, 255
Moisi, Dominique, 280
monogenism, 173, 194
Montesquieu, Baron De, 154, 155, 159
Montgomery, Helen Barrett, 199-200
Moon, Rev. Sun Myung, 24
Moravians, 124
Morton, Samuel George, 174-75
Moses, 16, 24, 32-33, 36, 56, 259, 302-04
Mote, Edward, 293
Muntzer, Thomas, 119
mutual aid, 256-57
My Utmost for His Highest (Chambers), 15
mysticism, 95, 102-03, 118, 128, 248, 295

Nasir, Awad, 280
National Council of Churches, 257
Nee, Watchman, 255, 307
Nero, Claudius, 92
Nero, Domitius, 74-75, 76, 92, 162
New Deal, 4
New Lights, 151-52, 158
new wine, 58, 60, 164
Newton, John, 167

INDEX

Newton, Isaac, 130-32, 140, 298, 300, 301
Nicolaitans, 23
Niemoller, Martin, 213, 231, 278
Nietzsche, Friedrich, 7, 229
Night (Wiesel), 282
Nikon, 249
Ninety-five Theses (Luther), 116
Noah, 29-30, 31, 33, 137
Notes on Virginia (Jefferson), 170
Nott, Josiah, 174

Obama, Barak, 273
Oberlin College, 182
Old Lights, 151-52, 158
One Day in the Life of Ivan Denisovich (Solzhenitsyn), 260, 262
One, the, 55, 288, 307
Onesimus, 85
Origen, 102-03
Orwell, George, 215-16, 230
Our Country (Strong), 197

Padina, 286-87
Paine, Thomas, 3, 138-42, 144, 146, 155-57, 177-78
Parker, Joseph, 75
Pascal, Blaise, 131
Passing of Peregrinus, The (Lucian), 75
Passover, 26, 32, 51-53, 77
Pasteur, Louis, 129, 131, 299
Paton, John G., 208-09
Pearl Harbor, 4
Pelagianism, 298
Penn, William, 191
Pescaru, Dr. Margaret, 255
Peter, the apostle, 63, 84, 98, 101, 102, 110, 297
Peter the Great, 249
Pharisees, 11, 40, 45-46, 60, 61, 72, 90, 91, 295
Philemon, 85
Philip, the apostle, 77
Philip, John, 205
philosophes, 138, 159
Pilgrims, the, 127
Pioneer Mission Society, 253
Pius XII, Pope, 235
Pizarro, Francisco, 167, 188-89
Plato, 79, 84, 88, 107, 298
Pliny the Younger, 73
Plutarch, 88
"Politics and the English Language" (Orwell), 215
Pol Pot, 264
Polycarp, 92
polygenism, 174-76, 194, 300
Pontius Pilate, 78

INDEX

Potter, Dr. Philip, 259
Potter, George and Rosella, 184
Powell, Colin, 284
President's Emergency Plan for AIDS Relief (Pepfar), 283-284
Presley, Elvis, 4
priesthood of the believer, 117, 154, 160
Principia Mathematica (Newton), 130
prophets of Baal, 17, 63
prosperity movement, 296
Ptolemy, Ptolemaic, 107, 300
Puritans, Puritanism, 127, 155, 191
Putnam, Frederic Ward, 195

Quirinius, 78

Rahab, 32-33
Raleigh, Sir Walter, 122
Ramsay, Sir William, 240
Ranke, Leopold von, 8, 226
Rauschenbusch, Walter, 257
Ray, John, 129, 131
Rayleigh, Lord, 131
Reagan, Ronald, 5, 264
red-letter Christians, 256
Reign of Terror, 159
Reimarus, H. S., 240
Religious Leaders for Sensible Priorities, 274
Renaissance, the, 113, 130, 223
Renan, J. E., 240
Report of the Parliamentary Select Committee on Aboriginal Tribes, (British Settlements), 193
Rhodes, Cecil, 193-94
Ridley, Bishop, 121
Riemann, Bernard, 131
Robespierre, Maximilien, 160
Romanov, Michael, 249
Roosevelt, Franklin D., 4
Rousseau, Jean-Jacques, 206
Royal Society of Great Britain, 129, 132
Rule of Faith, the, 102
Russell, Bertrand, 257
Russett, Bruce, 5, 290
Russian Bible Society, 250
Russian Orthodox Church, 248-50
Rutherford, Samuel, 134

Sabbath, the, 12, 50, 52, 53, 62, 63, 126
Sagan, Carl, 1, 54
Salvation Army, the, 157, 187
Sandinistas, 265
Satan, 15, 49, 54, 56, 69, 95, 106, 158, 261
Sayed, Juad Amir, 280
scarlet thread, 9, 33, 306

INDEX

Schindler, Oskar, 235
Schleiermacher, Friedrich, 226
scholasticism, 107, 115, 130
Scholl, Hans and Sophie, 234-35
Schopenhauer, Arthur, 216, 245
scientific method, 128, 226, 230, 243
scientific racism, 170-77, 194-200, 300-01
Scientific Revolution, 128-32, 172, 295, 298
Scotus, Dun, 107
Second Great Awakening, the, 180-82, 187
Seely, J. R., 240
Selling of Joseph, The (Sewall), 164
Selwyn, Bishop, 207
Seneca, 88, 92
Seneca Falls Convention, 185
September 11th, 306
Servetus, Michael, 126
Seutonius, 74, 92
Sewall, Samuel, 164
Shaftesbury, Lord, 186
Shah, Saira, 269
Shakespeare, William, 45
Shater, Dominique, 281
Shaw, George Bernard, 257
Shelley, Mary, 3
Shepherd of Hermas, The, 82, 87
shepherding movement, 296
Shiite, 269, 280
signs and wonders, 15, 47
Simmons, Menno, 124
Simpson, James, 131
Skeptical Chymist (Boyle), 129
Skripnova, Aida, 254
Slessor, Mary, 209-11
Smith, Adam, 238, 267
Smith, Captain John, 190
Smith, Joseph, 76
Smith, Oswald J., 250
Snow, John, 299
social Darwinism, 188, 193-98, 200-03, 226-27, 236, 238, 300-01
Social Gospel, 197, 256-57
Socrates, 222
Sodom and Gomorrah, 298
sola scriptura, 119, 122
Solomon, King, 6, 33, 65, 244
Solzhenitsyn, Alexander, 254, 260, 263
Sons of Ishmael, 288-89, 291
Sorsky, Nil, 248
Spartacus, 85
Spencer, Herbert, 195, 226
spontaneous generation, 129, 299-300
Spurgeon, Charles, 250, 253

INDEX

Stalin, Joseph, 254, 259
Stanton, Elizabeth Cady, 185
Steno, Nicholas, 132
Stoicism, 75, 222
Stokes, George, 131
Stowe, Harriet Beecher, 183, 185
Strauss, David F., 226, 240
Strong, Josiah, 197
Sturge, Joseph, 174
Sumner, John Bird, 175
Sunni, 269
super-apostles, 57, 98
superstition, 74, 88, 106, 109, 142, 294
survival of the fittest, 195, 214, 238, 257, 301
Symeon the Stylite, 103

Tacitus, Cornelius, 74, 89
Tale of Two Cities, A (Dickens), 306
Taliban, 37, 269
Tappan, Lewis, 185
Taylor, Hudson, 209
Ten Boom, Corrie, 234
Tenney, Tommy, 18, 63
Tetzel, 116-17
Third Wave, 296
Thirty Years War, 120, 141, 164
Tiananmen Square, 5, 273
Tillich, Paul, 21, 233
tithe, 10, 47, 50, 52, 58, 61, 62, 155
Titus, 100
To the Christian Nobility of the German Nation (Luther), 117
Tolkien, J. R. R., 264
Tolstoy, Leo, 243-48, 250
Toronto laughter, 250, 296
totalitarianism, 5, 238
Tower of Babel, 6, 7, 30, 56, 204
tradition, 48, 61, 90, 93, 99, 101-02, 108, 113, 119, 122, 134, 163, 213, 241, 247, 250, 258, 294
transubstantiation, 56, 102
Treatise on the Records of the Creation, A (Sumner), 175
Treaty of Westphalia, 120, 141
Tree of Life, 13-14, 25, 27, 28, 33, 50, 58-60, 234
Tree of the Knowledge of Good and Evil, 7, 13, 25, 27, 33, 60, 211
Tubman, Harriet, 185
Twain, Mark, 187
Twelve Caesars, The (Seutonius), 74, 92
Twelve Tables, 88
Tyndale, William, 9, 121, 134, 163, 307
Types of Mankind (Gliddon and Nott), 174

Uncle Tom's Cabin (Stowe), 179, 185
Underground Railroad, 183, 185

INDEX

United Church of Christ, 273, 297-98
United Nations, 6, 270, 273, 278, 279

Valentinus, 99
Vietnam, 4, 255, 264
Vins, Georgi, 255
Virchow, Rudolph, 131
Virginia Company of London, 190
Voice of the Martyrs, 240, 258, 260, 287
Volkgeist, 218
Voltaire, 1, 138, 140, 142-44, 156, 173, 175, 191
Von Bodelschwing, Pastor, 234
Von Bora, Katherine, 133

Waldensians, 110
Wallenberg, Raoul, 235
War on Terror, 37, 267
Ward, Harry F., 256-58
Watchman Nee, 255, 307
Watergate, 4, 278
weapons of mass destruction, 270, 278, 279
Webb, Beatrice Potter, 257
Webb, Sidney, 257
Weld, Theodore Dwight, 182
Wellhausen, Julius, 240
Wells, H. G., 72, 85, 94, 159, 160, 257
Wesley, John, 49, 63, 149, 250
Westcott, B. F., 240
Western imperialism, 188, 199, 238, 300
What Ever Happened to Baby Jane?, 2
white man's burden, 188, 193-97
White, Harry Dexter, 257
Whitefield, George, 49, 63, 143, 149-53, 160, 167, 307
Wiesel, Elie, 282
Wilberforce, William, 8, 167-69, 174, 181, 186, 192, 206
Williams, John, 207
Williams, Roger, 145, 155
Winthrop, John, 157
witch trials, witch hunts, 11, 13, 15-16, 94, 108, 109, 110, 140, 160
Witness (Chambers), 265
Woodward, John, 131
woolen and linen, 18-19, 47, 58, 63
Wordsworth, William, 216
World Council of Churches, 258-60
Wurmbrand, Rev. Richard, 240, 254, 258-60, 307
Wycliffe, John, 110-11, 113, 134, 163, 307

Yakovlena, Vera, 254

Zakharov, Pavel, 255
Zeitgeist, 226, 230
Zeno, 75
Zwingli, Ulrich, 122-24, 133, 134